*New Beacon

PHILIPPIANS
A Commentary in the Wesleyan Tradition

DEAN FLEMMING

BEACON HILL PRESS
OF KANSAS CITY

Copyright 2009
by Dean Flemming and Beacon Hill Press of Kansas City

ISBN 978-0-8341-2411-0

Printed in the United States of America

Unless otherwise indicated all Scripture quotations are from the *Holy Bible, New International Version*® (NIV®). Copyright © 1973, 1978, 1984 by International Bible Society. Used by permission of Zondervan Publishing House. All rights reserved.

King James Version (KJV).

The following copyrighted versions of the Bible are used by permission.

The *Contemporary English Version* (CEV). Copyright © by the American Bible Society, 1991, 1992.

The *Good News Translation* (GNT). Copyright © 1966, 1971, 1976, 1992.

The *New American Standard Bible*® (NASB®), © copyright The Lockman Foundation 1960, 1962, 1963, 1968, 1971, 1972, 1973, 1975, 1977, 1995.

The New English Bible (NEB). Copyright © by the Delegates of the Oxford University Press and the Syndics of the Cambridge University Press, 1961, 1970.

The *New King James Version* (NKJV). Copyright © 1979, 1980, 1982 Thomas Nelson, Inc.

The *Holy Bible, New Living Translation* (NLT), copyright © 1996, 2004. Used by permission of Tyndale House Publishers, Inc., Carol Stream, IL 60188. All rights reserved.

The *New Revised Standard Version* (NRSV) of the Bible, copyright 1989 by the Division of Christian Education of the National Council of the Churches of Christ in the USA. Used by permission. All rights reserved.

The *New Testament in Modern English* (PHILLIPS), Revised Student Edition, by J. B. Phillips, translator. Copyright 1958, 1960, 1972 by J. B. Phillips.

The *Revised Standard Version* (RSV) of the Bible, copyright 1946, 1952, 1971 by the Division of Christian Education of the National Council of the Churches of Christ in the USA. Used by permission.

The Living Bible (TLB), © 1971. Used by permission of Tyndale House Publishers, Inc., Wheaton, IL 60189. All rights reserved.

The Message: The Bible in Contemporary Language (TM), copyright 2002 by Eugene Peterson. All rights reserved.

The *Holy Bible, Today's New International Version*™ (TNIV®). Copyright © 2001, 2005 by International Bible Society. All rights reserved worldwide.

Library of Congress Cataloging-in-Publication Data

Flemming, Dean E., 1953-
  Philippians / Dean Flemming.
    p. cm. — (New Beacon Bible commentary)
  Includes bibliographical references.
  ISBN 978-0-8341-2411-0 (pbk.)
  1. Bible. N.T. Philippians—Commentaries. I. Title.

BS2705.53.F54 2009
227'.607—dc22

2008053475

DEDICATION

For my father, Floyd O. Flemming,
preacher of the gospel and
example of joy in the Lord

COMMENTARY EDITORS

General Editors

Alex Varughese
Ph.D., Drew University
Professor of Biblical Literature
Mount Vernon Nazarene University
Mount Vernon, Ohio

George Lyons
Ph.D., Emory University
Professor of New Testament
Northwest Nazarene University
Nampa, Idaho

Roger Hahn
Ph.D., Duke University
Dean of the Faculty
Professor of New Testament
Nazarene Theological Seminary
Kansas City, Missouri

Section Editors

Joseph Coleson
Ph.D., Brandeis University
Professor of Old Testament
Nazarene Theological Seminary
Kansas City, Missouri

Kent Brower
Ph.D., The University of Manchester
Vice Principal
Senior Lecturer in Biblical Studies
Nazarene Theological College
Manchester, England

Robert Branson
Ph.D., Boston University
Professor of Biblical Literature
Olivet Nazarene University
Bourbonnais, Illinois

George Lyons
Ph.D., Emory University
Professor of New Testament
Northwest Nazarene University
Nampa, Idaho

Alex Varughese
Ph.D., Drew University
Professor of Biblical Literature
Mount Vernon Nazarene University
Mount Vernon, Ohio

Jeanne Serrão
Ph.D., Claremont Graduate University
Dean of the School of Theology and
    Philosophy
Professor of Biblical Literature
Mount Vernon Nazarene University
Mount Vernon, Ohio

Jim Edlin
Ph.D., Southern Baptist Theological
    Seminary
Professor of Biblical Literature and
    Languages
Chair of the Division of Religion and
    Philosophy
MidAmerica Nazarene University
Olathe, Kansas

CONTENTS

General Editors' Preface	7
Acknowledgments	9
Abbreviations	10
Bibliography	13

INTRODUCTION — 21

- A. The Context of Philippians — 22
  1. The City and People of Philippi — 22
  2. Paul's Mission in Philippi — 23
  3. The Place and Date of Writing — 24
  4. Paul's Imprisonment — 26
  5. The Occasion and Purpose of the Letter — 27
- B. The Form, Structure, and Persuasive Strategy of Philippians — 30
  1. Philippians as a Letter — 30
  2. Philippians as Rhetoric — 33
  3. Authorship and Unity — 38
- C. Key Themes — 39
  1. The Defining Story of Christ — 39
  2. The Surpassing Knowledge of Christ — 40
  3. The Gracious Work of God — 41
  4. Cruciform Living — 42
  5. Partnership in the Gospel — 42
- D. The Approach and Intent of the Commentary — 43

COMMENTARY — 45

- I. Letter Opening: Philippians 1:1-11 — 45
  - A. Greeting (1:1-2) — 47
  - B. Thanksgiving and Prayer (1:3-11) — 51
    1. Thanksgiving (1:3-8) — 51
    2. Intercession (1:9-11) — 56
- II. Paul's Circumstances: An Example of Faithfulness to the Gospel: Philippians 1:12-26 — 63
  - A. The Gospel Progresses Through Paul's Imprisonment (1:12-14) — 65
  - B. Christ Is Proclaimed—Through True or False Motives (1:15-18a) — 67
  - C. Christ Is Glorified Through Paul's Living or Dying (1:18b-26) — 69
- III. Conduct Worthy of the Gospel: Exhortations and Examples: Philippians 1:27—2:18 — 83
  - A. An Appeal to Firmness and Unity in the Face of Opposition (1:27-30) — 84
  - B. An Appeal to Unity Through Unselfish Humility (2:1-4) — 94

	C. An Appeal to the Example of Christ (2:5-11)	105
	1. Paul's Exhortation: Adopt the Mind-set of Christ (2:5)	110
	2. Christ's Humiliation (2:6-8)	112
	3. Christ's Exaltation (2:9-11)	119
	D. An Appeal to Obedience (2:12-18)	127
	1. Work Out Your Own Salvation by God's Enabling Power (2:12-13)	129
	2. Live as God's Holy People in a Dark World (2:14-16)	132
	3. Share in Paul's Sacrificial Ministry (2:17-18)	136
IV.	Two Christlike Examples: Philippians 2:19-30	143
	A. Timothy (2:19-24)	145
	B. Epaphroditus (2:25-30)	147
V.	Standing Firm in the Face of Threats to the Gospel: Warnings and Examples: Philippians 3:1—4:1	155
	A. True and False Confidence (3:1-11)	155
	1. The Transition (3:1)	158
	2. A Warning Against "the Dogs" (3:2-4a)	159
	3. Paul's Jewish Pedigree (3:4b-6)	162
	4. The Surpassing Value of Knowing Christ (3:7-11)	165
	B. Pressing on Toward the Prize (3:12-14)	181
	C. Good and Bad Examples (3:15—4:1)	189
	1. Adopt a Mature Mind-set (3:15-16)	192
	2. Examples to Imitate: Paul and Others like Him (3:17)	195
	3. Examples to Avoid: Enemies of the Cross (3:18-19)	197
	4. A Heavenly Commonwealth and a Hope for the Future (3:20-21)	199
	5. Stand Firm in the Lord (4:1)	203
VI.	Final Exhortations: Philippians 4:2-9	211
	A. An Appeal for Unity (4:2-3)	213
	B. A Call to Joy and Peace in All Circumstances (4:4-7)	218
	C. A Call to Focus on the Excellent and Follow Paul's Example (4:8-9)	222
VII.	Concluding Matters: Philippians 4:10-23	233
	A. Gratitude for the Philippians' Gift (4:10-20)	233
	1. Rejoicing and Contentment (4:10-13)	237
	2. A Partnership in Giving and Receiving (4:14-17)	241
	3. Gratitude and God's Provision (4:18-20)	245
	B. The Letter Closing (4:21-23)	251

GENERAL EDITORS' PREFACE

The purpose of the New Beacon Bible Commentary is to make available to pastors and students in the twenty-first century a biblical commentary that reflects the best scholarship in the Wesleyan theological tradition. The commentary project aims to make this scholarship accessible to a wider audience to assist them in their understanding and proclamation of Scripture as God's Word.

Writers of the volumes in this series not only are scholars within the Wesleyan theological tradition and experts in their field but also have special interest in the books assigned to them. Their task is to communicate clearly the critical consensus and the full range of other credible voices who have commented on the Scriptures. Though scholarship and scholarly contribution to the understanding of the Scriptures are key concerns of this series, it is not intended as an academic dialogue within the scholarly community. Commentators of this series constantly aim to demonstrate in their work the significance of the Bible as the church's book and the contemporary relevance and application of the biblical message. The project's overall goal is to make available to the church and for her service the fruits of the labors of scholars who are committed to their Christian faith.

The *New International Version* (NIV) is the reference version of the Bible used in this series; however, the focus of exegetical study and comments is the biblical text in its original language. When the commentary uses the NIV, it is printed in bold. The text printed in bold italics is the translation of the author. Commentators also refer to other translations where the text may be difficult or ambiguous.

The structure and organization of the commentaries in this series seeks to facilitate the study of the biblical text in a systematic and methodical way. Study of each biblical book begins with an ***Introduction*** section that gives an overview of authorship, date, provenance, audience, occasion, purpose, sociological/cultural issues, textual history, literary features, hermeneutical issues, and theological themes necessary to understand the book. This section also includes a brief outline of the book and a list of general works and standard commentaries.

The commentary section for each biblical book follows the outline of the book presented in the introduction. In some volumes, readers will find section ***overviews*** of large portions of scripture with general comments on their overall literary structure and other literary features. A consistent feature of the commentary is the paragraph-by-paragraph study of biblical texts. This section has three parts: ***Behind the Text***, ***In the Text***, and ***From the Text***.

The goal of the ***Behind the Text*** section is to provide the reader with all the relevant information necessary to understand the text. This includes specific historical situations reflected in the text, the literary context of the text, sociological and cultural issues, and literary features of the text.

In the Text explores what the text says, following its verse-by-verse structure. This section includes a discussion of grammatical details, word studies, and the connectedness of the text to other biblical books/passages or other parts of the book being studied (the canonical relationship). This section provides transliterations of key words in Hebrew and Greek and their literal meanings. The goal here is to explain what the author would have meant and/or what the audience would have understood as the meaning of the text. This is the largest section of the commentary.

The *From the Text* section examines the text in relation to the following areas: theological significance, intertextuality, the history of interpretation, use of the Old Testament scriptures in the New Testament, interpretation in later church history, actualization, and application.

The commentary provides **sidebars** on topics of interest that are important but not necessarily part of an explanation of the biblical text. These topics are informational items and may cover archaeological, historical, literary, cultural, and theological matters that have relevance to the biblical text. Occasionally, longer detailed discussions of special topics are included as ***excurses.***

We offer this series with our hope and prayer that readers will find it a valuable resource for their understanding of God's Word and an indispensable tool for their critical engagement with the biblical texts.

Roger Hahn, Centennial Initiative General Editor
Alex Varughese, General Editor (Old Testament)
George Lyons, General Editor (New Testament)

ACKNOWLEDGMENTS

I never planned to write a commentary. But when I was invited to do so on Philippians, a letter I have loved and taught for many years, I could not decline. What began as a seemingly overwhelming assignment has become a labor of love. I did not expect that writing a commentary could be such a spiritually enriching task.

Many people have helped to make this book possible. Thanks goes to Beacon Hill Press and its director, Bonnie Perry, for enabling this commentary project. I am also grateful to the administration of European Nazarene College for allowing release time from teaching in the latter stages of writing. And I cannot neglect to thank my students, both in Asia and in Europe, who have sharpened my thinking about Philippians over the years.

Special appreciation goes to a number of faithful friends who have read part or all of the commentary. They include Tim Isbell, Jonathan Falkenstein, Bruce Petersen, Kevin Peacock, Darrell Ranum, John M. Nielson, Ayo Adewuya, and Stephen Merki. The latter three deserve my particular gratitude for reading the entire manuscript. Without the encouragement and incisive comments of these readers, the end product would surely have been much the poorer.

I am also deeply grateful to George Lyons for his investment of many, many hours in carefully editing the commentary. His broad understanding of Paul's writings and attention to detail have constantly challenged me to think more clearly about the meaning of this letter.

My thanks goes as well to the members of the Monday evening Bible study I lead. They have consistently prayed for me and encouraged me throughout this project. In addition, my father, Floyd O. Flemming, deserves special mention. He has been a source of encouragement and unwavering support at every point of this journey. Growing up in a pastor's home, I heard my father preach from Philippians on many occasions. His passion for God's Word has significantly shaped my own love for Scripture. I gratefully acknowledge his example and prayers.

Finally, thanks be to God for his guidance, inspiration, and strength. For whatever small help this commentary may offer to the church and its ministers, God alone deserves the honor. "To our God and Father be glory for ever and ever" (Phil 4:20).

—Dean Flemming

ABBREVIATIONS

With a few exceptions, these abbreviations follow those in *The SBL Handbook of Style* (Alexander 1999).

General

A.D.	anno Domini
ACCS	Ancient Christian Commentary on Scripture
B.C.	before Christ
ch	chapter
chs	chapters
CEV	Contemporary English Version
DPL	*Dictionary of Paul and His Letters*. Edited by G. F. Hawthorne and R. P. Martin. Downers Grove, Ill.: InterVarsity Press, 1993.
EDNT	*Exegetical Dictionary of the New Testament*. Edited by H. Balz and G. Schneider. Grand Rapids: Eerdmans, 1990–93.
e.g.	*exempli gratia*, for example
esp.	especially
etc.	*et cetera*, and the rest
i.e.	*id est*, that is
GNT	Good News Translation: Today's English Version
JSNTSup	Journal for the Study of the New Testament: Supplement Series
KJV	King James Version
ktl.	etc. (in Greek transliteration)
LXX	Septuagint
n	note
NASB	New American Standard Bible
n.d.	no date
NEB	New English Bible
NIDNTT	*New International Dictionary of New Testament Theology*. Edited by C. Brown. 4 vols. Grand Rapids: Zondervan, 1975–85.
NIV	New International Version
NKJV	New King James Version
NLT	New Living Translation
NovTSup	Novum Testamentum Supplements
NRSV	New Revised Standard Version
NT	New Testament
OT	Old Testament
Phillips	The New Testament in Modern English
SNTSMS	Society for New Testament Studies Monograph Series
TDNT	*Theological Dictionary of the New Testament*. Edited by G. Kittel and G. Friedrich. Translated by G. W. Bromiley. 10 vols. Grand Rapids: Eerdmans, 1964–76.
TLB	The Living Bible
TM	The Message
TNIV	Today's New International Version
v	verse
vv	verses

Print Conventions for Translations

Bold font	NIV (bold without quotation marks in the text under study; elsewhere in the regular font, with quotation marks and no further identification)
Bold italic font	Author's translation (without quotation marks)

Behind the Text:	Literary or historical background information average readers might not know from reading the biblical text alone
In the Text:	Comments on the biblical text, words, phrases, grammar, and so forth
From the Text:	The use of the text by later interpreters, contemporary relevance, theological and ethical implications of the text, with particular emphasis on Wesleyan concerns

Old Testament

Gen	Genesis	Dan	Daniel		
Exod	Exodus	Hos	Hosea		
Lev	Leviticus	Joel	Joel		
Num	Numbers	Amos	Amos		
Deut	Deuteronomy	Obad	Obadiah		
Josh	Joshua	Jonah	Jonah		
Judg	Judges	Mic	Micah		
Ruth	Ruth	Nah	Nahum		
1–2 Sam	1–2 Samuel	Hab	Habakkuk		
1–2 Kgs	1–2 Kings	Zeph	Zephaniah		
1–2 Chr	1–2 Chronicles	Hag	Haggai		
Ezra	Ezra	Zech	Zechariah		
Neh	Nehemiah	Mal	Malachi		
Esth	Esther				
Job	Job				
Ps/Pss	Psalms				
Prov	Proverbs				
Eccl	Ecclesiastes				
Song	Song of Songs / Song of Solomon				
Isa	Isaiah				
Jer	Jeremiah				
Lam	Lamentations				
Ezek	Ezekiel				

(Note: Chapter and verse numbering in the MT and LXX often differ compared to those in English Bibles. To avoid confusion, all biblical references follow the chapter and verse numbering in English translations, even when the text in the MT and LXX is under discussion.)

New Testament

Matt	Matthew
Mark	Mark
Luke	Luke
John	John
Acts	Acts
Rom	Romans
1–2 Cor	1–2 Corinthians
Gal	Galatians
Eph	Ephesians
Phil	Philippians
Col	Colossians
1–2 Thess	1–2 Thessalonians
1–2 Tim	1–2 Timothy
Titus	Titus
Phlm	Philemon
Heb	Hebrews
Jas	James
1–2 Pet	1–2 Peter
1–2–3 John	1–2–3 John
Jude	Jude
Rev	Revelation

Apocrypha and Ancient Jewish Writings

Bar	Baruch
Let. Aris.	*Letter of Aristeas*
4 Macc.	4 Maccabees
Sir	Sirach
T. Benj.	*Testament of Benjamin*
Wis	Wisdom of Solomon

Qumran / Dead Sea Scrolls
- *1QH* — *Hodayot*, Thanksgiving Prayers
- *1QS* — *Serek Hayahad*, Rule of the Community

Josephus
- *Ag. Ap.* — Against Apion

Philo
- *Cong.* — *De congressueru ditionis gratia*, On the Preliminary Studies
- *Virt.* — *De Virtutibus*, On the Virtues

Early Christian Writings

1 Clem.	1 Clement
2 Apol.	Justin Martyr, *Apologia ii*, Second Apology
Diogn.	*Diognetus*
Hom. Phil.	John Chrysostom, *Homiliae in epistulam ad Philippenses*, Homilies on the Letter to the Philippians
Ign. Rom.	Ignatius, *To the Romans*
Pol. Phil.	Polycarp, *To the Philippians*

Other Ancient Writings

Aeschylus, *Prom.* — *Prometheus vinctus*
Appian, *Bell. Civ.* — *Bella civilia*
Aristotle
- *Eth. Nic.* — *Ethica nichomachea*
- *Rhet.* — *Rhetorica*

Cicero
- *Amic.* — *De Amicitia*
- *Rab. Perd.* — *Pro Rabirio Perduellionis Reo*

Plato, *Apol.* — *Apologia*
Ps-Isocrates, *Dem.* — Pseudo-Isocrates, *Ad Demonicum*
Quintilian, *Orat.* — *Institutio oratoria*

Seneca
  Ben.   *De beneficiis*
  Ep.   *Epistulae morales*
  Vit. Beat. *De vita beata*
Papyri
  BGU   *Aegyptische Urkunden aus den Königlichen Staatlichen Museen zu Berlin, Griechische Urkunden.* 15 vols. Berlin, 1895–1983.
  CPJ   *Corpus papyrorum judaicorum.* Ed. V. Tcherikover. 3 vols. Cambridge, Mass.: Harvard University Press, 1957–64.
  Pmich. Michigan Papyri
  PTebt. Tebtunis Papyri

Greek Transliteration

Greek	Letter	English
α	alpha	a
β	bēta	b
γ	gamma	g
γ	gamma nasal	n (before γ, κ, ξ, χ)
δ	delta	d
ε	epsilon	e
ζ	zēta	z
η	ēta	ē
θ	thēta	th
ι	iōta	i
κ	kappa	k
λ	lambda	l
μ	my	m
ν	ny	n
ξ	xi	x
ο	omicron	o
π	pi	p
ρ	rhō	r
ρ	initial *rhō*	rh
σ/ς	sigma	s
τ	tau	t
υ	upsilon	y
υ	upsilon	u (in diphthongs: au, eu, ēu, ou, ui)
φ	phi	ph
χ	chi	ch
ψ	psi	ps
ω	ōmega	ō
῾	rough breathing	h (before initial vowels or diphthongs)

Hebrew Consonant Transliteration

Hebrew/Aramaic	Letter	English
א	alef	ʼ
ב	bet	b
ג	gimel	g
ד	dalet	d
ה	he	h
ו	vav	v or w
ז	zayin	z
ח	khet	ḥ
ט	tet	ṭ
י	yod	y
כ/ך	kaf	k
ל	lamed	l
מ/ם	mem	m
נ/ן	nun	n
ס	samek	s
ע	ayin	ʽ
פ/ף	pe	p
צ/ץ	tsade	ṣ
ק	qof	q
ר	resh	r
שׂ	sin	ś
שׁ	shin	š
ת	tav	t

BIBLIOGRAPHY

Abate, Eshetu. 2006. Philippians. Pages 1439-48 in *Africa Biblical Commentary*. Grand Rapids: Zondervan.
Alexander, Loveday. 1989. Hellenistic Letter-Forms and the Structure of Philippians. *Journal for the Study of the New Testament* 37:87-101.
Alexander, Patrick H., and others, eds. 1999. *The SBL Handbook of Style for Ancient Near Eastern, Biblical, and Early Christian Studies*. Peabody, Mass.: Hendrickson.
Aquinas, Thomas. 1969. *Commentary on Saint Paul's First Letter to the Thessalonians and Letter to the Philippians*. Translated by F. R. Larcher and M. Duffy. Albany, N.Y.: Magi Books.
Arnold, Clinton E. 1992. *Powers of Darkness: Principalities and Powers in Paul's Letters*. Downers Grove, Ill.: InterVarsity Press.
Aune, David E. 1988. *The New Testament in Its Literary Environment*. Philadelphia: Westminster.
Barth, Karl. 1962. *The Epistle to the Philippians*. Translated by J. W. Leitch. London: SCM.
Basevi, Claudio, and Juan Chapa. 1993. Philippians 2.6-11: The Rhetorical Function of a Pauline "Hymn." Pages 338-56 in *Rhetoric and the New Testament: Essays from the 1992 Heidelberg Conference*. Edited by S. E. Porter and T. H. Olbricht. Sheffield: JSOT Press.
Bassett, Paul M., ed. 1997. *Great Holiness Classics*. Vol. 1. *Holiness Teaching—New Testament Times to Wesley*. Kansas City: Beacon Hill Press of Kansas City.
Bauckham, Richard. 1998. *God Crucified: Monotheism and Christology in the New Testament*. Grand Rapids: Eerdmans.
Bauer, Walter. 1979. *A Greek-English Lexicon of the New Testament and Other Early Christian Literature*. 2nd ed. Translated and adapted by F. W. Arndt, F. W. Gingrich, W. Danker. Chicago and London: University of Chicago Press.
Bauernfeind, O. 1964. *aret*. TDNT 1:457-61.
Beare, F. W. 1959. *A Commentary on the Epistle to the Philippians*. Harper's New Testament Commentaries. Peabody, Mass.: Hendrickson.
Behm, J. 1967. *morphē, ktl*. TDNT 4:742-52.
Berry, Ken L. 1996. The Function of Friendship Language in Philippians 4:10-20. Pages 107-24 in *Friendship, Flattery, and Frankness of Speech: Studies on Friendship in the New Testament World*. Edited by J. T. Fitzgerald. Leiden: Brill.
Best, Ernest. 1988. *Paul and His Converts: The Sprunt Lectures 1985*. Edinburgh: T & T Clark.
Black, David A. 1985. Paul and Christian Unity: A Formal Analysis of Philippians 2:1-4. *Journal of the Evangelical Theological Society* 28:299-308.
———. 1995. The Discourse Structure of Philippians: A Study in Textlinguistics. *Novum Testamentum* 37:16-49.
Blomberg, Craig L. 1999. *Neither Poverty nor Riches: A Biblical Theology of Material Possessions*. Grand Rapids/Cambridge: Eerdmans.
Bloomquist, L. Gregory. 1993. *The Function of Suffering in Philippians*. JSNTSup 78. Sheffield: Sheffield Academic Press.
Blum, G. G. 1972. The Office of Woman in the New Testament. Pages 63-77 in *Why Not? Priesthood and the Ministry of Women*. Edited by Michael Bruce and G. E. Duffield. Appleford, U.K.: Marcham.
Bockmuehl, Markus. 1995. A Commentator's Approach to the "Effective History" of Philippians. *Journal for the Study of the New Testament* 60:57-88.
———. 1998. *The Epistle to the Philippians*. Black's New Testament Commentary. Peabody, Mass.: Hendrickson.
Bonhoeffer, Dietrich. 1954. *Life Together*. Translated by J. W. Doberstein. New York: Harper and Row.
Bormann, Lukas. 1995. *Philippi: Stadt und Christengemeinde zur Zeit des Paulus*. NovTSup 78. Leiden: Brill.
Braumann, G. 1975. Form. *NIDNTT* 1:703-10.
Brewer, Raymond R. 1954. The Meaning of *Politeusthe* in Phil 1:27. *Journal of Biblical Literature* 73:76-83.
Bruce, F. F. 1983. *Philippians*. Good News Bible Commentary. Basingstoke, U.K.: Pickering and Inglis.

Calvin, John. 1965. *The Epistles of Paul the Apostle to the Galatians, Ephesians, Philippians and Colossians.* Translated by T. H. L. Parker. Grand Rapids: Eerdmans.

Capes, David B., Rodney Reeves, and E. R. Richards. 2007. *Rediscovering Paul: An Introduction to His World, Letters and Theology.* Downers Grove, Ill.: InterVarsity Press.

Carson, D. A. 1996. *Basics for Believers: An Exposition of Philippians.* Grand Rapids: Baker.

Chrysostom, St. John. 1983. *Homilies on Galatians, Ephesians, Philippians, Colossians, Thessalonians, Timothy, Titus, and Philemon.* In vol. 13 of *The Nicene and Post-Nicene Fathers.* Series 1. Edited by Philip Schaff. Repr. Grand Rapids: Eerdmans.

Clarke, Adam. n.d. *The New Testament of Our Lord and Saviour Jesus Christ.* Vol. 2. *Romans to Revelation.* Nashville: Abingdon.

Coenen, L. 1975. Call. *NIDNTT* 1:271-76.

Couslan, J. R. C. 2000. Athletics. Pages 140-42 in *Dictionary of New Testament Background.* Edited by Craig A. Evans and Stanley E. Porter. Downers Grove, Ill.: InterVarsity Press.

Craddock, Fred. 1985. *Philippians.* Interpretation. Atlanta: John Knox.

Croy, N. Clayton. 2003. "To Die Is Gain" (Philippians 1:19-26): Does Paul Contemplate Suicide? *Journal of Biblical Literature* 122:517-31.

Cullmann, Oscar. 1963. *The Christology of the New Testament.* 2nd ed. Translated by Shirley C. Guthrie. London: SCM.

Culpepper, R. Alan. 1980. Co-Workers in Suffering: Philippians 2:19-30. *Review and Expositor* 77:349-58.

Dahl, Nils A. 1995. Euodia and Syntyche and Paul's Letter to the Philippians. Pages 3-14 in *The Social World of the First Christians: Essays in Honor of Wayne A. Meeks.* Edited by L. M. White and O. L. Yarbrough. Minneapolis: Fortress.

Deasley, Alex R. G. 2005. Commentary on Philippians. *Illustrated Bible Life* 29, 1:4-53.

———. 2007. Philippians. Pages 147-240 in E. L. Wilson, A. R. Deasley, and B. L. Callen, *Galatians, Philippians, Colossians: A Commentary for Bible Students.* Wesleyan Bible Commentary. Indianapolis: Wesleyan Publishing House.

Delling, G. 1972. *teleios.* TDNT 8:67-78.

deSilva, David A. 2000. *Honor, Patronage, Kinship, and Purity: Unlocking New Testament Culture.* Downers Grove, Ill.: InterVarsity Press.

———. 2004. *An Introduction to the New Testament: Contexts, Methods, and Ministry Formation.* Downers Grove, Ill. / Leceister, U.K.: InterVarsity Press.

Droge, Arthur J., and James D. Tabor. 1992. *A Noble Death: Suicide and Martyrdom Among Jews and Christians in Antiquity.* San Francisco: HarperSanFrancisco.

Dunn, James D. G. 1980. *Christology in the Making: An Inquiry into the Origins of the Doctrine of the Incarnation.* London: SCM Press.

———. 1997. Once More, *PISTIS CRISTOU.* Pages 61-81 in *Pauline Theology.* Vol. 4: *Looking Back, Pressing On.* Edited by E. Elizabeth Johnson and David M. Hay. Atlanta: Scholars Press.

———. 1998. *The Theology of Paul the Apostle.* Grand Rapids: Eerdmans.

Dunning, H. Ray. 1988a. *Grace, Faith, and Holiness: A Wesleyan Systematic Theology.* Kansas City: Beacon Hill Press of Kansas City.

———. 1988b. Christian Perfection: Toward a New Paradigm. *Wesleyan Theological Journal* 33:151-63.

Dyrness, William A. 1995. *The Earth Is God's: A Theology of American Culture.* Maryknoll, N.Y.: Orbis.

Edwards, Mark J., ed. 1999. *Galatians, Ephesians, Philippians.* Ancient Christian Commentary on Scripture. Vol. 8. Downers Grove, Ill.: InterVarsity Press.

Ezell, Douglas. 1980. The Sufficiency of Christ: Philippians 4. *Review and Expositor* 77:373-81.

Fee, Gordon D. 1995. *Paul's Letter to the Philippians.* New International Commentary on the New Testament. Grand Rapids: Eerdmans.

———. 1999. *Philippians.* IVP New Testament Commentary. Downers Grove, Ill.: InterVarsity Press.

Fitzgerald, John T. 1992. Epistle to the Philippians. Pages 318-26 in vol. 5 of *Anchor Bible Dictionary.* Edited by David N. Freedman. New York: Doubleday.

———. 1996. Philippians in the Light of Some Ancient Discussions of Friendship. Pages 141-60 in *Friendship, Flattery, and Frankness of Speech: Studies on Friendship in the New Testament World.* Edited by J. T. Fitzgerald. Leiden: Brill.

———. 2007. Christian Friendship: John, Paul, and the Philippians. *Interpretation* 61:284-96.

Fitzmyer, Joseph A. 1993. The Consecutive Meaning of *EPH' HŌ* in Romans 5.12. *New Testament Studies* 39:321-39.
Flemming, Dean. 1994. The Clergy/Laity Dichotomy: A New Testament Exegetical and Theological Analysis. *Asia Journal of Theology* 8:232-50.
———. 2005. *Contextualization in the New Testament: Patterns for Theology and Mission*. Downers Grove, Ill./Leicester, U.K.: InterVarsity Press / Apollos.
Foster, Richard. 1985. *Money, Sex and Power: The Challenge of the Disciplined Life*. London: Hodder and Stoughton.
Fowl, Stephen E. 1990. *The Story of Christ in the Ethics of Paul*. JSNTSup 36. Sheffield: JSOT Press.
———. 2005. *Philippians*. Two Horizons New Testament Commentary. Grand Rapids: Eerdmans.
———. 1998. Christology and Ethics in Philippians 2:5-11. Pages 140-53 in *Where Christology Began: Essays on Philippians 2*. Edited by R. P. Martin and B. J. Dodd. Louisville, Ky.: Westminster/John Knox.
France, R. T. 1995. *Women in the Church's Ministry: A Test-Case for Biblical Hermeneutics*. Carlisle, U.K.: Paternoster.
Furnish, Victor P. 1985. *The Moral Teaching of Paul: Selected Issues*. Nashville: Abingdon.
Garland, David E. 1985. The Composition and Unity of Philippians: Some Neglected Literary Factors. *Novum Testamentum* 27:141-73.
Gaventa, Beverly R. 1986. Galatians 1 and 2: Autobiography as Paradigm. *Novum Testamentum* 28:309-26.
Geoffrion, T. C. 1993. *The Rhetorical Purpose and the Political and Military Character of Philippians: A Call to Stand Firm*. Lewiston, N.Y.: Mellen.
Giesen, H. 1991. *eritheia*. EDNT 2:52.
Gorman, Michael J. 2001. *Cruciformity: Paul's Narrative Spirituality of the Cross*. Grand Rapids: Eerdmans.
———. 2004. *Apostle of the Crucified Lord: A Theological Introduction to Paul and His Letters*. Grand Rapids: Eerdmans.
Greathouse, William, and George Lyons. 2008. *Romans 1-8: A Commentary in the Wesleyan Tradition*. Kansas City: Beacon Hill Press of Kansas City.
Green, Gene. 2002. *The Letters to the Thessalonians*. Pillar New Testament Commentary. Grand Rapids: Eerdmans.
Gregory of Nyssa. 1995. *From Glory to Glory: Texts from Gregory of Nyssa's Mystical Writings*. Introduction by Jean Daniélou. Translated and edited by Herbert Musurillo. New York: Charles Scribner's Sons, 1961. Repr. Crestwood, N.Y.: St. Vladimir's Seminary Press.
Grundmann, W. 1972. *tapeinos, ktl*. TDNT 8:1-26.
Gutbrod, Walter. 1965. *Hebraios*. TDNT 3:389-91.
Hahn, H.-C. 1976. Openness, Frankness, Boldness. NIDNTT 2:734-37.
Hainz, J. 1991. *koinōnos*. EDNT 2:303-5.
Hawthorne, Gerald F. 1993. Letter to the Philippians. Pages 707-13 in *DPL*.
———. 1996. The Imitation of Christ: Discipleship in Philippians. Pages 163-79 in *Patterns of Discipleship in the New Testament*. Edited by R. N. Longenecker. Grand Rapids: Eerdmans.
Hawthorne, Gerald F., and Ralph P. Martin. 2004. *Philippians*. Word Biblical Commentary. Rev. ed. Nashville: Thomas Nelson.
Hays, Richard B. 1989. *Echoes of Scripture in the Letters of Paul*. New Haven, Conn.: Yale University Press.
———. 1992. Justification. Pages 1129-33 in vol. 3 of *Anchor Bible Dictionary*. Edited by David N. Freedman. Garden Grove, N.Y.: Doubleday.
———. 1996. *The Moral Vision of the New Testament: A Contemporary Introduction to New Testament Ethics*. San Francisco: HarperSanFrancisco.
———. 1997a. *PISTIS* and Pauline Christology: What Is at Stake? Pages 35-60 in *Pauline Theology, Vol. 4: Looking Back, Pressing On*. Edited by E. Elizabeth Johnson and David M. Hay. Atlanta: Scholars Press.
———. 1997b. *First Corinthians*. Interpretation. Louisville, Ky.: John Knox.
———. 2000. Galatians. Pages 181-348 in *The New Interpreter's Bible*. Vol. 11. Nashville: Abingdon.
Hegermann, H. 1990. *doxa*. EDNT 1:344-48.
Hellerman, Joseph H. 2005. *Reconstructing Honor in Roman Philippi: Carmen Christi as Cursus Pudorum*. SNTSMS 132. Cambridge: Cambridge University Press.
Hengel, Martin. 1977. *Crucifixion*. Translated by J. Bowden. London: SCM.

———. 1991. *The Pre-Christian Paul*. Translated by J. Bowden. London: SCM.
Holloway, Paul A. 2001. *Consolation in Philippians: Philosophical Sources and Rhetorical Strategy*. SNTSMS 112. Cambridge: Cambridge University Press.
Holmes, Michael W., ed. and trans. 2007. *The Apostolic Fathers: Greek Texts and English Translations*. 3rd ed. Grand Rapids: Baker.
Hooker, Morna D. 1994. *Not Ashamed of the Gospel: New Testament Interpretations of the Death of Christ*. Carlisle, U.K.: Paternoster.
———. 2000. Pages 467-549 in *The New Interpreter's Bible*. Vol. 11. Nashville: Abingdon.
Hoover, Roy. 1971. The HARPAGMOS Enigma: A Philological Solution. *Harvard Theological Review* 64:95-119.
Horstmann, A. 1990. *aischnomai*. *EDNT* 1:42-43.
Houston, James. M. 2006. *Joyful Exiles: Life in Christ on the Dangerous Edge of Things*. Downers Grove, Ill.: InterVarsity Press.
Hunt, A. S., and C. C. Edgar, eds. 1970. *Select Papyri I. Non-Literary Papyri*. Repr. Cambridge, Mass./London: Harvard University Press/William Heinemann.
Hurtado, L. W. 1984. Jesus as Lordly Example in Philippians 2:5-11. Pages 113-26 in *From Jesus to Paul: Studies in Honour of Frances Wright Beare*. Edited by P. Richardson and J. C. Hurd. Waterloo, Ont.: Wilfrid Laurier University Press.
Jewett, Robert. 2007. *Romans*. Hermeneia. Minneapolis: Fortress.
Johnson, Luke T. 1999. *The Writings of the New Testament: An Interpretation*. Rev. ed. Minneapolis: Fortress.
Jowers, Dennis W. 2006. The Meaning of MORPH in Philippians 2:6-7. *Journal of the Evangelical Theological Society* 49:739-66.
Käsemann, Ernst. 1968. A Critical Analysis of Philippians 2.5-11. Pages 45-88 in *God in Christ: Existence and Province*. Edited by Robert W. Funk. New York: Harper and Row.
Keener, Craig S. 1992. *Paul, Women, and Wives: Marriage and Women's Ministry in the Letters of Paul*. Peabody, Mass.: Hendrickson.
———. 2000. Friendship. Pages 380-88 in *Dictionary of New Testament Background*. Edited by Craig A. Evans and Stanley E. Porter. Downers Grove, Ill.: InterVarsity Press.
Koperski, Veronica. 1996. *The Knowledge of Jesus Christ My Lord: The High Christology of Philippians 3:7-11*. Kampen: Kok Pharos.
Kreitzer, Larry J. 1993. Body. Pages 71-76 in *DPL*.
———. 1998. "'When He at Last Is First!': Philippians 2:9-11 and the Exaltation of the Lord." Pages 111-27 in *Where Christology Began: Essays on Philippians 2*. Edited by R. P. Martin and B. J. Dodd. Louisville, Ky.: Westminster/John Knox.
Kruse, Colin. 1993a. Call, Calling. Pages 84-85 in *DPL*.
———. 1993b. Afflictions, Trials, Hardships. Pages 18-20 in *DPL*.
Kurz, William S. 1985. Kenotic Imitation of Paul and of Christ in Philippians 2 and 3. Pages 103-26 in *Discipleship in the NT*. Edited by Fernando F. Segovia. Philadelphia: Fortress.
Lang, Friedrich. 1971. *skybalon*. *TDNT* 7:445-47.
Liddell, Henry George, Robert Scott, Henry Stuart Jones, and Roderick McKenzie. 1996. *A Greek-English Lexicon*. Rev. and augm. throughout. Oxford: Clarendon Press.
Lightfoot, J. B. 1953. *St. Paul's Epistle to the Philippians*. Repr. Grand Rapids: Zondervan.
Lincoln, Andrew T. 1981. *Paradise Now and Not Yet: Studies in the Role of the Heavenly Dimension in Paul's Thought with Special Reference to His Eschatology*. SNTSMS 43. Cambridge: Cambridge University Press.
Link, H.-G., and A. Ringwald. 1978. Virtue. *NIDNTT* 3:925-28.
Lohmeyer, Ernst. 1929. *Die Briefe an die Philipper, an die Kolosser und an Philemon*. Göttingen: Vandenhoeck und Ruprecht.
Lüderitz, Gerd. 1994. What Is the *Politeuma*? Pages 183-225 in *Studies in Early Jewish Epigraphy*. Edited by J. W. Van Heuten and P. W. Van der Horst. Leiden: Brill.
Luter, Boyd. 1996. Partnership in the Gospel: The Role of Women in the Church at Philippi. *Journal of the Evangelical Theological Society* 39:411-20.
Luther, Martin. 1972. *Luther's Works*. Vol. 25. *Lectures on Romans*. Edited by H. C. Oswald. St. Louis: Concordia Publishing House.
Lyons, George. 1985. *Pauline Autobiography: Toward a New Understanding*. Atlanta: Scholars Press.
———. 1996. Money. Graduation Address, Nazarene Theological College. Brisbane, QLD. No pages. Accessed 25 September 2008. Online: http://wesley.nnu.edu/misc_sermons/money.htm#_edn6.

Lyons, George, and William H. Malas. 2007. Paul and His Friends Within the Greco-Roman Context. *Wesleyan Theological Journal* 42:50-69.
Maddox, Randy L. 1994. *Responsible Grace: John Wesley's Practical Theology*. Nashville: Kingswood Books.
Magaay, Melba P. 1987. *The Gospel in Filipino Context*. Manila: OMF Literature.
Malherbe, Abraham J. 1986. *Moral Exhortation, A Greco-Roman Sourcebook*. Philadelphia: Westminster.
———. 1996. Paul's Self-Sufficiency (Philippians 4:11). Pages 125-39 in *Friendship, Flattery, and Frankness of Speech: Studies on Friendship in the New Testament World*. Edited by J. T. Fitzgerald. Leiden: Brill.
———. 2000. *1 and 2 Thessalonians*. Anchor Bible. Vol. 32B. Garden City, N.Y.: Doubleday.
Manning, Brennan. 2002. *The Wisdom of Tenderness*. San Francisco: HarperSanFrancisco.
Marchal, Joseph A. 2006. With Friends Like These . . . : A Feminist Rhetorical Reconsideration of Scholarship and the Letter to the Philippians. *Journal for the Study of the New Testament* 29:77-106.
Marshall, I. Howard. 1991. *Philippians*. Epworth Commentaries. London: Epworth.
———. 1993. The Theology of Philippians. Pages 115-91 in Karl P. Donfried and I. Howard Marshall. *The Theology of the Shorter Pauline Letters*. Cambridge: Cambridge University Press.
———. 2004. *New Testament Theology: Many Witnesses, One Gospel*. Downers Grove, Ill.: InterVarsity Press.
Martin, Ralph P. 1976. *Philippians*. New Century Bible. London: Marshall, Moran and Scott.
———. 1997. *A Hymn of Christ: Philippians 2:5-11 in Recent Interpretation and in the Setting of Early Christian Worship*. Downers Grove, Ill.: InterVarsity Press. Repr. *Carmen Christi*. London: Cambridge University Press, 1967.
Mason, Steve. 2000. Pharisees. Pages 782-87 in *Dictionary of New Testament Background*. Edited by Craig A. Evans and Stanley E. Porter. Downers Grove, Ill.: InterVarsity Press.
McEwan, David B. 2002. Being Holy Is Being Christlike: To What Extent Is This a Definable and Useful Model in an Australian Context? *Didache* 2, 1. 17 pages. Accessed 25 September 2008. Online: http://didache.nts.edu/index.php?option=com_docman&task=doc_view&gid=278&Itemid=.
Meeks, Wayne A. 1983. *The First Urban Christians: The Social World of the Apostle Paul*. New Haven, Conn.: Yale University Press.
Michael, J. H. 1928. *The Epistle of Paul to the Philippians*. Moffatt New Testament Commentary. London: Hodder & Stoughton.
Morrice, W. G. 1993. Joy. Pages 511-12 in *DPL*.
Morris, Leon. 1993. Truth. Pages 954-55 in *DPL*.
Moule, C. F. D. 1970. Further Reflection on Philippians 2:5-11. Pages 264-76 in *Apostolic History and the Gospels*. Edited by W. Ward Gasque and Ralph P. Martin. Grand Rapids: Eerdmans.
Murphy-O'Connor, Jerome. 1995. *Paul the Letter-Writer: His World, His Options, His Skills*. Collegeville, Minn.: Michael Glazier/Liturgical Press.
Nouwen, Henri, Donald P. McNeill, and Douglas A. Morrison. 1982. *Compassion: A Reflection on the Christian Life*. New York: Image Books.
Oakes, Peter. 2001. *Philippians: From People to Letter*. SNTSMS 110. Cambridge: Cambridge University Press.
O'Brien, Peter T. 1977. *Introductory Thanksgivings in the Letter of Paul*. NovTSup 49. Leiden: Brill.
———. 1986. The Importance of the Gospel in Philippians. Pages 213-33 in *God Who Is Rich in Mercy. Essays presented to D. B. Knox*. Edited by P. T. O'Brien and D. G. Peterson. Homebush, NSW: Lancer.
———. 1991. *Commentary on Philippians*. New International Greek Testament Commentary. Grand Rapids: Eerdmans.
Oden, Thomas C. 1994. *John Wesley's Scriptural Christianity: Plain Exposition of His Teaching on Christian Doctrine*. Grand Rapids: Zondervan.
Onesti, K. L., and M. T. Brauch. 1993. Righteousness, Righteousness of God. Pages 827-37 in *DPL*.
Osiek, Carolyn. 2000. *Philippians, Philemon*. Abingdon New Testament Commentaries. Nashville: Abingdon.
Perkins, Pheme. 1991. Philippians: Theology for the Heavenly Politeuma. Pages 89-104 in *Pauline Theology*. Vol. 1. *Thessalonians, Philippians, Galatians, Philemon*. Edited by Jouette M. Bassler. Minneapolis: Fortress.
Peterlin, Davorin. 1995. *Paul's Letter to the Philippians in the Light of Disunity in the Church*. NovTSup 79. Leiden: Brill.

Peterman, Gerald W. 1991. "Thankless Thanks": The Epistolary Social Convention in Philippians 4:10-20. *Tyndale Bulletin* 42: 261-70.
———. 1997. *Paul's Gift from Philippi: Conventions of Gift Exchange and Christian Giving.* SNTSMS 92. Cambridge: Cambridge University Press.
Peterson, Eugene. 2006. *Eat This Book: A Conversation in the Art of Spiritual Reading.* Grand Rapids: Eerdmans.
Pfitzner, Victor C. 1967. *Paul and the Agon Motif: Traditional Athletic Imagery in the Pauline Literature.* NovTSup 16. Leiden: Brill.
Poythress, Vern S. 2002. "Hold Fast" Versus "Hold Out" in Philippians 2:16. *Westminster Theological Journal* 64:45-53.
Pucci, M. 2000. Circuses and Games. Pages 209-12 in *Dictionary of New Testament Background.* Edited by Craig A. Evans and Stanley E. Porter. Downers Grove, Ill.: InterVarsity Press.
Rapske, Brian. 1993. Prison, Prisoner. Pages 827-30 in *DPL.*
———. 1994. *The Book of Acts and Paul in Roman Custody.* Vol. 3. *The Book of Acts in Its First Century Setting.* Grand Rapids: Eerdmans.
Reed, Jeffrey T. 1991. The Infinitive with Two Substantival Accusatives, An Ambiguous Construction? *Novum Testamentum* 33:1-27.
Reumann, John. 1996. Philippians, Especially Chapter 4, as a "Letter of Friendship": Observations on a Checkered History of Scholarship. Pages 83-106 in *Friendship, Flattery, and Frankness of Speech: Studies on Friendship in the New Testament World.* Edited by John T. Fitzgerald. Leiden: Brill.
Richards, E. Randolph. 2004. *Paul and First-Century Letter Writing.* Downers Grove, Ill.: InterVarsity Press.
Sampley, J. Paul. 1980. *Pauline Partnership in Christ.* Philadelphia: Fortress.
Schippers, R. 1976. telos. *NIDNTT* 2:59-66.
Schlimm, Matthew R. 2003. The Puzzle of Perfection: Growth in John Wesley's Doctrine of Perfection. *Wesleyan Theological Journal* 38, 2:124-42.
Schrenk, G. 1964. dikaios. *TDNT* 2:182-91.
Schütz, John Howard. 1975. *Paul and the Anatomy of Apostolic Authority.* SNTSMS 26. Cambridge: Cambridge University Press.
Schweizer, E. 1971. sarx, ktl. *TDNT* 7:98-151.
Silva, Moises. 1993. Old Testament in Paul. Pages 630-42 in *DPL.*
———. 2005. *Philippians.* Baker Exegetical Commentary on the New Testament. 2nd ed. Grand Rapids: Baker.
Staples, Rob L. 1993. Holiness as Christlikeness (Phil. 2:5-11). Pages 211-20 in *Biblical Resources for Holiness Preaching: From Text to Sermon.* Vol. 2. Edited by H. Ray Dunning. Kansas City: Beacon Hill Press of Kansas City.
Stowers, Stanley K. 1986. *Letter Writing in Greco-Roman Antiquity.* Philadelphia: Westminster.
———. 1991. Friends and Enemies in the Politics of Heaven: Reading Theology in Philippians. Pages 105-21 in *Pauline Theology.* Vol. 1. *Thessalonians, Philippians, Galatians, Philemon.* Edited by Jouette M. Bassler. Minneapolis: Fortress.
Sumney, Jerry L. 2007. *Philippians: A Greek Student's Intermediate Reader.* Peabody, Mass.: Hendrickson.
Swift, Robert C. 1984. The Theme and Structure of Philippians. *Biblioteca Sacra* 141:234-54.
Talbert, Charles H. 2002. *Romans.* Smyth and Helwys Bible Commentary. Macon, Ga.: Smyth and Helwys.
Tarn, William, and G. T. Griffith. 1959. *Hellenistic Civilisation.* 3rd ed. London: Edward Arnold.
Thielman, Frank. 1995. *Philippians.* The NIV Application Commentary. Grand Rapids: Zondervan.
Thiselton, Anthony C. 1978. Truth. *NIDNTT* 3:874-902.
———. 2000. *The First Epistle to the Corinthians.* Grand Rapids: Eerdmans.
Thomas à Kempis. 1973. *Of the Imitation of Christ.* New Canaan, Conn.: Keats Publishing.
Thompson, Alan J. 2002. Blameless Before God? Philippians 3:6 in Context. *Themelios* 28:5-12.
Thompson, James W. 2007. Preaching to Philippians. *Interpretation* 61:298-309.
Thurston, Bonnie B., and Judith M. Ryan. 2005. *Philippians and Philemon.* Sacra Pagina. Collegeville, Minn.: Liturgical Press.
Vincent, Marvin R. 1897. *A Critical and Exegetical Commentary on the Epistles to the Philippians and to Philemon.* International Critical Commentary. Edinburgh: T & T Clark.
Volf, Miroslav. 1996. *Exclusion and Embrace: A Theological Exploration of Identity, Otherness, and Rec-*

onciliation. Nashville: Abingdon.
Wallace, Daniel B. 1996. *Greek Grammar Beyond the Basics.* Grand Rapids: Zondervan.
Walton, John H. 2001. *Genesis.* The NIV Application Commentary. Grand Rapids: Zondervan.
Wagner, J. Ross. 2007. Working Out Salvation: Holiness and Community in Philippians. Pages 257-74 in *Holiness and Ecclesiology in the New Testament.* Edited by Kent E. Brower and Andy Johnson. Grand Rapids/Cambridge: Eerdmans.
Wansink, C. 1996. *Chained in Christ.* JSNTSup 130. Sheffield: Sheffield Academic Press.
Ware, James. 2005. *The Mission of the Church in Paul's Letter to the Philippians in the Context of Ancient Judaism.* NovTSup 120. Leiden: Brill.
Watson, D. F. 1988. A Rhetorical Analysis of Philippians and Its Implications for the Unity Question. *Novum Testamentum* 30:57-88.
Weima, J. A. D. 1994. *Neglected Endings: The Significance of the Pauline Letter Closings.* JSNTSup 101. Sheffield: Sheffield Academic Press.
Welch, Reuben R. 1988. *The Open Secret of Strength.* Grand Rapids: Zondervan.
Wesley, Charles. 1983. Hymn 461. Pages 643-44 in *The Works of John Wesley.* Vol. 7: *A Collection of Hymns for the Use of the People Called Methodists.* Edited by Franz Hilderbrandt and Oliver A. Beckerlegge. Oxford: Oxford University Press, 1983. Repr. Nashville: Abingdon.
Wesley, John. n.d. *Explanatory Notes upon the New Testament.* Repr. Salem, Ohio: Schmul.
———. 1975—. *The Works of John Wesley.* Begun as the Oxford Edition. 1975-83. Oxford: Oxford University Press. Continued as the Bicentennial Edition, 1984—. Projected 35 vols. Nashville: Abingdon.
———. 1978-79. *The Works of John Wesley.* 3rd ed., 14 vols. Repr. Kansas City: Beacon Hill Press of Kansas City.
Westerholm, Stephen. 1992. Pages 609-14 in *Dictionary of Jesus and the Gospels.* Edited by J. B. Green, S. McKnight, and I. H. Marshall. Downers Grove, Ill.: InterVarsity Press.
White, John L. 1986. *Light from Ancient Letters.* Philadelphia: Fortress.
White, Michael L. 1990. Morality Between Two Worlds: A Paradigm of Friendship in Philippians. Pages 201-15 in *Greeks, Romans, and Christians: Essays in Honor of Abraham J. Malherbe.* Edited by D. L. Balch and others. Minneapolis: Fortress.
Willard, Dallas. 1988. *The Divine Conspiracy: Rediscovering Our Hidden Life in God.* San Francisco: HarperSanFrancisco.
Williams, David J. 1999. *Paul's Metaphors: Their Context and Character.* Peabody, Mass.: Hendrickson.
Williams, Demetrius K. 2002. *Enemies of the Cross of Christ: The Terminology of the Cross and Conflict in Philippians.* JSNTSup 223. Sheffield: Sheffield Academic Press.
Witherington, Ben, III. 1994. *Friendship and Finances in Philippi: The Letter of Paul to the Philippians.* Valley Forge, Pa.: Trinity Press International.
———. 1998. *Women in the Earliest Churches.* SNTSMS 59. Cambridge: Cambridge University Press.
Wright, N. T. 1991. *The Climax of the Covenant: Christ and the Law in Pauline Theology.* Minneapolis: Fortress.
———. 1997. *What Saint Paul Really Said: Was Paul of Tarsus the Real Founder of Christianity?* Grand Rapids: Eerdmans.
———. 2000. Paul's Gospel and Caesar's Empire. Pages 160-83 in *Paul and Politics:* Ecclesia, *Israel,* Imperium, *Interpretation.* Edited by R. A. Horsley. Harrisburg, Pa.: Trinity Press International.
———. 2003. *The Resurrection of the Son of God.* London: SPCK.
———. 2005a. Book of Philippians. Pages 588-90 in *Dictionary for the Theological Interpretation of the Bible.* Edited by Kevin J. Vanhoozer. Grand Rapids: Baker.
———. 2005b. *Paul: Fresh Perspectives.* London: SPCK.
———. 2007. *Surprised by Hope.* London: SPCK.
Ziesler, John A. 1972. *The Meaning of Righteousness in Paul: A Linguistic and Theological Enquiry.* Cambridge: Cambridge University Press.

INTRODUCTION

Paul's letter to the Philippians is "a small gem" (Wright 2005a, 588). One of the shortest of Paul's letters, it is perhaps the most beloved by the church. No doubt, this is due in part to its high concentration of memorable passages that constantly challenge and encourage the people of God (e.g., 1:6, 21; 2:5-11; 3:7-14, 20-21; 4:4-7, 13, 19). What is more, the letter glows with affection and joy. The imprisoned Paul who writes Philippians is not hard to love. But we should not allow the letter's warm and pastoral tone to mask its theological importance. Philippians is practical, but it is hardly "lightweight." It holds some deeply theological reflections, particularly about Christ (2:6-11) and the cruciform character of life in Christ (e.g., 1:27—2:5; 3:4-11).

Philippians is arguably Paul's most personal letter. It gives us an intimate glimpse into the self-understanding of this incarcerated apostle to the Gentiles. Paul airs his inmost thoughts (1:18-26), tells his personal story (1:12-26; 3:4-14; 4:11-13), and testifies to his burning passion to know Christ his Lord (3:8, 10-11) and to make him known. He also reveals his deep love and affection for this church, which has faithfully partnered with him in ministry from its earliest days.

But this letter is not *about* Paul. Above all, Philippians is concerned with the advance of the gospel and the formation of a local Christian community—a congregation that faces pressures from both inside and outside the church. Paul's theological response to his own situation and that of his audience yields a Christ-centered letter that continues to shape Christian communities today.

A. The Context of Philippians

1. The City and People of Philippi

First-century Philippi was located in the northeastern corner of the Roman province of Macedonia (in present-day Greece). With perhaps ten to fifteen thousand inhabitants, it was not a large city (Oakes 2001, 44-45). But it was strategically situated on the Via Egnatia, the main road linking Rome with the East. In addition, the important seaport of Neapolis (present-day Kavala) was only 10 miles (16 km) away. This "gateway between Europe and Asia" (Appian, *Bell. Civ.* IV, 106; cited by Oakes 2001, 12) became a vital crossroads for travel and trade, both by land and by sea. Inscriptional evidence indicates that among its merchants were traders in purple dye, like Lydia mentioned in Acts 16 (Gorman 2004, 414).

Map of the Via Egnatia

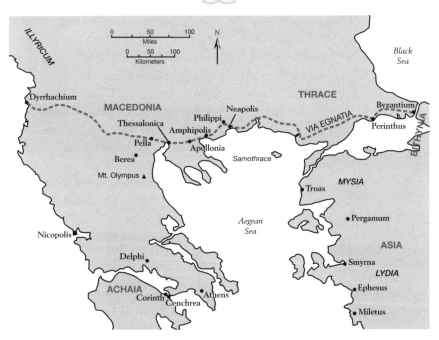

Philippi took its name from Alexander the Great's father, Philip II of Macedon, who fortified an earlier Greek city (356 B.C.) on this site. Two centuries later, Philippi came under Roman rule (168-67 B.C.). The city was the location of a famous battle in 42 B.C., in which Antony and Octavian (later emperor Augustus) defeated the assassins of Julius Caesar. The victorious generals founded Philippi as a Roman colony (Acts 16:12) and rewarded veteran soldiers with free grants of land there. Later, in 31 B.C., Augustus refounded the colony under his personal patronage and boosted the population with an influx of Italian colonists.

The status of a Roman colony gave the people of Philippi many privileges. They enjoyed, for example, considerable property and legal rights and exemption from taxes. Citizens of the colony were citizens of Rome. In most ways, a Roman colony like Philippi was considered an extension of Rome itself.

When Paul arrived in Philippi, he would have found a city with a sizable Roman population, a Roman civil administration, and a largely Roman public identity and appearance (in Acts 16:21, the citizens identify themselves as "Romans"). One evidence of this is that most public inscriptions were written in Latin, not Greek. While not all of the inhabitants were Roman citizens, all were expected to show loyalty to Rome and its emperor. Philippi's colonial status and identity provide a backdrop for Paul's "political" language in passages like 1:27 and 3:20. Paul urges Christians in Philippi to find their identity in a higher "citizenship" than that of Rome.

Despite the dominant influence of Roman culture and politics, Romans were probably in the minority in the region. There were sizable populations of native Thracians and Greeks, who were agricultural workers, tradespersons, and slaves. Greek, rather than Latin, was the common language. Using archaeological and other evidence, Oakes estimates that the city was comprised of roughly 40 percent Roman colonists and 60 percent non-Roman, Greek-speaking people (2001, 50).

Religion in the Roman colony of Philippi was a diverse mix. Not surprisingly, the official emperor cult was strong. In addition, there is evidence of the worship of various other traditional and local deities, including Zeus, the Roman god Silvanus, Dionysus, and Diana. There is, however, no archaeological evidence for a significant Jewish presence in first-century Philippi, and Acts makes no reference to a synagogue there (Acts 16:13 mentions a "place of prayer"). It appears that the population, as well as Paul's converts, were almost entirely Gentiles.

2. Paul's Mission in Philippi

Most of what we know about the origins of the church in Philippi comes from Acts 16 (on the historical reliability of the narrative in Acts, see Bockmuehl 1998, 10-12, 16-17). The events in Acts take place during what is widely called Paul's second missionary journey, probably in A.D. 49 or 50. In response to a vision of a man from Macedonia, Paul and his coworkers Silas and Timothy (vv 1-5) set sail from Asia (the "we" passages start at this point [v 10], implying that the narrator [traditionally Luke] joined the missionary party there). Landing at the port of Neapolis, they follow the Via Egnatia to Philippi. Paul finds several Gentile women who worshipped the God of Israel meeting for prayer outside the city gate. One of them, a businesswoman named Lydia, becomes the first Christian convert and provides hospitality for the newborn church (vv 14-15).

Paul's ministry in Philippi is earmarked by conflict (see Phil 1:29-30; 1 Thess 2:2). He ignites a public commotion when he casts out a demon from a fortune-telling slave girl. Her owners drag Paul and Silas before the Roman magistrates and accuse them of propagating anti-Roman, Jewish behavior among Gentiles (Acts 16:19-21). In response, the Roman officials have the two missionaries publicly beaten with rods and jailed (vv 22-35, 37-39). Their imprisonment, however, leads to the conversion and baptism of the jailer and his household (vv 25-34). Paul and Silas depart the city prematurely, but not before getting an apology from the magistrates for their unlawful treatment of Roman citizens. The missionaries leave behind a nucleus of new believers meeting in Lydia's home (vv 35-40). The founding of the church at Philippi represents a key development in Paul's missionary work, opening up a new area of ministry in Europe (for detailed discussions of Paul's Philippian ministry in Acts, see Bockmuehl 1998, 10-17; and Thurston 2005, 10-15).

Acts reports Paul's sustained contact with the churches in Macedonia through Timothy (19:21-23; see Phil 2:19-20). Paul himself probably visited Philippi on at least two more occasions during his third missionary journey (Acts 20:1-6; compare 1 Cor 16:5-6; 2 Cor 2:13; 7:5).

3. The Place and Date of Writing

Philippians is identified as one of Paul's "prison epistles" (along with Philemon, Colossians, and Ephesians), because the letter shows that he was a prisoner at the time of writing (1:7, 12-14, 17). What is much less certain is *where* he was being detained. Any attempt to answer that question must try to account for certain clues within Philippians itself (see Hawthorne 1993, 709): (1) Wherever Paul is in prison, his life hangs in the balance (vv 20-23), although he hopes for release (vv 23-26) and a subsequent visit to Philippi (2:24). (2) Timothy is with him (1:1) and will soon be sent as Paul's representative to Philippi (2:19-24). (3) Paul has the freedom to bear witness to believers and unbelievers alike, including some among the praetorium ("imperial guard," 1:13 NRSV). (4) He is able to receive visitors, including, on several occasions, representatives traveling to and from Philippi during the time of his imprisonment. (5) There is a Christian congregation nearby, which includes members of "Caesar's household" (4:22). Furthermore, significant evangelistic efforts are taking place in the city of his imprisonment (1:14-17). (6) It seems, however, that few of Paul's loyal friends are present there (2:20; see 1:15-17).

The traditional view, espoused since the second century, is that Paul wrote the letter from Rome. This seems to match up well with the evidence.

Acts relates that Paul was a prisoner in Rome under something like house arrest for at least two years (28:30). Although soldiers guarded him (v 16), he had the freedom to receive visitors and gifts, as well as to preach (vv 17, 30-31). There was also a sizable church in Rome, but one with few direct ties to Paul (Bockmuehl 1998, 30).

Furthermore, a Roman imprisonment also best accounts for the references to the praetorium and to "Caesar's household." The praetorium referred to a building as well as to the imperial guard. But the context favors the latter. Paul's mention of the **whole praetorium** (1:13) is more natural and impressive if it points to the emperor's elite troops stationed in Rome (see the sidebar at 1:13). "Caesar's household" referred to the imperial civil servants and administrators, who could be found throughout the empire. The majority of them, however, were located in the imperial capital. If there were a sufficient number of Christians among this group to merit special mention, Rome would be the strongest candidate for their place of residence (Bockmuehl 1998, 31).

There are objections, however, to Rome as the matrix of the letter. The main obstacle is accounting for the comings and goings of Paul's visitors between Rome and Philippi implied within the letter. Philippi is some 800 miles (1,300 km) from the capital city. In antiquity, time and arduous travel would have been needed for the following journeys: (1) News of Paul's imprisonment was taken to Philippi. (2) Epaphroditus traveled with the Philippians' gift to Paul. (3) Word of Epaphroditus's illness was sent to Philippi. (4) The Philippians dispatched word of their concern for Epaphroditus to Paul. And (5) Paul sent Epaphroditus home with the letter. The two-year period of Paul's imprisonment is too short, some claim, for so many trips over such a distance.

This difficulty, however, may be overblown. Two major roads (the Via Egnatia in Macedonia and the Via Appia in Italy) and a two-day sea voyage linked Rome and Philippi. Journeys could be made in a relatively short time by ancient standards. Silva estimates that the trip could have taken between four and seven weeks (2005, 5-6, n 5). Given that Paul was imprisoned in Rome for at least two years, there would have been ample time for multiple journeys. Moreover, it is possible that Epaphroditus fell ill en route to Rome and sent word back, shortening the time line (O'Brien 1991, 25).

There are two main alternates to a Roman imprisonment. *Caesarea Maritima* has in its favor the testimony of Acts that Paul was jailed there for two years (24:27; A.D. 58-60). Furthermore, Acts says that he was held in the praetorium of Herod (23:35) and that he had the freedom to receive material help from his friends (24:23). But perhaps the fatal flaw of this theory is that Paul was never under threat of execution while in Caesarea. He had the option to purchase his freedom (v 26) or use his Roman citizenship to appeal to the emperor, as in fact he did (25:10-12). This makes a Caesarean origin for the letter hard to square with Paul's readiness to face either death or release from prison in Phil 1:19-26.

A third possibility, *Ephesus*, has garnered wide support in recent decades. Its main attraction is that the city is much closer to Philippi. As a result, it more easily accounts for the travels between Philippi and the place of Paul's incarceration. What is more, Timothy was with Paul in Ephesus (Acts 19:22; Phil 1:1); and Acts is silent about his presence with Paul in Rome. Ephesus was also a center of energetic missionary activity while Paul was there (Acts 19:10, 25-26). If the letter came from Ephesus, it would have been written sometime during Paul's three-year mission there (ca. A.D. 52-55).

A major difficulty, however, is that we have no indication that Paul was ever jailed in Ephesus, let alone under a capital charge. Such a scenario must be inferred from his rather general allusions to struggles in Asia and imprisonments (see 1 Cor 15:32; 2 Cor 1:8-9; 6:5; 11:23). In addition, Paul had many friends in Ephesus; but he seems to feel extremely isolated when writing to Philippi (Hooker 2000, 474). Finally, the reference to the praetorium is an obstacle. Ephesus was the capital of a senatorial province, not an imperial province controlled by the emperor. F. F. Bruce, for one, insists that there is no evidence of a governor's headquarters being called a praetorium in a senatorial province at this time (1983, xxii).

In sum, there are plausible arguments for all three options. But there is no compelling reason to overturn the early tradition that Paul wrote Philippians from Rome. If this is so, the letter may be dated in the early 60s, probably toward the end of Paul's Roman imprisonment (A.D. 60-62). In this case, Paul writes as a battle-tested, mature apostle, late in his monumental missionary career. However, all conclusions about the place of origin and date for Philippians must remain tentative (see Bockmuehl 1998, 25-32; and Hawthorne 1993, 709-11, for useful discussions of the place and date of the letter).

4. Paul's Imprisonment

What do we know about the conditions of Paul's detention? The apostle gives us no specific information in the letter, other than speaking repeatedly of his "chains" (1:7, 13, 14, 17). Although the term "chains" can be used in a figurative way for imprisonment, it was a common practice for prisoners to be manacled to a soldier guard (see Rapske 1994, 181; Wansink 1996, 46-47). This would fit Acts' description of Paul's custody in Rome (28:20).

Generally, ancient prisons did not seek to rehabilitate people. Nor were they intended for punishment as such. They were more like "holding tanks," where prisoners awaited a court trial or perhaps execution. Jails were usually places of horrific squalor; and it was not uncommon for prisoners to die of illness or to take their own lives. Prison rations were meager and intended only for the prisoner's bare survival. Consequently, material help from family members and friends was vital. Both Philippians and Acts (28:23, 30-31) testify that Paul's friends assisted him through visits, bearing letters, and giving him money and other material support. At the same time, since imprisonment meant devastating public shame, even associating with prisoners could be socially degrading (Fowl 2005, 10; on imprisonment in the Roman world, see Rapske 1993, 827-30; Rapske 1994; Wansink 1996, ch 1).

If Paul wrote to the Philippians from Rome, the description of his conditions of imprisonment in Acts 28 becomes quite relevant. Acts indicates that in Rome Paul was not held in the severest form of confinement, the state prison (*carcer*). Instead, he experienced a lighter form of military custody. He was under the guard of a single soldier (two was the norm), and probably chained to his wrist (28:16, 20). Paul was allowed to live on his own (v 16), perhaps in one of the thousands of tenement buildings in Rome (Rapske 1994, 178-80, 236-39). Furthermore, he was given considerable freedom to receive visitors and to evangelize (vv 17-31). None of this is inconsistent with what Paul says about his situation in Philippians.

Whatever gaps remain in our understanding of Paul's custody at the time he wrote this letter, his attitude toward his bonds is clear. As Stephen E. Fowl puts it, "In a world in which being in chains was dangerous and degrading, in which one became utterly dependent and easily victimized, in which control over one's future was taken out of one's own hands, the progress of the gospel cannot be impeded by Paul's imprisonment" (2005, 10).

5. The Occasion and Purpose of the Letter

The issues that prompted Paul to write this letter are related both to Paul's own circumstances and to those of the congregation in Philippi. In part, they are rooted in his unusually warm relationship with the church. Paul has enjoyed a long-term ministry partnership with the Philippians. From the outset, they supported him financially and in other ways (1:5; 4:10-20). More recently, they had sent Epaphroditus, one of their own, to deliver a gift of money and to minister to Paul's needs in prison (2:25, 30; 4:19). But Epaphroditus fell gravely ill, either while on the journey or after he arrived. Now recovered, Epaphroditus became distressed over the anxiety that news of his illness might have created in Philippi (2:26). As a result, Paul had decided to send Epaphroditus home. This presents Paul with the opportunity to dispatch a letter to the church.

The letter's direct occasion is probably tethered to these circumstances. First, Paul wants to thank the Philippians for their generosity and care sent through Epaphroditus (4:10-20). Second, he commends their envoy Epaphroditus and explains why this coworker is returning so soon (2:25-30).

Third, Paul takes the opportunity to update his friends on his own situation. He especially wants to assure them that his present detention will in no way impede the progress of the gospel (1:12-26). Fourth, Paul seeks to prepare the congregation for prospective visits by Timothy (2:19, 23), and, hopefully, himself (v 24).

But there are other reasons for the letter, related to the challenges of the church itself. Most likely, Paul has heard of the situation in Philippi from their messenger Epaphroditus. Three factors help shape Paul's exhortations in the letter. First, this congregation is suffering as a result of opposition in their city (1:27-30). Paul says two things about their affliction: it is "on behalf of Christ" (v 29) and the Philippians are engaged in "the same struggle" as Paul faces (v 30). We know that Paul's suffering is both in the defense of the gospel (v 7) and at the hands of the Roman Empire (Fee 1995, 31). It is probable, then, that the source of the Philippians' opposition and suffering is the pagan populace in this Roman colony, people who are fiercely loyal to the emperor (see BEHIND THE TEXT, vv 27-30).

Paul tells us neither the specific cause of this hostility, nor the forms it took. However, in an imperial colony like Philippi, civic duty was measured in terms of loyalty to Caesar and his empire. Virtually every public event (festivals, the assembly, etc.), as well as meetings of private clubs and associations, would have been occasions to give honor to the emperor and the traditional deities. It is not hard to imagine that Christians, who worshipped a "Lord" other than Caesar, would be read as dangerously un-Roman, a threat to the public order (see Acts 16:20-21).

Even if there was no organized, government-sponsored persecution in Philippi at this time, Christians could have experienced harassment from their neighbors and various forms of economic suffering (see Oakes 2001, 89-99). We might imagine that Christian tradespeople would lose their customers. Pagan owners might punish Christian slaves. Patrons could withdraw financial support from Christian clients. Magistrates might drag believers to court. In short, Christians in Philippi might experience the kind of ostracism, discrimination, or even violence that has accompanied loyalty to Christ in many times and places. Such adversity might tempt Paul's readers to be discouraged or even to abandon the struggle. Throughout the letter Paul calls them to steadfastness and joy (e.g., 1:27-28; 2:18; 3:1; 4:1, 4).

Second, Paul apparently responds to tensions and disagreements within the fellowship. He takes the unusual step of singling out two church leaders, Euodia and Syntyche (4:2-3). This suggests that discord among people in leadership roles was near the heart of his concern. Presumably, such frictions had the potential to infect the whole congregation. Furthermore, grumbling and arguing within the church could tarnish its witness to the pagan world (2:14-

16). As a result, Paul is adamant that the church needs to be unified in mind and spirit (1:27; 2:1-4; 3:15).

We are not privy to the specific cause of these tensions. However, given Paul's emphasis on humility as an antidote for "selfish ambition" (2:3-4, 6-8; see vv 20-21), the unrest may have involved interpersonal rivalry and self-promotion. For Paul, it is essential that the church be united in order to stand firm in the ministry of the gospel in Philippi (1:27).

Third, Paul's strong words in ch 3 (vv 2-3, 18-19) suggest that one of his reasons for writing is to warn his friends to watch out for agitators who could threaten the church. First, he aims his rhetorical arrows at people he calls "dogs" and "evil workers" who "mutilate the flesh" (v 2 NRSV). This is best understood as a reference to so-called Judaizers—Jewish Christian missionaries who insist that even Gentile followers of Jesus need to be circumcised and obey the Jewish law. In the second passage Paul weeps over some "enemies of the cross of Christ" who are headed for destruction. Paul depicts them as worshipping their belly, glorying in their shame, and setting their mind on earthly things (vv 18-19).

Scholars debate over who these people are, whether they represent one group or two, and the extent to which these are actual opponents or simply part of Paul's rhetorical argument (for a discussion of these questions, see the relevant passages in the commentary). In any case, the threat of opponents is not Paul's primary reason for writing this letter. In both cases, Paul has told the Philippians about such people on other occasions (3:1, 18). And there is no evidence that the troublemakers Paul mentions in ch 3 have already infiltrated the church, or even that they are standing on the doorstep. It seems likely that the threat is on the horizon and that this is an advance warning (on Paul's opponents in Philippi, see O'Brien 1991, 116-20; Thurston 2005, 116-20).

Paul's theological responses to the situations and needs of his friends in Philippi give us a clue toward understanding his overarching purpose for the letter. He seeks the Christian formation of a young community of believers, in light of challenges from both within the church and outside of it. In short, he desires their "progress and joy in the faith" (1:25). As we will observe shortly, Paul advances that aim through both exhortations and examples. The Philippians are to live out their public and communal life "in a manner worthy of the gospel of Christ" (v 27). Embodying the gospel will mean standing firm in the face of opposition and being united in Christian love. For Paul, such a gospel-worthy life is defined by the self-giving love of Jesus Christ (2:5-11). Paul's goal for the Philippians is Christlikeness.

At the same time, the Philippians' progress in the faith is linked to the continued "advance [of] the gospel" (1:12; Fee 1995, 39). Only if they walk in a manner worthy of the gospel, steadfast and united, can they expect to advance the work of the gospel in the world (Swift 1984, 250).

To summarize, although the initial reason for the letter is tied to Paul's own circumstances—his gratitude for the Philippians' gift, Epaphroditus's recovery and return, and so forth—he has a larger purpose for the letter. It is the formation of the community into the cruciform image of Christ and their ongoing partnership with Paul in the gospel (1:5). In the next section, we will see that this aim is reflected in the form and layout of the letter.

B. The Form, Structure, and Persuasive Strategy of Philippians

1. Philippians as a Letter

It may simply be stating the obvious, but Philippians is a *letter*, not a narrative, history, or apocalypse. Just as letters today have a standard form ("Dear so-and-so . . . Sincerely, Dean"), ancient letters share a fairly consistent formal structure. This format begins with a salutation (X to Y, greetings), followed by a health wish for the receiver or (much less often) a thanksgiving to the gods. Then comes the letter body, which unfolds the main themes and purpose. Ancient letters end with a brief closing, usually including a wish for the receiver's well-being and a farewell (for a more detailed standard letter outline, see Capes, Reeves, and Richards 2007, 57). As with all of his letters, Paul follows this basic form but significantly adapts it for his own purposes (on Paul's use of ancient letter forms, see Murphy-O'Connor 1995 and Richards 2004). Analyzing Philippians according to its formal letter structure yields the following outline:

    I. Letter Opening (address and greeting) (1:1-2)
    II. Thanksgiving Section (1:3-11)
    III. Letter Body (1:12—4:20)
        A. Body Opening (1:12-26)
        B. Body Middle (1:27—4:1)
        C. Body Closing (4:2-20)
    IV. Letter Closing (greeting and blessing) (4:21-23)

A Letter of Friendship? In addition, Greco-Roman letters could be classified by different types, based on the situation they addressed and the letter's intended effect. In other words, a letter should fit the occasion. Ancient manuals for letter writing gave instruction in different styles of letters. One handbook by Pseudo-Demetrius (Malherbe dates it from around the beginning of the Christian era; 1986, 18) lists and illustrates 21 different letter types. In recent years, scholars have tried to classify Philippians according to one or more of these letter styles.

A number of interpreters argue that Philippians follows the conventions of a letter of *friendship* (e.g., Stowers 1991; Fee 1995, 2-10; Fitzgerald 1992, 1996; Fowl 2005, 8, 207). Pseudo-Demetrius provides a sample of a "friendly letter" (*epistolē philikē*) in his handbook, which reads in part:

> Even though I have been separated from you for a long time, I suffer this in body only. For I can never forget you or the impeccable way we were reared together from childhood up. Knowing that I myself am genuinely concerned about your affairs, and that I have worked unhesitatingly for what is most advantageous to you, I have assumed that you, too, have the same opinion of me, and will refuse me nothing. (Cited by Stowers 1986, 58-59)

This example illustrates a number of common elements in letters of friendship, which have parallels in Philippians (see Stowers 1991, 54, 108-14; Fee 1995, 2-4). For instance, friendly letters regularly feature expressions of affection and concern between friends. Paul longs for his friends "with the affection of Christ Jesus" (1:7-8). They are his "beloved" (NRSV) and his "joy and crown" (2:12; 4:1). Another commonplace is the theme of presence and absence. The letter writer attempts to maintain friendship during a time of separation. In Philippians, Paul speaks repeatedly about his absence from his friends and his desire to be present with them (1:7-8, 25-26, 27; 2:12, 24; 4:1).

Despite such common features, classification as a letter of friendship does not completely fit Philippians, and there is much in the letter for which it does not account (Osiek 2000, 24; Reumann 1996, 105-6). One crucial difference is that the context of Philippians is not the private interchange between two friends but the formation of a Christian *community*. What is more, Paul completely avoids using the usual words for "friend" (*philos*) or "friendship" (*philia*) in the letter. It is also telling that there is no evidence that John Chrysostom or the other early Greek Fathers recognized Philippians as a letter of friendship (see Reumann 1996, 100-104).

The Language of Friendship. Even if Philippians does not altogether fit the literary category of a friendly letter, we can still observe that Paul draws deeply from the well of friendship *language*. It is hard for us today to appreciate how seriously Greeks and Romans took the matter of friendship (see Fee 1995, 4-7). Moral philosophers like Aristotle, Cicero, and Seneca were fascinated with the subject (see, e.g., Aristotle, *Eth. Nic.* 8-9; Cicero, *Amic.*; Seneca, *Ep.* 11). The concept of friendship was wide-ranging. It could refer to a relationship of dependence or equality, of political alliances or bonds of personal affection (Keener 2000, 380-81). Ancient writers, however, tended to concentrate on personal friendships between social equals.

Paul uses typical friendship language throughout the letter, especially in chs 1—2 and 4 (see Fitzgerald 1996, 144-60; Johnson 1999, 372-73). For example, a common description of ancient friendship is that friends are of "one soul" (*mia psychē*; e.g., Aristotle, *Eth. Nic.* 9.8.2; Phil 1:27; see 2:2, 20) and share the same mind (*to auto phronein*; Phil 2:2; 4:2). Likewise, Paul's striking use of the language of "partnership" (*koinōnia*; 1:5, 7; 2:2; 3:10; 4:14-15) relates to the ancient notions that friendship is *koinōnia* (Aristotle, *Eth. Nic.* 8.12.1) and that "friends have all things in common."

This idea of sharing something in common is also picked up in the many words that begin with the prefix "with" (*syn-*; 1:7, 27; 2:17-18, 25; 3:10, 17; 4:3, 14). And friendship typically involved the mutual exchange of benefits (gifts and services). Not surprisingly, we find a heavy dose of friendship terms in 4:10-20, where Paul talks about the Philippians sharing with him in "giving and receiving" (v 15).

Paul's friendship language is rhetorically powerful. On the one hand, it reinforces the Philippians' ongoing "partnership in the gospel" (1:5) with the apostle. On the other, it invites a community dealing with internal frictions to "be of the same mind" (NRSV) in the Lord (4:2; 2:2). But Paul not only uses the traditional language of friendship but also reshapes its content in light of the gospel. Gordon D. Fee is on target that for Paul "friendship is transformed from a two-way to a three-way bond—between him, the Philippians, and Christ. And obviously it is Christ who is the center and focus of everything" (1995, 13). *Koinōnia*, then, is not simply about human friendships. Christian "fellowship" is a Christ-oriented notion (for more on ancient friendship and how that sheds light on Philippians, see Stowers 1986, 58-70; 1991; White 1990; Fee 1995, 2-14; 1999, 12-22; Fitzgerald 1996; 2007, 293-96; Malherbe 1996; Reumann 1996; Berry 1996; Keener 2000; Marchal 2006).

Other Letter Forms. Scholars have made other suggestions for how Philippians best fits into the types of ancient letters. These include "family letters," which reinforced close family relationships (see, literally, "brother," 1:12; 3:1, 17; 4:1, 8; Alexander 1989). Similarly, "letters of consolation" addressed the problem of discouragement. In the latter case, Paul would be writing to encourage a church that was despondent over the apostle's imprisonment and its own suffering (Holloway 2001).

Finally, some compare Philippians to letters of *exhortation*. In antiquity Demetrius calls these the "advisory" type; and Libanius, the "paraenetic" letter. Such letters urged people to pursue something or dissuaded them from some course of action. They regularly offered positive models to emulate or negative models to avoid. Persuasion of this kind is a regular feature in Philippians (e.g., 2:5-11; 3:17). In addition, letters of exhortation came from one who had a positive relationship with the recipients (e.g., parent, friend, or mentor; Stowers 1986, 95-96). Paraenetic letters often combined affirmation, correction, and exhortation, all three of which we find in Philippians.

Of the various ancient letter types, the letter of exhortation perhaps best fits the content and purpose of Philippians. The major part of the letter is comprised of exhortations to Paul's Christian friends in Philippi (1:27—2:18; 3:1—4:1; 4:2-9). Paul seeks to persuade his audience to adopt a particular pattern of thinking and behaving (e.g., 1:27; 2:5; 3:15; 4:8), shaped by the example of Christ (2:5-11). This likewise involves steering them away from the influence of "evildoers" (NRSV) and "enemies of the cross" (3:2, 18). Nevertheless, whereas Greco-Roman letters of exhortation offered moral guidance to individuals, Paul had a different goal. For the apostle, moral formation could happen only in the context of a community of faith.

Conclusion. Even a letter as comparatively brief as Philippians is longer and more complex than most ancient letters. This is one reason why scholars have failed to agree about what style of letter best fits Philippians. Paul's word to this church simply cannot be pinned down to a single literary category. It has elements of encouragement, friendship, thanksgiving (4:10-20 has some expected features of a "thankful" letter), and especially moral exhortation, all of which relate to different letter forms. This letter, then, probably corresponds to what Libanius calls a "mixed" style (*Epistolary Styles*, 45, 92; cited in Aune 1988, 203). Paul had more than one aim in writing to his audience, and along the way he addressed various themes and subjects. As a result, he was free to draw upon aspects of different letter-writing conventions.

Did Paul consciously follow any contemporary models for letter types? It's hard to say. Perhaps he was no more self-conscious than we are about the differences between, say, a love letter and business correspondence. But he does seem to have been aware of elements of how writers in his world used letters to reach their aims in writing. Typically, Paul adapts and reworks traditional forms in the service of the gospel and with the goal of his readers' progress in the faith.

2. Philippians as Rhetoric

Paul writes letters within a largely oral culture. What is more, he normally writes to a community, not to an individual. His letters are stand-ins for what he would say to the church if he were present among them. Letters like Philippians were intended to be "read publicly to a corporate audience who use their ears rather than their eyes" (Thiselton 2000, 49). In this setting, Philippians would have had the character of an oral *sermon* to the congregation.

Because of this oral dimension to Paul's letters, scholars have studied them in light of the conventions of ancient rhetoric—the art of persuasion. In the Greco-Roman world, saying something well was a highly valued skill. It appears that Paul carefully constructed his letter to the Philippians so that it would have a maximum persuasive impact on his Gentile audience. Observing Paul's rhetorical strategies can help us understand how the letter "works" to advance Paul's pastoral goals and to bring about transformation in the lives of his hearers. We will observe these strategies throughout the commentary. But an introduction to several aspects of Paul's use of rhetoric is called for at present.

Arguments and Examples. First, Paul uses well-established kinds of arguments (in classical rhetoric, called "invention") to build a persuasive case for his audience. Long before Paul, Aristotle spelled out three modes of persuasion, based on three essential elements in effective communication—the speaker, the audience, and the word (*Rhet.* 1.2). Appeals to *ethos* build on the character and credibility of the speaker. We find this particularly in the autobiographical sections of the letter, in which Paul tells his own story (1:12-26; 3:4-14; 4:11-13). Moreover, his direct calls for the Philippians to follow his Christlike example (3:17; 4:9) are striking arguments from *ethos.*

Arguments from *pathos* appeal to the emotions. The goal is that the audience would be put in a fitting frame of mind to receive the message. Paul's expressions of his personal and affectionate bond with the community are filled with *pathos* (1:7-8, 24-25; 2:16-18; 4:1). In a quite different way, he arouses his hearers' emotions by painting a foreboding picture of the "dogs" and "enemies of the cross" who would lead them astray (3:2, 18-19).

Finally, Paul builds arguments that rely on logical persuasion (*logos*) in all of his letters. Due to its personal character, Philippians does not feature the kind of sustained, closely reasoned discussions we find in Rom 9—11 or 1 Cor 15. Nevertheless, appeals to *logos* are still prominent. For example, in Phil 2, Paul calls the community to work out its salvation (v 12). He then gives that action a cause and basis in the prior work of God (v 13).

Of the basic categories (genres) of ancient rhetoric, Paul's argumentation in Philippians leans toward the *deliberative* type. Deliberative rhetoric seeks to persuade an audience to take a particular course of action, primarily by showing what is to their advantage or harm. One type of argument that particularly fits this kind of persuasion is an argument from example (Witherington 1994, 96-97).

It was commonplace for ancient orators and philosophers to appeal to worthy examples to follow, including their own. Paul uses this strategy extensively in Philippians; he tells exemplary stories (1:12-26; 2:6-11, 19-30; 3:4-14; 4:11-13). But unlike the philosophers, Paul relates all other stories in the letter to a *master* story, the story of Christ's self-humbling and exaltation by God (2:6-11; see Gorman 2004, 418-23). Jesus himself is the supreme model for steadfastness in the face of suffering. And Christ's self-giving humility will be the ground of relationships within the church. Later in ch 3, Paul tells his own story in a way that is patterned after the cruciform story of Christ (3:4-14; see 3:1-11, BEHIND THE TEXT). Within the text, both the story of Christ and the story of Paul become explicit models for the Philippians' own way of thinking and behaving (2:5; 3:15, 17; see 4:9; Fee 1999, 19).

Even when Paul's personal narrative is not explicitly paradigmatic, it can serve as an example for his audience to follow. Thus, Paul's experience of joy and steadfastness in the midst of suffering (1:12-26; compare 2:17) can shape the Philippians' response to their own struggles. Likewise, Paul narrates the stories of two other faithful servants of Christ, Timothy and Epaphroditus (2:19-30). They, too, become models of people who embody the unselfish mind-set of Christ.

Furthermore, Greco-Roman philosophers often appealed to contrasting models—positive examples to imitate and negative ones to avoid. This seems to be Paul's strategy in ch 3, when he appeals to his own Christ-oriented example (vv 4-14, 15, 17) over against people who should *not* be imitated (3:2-3, 18-19). Good and bad examples are a key to understanding Paul's rhetoric and moral exhortation in Philippians.

Arrangement. Ancient orators believed that the persuasive power of a speech in part depended on its careful arrangement. One evidence of Paul's concern for how he constructs his case is his use of rhetorical "bookends" (*inclusio*). For example, there are a number of parallels between Paul's opening thanksgiving (1:3-11) and his closing "thank you" to the Philippians (4:10-20; see 4:10-20, BEHIND THE TEXT). These two passages serve to frame the whole letter (see Thompson 2007, 303).

Aristotle and his successors also noted that a certain pattern of development was important for an effective oration. The major elements are: (1) the *exordium*, or introduction; (2) the *narratio*, the history of the case; (3) the *propositio* or thesis statement; (4) the *probatio*, the arguments to support the case; and (5) a conclusion, called the *peroratio*. No one followed this pattern mechanically, least of all Paul, who adapted rhetorical conventions to his own ends. Nevertheless, understanding what different parts of a speech sought to accomplish may help to clarify how the letter makes its case. It will, therefore, be useful to trace Paul's argument in the Philippians, pointing out where the categories of ancient rhetoric shed light on his persuasive strategy.

Following the normal letter opening (1:1-2) comes Paul's customary thanksgiving section (vv 3-11). Here he expresses gratitude and affection for his audience (vv 3-8) and intercedes for them in prayer (vv 9-11). Rhetorically, vv 3-11 function as an *exordium*. The purpose of the *exordium* is to introduce the subject and to secure the goodwill of the audience. Paul's thanksgiving passage previews a number of the key themes in the letter. These include: joy, partnership in the gospel, the Christian mind, and God's good work among the Philippians (see BEHIND THE TEXT, 1:1-11). At the same time, Paul's expressions of confidence (v 6), care, and affection (vv 7-8) would lead to a favorable hearing from his audience.

We then encounter the first of Paul's autobiographical reflections (vv 12-

26). Here the apostle joyfully narrates his present circumstances in light of what God is doing to advance the gospel. Whatever he faces, whether a prisoner's chains (vv 12-14) or the attacks of rival preachers (vv 15-18a), Christ is being proclaimed. Moreover, he knows that Christ will be exalted and the Philippians' faith will progress, no matter what the outcome of his pending trial (vv 18b-26). This autobiographical passage probably corresponds to the rhetorical *narratio*, which states the past facts of the case as a background to the main argument to come. But its chief function in the letter is to give encouragement to Paul's audience and an example of how they should respond to adverse circumstances.

With 1:27, the focus shifts from Paul and his situation to the Philippians and their behavior. This begins the first of two main sections of pastoral exhortations and examples in Philippians (along with 3:1—4:1), running through 2:18. Philippians 1:27-30 corresponds to the rhetorical *propositio*—the main thesis that will be developed in the letter. Paul calls God's people to live out their public, communal, and personal lives in a manner worthy of the gospel (v 27). Such a life will require two responses: standing together in unity and standing firm in the face of opposition and suffering (vv 27-30). The two are no doubt connected. A divided community will struggle to withstand pressures from outside.

The theme statement is usually followed by the *probatio*, which offers arguments and examples to support the case. This is the heart of the oration, normally the longest part. In Philippians, this could be seen to comprise Paul's arguments from exhortation and example that run from 2:1 through 4:1. Philippians 2:1-18 constitutes the first main section of these arguments. Its centerpiece—arguably, the centerpiece for the entire letter—is the "Christ hymn" in vv 5-11. Paul narrates the story of Christ in two movements, his self-emptying to the point of death on a cross (vv 6-8) and his exaltation to universal sovereignty by God (vv 9-11). This Christ-drama provides the ultimate model for a life worthy of the gospel. Paul wants the Philippian church to place its own story within the narrative of Christ (Thompson 2007, 306). They should adopt the same "mind" as that of their Lord (v 5).

As a result, vv 5-11 ground the appeals that both precede and follow it. In vv 1-4, Paul calls the church to unity based on the same kind of selfless love and humility they see in the story of Christ. And vv 12-18 draw out practical implications from the hymn for the church. Following Christ's own sacrificial obedience (vv 8, 12), they should live out their salvation with God's enabling power (vv 12-13). As a result, they will have a shining witness to outsiders within a crooked culture (vv 14-16). This is a life worthy of the gospel.

Sandwiched between Paul's two main sections of exhortation is an argument from example (vv 19-30). This is more than just an update on the future travel plans of two trusted coworkers, Timothy and Epaphroditus (although it serves that purpose). The community needs to see living examples of those known to them who embody the story of Christ. Swimming against the stream, Timothy puts the interests of others above his own (vv 19-24). And Epaphroditus risks his very life in loving service to Christ and others (vv 15-30).

Philippians 3:1—4:1 comprises the third main section in Paul's body of arguments. In one sense, it unexpectedly introduces a new topic—a warning against rival teachers who could threaten the spiritual progress of the church (see 3:2-3, 18-19). The Philippians need to stand firm in the face of such a potential danger. But Paul addresses this problem by contrasting the negative examples in the chapter with his own autobiography (vv 4-14). Paul's story conforms to the pattern of Christ narrated in ch 2: He has renounced his former glories (vv 7-9), and he participates in the suffering and death of Christ (v 10). Furthermore, his ultimate goal is to share in Christ's resurrection in the future (vv 11-14). Philippians 3:15—4:1 then apply Paul's story to the church through exhortation and example. His audience must imitate his mature and cruciform mind-set (3:15-17), over against other competing models (vv 18-19). Like Paul, their focus must be on the future, even as they already live as citizens of heaven (vv 20-21).

The concluding section of the letter features some final practical instructions (4:2-9), an expression of gratitude to the church for their recent gift (vv 10-20), and a simple letter closing (vv 21-23). From a rhetorical standpoint, vv 2-20 correspond to the conclusion (*peroratio*) of an oration. One of the functions of the rhetorical conclusion is to summarize the main themes of the speech. The imperatives in vv 2-9 recall earlier appeals to unity (vv 2-3), rejoicing (v 4), striving together in the gospel (v 3), and imitating Paul and Christ (v 9).

Likewise, Paul's thank-you note in vv 10-20 reinforces his longstanding "partnership" with the Philippians in both suffering and the work of the gospel (vv 14-15). This expression of gratitude fulfills other aims of the rhetorical conclusion (see Aristotle, *Rhet.* 3.19). It encourages a favorable response from the audience by affirming their past and present generosity. It also arouses their positive emotions by leaving them with a promise of God's provision and a praise of God's glory (vv 19-20). This concluding section is not out of place, as is sometimes thought. It is a fitting end to the letter.

Any rhetorical outline must be tentative, not least because scholars seldom agree about precisely how to structure Philippians from a rhetorical perspective (compare, e.g., Watson 1988; Witherington 1994; Black 1995, 48). However, our analysis of the rhetorical flow of Philippians suggests the following outline:

Exordium (1:3-11)
Narratio (1:12-26)

Propositio (1:27-30)
Probatio (2:1—4:1)
    Exhortations and the Example of Christ (2:1-18)
    Two Christlike Examples (2:19-30)
    Warnings and Examples (3:1—4:1)
Peroratio (4:2-20)

The more detailed outline, the table of contents of the commentary combines elements of both the letter and rhetorical structures.

Again, we must be wary of forcing Paul into rhetorical pigeonholes. But recognizing Paul's persuasive strategies in Philippians helps us see how the apostle uses rhetoric as a means of "preaching for a verdict." As James W. Thompson points out, preachers today could learn from this (2007). First, it helps us appreciate the rhetorical effect of each textual unit within the larger argument of the letter. Second, Paul's practice of weaving together different types of arguments (*ethos, pathos, logos*) reminds us that the effective preacher cannot live by cognitive arguments alone. Persuasiveness also depends on our own embodiment of the message and on our personal and emotional bond with the listeners. Third, testimony and personal examples are still powerful tools for shaping the people of God (Thompson 2007, 302-8).

3. Authorship and Unity

Paul's authorship of Philippians is almost universally accepted. On the other hand, many have questioned the letter's unity. Some interpreters read Philippians as a patchwork of different documents that have been sewn together into its present form. Two passages, in particular, are the crux of the problem.

First, scholars point to what appears to be an abrupt shift in tone and topic between 3:1 and 3:2. Paul seems to be winding things down ("finally") in v 1, only suddenly to rev up his engines into an attack on the "dogs" in v 2. What is more, Paul's call to "rejoice in the Lord" in 3:1 flows more smoothly into 4:4, where he repeats the same command. This suggests to some that another letter fragment about rival teachers has been carelessly inserted between these two verses.

Second, some interpreters argue that 4:10-20 comprises a separate letter. If Paul is writing, as least in part, to thank the Philippians for their gift, then why would he wait until the very end of the letter to do it? It is argued that 4:10-20 was originally an independent "thank you" dashed off soon after Paul received the gift.

Recent scholarship in English, however, has increasingly steered away from such partition theories and toward affirming the unity of the letter (e.g., Garland 1985; O'Brien 1991; Fitzgerald 1992; Witherington 1994; Black

1995; Fee 1995; Bockmuehl 1998; Osiek 2000; Hawthorne and Martin 2004; Silva 2005; Fowl 2005; Thurston 2005). There are good reasons to agree:
- Manuscript evidence fully supports the canonical form of Philippians.
- Partition theories assume a highly sophisticated process of piecing together various letter fragments. But if this is the case, why did the editor connect them in such a clumsy way (see Bockmuehl 1998, 24)?
- We saw in the last section that the letter can be understood as having a coherent structure. This would disappear if Philippians were divided up (Marshall 1991, xxxii).
- We find key terms distributed throughout canonical Philippians. This gives a *thematic* coherence to the letter as it stands. For example, the words for joy and rejoicing, partnership (*koinōnia*), and "to think, have a mindset" (*phroneō*) appear in all three supposed fragments of the letter. In particular, many of the words from the Christ hymn in 2:5-11 resurface in 3:2-21 (see deSilva 2004, 648-49).
- There are plausible explanations for why both of the passages in question (3:2—4:3 and 4:10-20) are situated where they are in the letter. I will argue that the "untidy" features of these sections are not as problematic as some allege.

In any case, as *readers*, our concern is above all with the canonical text of Philippians in the form that has come to the church.

C. Key Themes

While the historical and literary aspects of this letter are surely important, it is Paul's *message* that is most critical to contemporary communities of faith. Historically, the church has read Philippians as a *theological* document. But Philippians is *not* simply a theological treatise. Nor is Paul a card-carrying systematic theologian. The apostle is primarily a missionary and a pastor. He planted churches and wrote pastoral letters to build up his converts in their faith in the crucified and risen Christ. Paul's "theology," then, emerges out of the encounter between the Christ-centered gospel and the concrete realities and challenges of the apostle and his audience. In Philippians, as everywhere else, Paul gives us theological reflections on the "stuff of life."

What, then, are some of the key theological concerns that arise out of this context-sensitive letter? To a large degree, theology in Philippians comes to us in the form of story (Fee 1995, 47). This is above all the story of God in Christ. But it is also the story of Paul and of the church in Philippi as the people of God. Theology in Philippians is story-shaped.

I. The Defining Story of Christ

Front and center in this letter is Jesus Christ. No other noun occurs more often than "Christ" (Bockmuehl 1998, 41). Paul begins Philippians by identifying himself as a servant of Christ (1:1) and ends it by blessing the church with the grace of Christ (4:23). The story of Christ in 2:6-11 is the "beating heart" of Philippians (Hawthorne/Martin 2004, lxxii). Its imprint is stamped on every other part of the letter.

The "Christ hymn" in 2:6-11 narrates a V-shaped pattern. The one who is equal with God empties himself, takes on a human form, and humbles himself to the extreme—dying a slave's death on a cross. In response to Christ's obedience, God the Father exalts him and grants him the divine title of "Lord." The story line reaches its climax when the whole of creation acknowledges Christ's lordship to the Father's glory. In Philippians, the way *up* is *down*.

The Christology of this passage has had an enormous influence on the development of Christian doctrine (see Bockmuehl 1995, 75-83). In the early centuries, 2:6-11 became a touchstone for the controversies over the relationship between the divine and human natures of Christ. Later theologians constructed "kenotic" theories of the incarnation from the Christ hymn. Their concern was to determine of what Jesus "emptied himself" (v 7 NRSV) when he took on humanity.

These questions are not irrelevant. But Paul has a different focus. He tells the story of Christ's downward plunge from the heights of glory to the depths of humiliation so that the community will reenact that story of self-giving love. As Morna D. Hooker observes, the direct link between theology (who God is and what God does) and ethics (who we should be and what we should do) is one of the great contributions of this letter to the church (2000, 476).

This is not to say that the Christology of 2:6-11 is unimportant. In reality, it is quite breathtaking. Verses 9-11 give us a stunning vision of Christ as the divine Lord of the cosmos. Furthermore, the language of vv 6 and 7 indicates that Christ shared a preexistent status of equality with God before his human birth.

Nevertheless, Paul does not write about either Jesus' preexistence or his exalted divine status for their own sake. Above all, he wants us to grasp that the very one who shared God's supreme status and glory, the same one on whom was bestowed the personal name of the Lord God himself, is precisely the one who took the form of a slave and died on a cross. This means that when Christ "made himself nothing," he did not cease to be divine. The truly revolutionary Christology of the Christ poem is that it is in Jesus' very self-emptying and cruciform love that we see the true identity of God.

2. The Surpassing Knowledge of Christ

One of the distinctive features of Philippians is its accent on the experience of a close relationship with Christ. Much of this relational language is embedded in Paul's autobiographical passages. Paul is a man obsessed by Christ. His singular passion is the "surpassing greatness of knowing Christ" (3:8, 10). His supreme goal is to know his Lord in a full and final sense (v 14). This intimate, personal knowledge of Christ means sharing in his suffering and death (v 10). It also involves participating in Christ's resurrection, both now and in the future (vv 10-11). Paul's own story is inextricably bound to that of Christ. But the paradigmatic character of Paul's story in Philippians means that he also envisions his readers sharing this same kind of intimate, transforming relationship to God in Christ.

For Paul, living *is* Christ (1:21). This helps to explain why he can also testify that dying is "gain" (v 21). Departing this life is "better" because it means being with Christ in an even fuller and closer sense (v 24). But, consistent with his teaching elsewhere, the consummation of our life with Christ lies in the future, when the Savior will return from heaven and transform our humble bodies into bodies of glory like his own. The Christian's relationship to Christ is also expressed in the frequent occurrence of the phrase "in Christ" or its equivalents. This rich language describes not only the believer's personal union with Christ (e.g., 3:9) but also the community's corporate experience of being interconnected with him (e.g., 1:1; 4:21).

In addition, Paul can characterize his Christian experience as a "righteousness that comes from God" that is "through faith in Christ" (or "through the faith of Christ," KJV; see the commentary on 3:9). This is more than a right standing bestowed on sinners. It is the renewing of a right relationship with God, which results in living and loving rightly (see 1:11). Paul sets this righteousness that comes as a gift from God over against his former achievement-oriented righteousness ("a righteousness of my own") that is based on performance of the Law.

The contrast between the old and the new ways of relating to God could not be more striking. Paul considers the old pattern that put confidence in human privileges and performance as so much filth to be abandoned (3:8). This is some of the strongest language Paul uses to reject achievements under the Law as a basis for a right relationship with God in Christ (Marshall 2004, 350).

3. The Gracious Work of God

Although Philippians is distinctively Christ-centered, it is God the Father who acts in Christ to bring about human salvation. It is God who initiates his gracious work in and among Christians, and God will bring it to a completion in the final day (1:6; see 3:9). Believers can work out their own salvation in daily life only because God is already at work in the community (2:12-13). Divine and human agency are bound together, but God's work is always prior. Both salvation (1:28) and righteousness (3:9) originate "from God."

God's sovereignty and providential care undergird the letter. God is working out his purposes through the events of Paul's imprisonment (1:12-26). Both believing in Christ and suffering for Christ are divine gifts (v 29). God acts in mercy on behalf of his faithful servants (2:27). The letter climaxes with the assurance of God's lavish generosity (4:19). Truly, "God is before, behind, in, with, and under all that the Philippians are called to be and to do" (Wagner 2007, 261). It is therefore appropriate that Paul's thanksgiving and prayers are directed to God (1:3; 4:6) and that God receives all the glory (1:11; 2:11; 4:20).

4. Cruciform Living

The community's response to God's gracious work among them is to live their lives in a manner worthy of the gospel *of Christ* (1:27). In Philippians, more than any other letter of Paul, the paradigm for such living is the story of Jesus (2:5-11). The Christian life is life conformed to Christ and his cross.

What are the implications of this for everyday Christian living? Above all, the church is to adopt a Christian "mind-set" (*phronein*)—a way of thinking, feeling, and behaving that reflects the self-giving attitude of Christ (2:5; see 1:7; 2:2; 3:15; 4:2, 10). In Philippians, having the mind of Christ is the basis for Christian unity. Mature believers will have the "same mind" in the Lord (3:15; 4:2; see 2:2). What is more, following Jesus, they will adopt an attitude of humility that puts the interests of others above their own (2:3-4, 20-21). A further consequence of cruciform living is that believers not only trust in Christ but also are given the privilege of sharing in his sufferings (1:29; 3:10).

Christ is also the pattern for Christian holiness in Philippians. The life of holiness involves growth in love, purity, and ethical righteousness, which continue until the day of Christ (1:9-11). Christian maturity is marked by a continual striving to know Christ in his fullness (3:12-15). Holiness is personal, but it is never individualistic. Christ-shaped holiness is incarnated in loving relationships and an others-oriented attitude (2:1-11).

Furthermore, because God is doing his saving work in their midst and conforming them to the loving pattern of Christ, believers must *rejoice*. This joy emerges from the crucible of suffering (1:18; 2:17-18, 28-29). Such joy is only possible because it is joy "in the Lord" (3:1; 4:4), not in themselves. As a result, Paul commands his audience to rejoice *always* (4:4; see 2:17-18; 3:1). As Fee comments, "Whatever else, life in Christ is a life of joy" (1995, 53).

5. Partnership in the Gospel

In Philippians, living in a manner worthy of the gospel presumes involvement in mission. From its beginnings, the church at Philippi has shared in a partnership (*koinōnia*) with Paul in the gospel (1:5). This shared mission has two notable dimensions. First, these Christians participate in Paul's gospel mission through their prayers (1:19) and generosity (4:14-15). The latter involves both financial support for Paul (vv 10-20), as well as sending coworkers like Epaphroditus to provide practical help (2:25-30).

Second, "Paul fully expected the local congregation to be active in striving together for the faith of the gospel and in holding out the word of life (Phil 2:16)" (Marshall 2004, 360). Part of why Paul continues to "preach Christ," even in the midst of personal attacks (1:15-18), is to encourage the congregation to be faithful to make Christ known in their own sphere of influence (Marshall 2004, 360). A faithful witness to the gospel is costly. It entails a willingness to suffer together on behalf of Christ (1:29-30).

But Paul does not need to command the church to participate in mission. As they live out their public life as citizens of a heavenly commonwealth (1:27; 3:20), as the integrity of their lives shines forth in the midst of a twisted world (2:14-15), as they corporately embody the self-giving love of Christ, they *become* a proclamation of the gospel (Wagner 2007, 273-74). Mission is the very identity of the holy people of God.

D. The Approach and Intent of the Commentary

I write this commentary from the perspective that Paul's letter to the Philippians is part of Holy Scripture. This means that we should expect to hear Paul's words to the Philippians in the mid-first century as God's word to us in the twenty-first century. This understanding profoundly shapes the character and intent of the commentary. It is written for the church, especially for those engaged in the ministry of the church. As a result, it is important to interpret the text of Philippians from at least three perspectives.

First, we must read the text *historically*. Because Paul's letter to the Philippians is an ancient document, we must listen to the text within its original historical and cultural world. This will involve not only the classical concerns of historical exegesis (e.g., language, grammar, historical context) but also the insights of newer interpretive approaches that shed light on aspects of the text. I therefore try to incorporate, when appropriate, the fruit of recent study in ancient rhetoric, Greco-Roman friendship, and the Roman political and religious setting of the letter (see the valuable survey of recent approaches to Philippians in Silva 2005, 17-20, 32-34). These historical concerns are primarily featured in the BEHIND THE TEXT and IN THE TEXT sections of the commentary.

Second, we must read the text *theologically*. The church's interpretation of Scripture never stops with a historical reading. This commentary intentionally seeks to discover the theological significance of Paul's words. Such theological exegesis will be a regular part of the IN THE TEXT sections of the commentary. But it will especially be featured in the FROM THE TEXT discussions.

There is no such animal as a "neutral" reading of Scripture, and that is particularly true of a theological reading. This commentary is unapologetically confessional. It pays particular attention to issues of concern to the Wesleyan theological tradition. At the same time, we must avoid imposing any conceptual grid over the text that prevents Scripture from challenging our own human and inevitably flawed theological understandings. It is crucial that we listen to other wise voices. This involves paying attention to the history of the church's interpretation of Philippians, particularly the early church fathers. This practice is too often neglected in Scripture study today, and we are much the poorer for it.

Moreover, the church of Jesus Christ is a global interpretive community. I have lived most of my adult life outside of North America. That experience has taught me that I have much to learn from sisters and brothers who read Scripture out of different cultural and life situations. Unfortunately, biblical interpretation and commentary writing is still dominated by male, Western voices. Despite my unavoidable identity, I attempt to include theological insights from the historical and global church at various points in the commentary.

Third, we must read Scripture *formationally*. Fowl is quite right that the interpretation of Scripture is always directed toward a more faithful worship and practice; it aims at a deeper relationship with God and one another (2005, 6). That is particularly true in the case of Philippians. The formation of Christian communities is fully in line with what Paul desires for his first audience.

The commentary will try to address formational issues that emerge from the text in the FROM THE TEXT sections. These are, by no means, exhaustive. At best, they are signposts that point to ways in which believing communities might begin to appropriate the text for their spiritual development and communal life.

A commentary such as this, then, does not substitute for a formational reading of the text as the Word of God, but complements it. For John Wesley, Scripture reading was a form of prayer. We would do well, he advised, if "we were frequently to pause, and examine ourselves by what we read, both with regard to our hearts, and lives" (Preface to the *Explanatory Notes on the Old Testament*, 1765). It is my hope that this commentary will serve as a catalyst for assisting readers and Christian communities to engage the text of Paul's letter to the Philippians with both mind and heart.

COMMENTARY

I. LETTER OPENING: PHILIPPIANS 1:1-11

BEHIND THE TEXT

During Paul's time, letters in the Greco-Roman world were comprised of three parts: a letter opening, a body, and a letter closing. The letter opening typically included the names of the sender and the receiver, a brief greeting, and sometimes a wish or prayer for good health on behalf of the recipient and/or a thanksgiving to the gods.

Examples of Ancient Letter Openings

The following letter openings from papyrus letters in Greek (second and third centuries) share common elements with Paul's letters:

- Clairemon to Serapion, greeting. Before all else I pray that you will be well, and I make your obeisance before the lord Serapis daily (*Pmich.* 8.513 in Richards 2004, 129).
- Apion to his father and lord, Epimachus, very many greetings. Before all else I pray that you are well and that you may prosper in continual health . . . I give thanks to the Lord Serapis because, when I was endangered at sea, he rescued me (*BGU* II 423 in White 1986, 159).
- Toubias to Apollonios, greeting. If you are well and if all your affairs and everything else is proceeding according to your will, many thanks to the gods; we also are well, always remembering you, as I should (*CPJ* 14 in White 1986, 39).

Paul follows these normal patterns in his letters, but he also transforms them. Paul's letter openings are never simply conventional. In a letter like Philippians, he adapts and expands the customary elements found in ancient letters in order to charge them with a powerful theological current.

Paul's thanksgiving section (1:3-11) is a prime example. Paul decisively transforms the customary prayer for health or a thanksgiving to the gods, enlisting it in the service of the gospel. Three distinctive features stand out: First, instead of being thankful for safety, health, or good fortune, Paul normally gives thanks for his readers themselves (Richards 2004, 131). Second, Paul regularly combines his thanksgiving with a prayer of intercession for the church. Third, the thanksgiving section frequently introduces some of the main themes of the letter.

The thanksgiving and prayer of Philippians (1:3-11), in particular, anticipate matters that Paul will take up as the letter unfolds. These include (partially following Witherington 1994, 36):

- joy/rejoicing (1:4; see 1:18, 25; 2:2, 17, 18, 28, 29; 3:1; 4:1, 4, 10)
- partnership/sharing (1:5, 7; see 2:1; 3:10; 4:14, 15)
- the gospel and its defense (1:5, 7; see 1:12, 16, 27; 2:22; 4:3, 15)
- God's saving work among the Philippians (1:6; see 1:28; 2:12-13; 3:20-21)
- the day of Christ (1:6, 10; see 2:16; 3:10-11, 20-21)
- the Christian mind (1:7; see 2:2, 5; 3:15; 4:2, 8, 10)
- gratitude for the Philippians and their ministry (1:3, 5; see 2:25; 4:10-20)
- Paul's imprisonment (1:7; see 1:12-18)
- love or affection (1:7-8, 9; see 1:16; 2:1-2; 4:1)
- discerning the things that matter (1:9-10; see 3:4-16; 4:8-9)
- purity/holiness (1:10, 11; see 2:15; 4:8)
- the grace and glory of God (1:7, 11; see 2:11; 4:19-20, 23)

In addition, J. B. Lightfoot is probably right that the repeated use of the word "all" (1:1, 4, 7, 8; see 1:25; 2:17; 4:21) in connection with the Philippians anticipates Paul's exhortations to Christian unity in the letter (1953, 83; see 1:27; 2:1-4; 4:2, 3, 5, 7, 9). Furthermore, Paul's prayer for the Philippians (1:9-11) previews his principal concern that the Philippians live lives that are worthy of the gospel (v 27). Paul's letter opening, then, serves as an important guide for understanding the message of Philippians as a whole.

In addition to the letter form, Paul's letters also show the influence of ancient *rhetoric*, the art of persuading an audience (see the Introduction). This is hardly surprising, since Paul wrote letters primarily to be *read aloud* to be *heard* in public, not to be read privately by individuals.

Philippians 1:3-11 corresponds to the component of rhetorical delivery called the *exordium*. Its function was to secure the goodwill of the audience and to introduce the subjects that were about to be discussed. The latter purpose we have already seen. As for the former, Paul's report of his prayers for the Philippians (vv 3-5), his confidence in them (v 6), and his expressions of deep affection for them (vv 7-8) would surely have helped him gain a positive hearing.

Such assurances of Paul's care for his audience and his longing to be with them (vv 7-8) appeal to the audience's emotions. Rhetorically, these are arguments from *pathos* (see the Introduction). Paul also builds on *ethos*, his own credibility, in this opening section. He does this when he calls himself a **slave of Christ** (v 1) or when he refers to his "chains" for the sake of the gospel (v 7).

What is more, we noted in the Introduction that Paul draws upon the language of friendship in the Greco-Roman world throughout this letter. Here, for example, Paul speaks of his relationship with the Philippians as a "partnership [*koinōniai*] in the gospel" (v 5; see v 7, **fellowsharers**, *synkoinōnous*; see also vv 7-8). But this friendship is not simply a common bond between two parties. It is a sharing that serves the gospel and is focused on Christ.

Philippians 1:1-11 can be divided into three sections: a greeting (vv 1-2), a thanksgiving (vv 3-8), and an intercessory prayer (vv 9-11).

IN THE TEXT

A. Greeting (1:1-2)

■ **1** The letter begins by identifying both **Paul and Timothy** as the senders. Timothy, Paul's closest colleague and "son in the faith" (1 Tim 1:2; see 1 Cor 4:17), is often mentioned at the beginning of his letters (1 and 2 Thessalonians, 2 Corinthians, Philemon, Colossians). Although the practice of naming present companions as co-senders is characteristic of Paul's writings, it is extremely rare in other Greco-Roman letters. Timothy is likely not an actual co-author of Philippians, since Paul speaks throughout in the first person singular ("I"). Rather, his name probably appears because of his close ties with the church in Philippi. Acts testifies that he was involved in the founding of the church (Acts 16:1, 13) and that he returned during Paul's third missionary journey (19:22; 20:3-4). He was apparently well known and highly regarded by the Philippians (Phil 2:19-24). We simply cannot be sure whether Timothy also served as Paul's secretary and actually wrote the letter at Paul's dictation (so Fee 1995, 61).

Even more significant is how Paul expands the customary naming of the sender to give it theological meaning. Paul identifies himself and Timothy as **servants of Christ Jesus** (see also Rom 1:1; Titus 1:1). This is the only time in all his letters that Paul and his co-sender share the same title. This seems subtly to forecast Paul's emphasis on "partnership" (*koinōnia*) and mutuality throughout the letter (Lyons and Malas 2007, 61-62).

The word **servants** (*douloi*) is better translated by the term ***slaves***. In the Greek OT (LXX), "servant" can be a title of honor for leaders like Moses or David who have a special relationship with God. We can assume, however, that Paul's mainly Gentile readers would have heard this word in its more common sense of a "slave." Slavery was as taken for granted in Paul's day as electrical appliances are in ours.

Unlike many modern forms of slavery, slaves in the Greco-Roman world came from a wide range of social backgrounds. At times, they could even hold positions of high responsibility in a household. Nevertheless, they still "belonged" to someone else. The word "slave" communicated humility, submission, and ownership in Paul's world (Fee 1995, 63; see the sidebar "Further Reading on First-Century Slavery" in Greathouse and Lyons 2008, 188).

It is, therefore, highly significant that Paul and Timothy are Christ's "slaves." They are completely at the disposal of their common master and Lord, bound to his loving service. In Philippians, the word "slave" takes on particular weight, since it later describes the attitude of Christ himself. The missionaries are slaves of the one who deliberately adopted "the form of a slave" (2:7 NRSV) for their sake (Bockmuehl 1998, 51). Already, Paul points to himself and to Timothy as examples of the kind of humility and self-giving service that is such a prominent theme in the letter.

This emphasis on lowly service may be part of the reason that Paul does not identify himself as an apostle, as he does in most of his letters. At the same time, the omission fits his warm relationship with his friends in Philippi; he does not need to remind them of his apostolic authority.

The letter is addressed to **all the saints in Christ Jesus at Philippi**. Three aspects of this description deserve our attention:

First, Paul identifies the recipients as **saints** (*hagioi*). This term applies to the church as a whole (**all**), not simply an elite group of especially holy Christians. Like Israel in the OT, the saints (literally, "holy ones") are "a people holy to the LORD" (Deut 7:6; 14:2, 21; see Ps 34:9). As a community, they are chosen and set apart to belong to God in a special way (Exod 19:6). The Philippians are saints because they participate in the holiness of God. At the same time, they are set apart in order to *be* holy people, even as God is holy (Lev 11:45; 19:2; 20:7). The saints are to reflect God's holiness in their character and everyday conduct, in contrast to the world around them. This is a theme to which Paul will consistently return in the letter (see Phil 1:10, 11; 2:1-5, 14-15; 3:17; 4:8-9).

Second, the Philippians are holy, not in themselves, but because they are **in Christ Jesus**. Of the approximately 165 times this or equivalent expressions occur in the Pauline collection of letters, 21 are in Philippians. Clearly, **in Christ** is a critical phrase for understanding Paul's vision of the Christian life.

The specific significance of **in Christ** varies from case to case; and interpreters have not come to full agreement about its precise meaning. At the very least, however, to be **in Christ** means that believers are in close personal union with Christ crucified and risen (see Phil 3:9-11). At the same time, it signifies that they are incorporated into the community founded by Christ through their relationship with Jesus. Consequently, "Being 'in Christ' refers to the experience not merely of the individual but of the community" (Gorman 2001, 37; see, e.g., Gal 3:28, "you are all one in Christ Jesus").

Bockmuehl notes that the phrase **in Christ** carries particular importance within Philippians. This is not just because it occurs repeatedly. It is also due to the letter's emphasis on the example of Christ (see 2:5), who determines the church's character and communal life (1998, 53).

Third, God's holy people are not only in Christ but are also *in Philippi.* We might easily pass over these words as no more than a geographical reference. But in the context of the letter, the phrase has more substance than that. It is in a concrete setting, the Roman colony *in Philippi,* that the church lives out its life **in Christ.**

Later Paul will remind these Christians that their true citizenship is in heaven, not in Roman Philippi, a place where the emperor is proclaimed as a divine lord and savior (3:20). Although they are situated in Philippi, their primary identity is determined by their relationship to another lord—the Lord Jesus Christ (1:2).

In addition to addressing the church as a whole, Paul singles out the **overseers and deacons** in Philippi. This is the first time in Paul's letters that such specific leadership functions are mentioned. Moreover, after Paul draws attention to them at the outset, we hear nothing more of them in the rest of the letter. It is difficult to be certain about the precise role they played in the Philippian church.

Overseers (*episkopoi;* "bishops," NRSV) apparently refers to those within the congregation who were engaged in a ministry of oversight and pastoral care for the fellowship. The terms "overseers" and "elders" (*presbyteroi*) are virtually interchangeable in the NT (see Titus 1:5-7; Acts 20:17, 28; 1 Pet 5:1, 2). **Deacons** (*diakonoi*) is the plural of the word for "servant" or "minister" (*diakonos*), and Paul uses the term in a variety of ways. The NT nowhere spells out the specific duties of "deacons." But here it seems to indicate local leaders who were involved in a ministry of practical service and material care.

We can make several further observations about these church leaders:
- Paul's mention of these two groups suggests that from early on there was some type of organized leadership structure within the Pauline churches (compare Acts 14:23).
- The terms "overseer" and "deacon" primarily represented ministry

functions. Well-defined *offices*, such as that of "bishop," came later in the history of the church. Paul's leadership language is flexible (see, e.g., 1 Thess 5:12). It is linked to leadership gifts that functioned within the body (e.g., "leadership" in Rom 12:8; "administration" in 1 Cor 12:28; "pastor" in Eph 4:11). Gift, function, and office are intertwined.

- Leadership in Philippi and elsewhere in Paul's churches was apparently *collective*. There is no evidence for a single person who was "in charge" of the community or who was expected to fulfill all of the leadership functions.
- The language that introduces these leadership functions, **together with** (*syn*), is telling. As Fee points out, the overseers and deacons are addressed "alongside of" the saints. They are not *above* the church or *outside* of it, but a part of the whole (1995, 67; for more on the NT understanding of ministry, see Lightfoot 1953, 95-99, 181-269; and Flemming 1994).

Why, then, do we find this unusual mention of church leaders at the beginning of Philippians? One explanation, which goes back to John Chrysostom, is that they were especially responsible for sending Epaphroditus and the money gift from the church to Paul. A second option is that by mentioning these leaders at the start, Paul anticipates the tensions among congregational leaders he will address later (4:2-3). Yet another suggestion is tied to the issue of status: Paul models the humble attitude he will press for in this letter by giving titles of honor to the church's leaders (overseer and deacon). This stands in contrast to his own lowly status as a slave (v 1; Hellerman 2005, 118-19). But there are simply not enough clues to solve this mystery with any measure of certainty. In any case, Paul writes this letter to the church as a whole, not just the leaders.

■ **2** Paul closes his salutation with his characteristic blessing of **grace and peace** on the community. He modifies the standard Greco-Roman letter greeting by changing the word "Greetings!" (*charein*) into the Christian term "grace" (*charis*), making a play on words. Paul then adds the traditional Jewish greeting, "peace" (*shalom;* here *eirēnē* in Greek). Both words are charged with theological content.

Grace represents the full scope of God's loving favor toward sinful humanity in Jesus Christ. **Peace** is the blessing of reconciliation and wholeness that results from God's gracious saving work. Paul ascribes the source of these magnificent blessings to **God our Father and the Lord Jesus Christ.** Sharing a common preposition in Greek (*apo*), God the Father and the Son are bound closely together in Paul's thought. God the Father and Christ the risen Lord are "entirely at one" in bestowing the gift of salvation (Bruce 1983, 4).

B. Thanksgiving and Prayer (1:3-11)

1. Thanksgiving (1:3-8)

■ **3** Paul's regular practice in his letters to churches is to follow the opening greeting with some form of thanksgiving (but compare Galatians; on Paul's thanksgiving sections, see O'Brien 1997). Here the thanksgiving section sets the tone for the entire letter. It exudes a positive spirit of joy, affection, and confidence in the faithfulness of God.

The headline verb in v 3, **I give thanks** (*eucharistō*), begins one long and complex sentence in Greek, which runs through the end of v 8. Paul begins by reporting his repeated prayer to **God**. By v 6, however, it is clear that the apostle is also addressing the Philippians. He expresses his warm feelings toward them in the course of giving thanks to God (Fowl 2005, 21). His reference to **my** God indicates his personal relationship, not possession.

In v 3 Paul says, literally, **I thank my God at your every remembrance.** The grammar of the phrase **at your every remembrance** (*epi pasēi tēi mneiai hymōn*) is ambiguous and can be taken in two ways. It could mean that Paul gives God thanks whenever he remembers *the Philippians*. Alternatively, Paul may be saying that he regularly thanks God for all the ways that the Philippians remember *him*. If the second reading is correct, then Paul's gratitude might be a response to the Philippians' ongoing generosity on his behalf—particularly their recent financial gift sent through Epaphroditus (4:15-18; so O'Brien 1991, 58-61).

However, in every other place that Paul talks about **remembrance** in his introductory thanksgivings (Rom 1:9; 1 Thess 1:3; Phlm 4; 2 Tim 1:3), it is his *readers* that are the object of his remembering. It seems better, then, to understand Paul as thanking God "upon [*epi*] every remembrance *of you*"—the Philippians (so the NIV, **every time I remember you;** see Fee 1995, 77-79). On every occasion that Paul remembers his beloved Philippian friends in prayer, he does so with thanksgiving to God.

■ **4** The double reference to prayer in v 4 highlights its crucial importance to Paul's pastoral care for the church. Paul claims, **I thank my God ... always in my every prayer** [*deēsei*] **for all of you, as I make my prayer** [*tēn deēsin*] **with joy** (vv 3-4). The word Paul uses for **prayer** (*deēsis*) normally refers to prayers of petition or intercession, as it does here (Bauer 1979, 171-72).

A striking feature of this verse is the way that Paul stacks up the words for **all** and **always** (*pantōn*). The rhetorical impact is strengthened by Paul's use of alliteration (each word begins with the letter *p*) and by a play on words with similar sounds (*pasē ... pantote ... pasē ... pantōn*). This serves to spotlight "the all-inclusiveness of his prayer ... none of the Philippians Christians for any reasons whatever was excluded from the apostles' love and concern" (Hawthorne and Martin 2004, 20).

At the same time, Paul stresses that his pattern of praying for the Philippians is ongoing. Paul **always** thanks God for the Philippians, in the context of his regular habit of praying for them (**all my prayers**; Fee 1995, 80). The word **always** does not, of course, mean that Paul does nothing but pray for them. His point is that he does so consistently.

Furthermore, Paul's prayer on behalf of the Philippians is characterized by **joy**. Here Paul models an attitude that he later urges his readers to embrace (3:1; 4:4).

Joy in Philippians

Joy (*chara*) is a golden thread that runs throughout Philippians (1:4, 18, 25; 2:2, 17, 18, 28, 29; 3:1; 4:1, 4, 10). The word appears in one cognate form or other no fewer than 16 times. For Paul, joy is more than a feeling of well-being or a positive mood. It is an attitude of exultation and delight that is grounded in what God is doing in Christ, both in ourselves and in the lives of others (1:18, 25; 2:28; 4:1, 10; Marshall 1991, 8). Joy is the basic orientation of the Christian life, the fruit of the Spirit's active presence in the believer (Gal 5:22; Rom 14:17). A joyless Christian makes no more sense than a waterless ocean.

In Philippians, Christian joy is not dependent on favorable circumstances or outward success. Paul can have joy even as he languishes in prison under a capital charge (1:4, 18; 2:2, 17; 4:10). At the same time, he exhorts his friends to rejoice (*chairete*; 2:18; 3:1; 4:4; see Rom 12:12, 15; 1 Thess 5:16) in the face of opposition and suffering (see Phil 1:28; 2:17). The joy they share together is a reason for encouragement, despite external hardships (2:17-18; Lyons and Malas 2007, 62). Indeed, joy in the midst of trying circumstances is a keynote of the letter to the Philippians. Such an attitude is possible because joy flows out of a relationship with God in Christ. Therefore, Christians should "rejoice *in the Lord*" (3:1; 4:4; see 2:29; 4:10).

For Paul, joy is also wed to hope. Christians can presently exult in the hope of sharing God's glory in the life to come (3:20—4:1; Rom 5:2; 12:12).

■ **5** Paul now gives the reason (*epi*) for his joy when he prays for the Philippians, and probably his basis for thanksgiving (v 3) as well. It is their **partnership with him in the gospel from the first day until now.** The word **partnership** (*koinōnia*) is another signature term in the letter. In Paul's world, the term could refer to people *participating* in something together, as well as to the *relationship* they share as a result of that common participation. Its frequent use in this letter (1:5, 7; 2:1; 3:10; 4:14, 15) brings out both of these dimensions. Paul and the Philippians actively share in the grace and work of God (1:5, 7; 4:14, 15). At the same time, through their participation in the work of the gospel, they are bound together in spiritual fellowship and love (see 2:1, which probably refers to their common "sharing in the Spirit," NRSV; see further, Marshall 1993, 149-52; Hainz 1991, 2:303-5). The language of partnership also reflects the deep mutual friendship that Paul and the Philippians share (see BEHIND THE TEXT for this section).

Here the focus is on their partnership **in the gospel** (on "the gospel" in Philippians, see O'Brien 1986). In the context, this means not that the Philippians have accepted the gospel message but that they have actively partnered with Paul in the advance of the gospel of Christ. Clearly this involves their practical financial support of Paul's efforts to proclaim the gospel (4:15; see Rom 15:26; 2 Cor 9:13). It is not limited to that, however. Paul's partnership with the Philippians presumably also includes their

- evangelistic witness to the gospel in Philippi (see 1:27, 28)
- suffering along with Paul for the gospel's sake (1:30; 4:14)
- intercessory prayer on Paul's behalf (1:19)
- living in a way that that is truly worthy of the gospel of Christ (1:27; O'Brien 1986, 217-18)

Paul thanks God for the Philippians and prays for them with joy because from the time of their conversion (**the first day**) until the time of Paul's writing this letter, they have shared in the ministry and progress of the gospel. This partnership in mission becomes a major theme of the letter as a whole (see Ware 2005, 168-69).

■ **6** Grammatically, v 6 could provide another reason that Paul gives thanks to God (v 3; so O'Brien 1991, 63) or that he prays for the church with joy (v 4; so Marshall 1991, 10). More likely, however, what Paul says in v 6 is harnessed to v 5. The Philippians' partnership in Paul's gospel ministry from the beginning till now is sure evidence of God's gracious work among them (Bruce 1983, 7). Paul is **confident** (*pepoithōs*; see 1:14, 25; 2:24; 3:3, 4) **of this**: **that** the **good work** God began in the church will carry on to a glorious completion when Christ returns.

The source of Paul's confidence (1:14, 25; 2:24; 3:3-4) is no less than the faithfulness of God himself to accomplish what he purposes to do (see 1 Thess 5:24). Bockmuehl says it well: "Paul's confidence is not in the Christianity of the Christians, but in the God-ness of God, who is supremely trustworthy, able, and committed to finish the work he has begun" (1998, 62).

But what is God's **good work** within the Philippians? Some interpreters take the good work of God to refer narrowly to the Philippians' generosity in support of Paul's evangelistic ministry. It is better, however, to understand it in a more comprehensive sense as the work of salvation that God has already initiated in the church.

Salvation begins and ends with God. But here it is of no small importance that Paul calls their salvation a **good work** (Fee 1995, 87). Elsewhere, Paul uses this language to refer to the ethical dimension of redemption (see, e.g., Rom 2:7; 2 Cor 9:8; Col 1:10; 2 Thess 2:17). For Paul, salvation that does not result in a transformed life is simply not worthy of the name (Fee 1995, 87). It is a recurring theme in Philippians that God's *good work* in his people enables them to do *good works*, living a way that is worthy of the gospel (1:27-28; 2:12-13; see Chrysostom, *Hom. Phil.* 1.1.6). The church actively participates in the saving activity of God. But God's work is prior. Here, the Philippians' partnership with Paul in the advance of the gospel is rooted in what God is already doing.

The phrase **in you** (*en hymōn*) probably has both a personal and a corporate ("among you," NRSV) dimension. God is graciously at work in the community as a whole and within the lives of each of its members.

What is more, God's good work in the Philippian congregation is oriented toward the future. Their salvation is not a point in time but rather a process of transformation that will only reach its goal at **the day of Christ Jesus** (Fowl 2005, 26). This phrase resounds with echoes of the OT idea of "the day of the Lord." For Paul, it invariably refers to the *Parousia*, the future event when Jesus will return as both Judge and exalted Lord (see Phil 1:10; 2:16; Rom 2:16; 1 Cor 1:8; 3:13; 2 Cor 1:14; 1 Thess 5:2; 2 Thess 1:10; 2:2).

Paul's perspective on the Christian life is robustly eschatological. The church's salvation is already in progress, but it will only be completed on the day they see Christ face-to-face in all his glory. The assurance that God **will carry it on to completion** (*epitelesei*) **until** that day does not suggest that their final salvation is automatic. It does, however, indicate that whatever their present circumstances, God's gracious work will continue in and among his people right up to the end. God will not abandon them at any point along the way (Marshall 1991, 12).

■ **7** The NIV begins a new paragraph with v 7. But in Greek the conjunction **even as** (*kathōs*) connects this verse with what has come before (so Fee 1995, 88; Vincent 1897, 8; but compare Bauer 1979, 391). Here Paul seems to offer a justification for his joyful thanksgiving for the Philippians in vv 3-6, which includes his unshakable confidence that God's present work in them will ultimately come to completion (see Fowl 2005, 28). **It is,** after all, only **right,** or appropriate (*dikaion*), for him **to feel this way about** them.

The verb translated **to feel** (*phronein*) by the NIV is a crucial term in Philippians (see 2:2, 5; 3:15, 19; 4:2, 10). But it is not an easy word to translate in English. Often rendered "to think," it has to do with more than just an intellectual activity. It involves a whole pattern of thinking, discerning, feeling, and acting (Fowl 2005, 6)—what might be called a Christian "mind-set" (see especially 2:2, 5; 3:15). In v 7 it describes Paul's attitude or frame of mind toward the Philippians. At the same time, Paul's positive disposition toward his friends prepares for the kind of mind-set he will call them to embrace as the letter unfolds. They must reflect no less than the attitude of Christ himself (2:5).

The reason that Paul is right to have the Philippians in mind in this way is because of his deep affection for them. The NIV's **since I have you in my heart** (*dia to echein me en tēi kardiai hymas,* v 7) seems to read the clause better than the NRSV's "because *you* hold *me* in *your* heart." The order of the words in Greek suggests that here Paul is describing his own positive feelings toward **all of you.** (In a clause in which an infinitive is followed by two accusatives, the first [here *me,* "I"] is normally the subject and the second [here *hymas,* "you"] the object; see Reed 1991.)

Paul can affirm such feelings for his dear friends in Philippi because they are his ***fellow participants in grace.*** The Greek is somewhat ambiguous, but overall it is better to read the phrase as *"my* fellow sharers in grace" than "fellow sharers in *my* grace" (so O'Brien 1991, 70). The word for ***fellow participants*** (*synkoinōnous*) is another form of the key term **partnership** (*koinōnia*) introduced in v 5.

In what sense are Paul's friends in Philippi ***fellow sharers*** with him in grace? Is Paul highlighting their mutual participation in God's saving grace and love toward his people? Or, might this be a reference to the church's sharing in Paul's ministry through their financial gifts (see 4:14, where the verb form "sharing together" appears)?

The key lies in the two preceding phrases, which describe *how* Paul and his readers partner together in God's grace. **Whether I am in chains** refers to Paul's imprisonment. The words "chains" and "prison" were often used interchangeably in the ancient world (Wansink 1996, 46). This is Paul's first reference to his own suffering in Philippians. It is a theme that he will take up in more detail later in this chapter.

When Paul calls the Philippians his ***partners in grace,*** he likely has in mind not only their financial support of his ministry while he is in prison but also their own participation in affliction (Fowl 2005, 30-31; see Wesley n.d., 506). In 1:29, Paul says that the church has been given grace in order to suffer for Christ. He explains in v 30 that the Philippians are going through the same struggle as Paul himself. Part of the **grace,** then, in which they share together is the privilege of suffering for the sake of the gospel.

A second way in which the Philippians partner with Paul in grace is in **defending and confirming the gospel.** Note that as Paul conceives it here, it is not the apostle, but *the gospel* that is on trial. ***Defense*** (*apologia*) can refer to a formal defense of oneself against accusations (see Acts 22:1; 2 Tim 4:16). Thus, it could allude to Paul's impending court appearance in Rome. More likely, however, Paul uses the term in a nontechnical sense, of answering objections to the gospel.

Confirmation (*bebaiōsei*) signifies the more positive vindication of the gospel's credibility. The Philippians share in this task, not only through supporting Paul in his own ministry, but also by standing firm in the face of similar kinds of hostility from the empire (1:29-30). The Philippians are partners in God's grace, both through their participation in the gospel ministry and their suffering for the gospel's sake.

■ **8** Paul extends what he has just said in the previous verse about holding the Philippians in his heart. In an emotion-charged expression, Paul invokes **God** as his ***witness*** (see 1 Thess 2:5, 10; Rom 1:9; 2 Cor 1:23; Gal 1:20) in order to reinforce the depth of his feelings for them. In effect he says, "only God knows how much **I long for all of you**" (Marshall 1991, 15). In the ancient world, such expressions of affection strengthened the bonds between friends who were apart. In other letters, Paul declares that he longs *to see* his readers (Rom 1:11; 1 Thess 3:6; 2 Tim 1:4). Only here does he yearn directly for them, which implies a passionate concern for this church. As Calvin wisely notes, "we long after the things that are dear to us" (1965, 231).

But this is more than Paul's own feeling. He gives his concern a christological focus, adding the phrase **with the affection of Christ Jesus** (Fowl 2005, 31). The word **affection** (*splanchna*) originally referred to the inner organs (heart, liver, lungs), which were seen as the seat of human emotions. In the Gospels, it expresses Jesus' heartfelt compassion toward others (Matt 9:36; Mark 1:41; Luke 7:13). And here Paul says that he loves his dear friends in Philippi with (*en*) the same affection that Christ has for them. At the same time, Christ loves the Philippians through Paul. This testifies to a "three-way bond" of love between Paul, the Philippians, and Christ (Fee 1995, 94).

2. Intercession (1:9-11)

■ **9** Having assured the Philippians that he was praying for them in v 4, Paul now articulates the content of his intercession on their behalf (**and this is my prayer**). This prayer-report flows naturally from Paul's testimony of his love for these friends in v 8. At the same time, it brings the opening section of the letter to a resounding climax.

First, Paul prays **that [their] love** (*agapē*) **may abound more and more** (v 9). Does this refer to love for God or love for others? If we go by how Paul speaks of love in the rest of the letter (1:16; 2:2; see 1 Thess 3:12), it is likely that love for one another is particularly in view. Above all, Paul urges the Philippians to adopt the pattern of love demonstrated by Jesus Christ, who poured himself out for others, even to the point of death on a cross (Phil 2:5-8). This love is not something the Philippians completely lack but something they continually need more of.

The verb **abound** (*perriseuō*) is a favorite of the apostle (it occurs 26 times in his letters; see Phil 1:26; 4:12, 18; 1 Thess 3:12). It speaks here of a love that is lavish and overflowing, like a river that floods its banks. It is love without limits; love beyond measure (Chrysostom, *Hom. Phil.* 2.1.9).

This overflowing love is accompanied by **knowledge and depth of insight.** This phrase reveals the *manner* in which the Philippians' love is to abound (Fowl 2005, 32). **Knowledge** (*epignōsis*), another of Paul's characteristic words, normally indicates true spiritual knowledge of God and his ways (e.g., Rom 1:28; 3:20; 10:2; Col 1:9, 10; Eph 4:13). It is not so much knowledge *about* something as it is a knowing that results from experience and personal relationship (Fee 1995, 100).

The term **depth of insight** (*aisthēsis*) occurs nowhere else in the NT. However, its use in ancient Greek literature and in the OT points toward the kind of practical moral perception that enables us to make sound ethical choices. Paul's point is that growth in love is incomplete apart from an increase in spiritual knowledge and moral discernment.

Love without knowledge and insight can be permissive and morally flabby. "Blind" love can result in poor moral judgments or selfish conduct. Paul is not so much praying for a more *intense* love as a more *intelligent* love. He desires for his Philippian friends a love that evidences a genuine experiential knowledge of God and a pattern of moral decisions that accord with God's will (see Rom 12:2).

■ **10** The purpose of this love penetrated by true insight is that **you may be able to discern what is best** (v 10). The verb translated **discern** (*dokimazein*) carries the idea of putting something to the test and approving it as genuine, as, say, precious metals or money. Here Paul talks about the ability to determine **the things that matter** (*ta diapheronta*). What matters, of course, is from the divine perspective. Such things stand in marked contrast to the things that are inconsequential so far as God is concerned (see the similar language in Rom 2:18).

Most of the church fathers applied this phrase specifically to the need to distinguish between true and false teaching. In the present context, however, Paul's concern centers on determining what is morally and spiritually excellent. This will not only mean distinguishing between right and wrong but also involves sorting out what is merely good or acceptable from what is *best*. Paul himself models this ability to recognize what is absolutely vital in Phil 3:7-14; he leaves all else behind to press on toward the goal to which Christ has called him (see 4:8; Bockmuehl 1998, 68).

A second purpose clause in this verse expresses the *ultimate* goal of Paul's prayer (Fee 1995, 102): that they **may be pure and blameless until the day of Christ.**

The first of these terms (*eilikrinēs*) has to do with moral purity and integrity. Elsewhere, Paul uses this word to describe his sincere motives as a minister of Christ (2 Cor 1:12; 2:17; see 1 Cor 5:8). Here it signifies Christian character that is genuine, authentic, and transparent before God and others.

The second term, **blameless** (*aproskopos*), is less straightforward. Commentators are divided as to whether it means being "without offense" in one's own life, or whether it has to do with not causing *others* to stumble. Paul's immediate concern with standing before Christ's judgment favors the first meaning. Yet, it could be argued that his wider appeal for Christian unity in this letter supports the second (compare 1 Cor 10:32). The word may carry both meanings here.

As in v 6, Paul sees God's work in the Philippians' lives in light of the future **day** when they will stand before **Christ.** The purity and integrity that Paul desires for the Philippians, however, is not merely a future goal that will happen when Christ returns (against Fowl 2005, 34; Silva 2005, 52). Rather, the moral character of their lives here and now will make them *ready* to stand the test of that great day, whenever it comes. The Greek preposition *eis* (**until**) would then mean "in preparation for" **the day of Christ.**

■ **11** Paul's intercessory prayer for the Philippians ends with his request that they be **filled with the fruit of righteousness.** The phrase **the fruit of righteousness** (*karpon dikaiosynēs*) can be taken in more than one sense. Does it mean the fruit that *results from* their being justified or brought into a right relationship with God? Or is it the fruit that *consists of* a righteous character? Both the OT background (see Prov 3:9; 11:30; Amos 6:12) and the present context strongly favor the second option. The **fruit of righteousness** refers to the ethical fruit that characterizes lives of purity and integrity. Elsewhere Paul calls it the "fruit of the Spirit" (Gal 5:22-23)

To be **filled** with the fruit of righteousness means in part to "abound" and "overflow" in love (Fee 1995, 104). It is to be formed into the righteous character of Christ himself (see Phil 2:5-11). Paul wants the lives of his audience to blossom forth in a harvest of **righteousness.** This righteous fruit is by no means a human achievement but is the gracious work of God **through Jesus Christ.** Wesley remarks, "The branch and the fruits must derive both their virtue and their very being from the all-supporting, all-supplying root, Jesus Christ" (n.d., 506).

Furthermore, the goal of this harvest of righteousness among the Philippians is **the glory and praise of God.** This concluding doxology underscores that everything Paul prays for his friends in Philippi has a single and ultimate aim. Paul desires that God will be honored through the sanctifying work God is doing in the lives of his people. These verses beautifully capture Paul's moral vision for the church: an ever-growing love, knowledge, and moral discernment, which leads to pure hearts and lives. This alone prepares God's people for the final test. And ultimately, the holy character of the church brings glory to God.

FROM THE TEXT

Paul's introduction to this letter is anything *but* a mere formality. By the end of v 11 he has set forth both his feelings for the Philippians and his vision for the kind of church they are called to be. As we try to build a bridge between the ancient text and the contemporary church, a number of important concerns emerge:

1. *Slaves of Christ.* The way that Paul introduces himself and Timothy is striking and carries implications for Christian life and ministry today. What does it mean for us to be **slaves of Christ Jesus** (1:1)?

For many contemporary readers, the word "slave" digs up degrading images of the race-based institution of slavery that scourged the history of the United States. It may remind others of more recent brutal kidnappings and enslavement of children in parts of Africa.

Slavery in the ancient world was more complex. It was not always as oppressive and could at times even be a means to upward social mobility. Nevertheless, masters could act cruelly and harshly toward their slaves. So we might wonder why Paul would choose this morally ambiguous metaphor to describe his relationship to Christ. Even Paul himself recognized the theological limitations of the image (Rom 6:19).

The metaphor of slavery, however, perhaps uniquely communicates the exclusive allegiance of the believer to Jesus Christ. Chrysostom noted long ago that to be a slave of Christ means that we cannot be a slave in any other realm (cited by Edwards 1999, 217). Slavery to Christ excludes service to sin, as Paul conveys so vividly in Rom 6:16-23. Yet, paradoxically, becoming Christ's slave is the only path to perfect freedom (Rom 6:18, 22; Gal 5:1). Some lines from a hymn by George Matteson capture this well:

> *Make me a captive Lord, and then I shall be free.*
> *Force me to render up my sword, and I shall conquenor be. . . .*
> *My will is not my own till thou hast made it thine;*
> *If it would reach a monarch's throne, it must its crown resign.*

Finally, of particular importance for the message of Philippians is the notion of humble, self-sacrificing service to the Master (e.g., 2:17). We are slaves of the one who took the form of a slave (2:7). Christian leaders, in particular, must tenaciously resist the temptation to use their ministries as a means to position, privilege, and power. Following Paul's lead, we must choose to find our fundamental identity in our lowly and loving service to Christ.

2. *Thanksgiving for others.* Paul models an attitude of gratitude for his fellow Christians in Philippi. This was not because he was addressing a perfect church, free from any problem people (see 4:2-3). But an important aspect of his pastoral ministry to this congregation was to thank God for all of them

(1:7); to express gratitude for the specific ways in which God was working in their lives and ministering through them. Surely this would have encouraged the Philippians in their faith. It would also have strengthened the bond between them and the apostle (Hooker 2000, 485).

Giving thanks for others and assuring them of our confidence and prayers is often much less of a priority in churches today. It is easier to criticize and complain. Those who care for others in the faith can learn from Paul's practice of consistently expressing thanks and affirming God's gracious activity in his church.

Bonhoeffer on Gratitude

> If we do not give thanks for the daily Christian fellowship in which we have been placed, even where there is no great experience, no discoverable riches, but much weakness, small faith, and difficulty; if on the contrary, we only keep complaining to God that everything is so paltry and petty, so far from what we expected, then we hinder God from letting our fellowship grow according to the measure and riches which are there for us in Jesus Christ.
>
> This applies in a special way to the complaints often heard from pastors and zealous members about their congregations. A pastor should not complain about this congregation, certainly never to other people, but also not to God.... What may appear weak and trifling to us may be great and glorious to God.... The more thankfully we daily receive what is given to us, the more surely and steadily will fellowship increase and grow from day to day as God pleases. (Bonhoeffer 1954, 29-30)

3. *Gospel fellowship.* What is Christian "fellowship"? We sometimes use the term almost nonchalantly in reference to the kind of warm and friendly feelings that Christians experience together at Bible studies, coffee hours, or church potluck dinners. This may be one dimension of Christian fellowship. But when Paul talks in this passage about the *koinōnia* that he and the Philippians share, he has in mind something more than good times shared with other believers. Here Christian fellowship means a partnership in mission that seeks the advance of the gospel. What's more, it entails a sharing in the grace of God that enables Christians to suffer on behalf of that gospel. This is fellowship with a "backbone."

Christian fellowship today will do well to focus on our common participation in the gospel of Christ. Such a partnership invites us into a shared calling to evangelism, giving, prayer for others, and a lifestyle that embodies the gospel. Donald Carson is right that our partnership *in the gospel* must be at the center of our relationships with other believers (1996, 19).

4. *Balancing love and knowledge.* Paul's prayer for the Philippians offers a crucial corrective to the mushy and romanticized versions of love that perme-

ate our contemporary cultures. Our love, this passage assures us, must be infused with true knowledge of God and moral insight. Otherwise, love can easily degenerate into selfishness or sentimental feeling. Parents' love for their children (for example) can take the form of an indulgence that is ultimately harmful to them. Like Shakespeare's tragic character Othello, we can discover that we have "loved not wisely but too well." Even our enthusiasm and zeal for Christ can become misdirected if it is not guided by a genuine knowledge of God's purposes (see Prov 19:2).

At the same time, knowledge apart from love is "nothing" (1 Cor 13:2). It can become a source of pride or cause us to be rigid and judgmental toward others. Christian formation involves the cultivation of love *and* knowledge, passion as well as discernment; it takes both the head and the heart. Growth in self-giving love and the experiential knowledge of God go hand in hand (Bockmuehl 1998, 67). A hymn written by Charles Wesley in 1763 pleads for such a balance (1983, 7:643-44):

> *Unite the pair so long disjoined,*
> *Knowledge and vital piety:*
> *Learning and holiness combined,*
> *And truth and love, let all men see*
> *In those whom up to Thee we give,*
> *Thine, wholly thine, to die and live.*

5. *Making the right choices.* Paul's prayer for the Philippians calls believers to excellence in their moral and spiritual choices. We must learn to discern what truly matters to God (v 10). This is a hallmark of Christian maturity. Often Christians have to make choices, not simply between good and evil, but between what is good and what is *best*.

Paul is never satisfied with spiritual mediocrity. Choosing what is best requires that we resist the pressure from our culture to conform or to compromise. Through the Spirit's guidance, we must learn to pursue what is best in our family relationships, in our Christian service, in our choice of entertainment, in maintaining lives of moral integrity.

This has nothing to do with the postmodern preoccupation with individual preference in the ethical realm. It has *everything* to do with discerning what is superior in the eyes of God, both individually and as a church (Bockmuehl 1998, 68). Those in roles of caring for others, whether parents, pastors, teachers, or youth workers, have a particular responsibility to guide and support the less mature in making choices that honor God.

6. *Practical holiness.* This opening section of Philippians spotlights the need for a holy church. Paul addresses God's people as "saints in Christ Jesus" (v 1). Unfortunately, the term "saints" is commonly misunderstood. For large segments of the Christian church, saints are especially holy people who are

venerated for their extraordinary piety. For many Christians, "saints" are people to be admired and emulated; but they're not *us*.

In contrast, the NT views the saints as the *whole* of God's people, set apart to belong to God in a special way. Even the church in Corinth, with all of its problems and moral blunders, is addressed as "those sanctified in Christ Jesus, called to be saints" (1 Cor 1:2 NRSV). This means that holiness is not simply a private or personal matter. The plural term "saints" brings out the communal dimension of our holiness.

At the same time, as God's "holy ones," our calling is to live in ways that reflect the character of *the* Holy One who called us (1 Thess 5:23-24). And so Paul prays for the church to embody a mature love, lives of moral purity and unswerving integrity, and the fruit of a Christlike character—in this present world. In short, God has purposed us to be "saints" in reality as well as in name.

7. Transforming cultural conventions. We can also learn from Paul's creative use of ordinary cultural conventions in the service of the gospel. We have seen that he adopts the traditional letter opening in the Greco-Roman world and transforms it into a vehicle for communicating a targeted theological message for his readers (see Thielman 1995, 46, 55-56). This is typical of Paul's way of doing theology.

Elsewhere, for example, Paul transforms a conventional form of instructing various members of a household in Greco-Roman society (the so-called household code) into a vision of what it means for husbands and wives, parents and children, masters and slaves to live under the lordship of Jesus (Col 3:18—4:1; Eph 5:22—6:9). Paul's way of contextualizing the gospel through adopting and adapting everyday cultural materials illustrates his principle of becoming "all things to all people so that by all possible means I might save some" (1 Cor 9:22 TNIV).

Here we can learn not only from Paul's message but also from his method. We, too, can appropriate the cultural resources available to us in order to express and embody the transforming good news of Christ. Missionaries and majority-world Christians often have more experience and expertise in contextualizing the gospel than churches in the West. But Western Christians must also think "missiologically."

In an increasingly postmodern context, contextualizing the gospel could involve supplementing traditional word-and-reason-based communication of our theology with more imaginative, visual, and aesthetic forms. As Paul co-opted the cultural forms of his day, so the church today must learn to speak the language of metaphor, story, and symbol, which connects with many contemporary people. In sum, we must learn to sing the old, old story in new keys (see Flemming 2005, 322).

II. PAUL'S CIRCUMSTANCES: AN EXAMPLE OF FAITHFULNESS TO THE GOSPEL: PHILIPPIANS 1:12-26

BEHIND THE TEXT

Philippians 1:12-16 begins the body of the letter. It was common for ancient letter writers to inform readers about their circumstances, as Paul does in this section. In fact, Paul uses a phrase typical in letters of friendship, **I want you to know . . . that** (v 12; formally called a "disclosure formula"; see Rom 1:13; Gal 1:11). To cite one ancient example (early second century), a young soldier named Theonas wrote to his mother:

> Theonas to his mother and lady, Tetheus, very many greetings. *I want you to know that* the reason I have not sent you a letter for such a long time is because I am in camp and not on account of illness; so that you do not worry yourself. I was very grieved when I learned that you had heard (about me), for I did not fall seriously ill. (Cited by White 1986, 158)

Similarly, Paul wants to alleviate the Philippians' concern about his situation in prison with news about himself. Once again, however, he transforms a common letter convention. It becomes an occasion for Paul to reflect theologically on how he *interprets* his personal circumstances in light of the purposes of God.

Such an extended reflection on Paul's present and future circumstances near *the beginning* of one of his letters is unique (Fee 1995, 106-7; compare Rom 15:14-33). But in the context of Philippians, it is likely that Paul's personal narrative serves as an example his readers should follow. Immediately following this passage, he urges his audience to live in a manner worthy of the gospel in the midst of their *own* trials (Phil 1:27-30). He then calls his friends in Philippi to adopt the mind-set of Jesus Christ (2:5-11; see 3:17). Paul wants them to embrace a Christ-focused response to difficulties, as he has done (Fowl 2005, 36-37; Oakes 2001, 113-14).

We should view this section, then, as more than simply an update on Paul's situation and attitudes as a prisoner of Caesar. It also challenges the Philippians to rethink and reshape their own perspectives as followers of Christ.

From the standpoint of ancient rhetoric, 1:12-26 seems to function as the *narratio*. Such a "narration of facts" provides a background to the main argument of the letter. It also corrects any false impressions on the part of the audience (see, e.g., Witherington 1994, 42-43; Black 1995, 48).

The passage is skillfully shaped to be persuasive. For example, Paul frames the section with two structural "bookends" (the literary device of *inclusio*): the phrases **for the progress of the gospel** (v 12) and **for your progress . . . in the faith** (v 25). This form of repetition calls the attention of his audience to both the boundaries of the section and its chief concern—how God is advancing the gospel in the midst of adverse circumstances (Thielman 1995, 58).

In addition, vv 15-17 point to a conscious use of rhetorical features such as antithesis and chiasm (see below, IN THE TEXT). And in vv 21-24, Paul apparently draws on the ancient rhetorical device of comparison (*synkrisis*), which was sometimes applied to the contrast between living and dying in the Greco-Roman world (see Hawthorne and Martin 2004, 54; Bockmuehl 1998, 87).

Finally, the rhetorical effect of vv 12-26 is enhanced by an appeal to *ethos*. Paul argues on the basis of his own character and credibility; he narrates the impact of the gospel on his life (Thompson 2007, 304-5). He also appeals to the emotions (*pathos*) of his readers. This is especially clear in his moving account of how he has sacrificed his personal desire for the sake of his ministry to the Philippians (vv 19-26).

Paul's personal reflections in vv 12-26 divide well into three parts:
1. The gospel progresses through Paul's imprisonment (vv 12-14)
2. Christ is proclaimed through true or false motives (vv 15-18*a*)
3. Christ is glorified through Paul's living or dying (vv 18*b*-26)

Fee points out that the themes of *Christ* (the name *Christ* appears nine times) and *the gospel* saturate this section (1995, 107). Paul is eager to show that whatever his present circumstances, the gospel is advancing and Christ is being preached. Moreover, he is convinced that whatever might happen to him as a result of his upcoming judicial trial, Christ would be exalted.

IN THE TEXT

A. The Gospel Progresses Through Paul's Imprisonment (1:12-14)

■ 12 Paul begins the section by saying that he wants to inform his dear friends (literally, **brothers**) in Philippi about his present circumstances. The term **brothers** (*adelphoi*) is not restricted to males. It was culturally appropriate language for expressing the close ties that bind Christians together in God's family. It is therefore inclusive of all believers, that is, **brothers and sisters,** or "friends."

Knowing of Paul's captivity, the Philippians were no doubt deeply concerned, perhaps even distressed, about his welfare. They might easily surmise that Paul's present condition would be a detriment to his ministry and to their mutual partnership in the gospel (v 5).

Contrary to conventional expectations, Paul assures his friends that his situation as a prisoner awaiting trial has **rather** (*mallon*) **served to advance the gospel.** This reveals not only Paul's own perspective on his present suffering but the attitude the Philippians should adopt as well. Paul does not tell us who caused this reversal of expectations. But the implied agent is clearly God (Fowl 2005, 37).

By **the gospel** Paul especially refers to his evangelistic ministry of proclaiming the good news of Christ to a sinful world. Here Paul's sufferings and his proclamation of the gospel are partners in mission (Ware 2005, 175). Paul, then, immediately shifts the spotlight from his own circumstances to their implications for the gospel. His identity as Christ's apostle is bound up with that of the gospel (see Barth 1962, 25-26).

■ 13 In vv 13-14 Paul gives two forms of evidence for this unexpected advancement of the gospel. First, the reason for his imprisonment **has become clear throughout the whole palace guard and to everyone else** (v 13). The **palace guard** probably refers to the emperor's crack troops based in Rome. **All the rest** is a rather vague reference to a wider circle of pagans who might have had contact with prisoners.

The Meaning of the Praetorium

The identity of the term translated **palace guard** (*praitōrion*) in v 13 is not fully clear. The Greek word is borrowed from the Latin *praetorium*. This could refer to either a place or to a group of people, depending on the context. Elsewhere in the NT (Matt 27:27; Mark 15:16; John 18:28, 33; 19:9; Acts 23:35), as in most ancient writings, the term identifies the official residence of a provincial governor. There was no governor's palace in Rome, however. Consequently, if Paul was writing from Rome (see the Introduction), *praetorium* likely refers to the Praetorian guard. These were the approximately nine thousand elite troops responsible for carrying out the emperor's orders (see Lightfoot 1953, 99-104). The additional phrase **and to everyone else** (v 13) lends support to the idea that Paul is talking about people, not a building.

What has been made known to the readers is that Paul's imprisonment (literally, *my chains*) is *in Christ.* Paul's choice of prepositions here is significant. He does not simply mean that he is in chains **for Christ**. That is, he is not imprisoned simply because of his commitment to Christ and the gospel (as opposed to other reasons, like criminal activity; so Marshall 1991, 21). More than that, Paul's imprisonment is *"in* Christ" (*en Christōi*). That is, it is part of what he later calls sharing in Christ's sufferings (see 3:10; O'Brien 1991, 92).

Paul's **chains,** then, are an aspect of living in union with Christ. This implies that he considers his sufferings as in no way inconsistent with what it means to be *in Christ* (Fowl 2005, 39). In fact, his suffering has become a conduit for the good news.

But how would the **whole** imperial guard come to know that Paul was in prison because of his commitment to Christ? Obviously, Paul could not have testified personally to a company of up to nine thousand troops. Nevertheless, those who guarded him on a rotating basis would have soon recognized that this was no ordinary prisoner. Word of his case apparently dispersed quickly among the ranks of Caesar's soldiers. For readers in the Roman colony of Philippi, this would have been a source of encouragement. Paul's imprisonment under the nose of the emperor enabled the gospel to penetrate into the very heart of Roman political power (Fee 1995, 114).

■ **14** The progress of the gospel is demonstrated through the effect of Paul's detention on unbelievers. His chains also have an impact on the Christian community: ***The majority of the brothers and sisters have become confident in the Lord*** to announce the gospel more boldly.

It is possible to connect the phrase **in the Lord** with the words that immediately precede it in Greek, literally, **most of the brothers.** But this is somewhat redundant, since **brothers** (*adelphoi*) refers to Christians. It is better, then, to take **in the Lord** with the verb, showing the source of their confidence. The Lord has emboldened them to join Paul in bearing witness to Christ, regardless of the consequences.

The reference here is to Paul's fellow believers in Rome. This statement is more significant than it might first appear. It is one of the rare occasions in Paul's letters when he describes the verbal proclamation of the gospel to unbelievers as the task of the whole Christian community (see Ware 2005, 181-

85). Paul's immediate point is that while the Roman Christians have not been without courage **to speak the word,** they now were doing it ***all the more.***

Paul gives two reasons for this increased daring. First, God has used the example of Paul's own courageous witness in the midst of suffering to inspire the Roman Christians to spread the gospel more fearlessly. Second, Paul's chains have served as a catalyst for the church to put its confidence *in the Lord.* This, in turn, has enabled them to speak out with increased boldness (Marshall 1991, 21). The phrase **in the Lord** makes it plain that the ultimate basis of their confidence is not Paul, but Christ.

In their evangelistic witness they speak **the word.** The additional phrase, found in most early manuscripts, **of God** (see the NIV), was probably inserted later into the text as a clarification. Here, **the word** is another term for "the gospel," the message of Christ that Paul proclaims (see Gal 6:6; Col 4:3; 1 Thess 1:6; 1 Tim 4:2).

Paul accents the fearless testimony of the Roman Christians as an example for his Philippian friends. Like the Romans, Paul calls for the Christian community at Philippi to partner courageously with him in the progress of the gospel (Ware 2005, 184-85; see v 5).

In sum, far from being an obstacle to the gospel, Paul's captivity has unexpectedly become a vehicle for its progress.

B. Christ Is Proclaimed—Through True or False Motives (1:15-18*a*)

■ **15** Paul has just testified that God used his chains to embolden the majority of Roman Christians to proclaim "the word." But in 1:15-18*a* we learn that the gospel's progress has not been without its problems. Some of those who preach Christ fearlessly are doing so out of less-than-pure motives.

In a beautifully crafted passage, Paul contrasts those who **preach Christ out of envy and rivalry** and those who do so **out of goodwill** (v 15). Paul uses a chiastic literary pattern, in which parallel terms in sentences or clauses that stand next to each other are placed in reverse sequence. This puts special emphasis on his self-seeking rivals, who appear at the beginning and the end (vv 15*a*, 17).

The Parallel Structure of 1:15-18*a*

Those with good motives	**Those with false motives**
preach Christ (v 15)	preach Christ (vv 15, 17)
because of goodwill (v 15)	because of envy and rivalry (v 15)
out of love (v 16)	out of selfish ambition, not sincerely (v 17)
knowing (v 16)	supposing (v 17)
that I am here for the defense of the gospel (v 16)	that they can stir up trouble for me while I am in chains (v 17)

in truth (v 18)	in pretense (v 18)
Christ is preached (v 18)	Christ is preached (v 18)
	(Adapted from Thielman 1995, 61)

Obviously, Paul's ministry in Rome has sparked contention. Some preachers envy Paul and perceive him as a rival. To characterize their motives as **envy** (*phthonon*) and **rivalry** (*erin*) is a strong denunciation. Paul uses these terms in other letters to describe the attitudes of those who will not inherit the kingdom of God (Gal 5:20-21; Rom 1:29; see also 1 Tim 6:4).

What it means to preach *because of* **goodwill** (*di' eudokian*) is less clear. Elsewhere in the Bible *eudokia* most often refers to God's will or good pleasure (see Phil 2:13). Paul could be saying that the second group proclaims the gospel in obedience to God's will and saving purpose, in contrast to those with selfish motivations (Ware 2005, 189-91; Bockmuehl 1998, 78-79). But since **goodwill** stands parallel to **envy and rivalry,** it more likely refers to those motivated by goodwill toward Paul. Because Paul can no longer preach publicly, his Christian friends are ready to fill the gap on his behalf (Marshall 1991, 22).

■ **16** The apostle describes the two groups in reverse order in vv 16-17. His supporters preach Christ from a motivation of **love** (literally, *out of love, ex agapēs*). In the context, this surely includes love *for Paul*. They preach Christ in this way *because they know* (*eidotes*) that Paul is in jail **for the defense of the gospel** (v 16).

Paul's friends perceive, as others do not, that Paul's circumstances are both the result of his defending the gospel and a divinely appointed opportunity (**I am put here**) for the good news to advance through Paul's ministry (Fowl 2005, 40). This is a practical example of the kind of discerning love that Paul prays would characterize the Philippians in 1:9-10 (Bockmuehl 1998, 79-80).

■ **17** Paul's rivals, on the other hand, operate **out of selfish ambition** (*ex eritheias,* see 2:3). They proclaim the message of Christ from self-seeking and impure motives. Unlike those who *know* that Paul's imprisonment is part of God's work to further the gospel, they *suppose,* quite wrongly, that their preaching can heap more **trouble** and irritation on the apostle.

Who are these rivals? And why would they try to bring Paul grief by "preaching Christ"? (For various attempts to identify this group, see O'Brien 1991, 102-5.) Some commentators identify them with "Judaizing" Christians, similar to the agitators who tried to compel Gentile Christians in Galatia to follow the Jewish law (so, e.g., Lightfoot 1953, 90; compare Silva 2005, 65). But in Galatians Paul blasts such people for preaching "a different gospel—which is really no gospel at all" (Gal 1:6-7). In contrast, Paul's competitors in Rome "preach Christ."

It seems better to take what Paul says in these verses more or less at face value. These Christian preachers oppose Paul, not because they disagree with his message, but out of personal rivalry (e.g., O'Brien 1991, 105).

The difficulty with this view is to find a convincing scenario that prompted such animosity against Paul (Marshall 1991, 23). Perhaps the rivals were seeking to safeguard their own status and influence in the church. They may have seen Paul's arrival in Rome as a threat to their power base (Ware 2005, 189, 194-95). The church has never been immune to preachers using their ministries for self-promotion and competitive advantage. In any case, these Christians apparently jumped at the chance to use Paul's misfortune (his **chains**) as a means of advancing their own cause.

■ **18a** Although Paul does not provide much information about the reasons for the bad motives of these fellow preachers, his response is both clear and stunning. Paul says that one thing is crucial (**the important thing is,** *plēn;* see Bauer 1979, 669): that **in every way, whether from false motives or true, Christ is preached** (v 18).

By beginning and ending this section with phrases that mirror one another in vv 15 and 18a, Paul spotlights the main point of the passage—the proclamation of *Christ.* Paul's ultimate concern is not with the opposing groups. Nor is it with his own trying circumstances. His singular focus is on the progress of the gospel. And in that he can **rejoice,** despite his chains and the personal attacks of fellow Christians. Verses 15-18a, then, reinforce the main burden of vv 12-14: whatever the outward situation, the gospel of Christ is paramount.

One question remains, however. Why does Paul choose to rehearse his struggles with Christians in *Rome* when he is writing to the church in *Philippi?* I agree with Fowl that this passage is paradigmatic. That is, it helps to lay the groundwork for what Paul will later say about the Philippians' own situation (2005, 43).

For instance, the attitude of "selfish ambition" (v 17) crops up again in 2:3. Paul's self-seeking rivals serve as a negative example that the Philippians should avoid (compare 3:2-3, 18-19). Positively, Paul demonstrates a mind-set that puts the progress of the gospel before the need to respond to personal attacks. This prepares the way for his later appeal to look out for the interests of others rather than our own (2:1-4). Further, Paul models for his audience that the gospel must be proclaimed, even if that results in more suffering (Oakes 2001, 114, see 1:27-30).

C. Christ Is Glorified Through Paul's Living or Dying (1:18b-26)

■ **18b** Verse 18b signals a shift in tense from the present to the future. The thought moves from Paul's report on the gospel's advance through his current circumstances in vv 12-18a to his confidence regarding what lies ahead for him (vv 18b-26). This paragraph also constitutes a more *personal* reflection on the implications of Paul's imprisonment than in the preceding section. Here the apostle mulls over his situation in first person ("I") narrative style.

The paragraph falls into three parts: First, Paul affirms that, no matter what happens at his trial, his joy will not be diminished. He is confident that in the end he will be saved and Christ will be exalted (vv 18b-20).

Second, Paul contemplates the two possible outcomes of his situation as a prisoner under a capital charge—life and death. There are advantages to both. But he is persuaded that to go on living is more necessary for the Philippians (vv 21-24).

Third, Paul expects that he will be released from his imprisonment and will visit the Philippians again. He fully intends to contribute more to the progress of their faith (vv 25-26).

The last part of v 18 picks up on the theme of joy that ended the previous section. Just as Paul is able to **rejoice** in his present circumstances (v 18a), he **will continue to rejoice** in the future (v 18b).

■ **19-20** Verses 19 and 20 go on to explain why Paul is confident that his joy will endure. He begins with a remarkable statement, which receives special emphasis in the Greek text. He writes literally, ***I know that this will turn out for my salvation*** (v 19). The demonstrative pronoun **this** likely refers to Paul's present circumstances as a prisoner, which he has just described in the previous verses (12-18a). His assurance can only flow out of the perspective that governs the whole section: no matter what happens to him, God can use it to bring about good, either for Paul or for the Philippians (see Thurston 2005, 66; compare Rom 8:28).

But what kind of **salvation** (*sōtēria*) does Paul have in mind? Is it release from his imprisonment (so, e.g., Hawthorne and Martin 2004, 49-50)? Does it mean vindication at his Roman trial? Or is it something more transcendent, such as final salvation? All three of these are possibilities.

An important clue is that Paul's words, ***this will turn out for my salvation,*** are an exact quotation of Job 13:16 in the Greek Bible (on v 19 as an example of "intertextuality," in which a later text consciously echoes an earlier one, see Hays 1989, 21-24, and Fowl 2005, 44-45). To anyone well versed in the language of the LXX, these words would have called to mind the story of the righteous sufferer, Job. Here Paul's unmarked quotation evokes clear analogies between the apostle's present situation and the former plight of Job. In Job 13, Job defends himself against the accusatory arrows of his pious "comforters." The charge is that his suffering is the direct result of harboring some secret sin. In response, Job pleads his innocence, declaring that ultimately he will be vindicated by God (Job 13:16, 18). Similarly, Paul, in the face of afflictions and the attacks of rival preachers, looks forward to vindication before God in the end.

What is more, the Greek word the NIV translates as **deliverance** (*sōtēria*) is normally used elsewhere in Philippians (1:28; 2:12) and Paul's other writings in the sense of eschatological *salvation*. It refers to God's final saving action already made partially present through Christ. In addition, Paul says in v 20 that he will experience God's deliverance, whether his trial results in physical **life or . . . death.** This makes it unlikely that the "deliverance" Paul anticipates is simply a matter of getting out of prison or escaping a Roman death sentence.

In the first place, then, Paul's expected *salvation* probably refers to his vindication in the heavenly court on the final day (Bruce 1983, 24; see Silva 2005, 69-71, for a full discussion). His present adversity, he believes, will lead to that end. But Paul may also have a more immediate vindication in mind. He is confident that, when he goes to trial, God will vindicate him and his gospel, and Christ will be exalted (v 20). Whatever the verdict, like Job, Paul is determined to be found faithful in the eyes of God, both in the present and in the future (see Fee 1995, 131-32).

Paul proceeds to qualify this confident expectation in two ways. First, God will bring about his *salvation* through their **prayers** and ***the provision of the Spirit of Jesus Christ*** (1:19). It is striking that Paul sees *both* the Philippians' prayers *and* God's gift of the Spirit as contributors toward his final salvation (Bockmuehl 1998, 83). Grammatically, "your prayers" and "the provision of the Spirit" are closely linked, since they are governed by a single preposition ("through") and one definite article.

Paul is convinced that God will work through the prayers of the Christian community to energize the Spirit's power on his behalf. This will enable Paul to testify boldly to Christ (1:20) and ultimately stand among God's redeemed on the last day. Bockmuehl notes that this kind of intercessory prayer is an especially vivid example of the Philippians' "partnership in the gospel" alongside Paul (1:5; 1998, 84).

The NIV's **help** (*epichorēgias*) is better rendered as the ***provision*** or "supply" of the Spirit, since this word consistently refers to the provision itself (Fee 1995, 13-33). Paul's language is similar to that in Gal 3:5, where he speaks of God's gift of the Spirit to his people. Here, as well, Paul seems especially to emphasize that the **Spirit** *is* God's ***provision***, rather than that the Spirit provides help of some other kind.

The unusual phrase **the Spirit of Jesus Christ** anticipates Paul's desire that Christ will be glorified, whatever the outcome of Paul's court trial (v 20). The key to that happening is for Paul to be indwelt with the Spirit of Christ himself, the empowering presence of the risen Lord (Fee 1995, 134-35; see 2 Cor 3:17).

Verse 20 offers a second qualification to Paul's confidence that God would work through his present circumstances toward his ultimate salvation.

It is in keeping with Paul's ***eager expectation and hope*** that he will boldly exalt Christ in his impending trial. The word the NIV translates **eagerly expect** (*apokaradokia*) is an exceptionally strong term. We find it only here and in Rom 8:19 in the NT. In Romans it is also linked with hope. There it refers to creation's intense watching (see J. B. Phillips' delightful paraphrase, "the whole creation is on tiptoe") for its future redemption, when it will "be liberated from its bondage to decay and brought into the glorious freedom of the children of God" (Rom 8:21).

Grammatically, the words **eager expectation** and **hope** are intimately bound together. They point to a "hope-filled expectation" of something that is certain to happen (Fee 1995, 135). This is surely more than simply a reference to Paul's hope that he will acquit himself well during his court appearance. It looks beyond that upcoming test toward the final salvation he earnestly expects and yearns for (Thielman 1995, 77).

But Paul's hope of final acceptance by God is connected with how he defends the gospel now. Consequently, Paul formulates his expectation in two parallel clauses, first negatively, then positively. He hopes

that	*in no way*	*I will be put to shame,*
but	*with all boldness*	*Christ will be magnified.*

Paul's language about being **ashamed** (*aischynthēsomai*) echoes OT passages in the LXX (e.g., Pss 25:3, 20; 31:1, 17; Isa 50:7). There it has to do not so much with an inner feeling of shame as with a condition of disgrace that comes from failing to trust God (Fee 1995, 136; see Horstmann 1990, 1:42). Paul is confident that when he stands before Caesar he will do nothing that will bring disgrace to the gospel.

But Paul's words would likely have carried a further significance for Paul's Greco-Roman audience. Unlike modern Western Christians, they lived in a society where honor and shame were pivotal cultural values. The experience of public disgrace and dishonor was something to avoid at all costs. Paul's arrest and detention as a prisoner in chains would have brought precisely such humiliation to him in the court of public reputation (see Rapske 1994, 283-98). His public trial and possible judicial condemnation would be a further source of disgrace in Paul's world.

Paul flips these cultural notions upside down. Although his imprisonment and impending trial may bring disgrace in the eyes of the dominant culture, he is confident that he will not suffer shame in the eyes of God, either in the present or the future. On the contrary, his very shame is an opportunity to bring honor to Christ (see Osiek 2000, 42-43).

Positively, then, Paul expects and hopes that **Christ will be exalted**. The word **exalted** (literally, ***magnified***, *megalynthēsetai*) has rich resonances in the Psalms, where it speaks of exalting and glorifying God. In some cases, the same connection between "magnifying" God and "being put to shame" occurs as we find in 1:20 (e.g., Pss 34:3-5; 35:26-27; 70:2-4).

With a shift from the first person ("I") to the third person, Christ becomes the subject and Paul simply the instrument through which Jesus will be magnified (O'Brien 1991, 115). Paul is confident that glory will come to Christ **with all boldness** (*parrēsia*). This not only involves free and open speech but also entails **courage** to bear witness and to act in a way that honors Christ, whether at Paul's court appearance or elsewhere (Marshall 1991, 26; Hahn 1976, 2:736).

Furthermore, Christ will be exalted **in** Paul's **body, whether by life or by death.** Here the apostle looks squarely at the possible outcomes of his looming trial. It could result in either continued life in the body or bodily death as a martyr. Although the Roman Empire claimed to have control over Paul's body, Paul exerts a counterclaim. "Whether I live or I die," he seems to say, "my body will belong to Christ, not to the empire" (Fowl 2005, 48). This is Paul's expectant hope, regardless of whether his appearance before Caesar's tribunal results in acquittal or condemnation. Whatever happens, **now** as in the past, Christ will be glorified.

■ **21** Having raised the possibility that his capital charge could lead to execution, Paul enters into a highly personal reflection (**to me** in v 21 is emphatic in Greek) on the alternatives of life and death. Verses 21-24 explain how it is that Christ will be exalted, even if Rome's verdict goes against him (Fee 1995, 139-40). Paul ratchets up the rhetorical impact of these thoughts by suggesting that he personally would prefer death. But he concludes that it is more necessary to remain alive and continue his ministry (Bockmuehl 1998, 87).

The flow of thought in these verses follows a pattern of alternating statements about life and death. Paul "draws up a kind of balance sheet," weighing the results of each (Deasley 2007, 174):

Life	To live	is Christ (v 21*a*).
Death	To die	is gain (v 21*b*).
Life	To live in the body	is fruitful work (v 22).
Death	To depart and be with Christ	is far better (v 23).
Life	To remain in the body	is more necessary (v 24).

Paul begins with the well-known contrast in v 21: **For to me, to live is Christ and to die is gain.** Although rhetorically effective in English, this claim is even more striking in Greek. This is due to the similar sound of the words *Christos* (**Christ**) and *kerdos* (**gain**; Hooker 2000, 490). For Paul, living *means* Christ.

Ever since his world was turned upside down by the risen Lord on the Damascus road, Paul's whole life has been about "know[ing] Christ" intimately (3:10) and serving him in the ministry of the gospel. Later in this letter, Paul declares that he considers everything else as filth that he may "gain Christ"

(3:8). He desires to share in both Christ's resurrection power and his sufferings (3:10). Elsewhere he affirms, "I no longer live, but Christ lives in me" (Gal 2:20; compare Col 3:4). Indeed, **to live is Christ** sums up Paul's whole existence as a Christian.

In the context, "to live" refers in the first place to Paul's earthly life **in the body** (1:20, 22, 24). The apostle's present life becomes a means of glorifying Christ through his **fruitful labor** in the gospel (1:22; see Rom 1:13; O'Brien 1991, 119-22).

Yet, because life on earth means Christ, Paul can also testify that death—if that should be the outcome of his trial—would be **gain** (*kerdos*; literally, "profit"). The notion that death is a form of gain has parallels in the ancient world. Socrates and others saw death as a release from the miseries of mortal existence (see Plato, *Apol.* 40C-D; Aeschylus, *Prom.* 747-51).

But Paul has a radically different perspective. For him, death is not an escape from earthly troubles (against Hawthorne and Martin 2004, 56). On the contrary, since living means Christ, Paul is overwhelmingly joyful about his present ministry, whatever the hardships and difficulties. Nor is it likely that Paul thinks that death is gain because it will give him a chance to witness to Christ in the ultimate sense as a martyr (so Lohmeyer 1929, 57-59). Rather, for Paul, death is gain precisely because it means experiencing a deeper, more intimate knowledge of Christ, a fuller sharing in his resurrection life (3:8, 10).

■ **22** Paul now begins to reflect further on the two possibilities he set forth in v 21. Verse 22 expands on what it would mean "to live" (see the discussion about the ambiguous Greek syntax of this verse in Fee 1995, 143-44). **Living in the body** (literally, "in the *flesh*," *en sarki*) involves **fruitful labor** (literally, "the fruit of labor"). This probably refers to Paul's future ministry of the gospel. God will use his apostolic labor to produce more fruit, both in terms of new converts and of the progress of the Philippians' faith (1:25; see Rom 1:13). Since this is also a form of gain, Paul suddenly thinks out loud about whether it would be better to opt for life or death: **Yet what shall I choose? I do not know!**

But does Paul have a real choice in the matter? Some interpreters, going back to John Chrysostom, think that he does. It is "a great mystery," Chrysostom suggests, "that his departure was in his own power" (*Hom. Phil.* 3.1.22; compare Wansink 1996, 96-125). Several recent interpreters have gone a step farther to suggest that Paul contemplates voluntarily taking his own life (Droge and Tabor 1992, 119-28; compare Wansink 1996, 124-25; for an evaluation of these views, see Fowl 2005, 55-59). But if Paul were considering suicide as a release from his present sufferings, what could we make of his confidence in God's ongoing work in the midst of our adversities (e.g., 1:6, 12-20; Fowl 2005, 58)?

It seems better, then, to take the last clause of v 22 as rhetorical language. It is highly unlikely that Paul thought the choice was really his to make (Marshall 1991, 28; Croy 2003, 525-30). Underlying the entire passage is the confidence that the ultimate decision about whether Paul lives or dies is in the hands of God. The verb translated **I know** (*gnōrizō*) normally means "to make known" in the NT. Here the English idiom "I cannot tell" (i.e., in light of the alternatives, I can't say what I would choose) seems to capture Paul's intent (Fee 1995, 145). Paul is looking at a "win-win" situation. If he had to choose, he would have difficulty making up his mind.

■ **23** Verses 23-24 underscore this inner tension. The NIV's **I am torn** (literally, "I am hard pressed," *synechomai*) **between the two** paints a lively image of Paul's dilemma. On one hand, his personal **desire** (*epithymia*, used here, unusually, in a positive sense; see 1 Thess 2:17) was **to depart and be with Christ.**

The verb **depart** (*analyō*) is a picturesque word. It sometimes described an army's breaking camp and moving on, or a ship's hoisting anchor and sailing away (see Hawthorne and Martin 2004, 58-59). Here Paul seems to follow its popular Hellenistic usage as a metaphor for death (Bockmuehl 1998, 91). But the apostle parts company with the ancient Greek notion of death as the soul's release from the body. For Paul, the sole destination of this departure is to **be with Christ.** The two infinitives, **to depart** and **to be,** are connected by a single article in Greek. Therefore "departing" and "being with Christ" are intimately related.

Precisely what Paul means by the phrase **to be with Christ** has sparked considerable debate (see FROM THE TEXT for this section). At the very least, he expects death to bring about a closer communion with Christ. "Being with Christ" signifies the fulfillment and goal of his present life "in Christ." For Paul, death means being "at home" in the very presence of his Lord (2 Cor 5:8). The apostle has no doubt that being with Christ is **better by far** (literally, "much more better," *pollō mallon kreisson*) than life in the body. It is Christ and Christ alone that makes departing this life a more attractive option for Paul.

■ **24** On the other hand, Paul recognizes that to **remain in the body** (literally, "flesh"; see v 22) is **more necessary** for his audience. Weighing the alternatives, he comes to this conclusion: to depart and be with Christ may be better for *Paul*. But to stay and serve in fruitful labor for Christ is better for *the Philippians* (Fowl 2005, 52). Paul, then, subordinates his personal preference in favor of what is beneficial for the spiritual progress of others (v 25).

This helps us answer the question: Why does Paul debate in front of the Philippians whether to live or die, if the decision is not really his to make? Paul models before his children in the faith what it means to put the interests of others above one's own (2:3-4; Thielman 1995, 79). In this, he is simply reenacting the drama of Christ's self-giving love (2:5-11).

■ **25** The next two verses resolve the tension of the life-or-death dilemma with which Paul has been wrestling. He can assert with confidence, **I know that I will remain, and I will continue with all of you.** (The verbs **remain** [*menō*] and **continue** [*parameno*] reflect a wordplay in Greek.)

How can Paul *know* this, since he has just admitted his uncertainty about the outcome of his trial? The answer is probably not that he received a fresh revelation from God (so, e.g., Wesley n.d., 507-8). More likely, Paul is fully **convinced** that God will act for the benefit of the church in Philippi (Hooker 2000, 491). He is not speaking as a prophet but as one who knows God's character. Given the congregation's continued need for his ministry (v 24), Paul fully expects to be released from bondage and to renew his service to the church (Bockmuehl 1998, 94).

The aim of Paul's ongoing ministry among his dear friends is their **progress and joy in** (literally, "of") **the faith.** Both **progress** and **joy** are governed by the same article in Greek. This indicates, first, that they are closely connected, and second, that both are related to **the faith.** Paul has already used the notions of progress and joy to describe his own situation in the letter (see 1:4, 12, 18). Now he applies the same themes to the Philippians (Bockmuehl 1998, 94).

Specifically, the word **progress** (*prokopē*) picks up on what Paul has said about the "advance" of "the gospel" in v 12. Here, however, the focus is on the Philippians' role in the gospel's advance. Just as God used Paul in prison to advance the word, so after his release, he will be a catalyst for the spiritual growth of the Philippians (Silva 2005, 75).

It is somewhat unusual for Paul to talk about **the faith,** without further definition. In this case, it probably refers to the gospel itself (as in 1:27, "the faith of the gospel"; see Gal 1:23), rather than to the Philippians' own trusting in Christ (see 2:17). Along with their increased understanding and living out of the gospel comes a fuller experience of joy; the two are hand in glove.

■ **26** The *immediate* aim of Paul's release and ministry to his friends is their progress and joy in the gospel. But the *ultimate* purpose is that, through Paul's return to them, Christ might be glorified (O'Brien 1991, 140-41). The word the NIV translates **joy** here actually means ***boasting*** (*kauchēma*). In the honor/shame culture of the Greco-Roman world, boasting was a common way of demanding public recognition of one's honor.

Paul turns this cultural practice on its head. He deflects their boasting from himself and onto **Christ Jesus**—one who was shamefully executed on a Roman cross (Fowl 2005, 54; see Witherington 1994, 47-49). In this way, ***boasting*** is viewed in a positive light, unlike the mainly pejorative connotations of the word today. It has nothing to do with conceit. Rather, it means to glory and exult **in Christ** (see 1 Cor 1:31; 2 Cor 10:17; Jer 9:23-24, "let him who boasts boast in the Lord"). Paul wants his friends' glorying in Christ to **overflow** (*perisseuē*; see comment on 1:9).

Although Paul is not the focus of the Philippians' boasting in Christ, he says: It will happen **on account of me** (*en emoi*). Here the reference is to Paul's ministry when he returns to the Philippians. Paul's **coming** (*Parousia*) to them becomes the occasion and the means for the church to excel in giving glory to Christ.

FROM THE TEXT

1. *A perspective on adverse circumstances.* This passage is drenched with expressions of confidence and joy. Behind Paul's entire personal reflection stands the bedrock belief that God is sovereign and uses human circumstances—even the darkest ones—to his glory. Paul understands his own story to be part of a larger ongoing narrative of God's reconciling the world to himself. As a result, he has eyes to see that his predicament of being held in jail on a capital charge is no hindrance to what God was doing in the world. In fact, it actually serves to further the gospel and to bring courage and growth to the church.

Such a perspective still gives hope and courage to Christians facing persecution from oppressive regimes or opposition from families or communities throughout our world. God continues to work through the suffering and weakness of his people to advance the gospel.

But Christians in the affluent West, as well, need to hear that God works not simply *in spite of* adverse circumstances, but *through* them (Thielman 1995, 65). Just as God chose the cross to bring about redemption, he continues to choose what is weak and despised to accomplish his purposes in the world (1 Cor 1:26-31). This theological outlook will help us to resist either complaining about our circumstances (as if God has let us down) or trying to manipulate our situation according to what we think is best (as if God can't be trusted).

If we envision our stories as part of the grand drama of God's saving purpose for his creation, then our focus will shift from our present circumstances to God. We, too, will have eyes to see what God is doing to advance the gospel of Christ crucified in the world. Grasping this bigger perspective can liberate us, like Paul, to rejoice in the midst of tough times.

2. *A perspective on evangelism.* Paul models an astonishing large-heartedness toward Christian preachers who oppose him personally and whose motives are questionable (1:15-18*a*). This does not mean that Paul is a pluralist, someone who happily tolerates any message that might be touted in the name of Jesus. When the truth of the gospel is at stake, Paul is in no mood for compromise (see Gal 1:6-9). However, the main issue here is not the integrity of the gospel but the motivation of the preacher. Because *Christ* is preached, Paul can rejoice. The gospel is bigger than the worthiness of its ministers (Hooker 2000, 492).

At the same time, it would be a misunderstanding of the passage to assume that the motives of those who witness to the gospel do not matter. A few verses later, Paul exhorts his audience to live in a manner that is worthy of the gospel (1:27). Elsewhere he goes to great lengths to show that his motives as an evangelist are pure (see 1 Thess 2:1-12).

Ministers of the Word whose lives and attitudes lack integrity run the risk of contradicting the message of the gospel for the hearers. Paul does not condone the selfish motives of Christian preachers, and neither must we. We must simply recognize that the gospel is the "power of God for salvation" (Rom 1:16 NRSV). God sometimes uses even faulty and insincere proclamation of the gospel for his saving purposes. This ought to caution us against too easily disparaging other Christians whose motives, methods, or message we might question. "Believer-bashing" is not becoming to the body of Christ.

This passage also underscores that the gospel is greater than our own reputations. When we are unfairly accused and our motives are questioned, our natural inclination is to defend our rights. We feel the need to expose those who oppose us. But Paul's example points us in a different direction. Are we willing to lay down our personal rights, our wronged reputations, our wounded feelings, for the greater good of the gospel in the world?

3. *A perspective on living.* For many of us, Paul's testimony that for him *to live is Christ* (v 21) is so familiar that we can miss its startling significance. Paul has a singular, consuming passion—Christ. And he clearly longs for other believers to share this passion (Fee 1995, 150).

Our problem is that this is a deeply countercultural mind-set. The pervading culture in which most of us live proclaims other priorities, other pulls, other passions: for to me, living is . . . my work, my family, my music, sports, entertainment, being successful, gaining wealth, and so forth. Although it is easy to pay lip service to a Christ-centered existence, far too many Christians conduct their everyday lives as if the values of the culture around them come first.

"Living" Christ is never introspective. Paul's burning passion for Christ meant that he was willing to continue to pour out his life in sacrificial service to others (1:24-26; see 2:17). If we genuinely embrace the words, "for to me, to live is Christ," it will require a radical shift in focus away from ourselves and toward a costly, loving ministry to God's people and to a sin-enslaved world. For us, as for Paul, this is the one road to true joy and fruitfulness.

4. *A perspective on death.* Paul's understanding that "to die is gain" (v 21) underscores that his whole earthly existence is oriented toward the future. The notion that ongoing physical life is the harder and *less* desirable option flies in the face of contemporary notions of life and death in the West. Our societies abound with people who are willing to go to nearly any measure or expense in order to prolong their biological lives. Stunning advances in medical technolo-

gies in recent decades, as well as a host of alternative treatments that claim to be able to extend life, have convinced many that they can "cheat death"—or at least have a say in when and how it happens.

What is more, many spend fortunes on cosmetic surgeries, in an attempt to give the *appearance* that aging and death are not inevitable. As Fowl astutely observes, "For many, death is simply presented as the last great opportunity to exert an autonomous consumer choice, rather than an occasion on which Christ might be magnified in our bodies" (2005, 49).

This preoccupation with preserving life masks a widespread fear and denial of death in contemporary Western culture. Unlike most people who have walked this earth, we work hard to avoid facing the reality of death, which affects our attitudes toward those who are dying.

Paul, in contrast, models a positive awareness of death. He sees death as the gateway to more direct and intimate fellowship with his Lord. This is no otherworldliness that disdains earthy life. Nor does Paul take the end of life into his own hands, either by seeking inappropriately to prolong his life or by ending it. The perspective in this passage relativizes *both* living and dying. Both are opportunities for Christ to be glorified.

It was this attitude that caused John Wesley to rejoice when he said of the early Methodists, "Our people die well!" It is also a perspective embraced by a host of persecuted Christians in our time, who face the ongoing possibility of martyrdom for their loyalty to Christ.

Whatever the specific circumstances, one of the most precious ministries of the Holy Spirit is to enable God's people to contemplate death with hope and assurance, rather than fear and denial. This is only possible when we embrace Paul's forward-looking perspective: what is of ultimate value is knowing and serving Christ, whether through life or through death.

5. *A perspective on the afterlife.* Perhaps the stickiest theological issue in this passage involves Paul's expectation that when he dies he will "be with Christ" (v 23). How do we square this with what Paul says in places like 1 Thess 4 and 1 Cor 15 about the return of Christ and the resurrection of the dead in the end? These passages seem to imply that those who have "fallen asleep" (died) in Christ await the final resurrection, at which time they "will be with the Lord" (1 Thess 4:17).

Paul's interpreters have tried to resolve this problem in various ways. Some early church fathers, for example, held that Paul would be directly ushered into the presence of Christ as a reward for his martyrdom, before the general resurrection of the vast majority of dead believers (see *1 Clem.* 5; Pol. *Phil.* 9). But nothing in this passage suggests that Paul thinks this hope is reserved exclusively for a special class of martyrs.

Others maintain the notion of "soul sleep." Here the soul loses consciousness at death and does not reawaken until the end-time resurrection. According to this explanation, the next moment of awareness after death, from the Christian's perspective, would be the resurrection. Therefore, Paul can talk about death as being with Christ. But this seems unlikely. If Paul had thought there would be a prolonged period of "sleep" between his death and being in the presence of Christ, it is hard to imagine that the choice between life and death would have been so difficult. Nor would he likely have considered death to be "better by far" (see Silva 2005, 74; Wright 2007, 183-84).

We must recognize that a certain tension exists in the metaphors Paul uses to describe the future hope of believers. On the one hand, Paul's "spatial" metaphors in texts like this one and 2 Cor 5:6, 8 speak of being "with Christ" upon death. On the other hand, the "temporal" images of 1 Thess 4 and 1 Cor 15 describe a sequence of sleeping and then "waking" (being raised) at the end (Fowl 2005, 51; see also Lincoln 1981, 101-9). In truth, Paul is speaking about mysteries. No single set of human images can fully describe them. Further, Paul is addressing different questions, in say, 1 Thessalonians than he is here in Philippians. As a result, he brings out different aspects of the Christian's future hope.

Apparently, Paul did conceive of some type of transition stage prior to the resurrection. Upon death, Christians are ushered immediately into the presence of the Lord, but apart from the body (2 Cor 5:8). Yet, this state was not to be our final destination, which would come in the bodily resurrection itself (e.g., 1 Cor 15). It is also likely that we will be *conscious* of Christ's presence, as we await the final day (Wright 2007, 184). Paul, however, does not address such questions directly, so we need to be careful not to read too much into what he says (for more on what happens to believers at death, see O'Brien 1991, 132-37; Lincoln 1981, especially 101-9; Wright 2007).

What this passage emphasizes is that death will mean being with Christ in a fuller and more immediate sense than is possible in our earthly existence. This hope has brought strength and comfort to believers throughout the centuries and continues to do so today. If life means communion with Christ, then surely death will not bring that to an end. Because Christ is alive on the other side of death, we, his people, will live on with him (Bruce 1983, 27).

6. *A perspective on prayer.* For Western Christians who are used to thinking of salvation in individualistic terms, it might seem a bit odd that Paul assumed that his own salvation was at least in some measure dependent on *the Philippians'* prayers (v 19). Our prayers largely center on our own needs. Even when we do pray for other believers, we tend to ask that they will be delivered from present difficulties or sickness. Yet, how often do we pray for their perseverance in the faith and their ultimate salvation? Alex R. G. Deasley is quite right: "It is a sobering thought that our prayers make a difference in the eternal destiny of others" (2005, 12). Paul surely believed this, for he regularly prayed

for the spiritual progress and ultimate salvation of his converts (e.g., 1 Cor 1:4-9; 1 Thess 3:10-13; 5:23-24; Phil 1:3-11; Col 1:9-14), and he counted on them to do the same for him.

Salvation is a journey; endurance to the end is not automatically guaranteed. Paul understood that continuance and ultimate vindication before God was not simply a private affair. We need the prayers of our fellow believers for our spiritual well-being on an ongoing basis, especially in times of testing. Paul's example encourages us to take seriously the responsibility to pray, not just for the sick, but also for the "healthy" (see Arnold 1992, 215). We can pray that they may be kept "strong to the end" and be found "blameless on the day of our Lord Jesus Christ" (1 Cor 1:8). Paul, I suspect, would say that we are on this salvation journey *together* . . . or we are not on it at all.

III. CONDUCT WORTHY OF THE GOSPEL: EXHORTATIONS AND EXAMPLES: PHILIPPIANS 1:27—2:18

The words **whatever happens, conduct yourselves in a manner worthy of the gospel of Christ** (1:27*a*) signal a turning point in the letter. Paul's style of writing shifts from first person ("I") narrative to mainly second person plural ("you all") imperative. With the shift he launches into a section of pastoral exhortations and encouragement to the community that continues through 2:18. Here Paul's own circumstances fade into the background. Instead, the Philippians' situation, which involves pressures from both without and within, takes center stage. This movement of thought flows naturally out of the previous section, where Paul expressed his concern for the Philippians' progress in the faith (1:25-26).

Verse 27 sounds the keynote for the larger unit of 1:27—2:18. The Philippians are to "live out their citizenship," that is, their public, communal life, in a way that is **worthy of the gospel of Christ** (see Wagner 2007, 258). The rest of the section expands and fleshes out what such "gospelized" living involves. In 1:27-30, this entails a call to unified steadfastness in the midst of suffering and resistance. The next paragraph, 2:1-4, is an exhortation to unity within the church through unselfish humility.

The climax of the section comes in 2:5-11. Here the celebrated story of Christ's loving actions offers a paradigm for how Christians should live. Finally, Paul admonishes his audience to obedience and holy living as a witness to those outside the church (2:12-18).

A. An Appeal to Firmness and Unity in the Face of Opposition (1:27-30)

BEHIND THE TEXT

Rhetorically, Phil 1:27-30 is pivotal for Paul's argument in the whole letter. This passage corresponds to the *propositio*, or thesis statement, which summarizes the basic course of action that Paul wants his audience to take (Witherington 1994, 50; see Black 1995, 47-48). The gospel pattern of living to which Paul calls the Philippians in this paragraph is one that plays out in different variations throughout the letter. It is a pattern of unity and faithfulness in the face of opposition and suffering.

To develop his thesis, Paul draws on two striking metaphors from his world. The first is the political metaphor of **living out their citizenship** (v 27). Second, he borrows language from the world of athletic contests or military battles ("stand firm," "contending," v 27; "struggle," v 30). In addition, the passage features concerns and language from ancient descriptions of friendship. Notably, friends were commonly depicted as people of "one soul" (v 27; see, e.g., Aristotle, *Eth. Nic.* 9.8.2). These familiar images and language would connect with Paul's audience and enhance the persuasiveness of his argument.

Stalking in the shadows behind this paragraph is some form of opposition to the church. Paul urges the Philippians not to be frightened by these opponents (v 28). But just who are these people? We cannot be certain, since Paul gives us no specific information about them. He simply assumes that his readers are well aware of them.

Some scholars link these adversaries with the "Judaizers" mentioned in 3:2. Such people insisted that Gentile Christians follow Jewish practices like circumcision and Jewish food laws (see, e.g., Silva 2005, 92; see Hawthorne and Martin 2004, 72). But there is little evidence to support this. As we will see, Paul's warning against the Judaizing teachers in ch 3 is probably preemptive. In contrast, the attacks of the opponents in 1:28 were very real. What is more, Paul says that the Philippians are going through the **same struggle** (1:30) in which Paul himself engaged when he first came to Philippi. This suggests a pagan, rather than a Jewish, opposition (see Acts 16:16-40; see further Oakes 2001, 79-82, 84-89).

More likely, then, the Philippians were facing some form of opposition from non-Christian pagans in Philippi, perhaps linked with the authorities there (see the Introduction for a fuller description). The presence of the imperial cult touched nearly every aspect of public life in the Greek cities during that time. Especially in a Roman colony like Philippi, civic virtue was expressed in devotion to the emperor. Paul's mission had already been attacked for disloyalty to Rome (Acts 16:20-21). The church in Philippi could well have faced pressure on similar grounds (Bockmuehl 1998, 100-101). Moreover, 1 Thess 2:14 suggests that Christians elsewhere in Macedonia were encountering persecution from pagans.

One important aspect of the church's suffering in Philippi must have been economic. Oakes makes a good case that Christians—especially those engaged in trade—would likely have faced social exclusion by fellow townspeople, broken reputations, and ultimately loss of income (see 2001, 89-99).

IN THE TEXT

■ **27** The first words of v 27, **whatever happens,** are an important transition marker, introducing a new section. They translate a single Greek word that means **only** (*monon*). Barth's paraphrase, "Just one thing!" seems to capture Paul's intent. This admonition is raised "like a warning finger" (1962, 45; see Chrysostom, *Hom. Phil.* 4.1.27). Whatever transpires in relation to Paul's potential visit (vv 25-26), the one essential thing for the Philippians is to **conduct themselves in a manner worthy of the gospel.**

The NIV's **conduct yourselves** fails to capture the full force of this imperative. What Paul literally commands is, "live as citizens" (*politeusthe*) or **live out your citizenship.** Why did Paul choose this rare political metaphor to represent the Christian lifestyle instead of his customary word "to walk" (*peripatein*)? It is surely no coincidence that both the verb and the related noun form, "commonwealth" (*politeuma*, 3:20), appear only in Philippians among Paul's letters. Paul plays on Philippi's privileged status as a Roman colony populated by many Roman citizens, probably including some Christians (on the term's political background, see Brewer 1954).

But when Paul tells the Philippians to **live out** [their] **citizenship,** this is more than a call to fulfill their civic duty to an earthly state. As ch 3 will show, the Philippians are citizens of an empire other than Rome, a *heavenly* commonwealth (3:20). Theirs is a higher, more compelling loyalty. Bockmuehl hits the nail on the head: "Against the colonial preoccupation with the coveted citizenship of Rome, Paul interposes a counter-citizenship whose capital and seat of power are not earthly but heavenly, whose guarantor is not Nero but Christ" (1998, 98).

This change in loyalty demands a change in lifestyle. Citizenship carries with it both privileges and obligations. Christians are called to live according to the values, norms, and priorities of their heavenly commonwealth, not those of the dominant Roman culture. In short, Paul co-opts political language that was meaningful to his readers in order to reconstruct their identity and conduct. The verb Paul uses also brings out that Christian behavior is not simply an individual matter. As fellow citizens, our visible life as a *community* must be worthy of the gospel (Hooker 2000, 496).

But what does it mean to exercise our heavenly citizenship **in a manner worthy of the gospel of Christ**? Elsewhere, Paul urges Christians to a life worthy of God (1 Thess 2:12), of the Lord (Col 1:10), or of their calling (Eph 4:1; see 2 Thess 1:11). This is the only time, however, that Paul calls for behavior worthy of **the gospel**.

Paul certainly does *not* mean that his audience must live in such a way that they *deserve* salvation or the good news. Rather, to live in a manner worthy of the gospel means living in ways that are consistent with the gospel. Their lives should incarnate the gospel. For Paul, **the gospel** is more than a body of propositional truths or correct beliefs. The gospel also establishes a norm for Christian conduct (Schütz 1975, 50). As the "power of God for salvation" (Rom 1:16 NRSV), the gospel transforms the world of Paul and his readers. It brings about a new way of seeing the world, which results in a new way of living.

Here it is the gospel **of Christ** (i.e., "the gospel *about* Christ") that the Philippians must embody. The Christian message centers on the good news of Christ's life, death, and resurrection. For Paul's audience, living in a way that is worthy of the **gospel of Christ** means that their common life must continually reflect Jesus' self-giving love for others (2:1-11; see Gal 2:20; 4:19).

In the rest of the paragraph, Paul gives a more specific content to what it means to live out their Christian citizenship in a manner worthy of the gospel. In particular, three phrases in vv 27 and 28 unpack the concrete significance of the opening imperative for the Philippians.

First, whether Paul is able to come and see them personally, or whether he hears about their situation (literally, "your affairs," which parallels "my affairs," 1:12) indirectly (presumably from Timothy [2:19]), they are to **stand firm in one spirit.**

The verb **stand firm** (*stēkete*) conveys the idea of steadfastness, like soldiers who refuse to leave their appointed posts. The main interpretive question here concerns the meaning of the words **one spirit**. "Spirit" (*pneuma*) could refer to the human *spirit*. In this case, it is parallel to the two words that immediately follow it in the sentence, **one person** (literally, "one soul," *mia psychē*; see Phil 4:23). If so, Paul is talking about the unity of disposition and purpose that is necessary for God's people to remain steadfast.

The phrase **in one spirit** (*en heni pneumati*), however, has no analogy in Greek literature. Thus, it seems better to take it to mean *in one Spirit,* as a reference to the Holy Spirit (see Fee 1995, 163-66; Chrysostom, *Hom. Phil.* 4.1.27). This is supported by Paul's reference to the Philippians' "partnership in the Spirit" in 2:1, as well as his use of the language of "one Spirit" in other contexts (1 Cor 12:13; Eph 2:18; 4:3-4). It is the Spirit who is the source of their unity. And it is the one Spirit who enables them to stand firm in the face of opposition (Hooker 2000, 496).

A second manifestation of gospel-worthy living involves **striving together as one person** for the faith of the gospel. (Grammatically, the participles "striving together" [*synathlountes*, v 27] and "not being intimidated" [*mē ptyromenoi*, v 28] are dependent on the verb "stand firm." Both clauses, however, serve to fill out the content of the main imperative, *live out your citizenship* [v 27].) The verb **striving together** (see 4:3) suggests athletes or soldiers engaged in a team effort. It emphasizes, first, that living in a way worthy of the gospel and standing firm involve strenuous effort. Second, it brings out that Christians do not struggle alone. They strive side by side as part of a community of faith, strengthening, reinforcing, and encouraging one another in the contest (Witherington 1994, 53). Like the Spirit-filled community described in Acts (4:32), they are united with *one soul* in their common task. This is "unity for action" (Oakes 2001, 178).

Here Paul spotlights, not what (or whom) they are striving *against*, but what they are contending *for:* **the faith of the gospel** (*tēi pistei tou euangeliou*; see Barth 1962, 47). It is not fully clear how we should take this phrase. There are a number of plausible options. Does it refer to the faith response demanded by the gospel? And, if so, are the Philippians striving on behalf of their own faith? Or does it have to do with their evangelistic efforts to lead others to faith in Christ (e.g., "struggling . . . to get others to believe the good news," CEV)?

Alternatively, does **faith** have to do with the Christian message itself, either "the faith which is the gospel" or "the faith proclaimed in the gospel"? Or, since *pistis* can also mean "faithfulness," does Paul call them to struggle together "for faithfulness to the gospel" (Sumney 2007, 36)?

In light of v 25 ("your progress . . . in the faith"), Paul's emphasis is probably on the *content* of the faith; that is, the gospel message. In the face of persecution, the Philippians are engaged in a unified struggle to resist the pressure to compromise the gospel's integrity. In the context, that would involve not only promoting and defending the truth of the gospel to outsiders but especially refusing to discredit the gospel through unworthy living (Marshall 1991, 37).

■ **28** A third way in which Paul urges the Philippians to live in a manner worthy of the gospel is through courage under pressure—**without being frightened in any way by those who oppose you.** The verb **being frightened** (*ptyromenoi*) is found only here in the Greek Bible. In classical Greek, however, it sometimes referred to people being intimidated, or to horses being startled into a stampede (O'Brien 1991, 152-53). Paul is concerned that when the Philippians come under attack from hostile opposition (on the identity of these "opponents," see BEHIND THE TEXT for this section), they do not allow it to throw them into panic. They must continue boldly to tell and live the gospel. Paul has already modeled such courage under fire. We see it expressed in his desire that Christ would be magnified through him, "whether by life or by death" (1:20).

The second part of v 28 is a challenge to interpret. The NIV's **this** (literally, "which") could simply point back to the idea of fearlessness in the face of opposition from the immediately preceding phrase. More likely, however, it also embraces the unity, steadfastness, and common striving for the truth of the gospel that Paul urges in v 27. In short, it refers to living a gospel-worthy lifestyle. A very literal translation of the clause in v 28 would be: ***which is to them a sign of destruction, but your salvation.*** Yet how is the Philippians' conduct simultaneously **a sign** of both ***destruction and salvation?***

Fowl argues that Paul here refers to two widely different perspectives on Christians' faithfulness to the gospel in the face of persecution—one by the adversaries, the other by the Philippians themselves. Thus, to the opponents, the Philippians' steadfastness "is a willful flaunting of Roman authority and a harbinger of the Christians' imminent destruction." But to the church in Philippi, it is just the opposite; it is a concrete manifestation of their salvation (Fowl 2005, 65-69, here 68; see also Hawthorne and Martin 2004, 72-74).

This is an attractive explanation. Nevertheless, it is a rather unnatural way of reading the phrase ***for them, a sign of destruction.*** Furthermore, in Paul's writings ***destruction*** (*apōleia*) normally refers, not to physical death, but to God's end-time judgment on unbelievers (see 3:19). It is better, then, to see the Philippians' courageous steadfastness as a "demonstration" (*endeixis*) that *the opponents* are headed for destruction. This is strong language, to be sure. But, as Bockmuehl points out, if **salvation** entails the victory of good and righteousness, it must also mean the ***destruction*** of that which opposes the purposes of God. Otherwise, that salvation would have little meaning (1998, 102).

We find a similar thought in 2 Thess 1:5-6. There Paul cites the church's faithfulness during persecution as "evidence" (*endeigma*) of God's righteous judgment on the enemies of the gospel (see 1 Cor 1:18). In our passage, Paul's language does not require that the opponents recognize this omen of God's impending judgment, but it relates to them nonetheless (Bockmuehl 1998, 101).

This is a twofold sign. The same endurance in opposition that shows that the adversaries are on the highway to destruction also serves as a token of the Philippians' salvation and vindication by God in the end (see 1:19). It is unclear whether this sign of coming salvation is intended primarily for the opponents or for the Philippians themselves. We probably do not need to choose between them. Either way, the Philippians' firmness under fire *speaks*. To the opponents it is a demonstration of God's vindication of his people. For the Philippians, it is a mark of assurance that they truly are the people of God, on the path to ultimate salvation.

Paul's point seems to be that when Christians live in a way that is worthy of the gospel, their lives "preach" the message. They become living proof of the gospel's offer of salvation and God's victory over his enemies. Their "behavior is thus at one and the same time evidence of the truth of the gospel and a warning to those who oppose it" (Hooker 2000, 497).

The final phrase in v 28, **and that by God,** bolsters the thought. What comes ***from God*** (*apo theou*) is probably not only the Philippians' salvation but also the double-sided ***sign*** of deliverance and judgment. (The NIV's **that** is actually "this," *touto*, in Greek. As a neuter noun, it must point back to more than ***salvation*** [*sōtēria*], which is feminine.) Moreover, the next verse implies that not only is the "sign" from God; so also is the perseverance in the face of suffering of which the sign consists (Hooker 2000, 497).

■ **29** This verse makes a remarkable statement: **for it has been granted to you on behalf of Christ not only to believe on him, but also to suffer for him.** Here Paul gives a theological explanation of *why* their endurance in the midst of adversity is God's proof that they are on the pathway to salvation. Indeed, the Philippians might be tempted to think just the opposite. They might conclude that their current opposition and suffering are evidence that God is displeased with them. But that is not the case, for this reason: **because** (*hoti*) their suffering for Christ is part of God's gracious activity in their shared life.

Two aspects of this explanation of the Philippians' suffering are especially striking. First, their suffering is a *gift* from God. The verb **granted** actually means "graciously given" (*echaristhē*, which has the word "grace," *charis*, at its root). The verb is in the passive voice, with God as the implied subject. This communicates that both the Philippians' faith in Christ *and* their suffering for the sake of Christ are gifts of God's grace. In other words, not only is their courage in the face of opposition a divine gift, but even the affliction itself is an expression of God's grace (Hooker 2000, 497). This is surely one aspect of their partnership in the grace of God along with Paul (1:7; see v 30).

Second, the reason the Philippians' suffering is a gracious gift is because it is **on behalf of Christ** (*hyper Christou*). The Greek text intensifies the Christ-centered character of this endowment by giving it a double emphasis: "It has been graciously given *on behalf of Christ* . . . to suffer *on his behalf*" (see Fee 1995, 171).

In what way is their suffering "for" Christ (NRSV)? Here Paul is probably not talking about every form of suffering that Christians might experience. Rather, it is suffering for the sake of Christ—as a result of their commitment to Christ and the gospel. This finds support in v 30, where Paul views the Philippians' suffering as sharing the same character as his own. When Christians live lives worthy of the gospel in the midst of "a crooked and depraved generation" (2:15), they should not be amazed if this provokes opposition from the worldly powers.

Paul does not view such suffering on behalf of Christ as an evil to be escaped. Rather, it is a grace—though a severe one—to be embraced (Thurston

2005, 72). Just as Christ willingly suffered and died "for us" (Rom 5:8; 8:32; 1 Thess 5:10), so we also are privileged to suffer **for him** (Phil 1:29; see 2 Cor 12:10; Col 1:24; see also Marshall 1991, 39). Later, Paul will speak of his desire to know Christ in terms of sharing his sufferings (Phil 3:10).

For Paul, suffering with Christ is a means of intimately identifying with the crucified one in his suffering and death. It is through this identification that Christians proclaim the story of Christ's self-giving death and life to the world (2 Cor 4:10-12). We should view Phil 1:29 against the backlight of the example of Christ in 2:5-11: "for believers, as for their Lord, the path to glorification leads through the suffering of the cross" (Fee 1995, 172; see Bloomquist 1993 and Oakes 2001 for differing perspectives on suffering in Philippians).

■ **30** Paul wraps up his argument in the paragraph by reminding the Philippians that he and they are involved in **the same struggle**. The word **struggle** (*agōn*, from which the English word "agony" is derived) draws on another athletic metaphor, which could also be used of military conflict in the ancient world (see Geoffrion 1993, 71-81). It pictures an athlete or soldier enduring intense strain and pain in the face of opposition.

The Philippians were eyewitnesses (**you saw I had**) to Paul's hardships at the hands of the Romans in Philippi (Acts 16:19-24). Elsewhere, Paul speaks of severe suffering in that city, using the same word *agōn* for the opposition he met there (1 Thess 2:2). Now, by means of this letter and Epaphroditus's report, they have learned of his current ordeal as a prisoner of Rome.

The text stresses that the struggle Paul and the Philippians face is **the same**. This shared experience is probably not limited to the fact they are partners in the gospel (1:5) and engaged in the same general conflict against evil. It likely also refers to their specific fellowship of suffering at the hands of the Roman Empire (Bockmuehl 1998, 103).

Paul's reason for highlighting this common struggle is not simply to let the Philippians know that they are all, so to speak, in the same boat (Hooker 2000, 498). Throughout this chapter, Paul's experience has served as a model for the Philippians to follow. Here, no less, Paul encourages them through his example to live worthily of the gospel, to see God's hand of grace in their sufferings, and to bear trials with fortitude "for the sake of Christ" (3:7).

FROM THE TEXT

The key themes of this paragraph—steadfastness, unity, striving for the gospel, suffering—all fall under Paul's banner headline at the top of the section: live a lifestyle that is "worthy of the gospel of Christ." How do these themes and this overarching exhortation address the twenty-first century church?

1. *By calling us to embody the gospel.* The imperative to live in a way that is worthy of the gospel (v 27) shatters all attempts to divorce belief and behavior. Beliefs are important, and Paul affirms that the truth of the gospel is worth contending for (v 27). But the saving story of Christ crucified and risen that is at the center of the gospel must be embodied in the everyday lives and relationships of Christians (2:5-11).

I suspect that Paul would be quite puzzled over the practice of most seminaries and universities today of separating the study of right thinking (theology) and right living (ethics). Richard B. Hays is on the mark: "There is no meaningful distinction between theology and ethics in Paul's thought, because Paul's theology is fundamentally an account of God's work of transforming his people into the image of Christ" (1996, 46). If we fail to allow the good news that has saved us to come to visible expression in our common life, we effectively deny the truth of the gospel (Hooker 2000, 514).

Heeding the call to embody the gospel visibly and authentically is perhaps the church's greatest need in our time. A gospel that will be plausible to an increasingly postmodern world will be one that is "preached" by the shared life of the people of God. Or as St. Francis of Assisi is reputed to have advised, "Preach the gospel . . . and if necessary, use words." Holy lives and genuinely loving relationships will stamp our message with a seal of authenticity. A community of believers that lives out the gospel story will, through the Spirit's empowering, authenticate the truth of the gospel to a broken world.

2. *By showing us the basis for ethical living.* Paul's exhortation to live in ways that are consistent with *the gospel of Christ* gives us a ground for our Christian conduct. The church's shared life is not rooted in any ethical system, church tradition, or list of moral directives. Rather, the wellspring for our conduct is the liberating gospel of God's loving intervention in Jesus "for us." Any attempts to live "worthy" lives by simply striving to follow a set of rules or a system of teaching will lead to perpetual moral frustration and failure.

In Philippians, "worthy" living is primarily a matter of being conformed to the self-giving love of God in Christ in our individual and corporate lives. Not surprisingly, the plea to "conduct yourselves in a manner worthy of the gospel of Christ" is comprehensive and nonspecific. It must be enfleshed in a multitude of concrete forms within our diverse cultures and circumstances. Nevertheless, Paul gives some clues in this passage as to what directions gospel-worthy living may take. In Philippians, a worthy response to the gospel involves:

- a lifestyle that reflects the values, norms, and practices of the kingdom of Christ rather than those of the dominant culture
- unity in the Spirit in our common life and mission
- steadfastness and courage in the face of opposition

- a shared passion to promote the gospel and to resist compromising its integrity
- a willingness to suffer for the sake of Christ

Living worthily of the gospel is not just a matter of personal holiness or refraining from a list of harmful activities. It is realized in a common life and purpose centered on Christ and the gospel (Welch 1988, 49).

3. *By teaching us the grace of suffering.* The prickliest theme in this passage, especially for Christians in the West, is no doubt the idea of suffering as a gift of God's grace. As one writer puts it, "We find it hard enough to accept that suffering happens at all, let alone that it is a gift from God" (Deasley 2005, 17). Too often, popular Christianity is fixated on how to live a happy life, and suffering simply does not fit into the program. How should we understand this arresting notion of the gracious gift of suffering?

First, Paul in this context does not make a claim about suffering in general. He writes particularly about suffering that is "on behalf of Christ" (1:29)—suffering that is the direct result of living lives worthy of the gospel in a world that is offended by the gospel. Jesus warned that a world that opposed him for who he was will no less oppose his followers for who they are and whom they represent: "Students are not above their teacher, nor servants above their master" (Matt 10:24 TNIV; see John 15:18-25).

For a host of Christians in our own world, persecution for the sake of Christ is a present experience and martyrdom a real possibility. Missiologists tell us that there have been more Christian martyrs over the past century or so than during the entire prior history of the church. My own understanding of Christian suffering has been shaped through the humbling privilege of encountering believers in places such as China, the Middle East, and the former sphere of Soviet power, who, like the earliest apostles, rejoiced "because they had been counted worthy of suffering disgrace for the Name" (Acts 5:41).

One aged Chinese pastor told me his story of imprisonment in a labor camp for 22 years because of his loyalty to Christ over the Communist state. During that time he had no Bible, no fellowship with other Christians, and very little contact with his wife and six children. He was subjected to the freezing cold, inadequate food, backbreaking labor; he did not expect to make it out alive. During the worst days of his punishment, he would quietly sing the words of Ps 27 as a testimony of his undaunted trust in God's grace in the midst of suffering: "The LORD is my light and my salvation—whom shall I fear? The LORD is the stronghold of my life—of whom shall I be afraid?" (v 1). After being released from prison, he endured ten more years of house arrest. Yet, this humble Christian servant spoke with a glow on his face about the privilege of taking up the cross daily and following his Lord on the path of suffering.

But how should Christians living in societies that are relatively free from such direct persecution handle a text like this? Often our tendency is either to feel guilty because what Paul says about suffering for Christ doesn't pertain to us or to read his words so broadly that they are applied to virtually any form of illness or inconvenience. A more adequate reading of the text, however, suggests a different perspective (see Thielman 1995, 98-99).

First, even though we may not face overt suffering at the hands of the "powers that be" for our loyalty to Christ, we are called to stand in solidarity with Christians who do. Just as Paul and the Philippians formed a community of fellow sufferers, supporting one another through prayer and practical assistance, surely we can stand side by side with powerless and persecuted fellow believers today, wherever they might be found.

Second, it is clear that Jesus and Paul fully expect that authentic Christian communities will be opposed by cultures that have a radically different system of values and allegiances. If that is true, then perhaps we should ask why we do not experience the gift of suffering more than we do. As Fowl incisively comments, "The question . . . becomes whether Christians in America or elsewhere testify in word and deed to a faith substantial enough to provoke opposition from powers that are either indifferent or hostile to the triune God" (2005, 71). Too often the church has so accommodated to the values of the dominant culture, or it is so preoccupied with internal wranglings, that it poses little threat to the powers of a world that is no friend of grace.

What would happen if Christians in the West repented of their complacency? What if we faithfully lived out our calling in cultures soaked with materialism, moral relativism, and religious pluralism, whose security lies in defense systems and social safety networks? Is it not likely that such Christians would also face forms of opposition, ridicule, and ostracism for the sake of Christ? When this happens, will we complain, "Why should this happen to me?" Or will we humbly enter the fellowship of those who have been given the grace, not only of believing in Christ, but also of suffering for him (1:29)?

Third, when our text says that suffering is a gift from God, it does not claim that suffering is good in itself. While living in the Philippines, I witnessed young men, so-called *flagellantes*, using metal-tipped whips to beat their backs until they were crimson from the blood streaming down them. Their hope was that, by inflicting suffering upon their bodies, they could purify themselves from sin and become more acceptable to God.

Such masochistic efforts to elevate suffering itself are oceans apart from Paul's meaning. The suffering that Paul and the Philippians experienced originated from sinful powers that were opposed to the gospel, not from God. In effect, this passage offers a form of *theodicy*—a defense of God's goodness in light of the presence of evil and suffering. Paul does not call suffering a gracious gift because it is good. Rather, it is because God can transform that suffering into something he can use to further his glory and to conform us to the image of Christ (see Rom 5:3-5).

The suffering Christians experience for the sake of Christ is real. It cannot be trivialized with a plastic smile or shallow words of praise. But our suffering is also an opportunity for God's grace to abound in and through our lives. It bears witness that believers are on the highway of salvation (Phil 1:28). It enables us radically to identify with the one who obediently suffered, even to the point of death on a cross (2:8).

B. An Appeal to Unity Through Unselfish Humility (2:1-4)

BEHIND THE TEXT

Philippians 2:1-4 is linked both to what comes before and to what comes after it in the letter. From one standpoint, this paragraph is a concrete application of the general principle that Paul set forth in 1:27: live out your citizenship "in a manner worthy of the gospel." Both the opening ***therefore*** (*oun*, not translated in the NIV) and the content of 2:1-4 connect it to the preceding paragraph (Fee 1995, 175). There Paul urges the Philippians to "stand firm in the one Spirit, striving together with one accord for the faith of the gospel" (1:27 TNIV). If these Christians are to withstand the struggle from without that Paul and they share (1:30), they must be united within. It is to this essential unity that Paul now turns his attention.

Likewise, the theme of humility that Paul addresses in 2:3-4 builds on previous examples in the letter, both negative and positive. The rival preachers who proclaim Christ "out of selfish ambition" (1:17) embody the attitude Paul tells the church *not* to embrace in 2:3. In contrast, Paul's story in 1:12-26 models the self-sacrificing mind-set described in 2:3-4. The apostle willingly lays down his own preference to "depart and be with Christ" (1:23) for the sake of the Philippians (vv 22-26).

But this passage, however, not only looks back but also points forward, especially to the Christ hymn that immediately follows. Philippians 2:1-4 and 5-11 are intimately bound in language, structure, and content (see BEHIND THE TEXT, 2:5-11). The story of Christ told in vv 6-11 is the supreme example of the kind of humility and self-giving love that Paul calls the community to embody in vv 1-4. Paul's countercultural call to forsake selfish ambition and to humbly look first to the interests of others only makes sense in light of the example of Christ that follows (Thurston 2005, 75).

Later, Paul ends the chapter with three models of selfless concern for others: Paul himself (v 17), Timothy (vv 20-22), and Epaphroditus (vv 25-30). These examples put flesh on the exhortations of vv 3-4.

Philippians 2:1-4 is one long and complex sentence in Greek. It is a highly rhetorical passage with a definite structure. We can divide it into three main parts, obvious in this rather literal translation (see Black 1995, 36; O'Brien 1991, 165):

1. a *If therefore there is any encouragement in Christ,*
   b *If*   *any consolation of love*
   c *If*   *any participation in the Spirit*
   d *If*   *any compassion and mercy*
2. *Then make my joy complete*
   a *by setting your minds on the same thing*
     b *by having the same love*
     b' *united in spirit*
   a' *by setting your minds on one thing*
3. a *by doing nothing out of selfish ambition or empty conceit*
     b *but in humility considering others better than yourselves*
   a' *by each not looking out for your own concerns*
     b' *but rather for the concerns of others*

The passage opens with four compelling "if" clauses in v 1. These give the basis for Paul's appeal to unity and humility—what the Philippians already experience "in Christ."

The second part (v 2) begins with a "then" clause in the form of an imperative (if you have known these blessings, *then* "make my joy complete"). Four statements follow, which in different ways describe the need for unity and harmony in the church. These four appeals to unity form a chiasm, in which the first and fourth statements say virtually the same thing, as do the second and third (Osiek 2000, 51).

Finally, the third division (vv 3 and 4) has two pairs of statements, each of which contrasts what the Philippians should *not* do (not this) with what they *should* do (but that). They should *not* live selfishly, but they *should* put the interests of others first. Only if believers practice this self-giving kind of living does the appeal to Christian unity in v 2 work (on the structure of this passage, see Black 1985).

From a rhetorical perspective, this paragraph is carefully crafted in order to have a maximum impact on the audience. In the arrangement of Philippians, ch 2 probably begins the main section of proof (*probatio*), in which the speaker sets forth the principal arguments supporting the case (see, e.g., Watson 1988, 67-68; Black 1995, 47-48). After stating his main thesis about living a life worthy of the gospel in 1:27-30, Paul offers exhortations and examples demonstrating what that will mean for the Philippians in ch 2.

We also find specific rhetorical features. For example, Paul launches an intensely emotional appeal (*pathos*) in v 1, based on the Philippians' own experience. Then in v 2 he stacks four phrases on top of each other, all of which bolster his call to unity. The power and persuasiveness of such arguments would only have been enhanced when delivered publicly by a skilled oral communicator in a worship setting.

Paul draws deeply from the well of ancient friendship language in this paragraph. Aristotle and others had used expressions like "to think the same thing" and "united in soul" (*sympsychoi* in v 2), "not looking out for your own concerns" (in v 4), and the theme of "sharing" (*koinōnia*, v 1) to describe ideal friendship (see Fitzgerald 1996, 144-46). Paul employs the traditional language of friendship to reinforce the need for inner cohesion in the church (Ware 2005, 221).

Finally, if the main thrust of the passage is the appeal for Christian unity, what prompted such a concern? Is this a congregation riddled with internal divisions that threaten to destroy the church (so, e.g., Peterlin 1995)? Or is Paul's call to harmony and humility more of a preemptive action (see Fee 1995, 32-33, 187)? In light of Paul's explicit plea for two female Christian leaders to "be of the same mind" (4:2 NRSV), it seems there was at least some measure of actual disunity within the congregation. What is more, "Normally one does not underscore the need for something that already exists" (Thurston 2005, 76).

Whatever the precise circumstances, Paul is apparently concerned about a real and present shortcoming in what is generally a healthy Christian community. Without addressing this crucial issue, the Philippians risk not being able to stand firm and to live lives worthy of the gospel in the face of suffering.

IN THE TEXT

■ **1** The passage begins with four conditional ("if") clauses. The "if" at the beginning of each clause, however, is not designed to cast doubt on whether the Philippians have experienced any of the blessings Paul names. The force of the Greek construction is, "As surely as . . . you have any encouragement . . . comfort . . ." (Deasley 2005, 20).

Paul's richly emotive language in this verse gives his friends both a basis for and a motivation to pursue the unity and unselfishness described in vv 2-4. Such an appeal would have carried particular force in the Greco-Roman world, where accepting a gift brought someone into a relationship of mutual obligation with the giver. As Oakes observes, acknowledging God's gracious blessings would motivate obedience in two ways: out of gratitude and out of the profound moral obligation involved in receiving such gifts from God (2001, 180).

We need to make several general observations about v 1 before looking at its individual phrases. First, the blessings Paul spotlights in v 1 apply to the church as a whole (the main verb of the sentence is plural: *you all* **make** [v 2]), not simply to individual believers. Each of the spiritual blessings Paul mentions is experienced in relationship with other Christians.

Second, the initial clause suggests that it is by virtue of their **being united with Christ** that the community enjoys this shared life. All the blessings in v 1 are characteristics of life "in Christ" and flow out of a relationship with Christ. Paul's appeal to the Philippians "is both communal and christocentric" (Fowl 2005, 78).

Third, because a highly rhetorical passage like this is more concerned with persuasion than precision, the language is quite compressed. So it is difficult to be certain about the specific meaning of each line. As a result, the cumulative effect of the series—*encouragement in Christ, consolation of love, participation in the Spirit, compassion and mercy*—is more important than the precise meaning of the individual phrases.

There is no Greek verb in the four "if" clauses (NIV adds **you have**). The first is literally, *if any encouragement in Christ.* Commentators are divided over whether *paraklēsis,* **encouragement,** has the force of "exhortation" or "comfort" (O'Brien 1991, 167-71). Paul uses the word in both senses, so we do not need to choose. This verse points back to 1:27-30 (indicated by the opening *therefore*), which speak of standing firm in the face of opposition and suffering. The Philippians need *both* the comfort *and* the strength that is theirs because they are **united with Christ** (Bockmuehl 1998, 106). The word **encouragement** conveys both ideas.

The NIV's **any comfort from his love** translates a phrase that literally means *consolation of love.* Only Paul uses the word **consolation** (*paramythion*) and its related forms in the NT (see 1 Cor 14:4; 1 Thess 2:12; 5:14). Its meaning is essentially synonymous with "encouragement" in v 1*a*.

The phrase no doubt means "the comfort afforded by love" (a subjective genitive in Greek). But Paul does not specify whose love he has in mind. It may identify the mutual affection he and the Philippians share (e.g., Thielman 1995, 96). More likely, however, this phrase refers to Christ's love, the love the Philippians experience "in Christ." It is the love of the crucified Christ that supplies them with consolation in the midst of suffering. At the same time, their experience of divine love in Christ makes Christian unity and love for others possible (Bockmuehl 1998, 106).

The NIV rightly interprets the third phrase, literally "sharing of spirit," as **fellowship with the Spirit** (see "fellowship of the Holy Spirit," 2 Cor 13:14), rather than as a human "spiritual partnership." But what kind of "fellowship" (*koinōnia*; see Phil 1:5, 7) *is* this? Is it a fellowship among Christians created by the Spirit? Or is it the church's experience of the Spirit? Certainly, the Holy Spirit is the origin of Christian community. But comparison with 1 Cor 1:9, "fellowship with his Son Jesus Christ," suggests the meaning **participation in the Spirit.**

In the first place, the Christian community (not simply individual Christians) shares in the life and empowering work of the Holy Spirit. And second, as a result, we participate in fellowship with one another in that same Spirit (Fee 1995, 181). Just as the Philippians' encouragement "in Christ" and the comfort they experienced in his love were incentives to Christian unity, so Paul here bases his appeal on their common sharing in the "Spirit of Christ Jesus" (Phil 1:19).

The last of the four conditional clauses in 2:1 is the most challenging to interpret: **if any tenderness or compassion.** The problem is not the meaning of the words themselves, which are near synonyms. The sticking point is that they appear, unlike the first three phrases, without qualification. There are several possible ways to take the phrase. It could refer to:

- the tenderness and compassion the Philippians have received from God or Christ
- the loving attitudes that the Philippians should display toward one another
- the affection Paul feels for the Philippians and they feel for him

A case could be made for each of these. Perhaps, Paul leaves the emotive language here deliberately ambiguous.

Both terms are divine qualities in Scripture. Paul has already said that he bases his longing for the Philippians on the "compassion [*splanchna*] of Christ Jesus" (1:8 NRSV). The second word (literally, "mercies"; *oiktirmoi*) is part of a word group often associated in Scripture with the loving mercy of God (e.g., Exod 34:6; Deut 4:31; Isa 63:15; Rom 12:1; 2 Cor 1:3; Jas 5:11).

These qualities of compassion and mercy are demonstrated above all in the story of Christ himself (Phil 2:6-11). Because believers have experienced God's compassion in Christ, they are enabled to extend mercy and love to others (see Col 3:12). Paul therefore grounds this final appeal to Christian unity not only on the Philippians' tenderness and compassion toward him but especially on their own experience of God's abundant mercy in Christ (Osiek 2000, 53).

■ **2** Paul now unfolds the implications of the benefits named in v 1. If the Philippians have experienced such extraordinary blessings by virtue of being in Christ, they have an obligation to respond appropriately. Paul urges them to fill his joy to the brim by the way they live in relation to one another (Marshall 1991, 43).

Technically, the imperative **make my joy complete** is the only main verb in the paragraph. But the context makes it plain that this is not the focus of

Paul's appeal. That comes in the dependent clauses that follow, which call for the unity and harmony of the church. Nevertheless, Paul's personal appeal for the Philippians to **complete** (*plērōsate*) his joy is entirely appropriate in this conversation between close friends.

Furthermore, it is in keeping with the whole tone of the letter (Fee 1995, 183). Fee is quite right that this "speaks volumes about Paul's pastoral heart" (1995, 183). The Philippians have already been a source of joy for Paul (1:4). Now he gives his dear friends a further motive for behaving in a way worthy of the gospel. In light of their deep bond of mutual affection, the Philippians can fulfill his joy by being like-minded in their life together. This means that Paul's joy is in some sense, at least, dependent on the Philippians' response to his call to unity and humility in this paragraph (Black 1985, 303).

Paul gives his appeal to unity rhetorical punch by piling up four phrases that have a similar meaning. The first and the last of these are almost identical: literally, **set your minds on the same thing** . . . **setting your minds on one thing.** The verb in each case is the key term *phroneō*, which will serve to call the church to a Christlike mind in 2:5. The repetition of this word in v 2 underscores Paul's chief concern in this exhortation—that the Philippians be **like-minded** (Silva 2005, 86).

Recall that *phroneō* is not so much an intellectual activity as it is a life attitude or mind-set, which results in a certain lifestyle. Consequently, when Paul urges the Philippians to be like-minded, he is not saying they must all have identical ideas, opinions, or points of view. In the context, having the same mind involves subordinating selfish desires for the good of the community. It means sharing the same priorities, having a unified purpose, and embracing a common way of seeing the world (Bockmuehl 1998, 109). The church is not an army, where everyone marches in step. It is more like a philharmonic orchestra, in which each member uses his or her gifts, contributing toward the goal of creating a harmonious symphony.

The goal of having "the same mind" (v 5 NRSV) is further explained by the two intervening phrases in the series. **Having the same love** points back to v 1, where the source of love is Christ. Perhaps Paul wants the Philippians to have the "same love" (v 2 NRSV) as Christ (see vv 5-11) and share this with one another (Fee 1995, 185). Only when Christ's love permeates the community is Christian unity possible.

The unusual term, "together in soul" (*sympsychoi*, **one in spirit**), reinforces the previous phrases. It recalls Paul's exhortation to struggle together "with one soul" (*mia psychē*) against outside opposition in 1:27. But here the emphasis shifts to living together in one accord within the community of faith.

■ **3** In vv 3 and 4 Paul shows the Philippians more specifically how to live out this unified attitude. He does this with two "not . . . but" statements. These give both the negative and the positive sides of adopting a mind-set that promotes unity in the church.

First, Christians should **do nothing out of selfish ambition and vain conceit** (v 3*a*). Calvin colorfully labeled these attitudes the "two most dangerous pests for disturbing the peace of the church" (1965, 245). They are polar opposites of the mind-set Christ modeled in vv 5-11. The word translated **selfish ambition** (*eritheia*) describes Paul's rivals who preach the gospel out of self-centered motives in 1:17. To live in this way signals a spirit of self-interest that disregards the well-being of others (Giesen 1991, 2:52).

The term **vain conceit** (*kenodoxia*) is formed from two Greek words meaning "empty" and "glory." It occurs only here in the NT. In the Greco-Roman world, however, it often referred to people who had an inflated sense of self-importance. In the highly competitive environment in which the Philippians lived, gaining honor depended largely on keeping up appearances in order to be praised by others. Consequently, the pressure was intense to project a false image that seemed like "glory," even when the substance of character behind it was lacking (Osiek 2000, 53). Such "empty glory" sits in striking contrast, not only to the second part of the verse, but also with the genuine glory that belongs to God alone (2:11; Hooker 2000, 499).

In Gal 5:26, Paul linked the related adjective "conceited" (*kenodoxos*) with a spirit of competitiveness and envy within the church. Paul is well aware that attitudes like selfish ambition and conceit can be devastating to the mind-set necessary for genuine Christian community. As Chrysostom perceptively comments, "There is nothing so foreign to a Christian soul as haughtiness" (*Hom. Phil.* 5.2.3, 207).

In contrast to this "strangely addictive and debasing cocktail of vanity and public opinion" (Bockmuehl 1998, 110), Paul urges his readers **in humility [to] consider others better than [them]selves** (v 3*b*). The noun **humility** (*tapeinophrosynē*) is related to the key verb *phroneō*; it represents the attitude or mind-set of being humble (Hooker 2000, 499). **Humility** generally did *not* make the virtue lists of the Greco-Roman world. Instead, it was viewed negatively as servility and self-abasement. It was the groveling mentality of a slave—hardly something to be admired or imitated (see Grundmann 1972, 8:1-5). It would scarcely have been lost on either Paul or the Philippians that the call to humility was a countercultural message.

Paul's understanding of humility, however, is rooted in Scripture. God consistently shows a special concern for the lowly and the humble (e.g., Pss 17:27; 25:9; 138:6; Prov 3:34; see Num 12:3). In the biblical view, the humble recognize their own inadequacies as created beings. Because of this, they are willing to entrust their case to God, rather than relying on their own strength and resources (Fee 1995, 188).

In contemporary Jewish writings at Qumran, humility was also recognized as the proper attitude toward God and others in the community (1QS 2:24; 4:5; 5:25). But above all, the Christian understanding of humility is shaped by the attitude and example of Jesus, who describes himself as being "gentle and humble in heart" (Matt 11:29). Thus, Paul's appeal to humility in Phil 2:3 anticipates the Christ hymn to follow. There we hear of the one who "humbled himself and became obedient to death . . . on a cross" (v 8). Humility, within a Christian framework, is transformed from a forced servility into a freely chosen service to others, in conformity to the crucified Christ (Thurston 2005, 74).

In the present context, humility is a key to unity. We find a similar connection in Col 3:12-14 and Eph 4:2-3, where a humble mind-set is considered essential to experiencing love and harmony in the body of Christ. In Phil 2:3-4, humility is the opposite of selfishness and looking out for one's own interests. On the contrary, an attitude of humility means regarding **others better than yourselves** (v 3).

This attitude has nothing to do with false modesty—the kind of manipulative mind-set found in the Dickens character Uriah Heep, whose insincere humility was a mask for his ambition. Nor is it connected to a self-deprecating inferiority complex. Rather, it means to value the needs, rights, and achievements of others as "surpassing" (*hyperechontes*) one's own (Fee 1995, 189). This is only possible when we **in humility** realize that we all stand in common need at the foot of the cross, as "slaves of the same Master" (Thurston 2005, 75). Chrysostom adds that giving preferential treatment to others should be extended without distinction—even to those who speak against us and ill-treat us (*Hom. Phil.* 5.2.3).

At the same time, Paul's exhortation in v 3 would have carried profound social implications for the Philippians. Dominant cultural values in the Greco-Roman world promoted a lifestyle of competing for honor and higher status. This was nowhere more so than in a Roman colony like Philippi (see Bormann 1995). In contrast, Paul teaches that unity depends on Christians considering others to be of *superior* status and deserving *greater* honor than themselves. Such thinking would have cut deeply into the cultural mind-set that sorted out peoples' values according to where they stood on the social ladder (see Witherington 1994, 63).

■ **4** Paul's second "not . . . but" statement gives the call to like-mindedness in v 2 further concrete application (Bockmuehl 1998, 112-13): **Each of you should look not only to your own interests, but also to the interests of others.** Significantly, the word **only** (*monon*) in the NIV does not appear in the Greek text. In addition, **also** (*kai*) in the second part of the statement is absent from some Greek manuscripts. To add an "also" seems to weaken the contrast. Without it, the clause resembles 1 Cor 10:24: "Do not seek your own advantage, but that of the other" (NRSV). Nevertheless, the *kai* has strong textual support and is most likely original. It seems that Paul's meaning is: Do not look out for your own interests, **but rather** (not "but also") the interests of others (Hooker 2000, 500; Bockmuehl 1998, 113-14).

In any case, the basic thrust of the contrast is clear. Our focus of attention (*skopountes*) should not be directed inwardly on our own rights and concerns. Instead, we should focus outwardly on what builds up others in the community of faith. This has both personal and corporate dimensions. When **each** member of the Christian community maintains an unselfish mind-set, menacing divisions in the fellowship tend to dissolve.

Paul's point is that without humility that prioritizes the needs and concerns of others, there can be no true unity in the church. Wesley calls the humility that esteems others above oneself "a glorious fruit of the Spirit, and an admirable help to your continuing of one soul" (n.d., 508). This all points to what follows: the supreme example of humility in attitude and action, Jesus Christ himself (2:5-8).

FROM THE TEXT

1. *Responding to our blessings in Christ*. Paul begins this passage by reminding the Christian community at Philippi of the blessings they have received by virtue of being united with Christ. Then on the basis of their experience of God's grace, he urges them to embrace a different way of thinking and acting in their common life.

The experience of what God has done in Christ should be a powerful incentive for renewal in the corporate life of the church today. Conduct that is worthy of the gospel is a response to God's transforming grace. If *we* have received the remarkable blessing of a relationship with Christ; if *we* experience his love and comfort in times of suffering; if *we* share a common fellowship in the Spirit; if *we* know the benefits of God's mercy and compassion—if these gifts matter to us—then we have an obligation to treat others in the same way we have been treated by God.

Our experience of the overflowing blessings of God, both individually and as a community, should translate into a reorientation of life in relationship to others. As John perceived so clearly, a genuine experience of God's love compels us "to love one other" (1 John 4:11). Only as we are in union with Christ, sharing in the empowering Spirit, will we have the resources for a communal life that reflects the selfless humility of Christ.

2. *A common mind-set*. This section gives a concrete application to Paul's exhortation to "conduct yourselves in a manner worthy of the gospel" (Phil 1:27). Central to his appeal is the desire that the church be a unified body

through becoming "like-minded" (2:2). This does not require everyone in the fellowship to march in lockstep or sign up to a detailed list of doctrines or behaviors. Nor ought members of a congregation uncritically accept everything their leaders ask them to think or do. God has no interest in creating "Christian clones" (see Marshall 1991, 44).

Rather, we are invited to embrace a common mind-set, a shared orientation and perspective. Part of what this means is defined by the content of the passage. We must exercise a common love for one another (2:2) as we subordinate our own rights and wishes to those of our Christian sisters and brothers (vv 3-4). The greatest obstacle to unity "is not . . . legitimate differences of opinion but self-centeredness" (Silva 2005, 87).

Just as we do not choose the members of our biological families, our relationships with others in the Christian community are generated out of faith and baptism, not out of our choice. In a world in which Christian communities are (or should be) increasingly pluralistic, our shared mind-set must be flexible enough to embrace differences in culture, generation, gender, social background, and life experience (Gal 3:28; Col 3:10).

For the past twenty years, I have had the privilege of teaching in international theological learning communities with students from diverse cultures and backgrounds. This experience has shown me the richness that such differences can bring to a community of faith. I have also learned that even in the midst of such diversity, it is possible (though never easy) to forge a common Christian mind-set and perspective that transcends human differences.

This can happen only because our corporate life is, above all, life *in Christ*. The mind-set of Christ (Phil 2:5) must take precedence over all other orientations and values, cultural or otherwise.

Christ-centered Unity

> Our community with one another consists solely in what Christ has done to both of us ... I have community with others and I shall continue to have it only through Jesus Christ. The more genuine and the deeper our community becomes, the more will everything else between us recede, the more clearly and purely will Jesus Christ and his work become the one and only thing that is vital between us. We have one another only through Christ, but through Christ we do have one another, wholly, and for all eternity. (Bonhoeffer 1954, 25-26)

3. *Humility and selflessness.* The kind of mutuality Paul expects of the church here is, in a word, staggering. It envisions a community filled with the love of Christ (2:1), in which the *whole* church voluntarily trades in competitive pride for lowliness, in which each Christian values the good of others ahead of his or her own.

Such a message is no more congenial in the twenty-first century than it was in the first. Particularly in contemporary Western democracies, we are expected to function as independent individuals. We look out for ourselves—our own needs and security, and those of our families. Popular culture encourages us to put our personal rights, choices, and happiness ahead of what would benefit others. Thus, our relationships function largely to meet our own felt needs. People who do not promote our interests become our competition (see Fowl 2005, 87).

Paul's uncomfortable words still beckon us to swim against the stream: "Look not to your own interests, but [***rather***] to the interests of others" (2:4 NRSV). This is a far more radical prescription than being a bit more congenial toward others in the fellowship. No wonder Calvin reflected on this passage: "Now, if anything in our whole life is difficult, this is the worst" (1965, 245).

Christian leaders are not immune to the siren call of "selfish ambition" (v 3). Even ministers can be tempted to climb the ecclesiastical ladder by seeking appointments to larger and more influential churches or aspiring to denominational positions. Christlike leaders do not inflate their own importance by trying to control and dominate those in their care. Pastors and professors must resist viewing their colleagues as competitors for recognition in the church or the academy. An experienced pastor once confided to me that, in his estimation, the hardest thing for people in ministry to do was to rejoice when their colleagues were honored and they were not.

This passage reminds us that the symbols of Christian ministry are the towel and the cross, not the throne and the crown. "De-throning" ourselves requires the end of self-centeredness, for the sake of others. Or, as Jesus put it, those who would follow him must deny themselves and take up their crosses daily (Luke 9:23). Only as we stand on level ground, as redeemed sinners beneath the cross, can we truly see the dignity, worth, and potential of other people. Instead of viewing others as competitors, we can freely choose to value and edify them, even at personal cost.

Such an others-oriented mind-set is not the product of trying harder. It is the fruit of the transforming work of the Spirit of God, within individuals and the community.

4. *Esteeming others better than ourselves.* Paul's language in Phil 2:3-4 has the potential for misunderstanding by contemporary readers. To look "not to your own interests, but to the interests of others" (v 4 NRSV) does not mean: "I must first love myself before I can love anyone else." Such concerns for self-love and healthy self-esteem are the province of modern psychology, mainly within the context of individualistic cultures. They are not, however, at the heart of Paul's understanding of our communal life in Christ (Osiek 2000, 54-55).

Granted, Paul would never suggest that Christians should despise themselves or that they should ignore their own good. Elsewhere he advises believers not to think of themselves *more highly* than they should. Instead, they must think of themselves appropriately *with sound judgment*, in accordance with the gifts God has given (Rom 12:3). What is more, Jesus' appeal to the great commandment to "love your neighbor as yourself" (Mark 12:31; Matt 19:19) assumes that Christ's followers have a proper self-regard.

Nevertheless, looking out for ourselves is simply not the issue in Philippians (note the CEV's questionable translation of v 4: "Care about them *as much as you care about yourselves*" [emphasis added]). From Paul's perspective, our personal dignity and significance flow from the fact that God has lavishly loved us in Christ (Rom 5:5; 8:27; Gal 2:20), and that we "know Christ" (Phil 3:10) and are "found in him" (v 9). Knowing who we are in Christ gives us the freedom to esteem others above ourselves (2:3).

This may not fit the popular psychological ideal for a healthy self-image. But it is surely a picture of the kind of other-regarding love that we find powerfully narrated in the story of Christ. We discover our true identity as persons in Christ, not through an introspective self-love, but in the common journey of giving ourselves away for the sake of others.

C. An Appeal to the Example of Christ (2:5-11)

BEHIND THE TEXT

Philippians 2:5-11 is one of the lofty peaks, not only of this letter, but of the entire NT. It narrates the story of Christ more fully than virtually any other passage in Paul's writings. But this is more than fine Christology. The goal of these verses is to call the Philippians to embody the pattern of Christ's story in their own lives and relationships.

Unfortunately, this paragraph's message and function in the letter have sometimes been overwhelmed by the torrent of scholarly attention vv 6-11 have received. Few passages in the Bible have generated more detailed discussion and sharp debate (see Martin 1997). Much of this interest has focused on three areas:
- the literary form and structure of the passage
- its possible original setting within the worship of the early church
- its religious background

Such issues are not the main focus in this commentary. Nevertheless, we must say a few things about them before discussing the meaning of these celebrated lines within the context of Philippians.

Is it a hymn? Most interpreters take Phil 2:6-11 to be an early Christian hymn (or hymn fragment) in honor of Christ, composed either by Paul or by someone else. Without question, the passage features exalted language and a poetic, rhythmic character. The NIV sets these verses in the form of poetry.

The problem comes when we try to define what we mean by a "hymn." In the ancient world, "hymns," both in classical Greek literature and the LXX, were generally songs of praise to the gods or to God. This is not the case with Phil 2:6-11 (see Fowl 1990, 31-45; Fowl, 2005, 108-9). Nor does this passage follow the typical meter structure of Greek hymns (Basevi and Chapa 1993, 341). Furthermore, although this "hymn" could conceivably have been sung when early Christians worshipped in Greek-speaking churches (see Col 3:16; Eph 5:19), we simply have no way of knowing whether or not this was the case.

If, then, we call this passage a "hymn," the term must be used in a broader, nontechnical sense, relating to its lyrical style and confessional language (see O'Brien 1991, 188). It is in this sense that I refer to Phil 2:6-11 as a *hymn*. But regardless of its specific classification, there is no doubt that these verses *sing*.

Is it pre-Pauline? Related to the issue of whether our text is an early hymn is the common view that it is a composition that predates Paul. Several factors raise such a possibility:
- It begins with the relative pronoun "who" (*hos*), like other poetic passages in the NT (Col 1:15; 1 Tim 3:16).
- It contains a number of unusual words and ideas, especially for Paul (e.g., Christ's incarnation as a "self-humbling" [Phil 2:8]).
- The carefully balanced structure of the passage is different from its surroundings in the letter and looks like a self-contained unit of poetry. Presumably, Paul could have taken over such a poem and adapted it for his own purposes.

These arguments may point to a text that Paul borrowed from the earliest Christian tradition. But I am less convinced than I once was that this is so (contrast Flemming 2005, 174-76). Passages such as 1 Cor 13 and Rom 8:31-39 show that Paul is certainly capable of writing in an elevated style. The unusual vocabulary and ideas could be attributed to the lyrical character of the passage (Bockmuehl 1998, 119). Moreover, the theology of the hymn seems quite consistent with what Paul says elsewhere (e.g., 2 Cor 8:9; see Marshall 1993, 129).

What's more, Phil 2:6-11 perfectly fits its context. In fact, much of the confusion surrounding the meaning of the Christ poem springs from the tendency to pry it from its letter context and inspect it for ideas that are different from those of Paul. Ultimately, whether Paul composed the lines of this "hymn" or took them over from Christians before him, *in the setting of the letter*, these are the apostle's words and thoughts. If they were not his to start with, he has surely made them his own.

What is its background? Scholars have devoted reams of print to the effort of identifying the religious background of 2:6-11 (see Martin 1997; O'Brien 1991, 194-98, 263-71). The once popular view that the hymn had its origin in a gnostic myth about a descending and exalted redeemer figure (see Käsemann 1968) has been rightly rejected by recent scholarship. If the passage reflects Paul's theology—not simply that of an earlier stage in the history of the church—it is more likely that the ideas we encounter are rooted in the OT and Jewish thought. In fact, there may be allusions to several different Jewish figures in the passage. These include:

- personified divine Wisdom, who descends from her dwelling place with God into the world of people (e.g., Prov 8:22-31; Wis 9:17-18)
- Adam, with whom Christ is contrasted (Gen 3; see Rom 5:12-21)
- the Suffering Servant of Isa 52:13—53:12

Concerning the last, Richard Bauckham has argued that Phil 2:6-11 can be viewed as a theological reinterpretation of Isa 40—55, especially chs 45 and 53 (1998, 56-61; see the sidebar "Echoes of the Servant Songs in the Christ Hymn"). There is a common pattern in both Phil 2 and the Isaiah passages. Because the Servant/Christ poured himself out to the point of death, *therefore* God exalted him to the divine throne. Paul apparently reads Isaiah to mean that through the Servant's suffering, humiliation, death, and exaltation, the one true Lord and God—here identified with Christ—is acknowledged by all the nations (Bauckham 1998, 59-61).

Echoes of the Servant Songs in the Christ Hymn

The following possible echoes of Isa 45 and 53 can be heard in Paul's language and ideas in Phil 2:6-11 (adapted from Bauckham 1998, 59):

Phil 2:6-11	Isa 52—53; 45
2:7 but *made himself nothing*	53:12 because he poured himself out ...
taking the *form* of a slave	(52:14; 53:2 form; appearance)
being made in human *likeness*	
and being found in human *appearance*	
2:8 he *humbled* himself	(53:7 he was brought low)
becoming obedient to *death*	53:12 ... to death
even *death* on a cross	
2:9 *Therefore* also God *exalted him to the highest place*	53:12 Therefore I will allot him a portion with the great ... 52:13 he shall be exalted and lifted up and shall be very high
and gave him the name that is above every name	
2:10 that at the name of Jesus every knee should bow ...	45:22-23 Turn to me and be saved all the ends of the earth! For I am God, and there is no other.
2:11 and every tongue confess	..."To me every knee shall bow, every tongue shall swear"
that Jesus Christ is Lord, to the glory of God the Father.	

But there are also clear differences between the two passages. For example, the Servant's sufferings are directly connected to the forgiveness of sins in Isa 53. This is not the case in Philippians. Nevertheless, it seems that the Servant passages in Isaiah helped Paul and other Christians to articulate the meaning of the story of what God has done in Christ (Fowl 2005, 117; for a criticism of this background to Phil 2:6-11, see Hooker 2000, 503).

What is the structure of the passage? Philippians 2:6-11 tells the story of Jesus in summary form. This Christ drama can be divided into two main units or "acts": Christ's *humiliation* (vv 6-8) and his *exaltation* (vv 9-11). The first act focuses on what Christ has done. He has voluntarily humbled himself to the point of death. The second act in the drama spotlights what God has done in response. God has exalted Jesus to the highest place.

We move onto thin ice, however, when we try to lay out the poetic structure of the passage. None of the various proposals as to how the hymn should be divided into stanzas has yet won the day (see O'Brien 1991, 188-93). The best efforts to uncover the hymn's structure are surely those that take into account both its content—the story of Christ it tells—and the structure of Paul's sentences (see Fee 1995, 194-95; Gorman 2001, 89-92).

With this in mind, one plausible way to view the flow of the passage is to recognize that the first act of Jesus' humiliation (vv 6-8) has three stanzas or "scenes" (see Gorman 2004, 103, for a similar structure):

(1) Christ's attitude toward his exalted preincarnate status (being in the form of God, he did *not* exploit his equality with God for his own advantage [v 6a-c])
(2) Christ's self-renunciation in his incarnation (*but* he emptied himself, becoming a slave and a human being [v 7a-c])
(3) Christ's self-humbling in his death (*and* being found in human appearance, he humbled himself, becoming obedient to the point of death on a cross [vv 7d-8c])

In the second act of Christ's exaltation, the rhythmic structure is not as strict. Nonetheless, it also appears to have three stanzas (so also Bockmuehl 1998, 125):

(1) God's response of vindicating him (*therefore* God highly exalted him and gave him the name above all names [v 9a-c])
(2) God's purpose in exalting Jesus—universal worship (*so that* at the name of Jesus every knee will bow in all of creation [v 10a-c])
(3) God's purpose in exalting Jesus—universal acknowledgment (*and* every tongue confess he is Lord, to the glory of God [v 11a-c])

In any case, it is the *content* of this majestic passage, rather than its poetic or hymnic form, which is most important for determining its meaning.

What is its function in the letter? Far from floating as a self-contained unit,

Phil 2:6-11 is tightly woven into the fabric of the letter. There are clear connections between the hymn and both the preceding and following sections of the letter.

Preceding context: Verse 5 provides a smooth transition from Paul's appeal to unity through humility in 2:1-4 to the exemplary model of Christ. There are also a number of parallels between vv 3-4 and vv 6-8. Paul, for example, urges the Philippians to *consider* others better than themselves in *humility* (v 3), even as Christ did not *consider* equality with God something to be used for his own advantage, but *humbled himself* (v 8; Thielman 1995, 112; see Gorman 2001, 168, 255-58).

This suggests that vv 1-4 and vv 6-11 interpret one another. On the one hand, the Christ drama of vv 6-11 puts flesh on Paul's call to forsake selfish ambition and humbly look to the good of others. On the other hand, vv 1-4 is a concrete application of the story of Jesus told in the hymn. The Philippians should have the same self-renouncing love toward one another (v 2) that Christ embodied in his downward descent to the cross (vv 6-8).

Following context: Looking forward, Paul uses a strong connecting word ("therefore") to tie his exhortations in vv 12-18 to the story of Christ in vv 5-11. And the Philippians' own obedience (v 12) is modeled after the actions of the one who obeyed to the point of death (v 8).

Letter context: Beyond the immediate context, vv 5-11 become the centerpiece of the entire letter. Everything in Philippians thus far may be seen to draw its coherence from this narrative of Christ. At the same time, this passage casts its shadow on much of what follows (Fowl 2005, 88-89). Note the following connections:

- Paul identifies himself and Timothy as "slaves" in the service of Christ (1:1), just as Christ is a "slave" in the service of others (2:8).
- Paul's own Christlike love for others puts the progress of the gospel (1:15-18) and the needs of the church (vv 19-25) ahead of his own interests.
- As Jesus willingly embraced suffering and death, the Philippians have been granted the privilege of suffering for Christ and like Christ (vv 27-30).
- Timothy (2:19-24) and Epaphroditus (vv 25-30) serve as examples of self-giving love.
- Paul's renunciation of his privileges in Judaism, sharing in Christ's suffering and death, and ultimately participating in his resurrection (3:4-11), echo the story of Christ.
- The extensive parallels in vocabulary between 2:6-11 and 3:20-21 (see the BEHIND THE TEXT section of 3:15-21 for specific examples) suggest a strong link between the two passages. Paul seems to presume

that if the Philippians follow their Lord on the path of obedient, self-humbling love, they, too, will be vindicated and experience a resurrection (v 21).

Plainly, the "master story" of Christ in Phil 2:5-11 (see Gorman 2004, 102) significantly shapes Paul's entire argument in the letter.

Our study of vv 5-11 divides naturally into three sections: (1) Paul's exhortation (v 5); (2) Christ's humiliation (vv 6-8); and (3) Christ's exaltation (vv 9-11).

IN THE TEXT

1. Paul's Exhortation: Adopt the Mind-set of Christ (2:5)

■ **5** This verse signals a transition from Paul's exhortations to the community in 1:27—2:4 to his appeal to the narrative of Christ in 2:6-11. But just how does it connect the Christ hymn with what precedes it?

The Greek in v 5 is compressed and can be read in more than one way. Literally, it says, **Think this among you, which also in Christ Jesus.** Commentators disagree about how to supply the missing verb in the second half of the verse.

The traditional interpretation adds some form of the verb "to be": **Have this mind-set among yourselves, which was also in Christ Jesus.** The NIV takes this approach: **Your attitude should be the same as that of Christ Jesus.** This supports the so-called ethical reading of the passage; the Philippians should adopt the same attitude that is demonstrated by Jesus in the following poem.

Others, however, argue that the real point of 2:5-11 is not an appeal to imitate Jesus. Instead, the hymn unfolds the drama of salvation (see especially Käsemann 1968 and Martin 1976, 90-102; Martin 1997). According to this so-called doctrinal interpretation, Paul urges Christians to live in light of the story of Christ's incarnation, death, and exaltation. That is, they are to live as people under the lordship of Christ.

On this reading, the supplied verb is the same one (*phroneō*) that occurs in the first part of the verse. The resulting translation is: "*Think* this way among yourselves, which you do indeed *think* in Christ Jesus." In other words, the Philippians should become (in practice) what they already *are* "in Christ." They should live out in their relationships with one another the attitude appropriate to their relationship with Christ.

Those who support this reading of v 5 cite Paul's characteristic use of the phrase "in Christ." Generally, it has to do with being in union with Christ as members of his body, not Christ's own attitude. Further, they ask, why would Paul include an account of Jesus' exaltation in vv 9-11 if the point of the passage is to appeal to Christ as an example of humility?

Overall, however, the traditional reading is stronger, both in regards to the grammar and the context (see Hurtado 1984; Moule 1970). **This** (*touto*) at the beginning of v 5 most naturally refers back to Paul's exhortations to the church in 1:27—2:4. In particular, it picks up on his appeal to unity through humility in 2:1-4. What is more, the imperative form of the key verb *phroneō* (***have this mind-set;*** "think") recalls the double use of the same word in v 2. Paul, then, urges the Philippians to embrace the kind of humble and unselfish mind-set in their common relationships that he has just described in vv 1-4 (Fowl 2005, 90).

At the same time, ***which also*** in the second half of v 5 points forward to the person of **Christ Jesus**—the one in whom this attitude of humility and self-giving love is found. Fee observes that this is not only the most natural way to take the grammar of v 5 but also how the Philippians probably would have *heard* the sentence when it was read to them aloud (1995, 201, n 33). Certainly the preceding verses would have prepared them for such an understanding. In addition, seeing Christ their Lord as a paradigm for how they should live would have been a quite natural way of thinking for Paul's audience. Both emperors and kings were often viewed as providing ethical examples for their subjects to imitate in the Greco-Roman world (Oakes 2001, 190).

The Philippians are to allow the story and attitude of Christ to shape their present mutual relations within the community. Consequently, **your attitude** does not simply refer to the attitude within each individual believer. "In you [*en hymin*]" (NRSV) probably means ***among yourselves.*** Paul urges his friends to adopt the same self-giving mind-set in their communal relationships as was modeled by Christ.

If Paul intended for 2:6-11 to be read as a paradigm for Christian conduct, how are we to handle vv 9-11? How might Christ's exaltation offer an example to follow? Here the analogy between the story of Christ and those who are in Christ is less direct. Nevertheless, the parallels with 3:20-21 noted above suggest that Paul views the Philippians' own future through the lens of the drama of Christ. The passage implies that just as God vindicated Jesus in response to his obedience unto death, so also the Philippians, if they remain faithful to the gospel in the face of suffering, will be exalted by God in the end (see 1:6). Put differently, if they are *conformed* to his likeness in humility now, they will be *transformed* into his glorious likeness in the future (3:21; see 3:10-11; O'Brien 1991, 253). Furthermore, Paul has already assured his readers that their present opposition and suffering is a sign that they are genuine followers of Christ and that they will indeed be saved by God (1:28-29).

Although 2:6-11 tells the story of Christ, v 5 and the surrounding context show that Paul has not scored this christological hymn for its own sake. Paul gives the Christ drama an ethical, not christological, application. Its function is not primarily to tell the Philippians what they should *believe* about Christ. It is rather to show them how they should *act* in light of the pattern of Jesus' cruciform love.

Conformity to the story of Christ, particularly his self-giving death, is fundamental to Paul's understanding of the Christian life (see, e.g., Rom 8:17, 29; 15:1-7; 2 Cor 8:9; Gal 2:19-20; Eph 4:32; 5:1-2, 25-33; Col 3:13; 1 Thess 1:6). Pivotal to Paul's strategy for moral transformation in Philippians, then, is his retelling of the story of Jesus (Wagner 2007, 266). He not only directly exhorts his friends to conduct themselves in ways that are worthy of the gospel (see 1:27—2:4) but also spotlights the narrative of Christ, which is at the heart of the gospel, as the supreme reason for doing so. By interpreting the story of Christ in light of the circumstances of the community, Paul reads his audience into the text of the hymn. What God has done in Jesus is both the source of their salvation and the pattern of their lives.

2. Christ's Humiliation (2:6-8)

■ **6** The story of Christ told in 2:6-11 follows a V-shaped pattern. From the lofty heights of Christ's preexistent glory, it plunges down, down to his earthly humility and death. Then, unexpectedly, it catapults upward as Jesus is exalted as Lord of the universe. Verse 6 begins with the relative pronoun **who** (*hos*), which identifies **Christ Jesus** (v 5) as the subject of this poetic rhapsody. From this point on, however, the road is dimpled with interpretive potholes, which have caused no end of lively debate.

First, Christ is identified as one who was **in very nature God** (v 6). The term the NIV renders "very nature" literally means *form* (*morphē*). This noun occurs only in this passage and Mark 16:12 in the NT. What does it mean that Christ was **in the *form* of God** (emphasis added)?

In its most conventional sense, the Greek word "form" referred to the visible, outward appearance of a person or object. But it could also denote the reality or characteristics that corresponded to the outward appearance (Braumann 1975, 1:705; Bockmuehl 1998, 126). The specific nuance of the term in this passage is far from clear. As a result, it has been taken in a variety of ways, including God's "essential nature," "mode of being," "image," "glory" and "status" (on the various options, see O'Brien 1991, 207-10).

One possible interpretation is that the ***form of God*** is an allusion to Adam, who was created in the image and likeness of God (Gen 1:26). If so, Paul was simply saying that Jesus was born as a *human*, like Adam. Thus, he shared the image of God. This view is especially associated with James D. G. Dunn, who claims that Paul's language makes no allusion to Christ's preexistent state (1980, 114-21; for a critique, see O'Brien 1991, 266-68; more recently, Dunn has somewhat modified his position; see 1998, 281-88). But this reading swims against the whole flow and logic of 2:6-8, which moves from a divine to a human state. Humanity is something Christ did *not* have, but "took" (v 7; Bockmuehl 1998, 132).

Since the expression **form of God** has a range of possible meanings, it is crucial that we consider its setting in Philippians. Two clues from the context are especially important.

First, there is a close grammatical connection between the two phrases **in the form of God** and **equality with God** that follows. Both point to the same basic reality (Fee 1995, 206).

Second, Christ's being in the **form of God** (*morphē theou*) in his pretemporal existence is placed in direct antithesis to his taking the **form of a slave** (*morphēn doulou*) on earth. This latter phrase spotlights Jesus' lowly status when he came **in human likeness** (v 7). Given the contrasting parallelism of the two phrases, we should expect the term *morphē* in both verses to be used in roughly the same way. It is, therefore, possible to take both **the form of God** and **the form of a slave** in the most basic sense of the word—as forms of appearance. The incarnate Jesus takes on the appearance of a slave. This appearance is visibly manifested in the lowliness and obedient submission that characterizes his human life.

But what would it mean for Christ to have the visible appearance of God? Although the OT affirms that God does not have a visible form as such, the LXX describes the appearance of God to humans in terms of glory (*doxa*; Exod 16:10; 24:16; 33:17-23; 1 Kgs 8:11; Isa 6:3; see Fowl 2005, 91, n 6, 92). Paul uses similar language to describe the visible manifestation of God's radiant splendor (Rom 1:23; 1 Cor 11:7; 2 Cor 3:18; 4:6). The **form of God,** then, is God's radiance and glory (Behm 1967, 4:750-52; O'Brien 1991, 210-11).

This understanding supports the broad, scholarly consensus that this passage refers to Christ's preexistence. Prior to his incarnation, Christ displayed the majesty and splendor of the divine glory. The thought fits beautifully with John 17:5, where Jesus speaks of the glory he shared with the Father "before the world began" (compare Heb 1:3).

In Phil 2, however, Paul's concern is not to extol Christ's preexistent glory for its own sake. The point he seems to make is this: If Christ shared the eternal glory and majesty of God, he also had the exalted *status* of his divine position. He then chose to exchange his lofty state for the lowly status of a slave (see 2 Cor 8:9; Fowl 1998, 142; Hellerman 2005, 131-33).

This perspective becomes clearer in the rest of v 6: the preincarnate Christ **did not consider equality with God something to be grasped.** The meaning of this clause hinges largely on *harpagmos*, the Greek word translated **something to be grasped,** which occurs only here in the Greek Bible. In the few secular Greek sources in which it appears, it means something like "robbery," or even "rape." But this hardly fits this context (note the KJV: "thought it not *robbery* to be equal with God" [emphasis added]).

Since the time of the church fathers, this term has evoked a whole shopping list of different interpretations (see the comprehensive survey of the options in Wright 1991, 56-98). At the heart of the debate is this issue: Was **equality with God** something Christ did *not yet* possess but might have desired or grasped after (so the GNT footnote: "he did not think that by force he should try to become equal with God")? Or was being equal with God something Christ *already* enjoyed but did not cling to selfishly (so the NLT)? The NIV translation, **something to be grasped,** is ambiguous and could be interpreted in either of these senses.

A major pitfall for the former reading is that it assumes that "equality with God" (which Christ did not have) is a *higher* status than being "in the form of God" (which he did have). But the grammar of the sentence closely links **the form of God** and **equality with God.** (The definite article in *to einei,* literally, *"the being* equal with God," refers back to "the form of God." The meaning, then, is *"this* previously mentioned equality with God.")

Thus, it is better to understand "equality with God" as something Christ *already* possessed in his preincarnate state. The careful linguistic research of Roy W. Hoover (1971) has persuaded most recent commentators that the term *harpagmos* has the idiomatic sense of "something to be exploited" (NRSV). The underlying idea is that people might use what they possess for their own advantage. For instance, the CEO of a large company might exploit his or her high position to promote self-seeking ends or to coerce people to cater to personal desires (see Marshall 1991, 51-52). Christ, however, deliberately chose *not* to use his equality with God for his own benefit.

This helps make sense of the phrase **equality with God** (*to einei isa theōi;* see John 5:18). Paul's main concern is to show Christ's *attitude* toward being equal with God, not to explain the specific nature of that equality (Fowl 2005, 94). There is a close relationship between this phrase and **the form of God** in the first part of the verse. Being equal with God has to do especially with Christ's sharing in God's eternal glory and divine status. In the present context, Paul says that the preexistent Christ possessed the same rank and supremacy as God the Father, but he refused to take advantage of this.

Within the Roman world, the language of not exploiting equality with God would surely have hit home. The Philippians would know that Roman emperors claimed divine status and used that status to increase their own glory and honor. In utter contrast, Christ, who actually possessed divine status, willingly surrendered it for the sake of others (Hellerman 2005, 135).

Considering v 6 as a whole, it is difficult to decide whether Paul intends the first clause to have a concessive or causal force. A concessive translation would be: *"although* he was in the form of God, he did not exploit that status." A causal reading would be: "precisely *because* he was in the form of God, he voluntarily laid down his right to take advantage of that position." Both readings make a valid point, and both are consistent with Paul's thought.

The former corresponds to a recurring theme in Paul's letters. Christ renounces something, *even though* it was his right to use it (see 2 Cor 8:9: "though he was rich, yet for your sakes he became poor"; see 1 Cor 8:1—9:23; Rom 15:1-13; Gorman 2001, 165, n 19). At the same time, this passage tells us something important about the character of God, as the causal reading shows. Christ redefines our perception of what God is like in terms of self-renunciation and servanthood. Perhaps it is best simply to leave the phrase ambiguous: **being in the form of God.** This lets us recognize that its possible meaning does not exclude either of these interpretations.

The Story of Christ and the Story of Adam?

Does the story of Christ in Phil 2:6-11 imply a contrast with the story of Adam in Genesis? This has been suggested since the time of the church father Irenaeus. Modern scholars find links such as these:
- Christ, who is in the "form of God," recalls Adam, who was in the "image of God" (Gen 1:26).
- Adam, who *did* grasp at equality with God (Gen 3:5), stands in contrast to Christ, who *did not* grasp at/exploit that equality (Phil 2:6).
- Adam's disobedience brought sin and death for all, whereas Christ's obedience to death reversed the effects of Adam's sin (Hooker 2000, 503-4; see also Dunn 1980, 114-21).

Moreover, Paul made use of the Adam/Christ connection elsewhere (Rom 5:12-21; 1 Cor 15:21-22, 45-49).

In spite of such intriguing possibilities, an allusion to the story of Adam's fall is far from explicit in the passage (see O'Brien 1991, 263-68; Fowl 2005, 114-17). There are no clear verbal or other precise links between Phil 2 and Gen 3. The "image of God" and the "form of God" are not interchangeable terms. In addition, what Adam and Eve wrongly sought was the knowledge of good and evil (Gen 3:22), not "equality with God."

It is true that both Rom 5:12-21 and Phil 2:8 mention Christ's obedience. But they look at it from different perspectives. In Romans the point of the contrast is to show that the obedience of Christ has undone the damage done by Adam's sin. In Phil 2, however, the focus is not on the reversal of Adam's disobedience. Instead, Christ's example of obedience served as a pattern for Christian obedience.

This evidence does not rule out an indirect echo of Adam's story in the Christ hymn of Phil 2. But it is unlikely that Paul deliberately reads the story of Christ through the lens of Adam's fall.

■ **7** This verse signals the start of Christ's downward descent. Immediately, we encounter the most controversial statement in the passage. Instead of using his exalted divine status to his own advantage, Christ **made himself nothing** (v 7). Literally, *he emptied himself.*

The clauses that follow in v 7 explain that this refers to what theologians call "the incarnation"—when the eternal Son of God took the form of a slave and was born in human likeness. The verb *emptied* (*ekenōsen*) probably refers not only to the moment when Christ became human but also to his whole earthly mission and death on a cross (v 8).

But what specifically did it mean for Jesus to empty himself? Some interpreters take the verb quite literally: Christ emptied himself of *something*, like emptying water from a glass. If we ask what that something was, different suggestions emerge; for example, his "equality with God" or his divine attributes. But nothing in the passage supports this. What is more, Paul's use of the verb "to empty" (*kenoō*) elsewhere is uniformly metaphorical. It has the sense of nullifying or making something void (Rom 4:14; 1 Cor 1:17; 9:15; 2 Cor 9:3). It is best, then, to take the verb *emptied himself* figuratively here, as well.

Christ, then, did not empty himself *of* anything. Rather, he "poured himself out." Or as Theodore of Mopsuestia put it, he became of no account (cited by Edwards 1999, 242). This surely involves abandoning his rights and giving up his high status as one equal with God. The NIV's idiomatic translation captures the thought beautifully: he **made himself nothing**. The word **himself** is emphatic in Greek. This self-renouncing attitude was Christ's deliberate, active choice.

How Christ *emptied himself* is defined more precisely in the two participial phrases that follow: *taking the form of a slave* and **being made in human likeness**. The *form of a slave* recalls the "form of God" in v 6. The contrast here is between what Christ originally was and what he became (Marshall 1991, 53).

It is important to read the word *slave* (*doulos*) in its Greco-Roman context. The Philippians would have understood that slaves were deprived of the most basic rights, that they usually had little or no status, and that they were subject to the will of a master (see comments on 1:1). For Christ willingly to take on the appearance and characteristics of a slave meant becoming a nobody. Spurning the right to rank and reputation in the eyes of people, he identified with the lowest of the low and the poorest of the poor.

Morna D. Hooker notes that the words *taking the form of a slave* create a shocking counterpoint to v 6. No one would expect slavery of the one who is in the form of God; the same one who could have, had he wanted, claimed equal status with God (Hooker 2000, 508). **But** (v 7a), astonishingly, he freely chose the lowly, submissive status of a slave. Such a move directly counters the status-obsessed value system of Roman Philippi.

This does not mean that Christ *gave up* **equality with God** in order to take on ***the form of a slave***. Nor did he *exchange* one "form" for another—a divine form for a human one. On the contrary, "it is *in his self-emptying and his humiliation that he reveals what God is like*, and it is through his taking the form of a slave that we see 'the form of God'" (Hooker 2000, 508, emphasis Hooker's; see Wright 1991, 84; Augustine, cited by Edwards 1999, 242). This mirrors the emphasis of the Fourth Gospel: It is in the utter humiliation of the cross that the divine glory is most on display. Likewise, it was with full consciousness of his divine authority that Jesus, in love, adopted the visible appearance of a slave and washed his disciples' feet (John 13:1-5).

Paul clarifies the manner of Christ's self-emptying in a second way: he was **made in human likeness.** The participle translated **being made** (*genomenos*) in the NIV means that Jesus entered into a human existence. Put differently, he "was born" like other human beings (Rom 1:3; Gal 4:4). Interpreters sometimes read too much into the word **likeness** (*homoiōmati*).

First, it does not suggest that Jesus simply *appeared* to be fully human, but in reality was not, as the Docetist heresy taught. Second, the phrase **in human likeness** does not stress the *difference* between Christ and the rest of humanity; i.e., that Jesus was not *merely* human; he was still fully God. This reading was popular among the church fathers (see, e.g., Chrysostom and Theodoret, cited by Edwards 1999, 248). This may be theologically correct, but the Greek word **likeness** cannot support such a subtle distinction.

Paul's point in the context is more straightforward. Christ became in every respect like other human beings: he was fully human (see Heb 2:17; O'Brien 1991, 225; Bockmuehl 1998, 137). Here Christ's self-emptying love is expressed in his wholly embracing the lowliness of the human condition rather than exploiting the privileges of his divine status. Once again, this humble attitude functions as a paradigm for the Philippians. As Cyril of Alexandria reflected, "he became like us that we might become like him" (Festal Letter 10:4, cited by Edwards 1999, 250).

The final phrase of v 7, ***and being found in human appearance,*** begins a new sentence. It marks a transition, summarizing the previous thought. But, at the same time, it sets the stage for Christ's further action of humbling himself to the point of death (Silva 2005, 106).

The word **appearance** (*schēma;* elsewhere in the NT only in 1 Cor 7:31) completes a triad of terms that point to the "form," "likeness," and "appearance" of Christ's humanity. Of the three, *schēma* most clearly emphasizes visible appearance. Instead of appearing as a glorious, divine figure, Jesus was recognized in every way as a human being (Marshall 1991, 54; see Martin 1997, 207-8). We should not press the distinctions between these three words too far, however. They all make the same basic point: Christ humbled himself in order to share fully our lowly human existence. Although the NIV translates the present phrase **being found in appearance as** a man, the Greek word *anthrōpon* focuses on Jesus' humanity, not his maleness.

■ **8** It was in this weak and vulnerable human condition that Jesus **humbled himself.** This echoes the language of v 3, where Paul describes the attitude of humility the whole Christian community should embrace. **He humbled himself** also stands parallel to *he emptied himself* in v 7. But v 8 takes the thought even further. Christ's humbling of himself represents the "final downward step of self-abasement," resulting in his death on the cross (Bockmuehl 1998, 138).

The reflexive pronoun **himself** accents the voluntary nature of Christ's actions. As Bockmuehl observes, Jesus can serve as a moral pattern for the Philippians only if his humility is self-willed, not a matter of fate or compulsion (1998, 138).

Verse 8 explains *how* Christ humbled himself, in two remarkable phrases. First, he **became obedient to death.** For the Sovereign One to become submissive to the will of another is part of Christ's self-humbling (Marshall 1993, 134). We are not told *to whom* Jesus was obedient. It is strongly implied, however, that his obedience was not to personified "Death" but to God (see Rom 5:19; Heb 5:7-8).

The first phrase of v 8 underscores that Jesus' obedience took him to the extreme limit of self-humiliation, even to the point of dying a shameful death. If our ears are tuned, we can hear echoes of Isa 53 in this passage. There Yahweh's Servant was lowly and obedient (53:7), and poured himself out to death (53:12; see BEHIND THE TEXT for this section).

Jesus' unflagging obedience serves as an example for the Philippians to follow (2:12). As he obeyed and suffered, so they must faithfully stand their ground in the midst of their own suffering (1:27-30).

The second phrase of v 8 brings the story of Christ's self-humbling to a chilling climax: **even death on a cross.** It is difficult for us today to imagine how repugnant and shocking these words sounded within a status-conscious Roman colony like Philippi. "Crucifixion was the ultimate instrument of Roman torture, used as a political tool to subjugate the provinces of the Empire. It was reserved for those with no status, like despised slaves, hardened criminals and rebellious peasants" (Flemming 2005, 141). The Roman writer Cicero called it "the most cruel and abominable form of punishment" (Verrine Orations 5.64; cited by Bruce 1983, 54). "The very word 'cross,'" he cautioned, "should be far removed not only from the person of a Roman citizen, but from his thoughts, his eyes and his ears" (*Rab. Perd.* 16; cited by Hengel 1977, 42). In other words, **cross** was an obscenity not to be mentioned in polite Roman society.

What made crucifixion so appalling in Paul's world was that it combined excruciating torture with total humiliation (Hooker 1994, 8). Victims were paraded through the streets publicly, open to ridicule from bystanders, crucified naked, left to hang sometimes for several days, with even their bodily excretions in full view. The victims' bodies were usually left exposed to be eaten by birds or wild animals, with the remnants tossed into a common pit (the Gospels note that Jesus' burial was an exception to this practice; see Matt 27:57-59). The absence of a proper burial heaped further humiliation on the victims and their families (see Osiek 2000, 63).

The social stigma attached to crucifixion was further extended by its close identification with slavery. In fact, it was so common for slaves to be crucified in the Roman world that crucifixion came to be known as the "slaves' punishment" (Hellerman 2005, 146-47). No one would have had to alert the Philippians to the connection between Jesus "taking the form of a slave" (NRSV) and his **death on a cross.** Everyone knew that crucifixion was the penalty for slaves (Hengel 1977, 62).

That Jesus willingly chose the path of obedience, not simply to death, but to death *on a cross*, takes his self-lowering to an unfathomable depth. The contrast with the first part of the hymn could not be more stunning. Christ came from the summit of glory to die the death of a slave—because such limitless love expresses what it means to be God (Thielman 1995, 119).

If we look at Phil 2:7-8 as a whole, the cumulative rhetorical impact of the language is astounding. All of the individual descriptions of Christ's career mutually interpret one another: he "emptied himself, taking the form of a slave, being born in human likeness, . . . found in human form, he humbled himself and became obedient to the point of death" (vv 7-8 NRSV). At the same time, the series intensifies as Jesus descends into the pit of humiliation and shame.

But we cannot forget the point of all this. Paul offers the Philippians a pattern to follow. They, too, must take the downward path of dishonor, suffering, and self-renouncing love. As Gerald Hawthorne sums things up, "The life of Christ shows that the way up is by stepping down, that the way to gain for oneself is by giving up oneself, that the way to life is by death, and that the way to win the praise of God is by steadfastly serving others" (1996, 169).

3. Christ's Exaltation (2:9-11)

■ **9** With the words "even death on a cross" reverberating in the ears of the readers, the story of Christ takes a dramatic turn. Following its V-shaped pattern, the narrative suddenly veers upward, climbing from the deepest of depths to the loftiest of heights: **Therefore God exalted him to the highest place** (v 9). This surprising reversal of fortunes also signals a change in subject. Whereas Christ was the agent of his own humiliation in vv 6-8, God becomes the leading actor in vv 9-11, as the author of Jesus' exaltation.

Verses 9-11 comprise one long sentence in Greek. The connecting term **therefore** (*dio kai* in Greek) is crucial. Jesus was elevated to the supreme status, not *in spite of* his self-humiliation, but precisely *because of* it. There is a causal relationship between the two actions. The implication is that Christ's humiliation is as much an expression of his divine identity as is his exaltation (Bauckham 1998, 61). God's exaltation of Jesus, then, is a direct consequence of Christ's obedience. God the Father vindicates Christ's obedient suffering. God places a seal of approval on Jesus' cruciform love.

In v 9, God's response to Christ's self-renouncing humility takes two forms: Christ is exalted **to the highest place** and he is given **the name that is above every name**. Paul uses a compound form of the verb "exalt" to express the extent of the honor conferred on Christ. Found only here in the NT, it literally means that God "super-exalted" (*hyperypsōsen*) Jesus. The point is not that Jesus was given a higher status than he had prior to his becoming a man (against Cullmann 1963, 174-81). Rather, the verb means that God lifted Jesus to the highest position possible. It is a place where he is publicly and universally recognized as equal in status with God the Father (vv 10-11).

Next, Paul says that God conferred on Christ the supreme **name**. In the ancient world, a name was more than a label. It was often a means of revealing a person's character and true identity (see Gen 25:26; 1 Sam 25:25). What is more, to give someone a name bestowed status and often signaled a new stage in life (see Gen 17:5; 32:28; Thurston 2005, 84). When Jesus gave Simon the name Cephas/Peter ("Rock"), for example, it communicated something important about who he was to become (John 1:42). Here God bestows on Jesus a name that reflects the character and supreme status of the exalted Christ.

But what is this **name that is above every name**? A number of the church fathers understood this name to be "God." Others have taken it, on the basis of v 10, to be the human name **Jesus** (e.g., Clarke n.d., 496; Moule 1970, 270; Thurston 2005, 84). "Jesus," however, is the name Christ had from birth, and the name in question was granted only after his death (Bruce 1983, 49).

More likely, we must look ahead to v 11, where Christ is universally acclaimed as **Lord** (*kyrios*). In the LXX, "Lord" is regularly used as the equivalent for *Yahweh*, the sacred personal name of the God of Israel. The designation "Lord" brings to mind OT passages such as Isa 42:8: "I am the LORD; that is my name! I will not give my glory to another or my praise to idols." For the crucified and exalted Jesus to receive the divine name Yahweh/Lord means that he has a unique and superior status. He is above all things. We find a similar thought in Ephesians, where Christ is positioned "far above all rule and authority, power and dominion, and every title that can be given" (1:21).

The verb **gave** (*echarisato;* from the Greek noun *charis*, "grace"; see 1:29) brings out that this supreme name and status is not a right Jesus claimed. Nor is it a coerced response to his obedience. Instead it is a gracious gift, freely bestowed by God the Father.

■ **10** Verses 10 and 11 state the *purpose* of God's exalting Christ. It was **that [*hina*] at the name of Jesus every knee should bow . . . and every tongue confess that Jesus Christ is Lord.** These words rework Isa 45:23 in light of what God has done in Christ. The wider context of this Isaianic passage is important. It affirms both God's unique sovereignty and his universal reign:

> I am the LORD, and there is no other. . . .
>
> Turn to me and be saved, all you ends of the earth; for I am God, and there is no other. . . .
>
> Before me every knee will bow; by me every tongue will swear. They will say of me, "In the LORD alone are righteousness and strength." (Isa 45:18, 22-24)

This OT language, which Paul elsewhere applies to God the Father (Rom 14:11), is transferred to Jesus (Bockmuehl 1998, 145). As a result, Jesus receives the worship from all of creation that is normally reserved for God the Father alone.

The picture of bowing the knee has to do with paying homage to someone of high authority. It invokes a throne room scene like that of Rev 4 and 5, where all created beings fall down in worship before God and the victorious Lamb. Here it is in honor of **the name of Jesus** (Phil 2:10) that every knee must bow. The very one who made himself nothing, took a human form, and died a slave's death on the cross, is now worshipped as Lord of the universe.

In addition to bending the knee, **every tongue** will **confess;** that is, the whole of creation will outwardly and openly acknowledge the lordship of Jesus. But Paul's depiction of the universal worship of Jesus in vv 10-11 raises three further questions.

First, who are the beings **in heaven and on earth and under the earth** (v 10; this phrase adds to the quotation from Isa 45:23)? Some interpreters have gone to great pains to identify specifically who or what makes up each of these categories. Others limit all three to the hostile spiritual powers conquered by Christ (e.g., Martin 1997, 257-65). It seems best, however, not to restrict this rhetorically powerful language to precise groups. Long ago Chrysostom recognized the comprehensive nature of the phrase: "It means the whole world, and angels, and men, and demons; or . . . both the just and the living and sinners" (*Hom. Phil.* 7.2.9-11). Paul's point is that the whole gamut of created beings will bend the knee and acclaim the supremacy of Lord Jesus. Nothing or no one is excluded.

Second, *when* will this universal worship of Jesus take place? Is it simply a future event reserved for the final day? Or is it a current possibility, based on the present exaltation of Jesus? Surely we do not need to choose between the two. Since God has already exalted Jesus to the heavens and given him the divine name of Lord, the church worships Jesus as Lord even now. But God's ultimate purpose that all would submit and confess Christ's lordship will only occur in the end-time future (see Kreitzer 1998, 119-20; O'Brien 1991, 242-43).

This brings us to the third question about this eschatological worship of Jesus. Will all creatures *willingly* acknowledge him as Lord or will some do so out of compulsion? A line of interpretation going back to the church father Origen claims that in the end everyone will unite in worship of God and as a result will be saved.

The wider context of the passage, however, argues against this. In 1:28 Paul has already mentioned the destruction of those who oppose Christ. Furthermore, in the Isaiah passage Paul quotes, the confession of God's lordship is followed by the words, "All who have raged against him will come to him and be put to shame" (45:24). This implies an unwilling submission. God's right to receive universal worship is tied to his right to judge the universe.

In Phil 2, as well, not all who bend the knee and acknowledge Christ's sovereignty on the final day will do so joyously. For some, it will be a "forced confession" (Aquinas 1969, 86; see O'Brien 1991, 243-50). Charles Wesley's hymn captures the thought:

> *Jesus! The name high over all,*
> *in hell or earth or sky;*
> *angels and mortals prostrate fall,*
> *and devils fear and fly.*

■ **11** The acknowledgment that **Jesus Christ is Lord** recalls the early Christian confession, "Jesus is Lord" (Rom 10:9; 1 Cor 12:3). In this case, however, **every tongue** will acknowledge him. Consequently, when Christians gather to worship and proclaim the lordship of Jesus, they anticipate the day when all of creation will confess the eternal sovereignty of God in Christ (Bockmuehl 1998, 147).

In light of the reworking of Isa 45:23 in this passage, the title **Lord** (*kyrios*) identifies Jesus as Yahweh, Israel's one and only God, the unique ruler and judge of the cosmos. But Paul does not compromise Jewish monotheism. The striking doxology that brings the whole passage to a climax makes that clear. This is all **to the glory of God the Father.** God the Father himself has exalted Jesus. As a result, Christ receives the glory God says he will not give to another (Isa 48:11). Here monotheism is magnificently redefined. Christ's deity and universal sovereignty, far from detracting from the Father's glory, only enhances it (Witherington 1994, 69).

Beyond its OT significance, what would the confession of Jesus as **Lord** have meant within the Philippians' Greco-Roman context? Certainly, in a world of "many 'gods' and many 'lords'" (1 Cor 8:5), Jesus' unique lordship would have brought assurance to the church. Christ is supreme over all the deities and spiritual powers that vie for human loyalty or threaten their lives (see 1 Cor 8:6; Rom 8:38; Col 1:15-20; 2:10, 15).

More specifically, acknowledging Jesus as **Lord** would have carried blatant political and religious implications within a Roman colony like Philippi. Inscriptions from the first century attest that Roman emperors were acclaimed "lord of all the world." The Philippians would surely have heard a challenge to imperial sovereignty in the language of Phil 2:9-11 (see Oakes 2001, esp. 149-50, 171-72; Hellerman 2005, 152-53). If Jesus is Lord, then Caesar *cannot* be Lord, whatever Rome or the growing imperial cult might claim. One cannot bow the knee to *both* Christ *and* the emperor. If Jesus reigns over the world, then no human ruler can demand ultimate authority and loyalty.

Philippians 2:6-11, therefore, amounts to a devastating critique of Caesar and his world (Wright 2005b, 589). That the one who was humiliated and crucified by Roman power is declared universally sovereign directly challenges the empire's version of how to achieve world rule. The story of a self-emptying Lord not only subverts Caesar's claims to universal dominion but also turns the whole Roman value system of what constitutes honor and power on its head.

FROM THE TEXT

1. *The divine identity of Jesus.* It is hardly surprising that Phil 2:6-11 has long been pivotal for the church's reflection on the nature of Jesus Christ. Facing teachings that questioned whether Christ was something less than fully God or other than wholly man, the church fathers focused on questions of being: Is the *form* of God the same as the *essence* of God? Did Christ empty himself of his divinity? What was the relationship between his human and divine natures? Such concerns ultimately led to the orthodox Christology that was forged in the Councils of Nicea and Chalcedon in the fourth and fifth centuries: the eternal Son, who had always shared the divine nature and substance as the Father, perfectly combined full divinity and full humanity in his incarnation.

Paul, however, is far more interested in Christ's *identity* than his essential being (but see Jowers 2006, 739-66). Verses 9-11 stunningly identify Jesus as Yahweh, the unique divine Lord of the universe. This amounts to one of the clearest affirmations of Christ's divinity in the NT. But Christ is exalted as sovereign Lord specifically *because* he emptied himself and in obedience embraced the cross (2:6-8). This means that self-giving and servanthood belongs as much to his divine identity as does his heavenly exaltation. Put another way, Jesus' "self-emptying and humiliation are not a step away from His true nature. His becoming as we are and dying on a cross is not a temporary interruption of His own divine existence. Rather, in the emptied and humbled

Christ we encounter God, we see who God really is, we come to know His true divinity" (Nouwen, McNeill, and Morrison 1982, 28).

It follows, then, that we cannot start with a definition of God and try to fit Jesus into it. We must look first to Jesus himself, who reveals to us the identity of God (Wright 2005b, 589). If we want to know what God is like . . . God is like *Jesus*.

Rather than trying to elaborate on Christ's divine attributes and nature, say, his omniscience or omnipresence, Phil 2:6-11 tells the story of Jesus. Jesus' *actions*—his refusal to take advantage of his rights, his humiliation, his obedience, his cruciform love—show us the true character of God (Hooker 2000, 514-15). Self-emptying is more than a single act. It is the basic disposition of the triune life of God (Fowl 2005, 96-97).

This is consistent with wider NT teaching. John's Gospel affirms that when Jesus is lifted up on the cross, his divine identity ("I am he") is revealed for all to see (John 8:28; compare 12:32-34). Revelation invites us to gaze upon the slaughtered Lamb, who is worshipped by all of creation (Rev 5:6-14). It is not without reason, Barth reflects, that when ancient Christian artists portray the exalted Christ enthroned in heaven, we still see the wounds of the cross (1962, 66).

2. *God incarnate.* This passage also reveals something profound about what we have come to call the *incarnation* of Christ. In the nineteenth and twentieth centuries, various "kenotic" theories (after the Greek word *kenōsis*, "emptying"; see the verb form in v 7) tried to answer the question, "Of what did Christ *empty* himself at the time of his incarnation?" Some of these speculations claimed that the preexistent Christ laid aside his divinity or his attributes of divinity (knowledge, power, omnipresence, and so forth) when he became a human being.

But Paul is apparently not interested in such questions. Instead, our text defines Jesus' self-emptying in terms of what he embraced—the human condition in all its lowliness (2:7-8). He did not abandon his divinity; he *added* humanity. Jesus was no less in the form of God when he took the form of a slave.

At the same time, the language Paul uses to express Jesus' incarnation—self-emptying, enslavement, humiliation—suggests a profound identification with our human situation. The Son of God stands in solidarity with the poor and the powerless, the suffering and the vulnerable, the lowly and the marginalized, because he has shared our fate. He is "God with us."

African scholar Eshetu Abate reflects that as hard as it is for us to imagine a slave owner voluntarily becoming a slave, this does not come close to communicating the depth of Christ's humiliation (2006, 1443). Jesus' incarnation meant not just becoming human. It also meant embracing the poverty, powerlessness, and death of a slave. It broadcasts the limitlessness of God's love in Christ.

Augustine on Jesus' Incarnation

What greater mercy is there than this, which caused to descend from heaven the maker of heaven; which reclothed with an earthly body the one who formed the earth; which made equal to us the one who, from eternity, is the equal of the Father; which imposed "the form of a servant" on the Master of the world—such that the Bread itself was hungry, Fullness itself was thirsty, Power itself was made weak, Health itself was wounded, and Life itself was mortal? And that so that our hunger would be satisfied, so that our dryness would be watered, our weakness supported, our love ignited. What greater mercy than that which presents to us the Creator created; the Master made a slave; the Redeemer sold; the One who exalts, humbled; the One who raises the dead, killed? (Augustine, *Sermon* 207, cited by Gorman 2004, 450)

3. *Living out the story of Jesus.* Most interpreters of Phil 2:5-11 have attempted to mine its christological riches. But we cannot forget that the function of these verses in their context is to offer a pattern for us to follow. The story of Jesus told in this hymn reveals one of the most compelling visions of Christian discipleship in the NT. Paul does not simply present a moral code and say, "Live up to this!" He tells the story of Jesus and says, in effect, "Live *into* this" (see Peterson 2006, 43-44). We are called to place our own stories within the story of Christ. Jesus' downward path of self-renouncing love is to be *our* journey, as well.

Some interpreters, however, are wary of a paradigmatic reading of this passage. This boils down the Christian response, they claim, to a naive notion of the "imitation of Christ." How, they ask, could humans possibly *imitate* the specific actions of Jesus described in the hymn—becoming a human being, dying on a cross, being exalted above all creation? What is more, some understandings of imitating Christ have viewed Jesus as *simply* a moral example for Christians to follow—an idea that undercuts Paul's doctrine of salvation by grace.

To be sure, the notion of imitating Jesus becomes problematic if we see it simply as a matter of aping Jesus' particular actions through our human efforts. At times, the imitation of Christ has taken highly literal forms. Consider, for example, the efforts by St. Francis and his followers to reproduce Jesus' wandering life of poverty; or the Filipino Christians who go so far as to have themselves literally nailed to a cross on Good Friday. How does and does not Christ serve as a pattern for Christians today?

First, Paul's focus is on adopting Christ's attitude or mind-set (2:5), not on mimicking the particulars of his earthly life and death. The correspondence between his story and ours, then, is not literal, but one of attitude and analogy. We are invited, both individually and corporately, to emulate his same attitude of obedience, humility, and self-emptying love. In other words, we must discover analogies that will enable us to live out the self-giving story of Jesus within our own circumstances (see Fowl 1998, 147-48).

How that is specifically manifested will surely vary. For the Philippians, in part, it meant standing firm in the face of suffering, as Christ also suffered (1:27-30). For Epaphroditus, it meant risking his life in the service of the gospel (2:30). Likewise, Christians today must find particular ways of becoming "a living exegesis of this narrative of Christ" where we live (Gorman 2001, 92).

Second, we cannot reenact the story of Jesus in our lives and communities in our own strength. In this sense, those who reject the idea of imitating Christ are right on target. Apart from the transforming work of God in Christ and the empowering of the Holy Spirit, living out the attitude of Christ isn't possible. This may not be stated as such in the Christ hymn, but it is surely implied. The mention of Christ's suffering and death presupposes the saving significance of those events "for us." Furthermore, the declaration that Jesus is *Lord* reminds us that we are living under his rule. It is the ongoing work of the living Lord, through his Spirit, that enables our obedience. The Christ hymn, therefore, sets forth *both* the source of our salvation and the shape of how we participate in his story (Gorman 2004, 105).

What this passage calls for is perhaps less "imitation" of Christ—"What would Jesus do?"—than *conformity* to Christ. We are transformed by the Spirit of Christ into the likeness of Christ. This enables us to retell the story of Christ through our attitudes and our relationships. In *The Divine Conspiracy*, Dallas Willard writes, "Jesus calls us to him to impart himself to us. He does not call us to do what he did, but to be who he was, permeated with love. Then the doing of what he said and did becomes the natural expression of who we are in him" (1988, 183).

4. *Holiness as Christlikeness.* The language of sanctification does not appear explicitly in this passage. But holiness is at the core of its message. At a basic level, holiness can be summed up as Christlikeness. John Wesley's favorite categories for speaking about holiness were christological. For him, Christian holiness meant "having all the mind which was in Christ, enabling us to walk as Christ walked. . . . loving God with all our heart, and our neighbour as ourselves" (1979, 11:444).

Unfortunately, we often read biblical descriptions of what it means to be like Christ through our own cultural lenses (McEwan 2002, 4). As a result, our definitions of Christlikeness (and holiness) have tended to focus on certain observable patterns of behavior (the avoidance of drinking or smoking, for example). What is more, particularly for Christians in the West, our understanding of what it means to be like Christ is shaped by our individualistic culture. "We see Christ," notes David B. McEwan, "as an 'individual' who possessed certain holy qualities that are essentially personal, private, interior and spiritual." Our experience of holiness, then, is viewed as the personal possession of those holy qualities by individual Christians (2002, 4).

This passage offers a corrective to such individualistic, law-based visions of holiness. The portrait of Christlikeness we find here is relational and community-oriented. It is the picture of a Christ who "made himself nothing" for others mirrored in a community that is called to embody his self-giving love toward one another. To the extent that sin is self-centeredness, holiness as Christlikeness is surely "other-centeredness" (Staples 1993, 217). Holiness means Christlike self-emptying; it involves living out the narrative of Christ on our streets.

5. *Recovering the shock of the cross.* Paul's language in v 8 is meant to shock—"even death on a *cross.*" The problem is that two millennia hence it sounds rather tame. When shiny crosses dangle from the necks of professional athletes and media celebrities, when golden crosses perch atop our church steeples, when polished wooden cross replicas adorn our sanctuary walls, it is hard for us to imagine that the cross was once a revolting symbol of horror and shame.

Perhaps if we hung large photos of the mass graves from the Holocaust or more recent genocides at the front of our church sanctuaries, or if we wore those same scenes emblazoned on our T-shirts, we might come closer to experiencing the shock effect of the symbol of the cross in Paul's world.

Until we can begin to fathom how disgusting and disgraceful it was for Jesus to die *on a cross,* we cannot fully grasp the extent of Jesus' humiliation in obedience to the Father. Nor can we truly comprehend what it means to identify with the cross personally and become like him in his death (3:10). Jesus' downward plunge from the glorious heights of heaven reaches its nadir on a Roman cross. That reality should cause us to shudder . . . and to bow in utter amazement at the depths of divine love.

D. An Appeal to Obedience (2:12-18)

BEHIND THE TEXT

The last section ended in the cosmic heights of Christ's end-time glory. But Paul brings his readers quickly back down to earth. **Therefore** (*hōste*) signals Paul's application of the Christ hymn of 2:6-11 to the concrete realities of the Christian community in Philippi. In particular, the theme of obedience (v 12) echoes v 8, which describes the one who was "obedient unto death." What is more, Paul's own willingness to be "poured out" for the sake of the Philippians in v 17 recalls Jesus' act of self-emptying love (v 7).

Verses 12-18 also pick up on themes and language from 1:27-30, the paragraph that began Paul's extended appeal regarding how the Philippians should live. There are various links between the two paragraphs. These include:

- the need to live out the gospel the Philippians have received, whether Paul is present or absent (1:27; 2:12)
- the assurance that their salvation is from God (1:28; 2:13)
- the call to unity (1:27; 2:14; see 2:2-4), which will be visible to an unbelieving world (1:27-28; 2:15-16)
- the reality of suffering for the gospel, which binds Paul and his converts together (1:29-30; 2:17)

The paragraphs of 1:27-30 and 2:12-18 thus bracket (the literary device of *inclusio*) the whole section of exhortation, like two bookends. Our present passage (2:12-18) further unpacks Paul's broader concern in this part of the letter—what it means for the Philippians to live "in a manner worthy of the gospel of Christ" (1:27).

Philippians 2:12-18 is made up of three sentences (vv 12-13, 14-16, 17-18). The structure plays out as follows: First, there is a general call to continue in obedience and work out their salvation, by God's enabling power (vv 12-13).

Second, Paul applies this appeal specifically to the situation in Philippi. His friends must avoid internal dissension, so that the integrity of their character will offer a shining testimony to those outside the church (vv 14-16a).

Third, Paul shows the Philippians how their Christlike witness is tied up with his own sacrificial ministry of the gospel. He urges them to rejoice with him, as together they present to God a sacrificial offering of their faith (vv 16b-18).

Rhetorically, this paragraph appeals strongly to the audience's emotions (*pathos*). Language such as the address "my beloved" (v 12 NRSV), the phrase "with fear and trembling" (v 12), and Paul's hope that his investment in the Philippians would not be "in vain" (v 16 NRSV), all carry an emotional charge. The pathos reaches its peak when Paul raises the possibility of his own life being poured out as a martyr on their behalf (v 17; Witherington 1994, 70-71).

Paul also continues his persuasive strategy of offering the Philippians positive and negative models for how to live. He starts by recalling the experience of the Israelites in the wilderness as a pattern *not* to follow (vv 14-15). Then, once again, the apostle himself becomes a positive, Christlike example for his converts (v 17).

Two further features of this paragraph add to its persuasive power. First, Paul draws upon familiar images from his world in order to spotlight his servant ministry on behalf of the Philippians. He asks his readers to picture him as an athlete (v 16), as a tentmaker/laborer (v 16), and as a drink offering that is poured out on an animal sacrifice (v 17). Second, the passage is brimming with echoes of biblical language (see esp. vv 14-16), which provides scriptural support for Paul's appeal.

IN THE TEXT

1. Work Out Your Own Salvation by God's Enabling Power (2:12-13)

■ **12** Paul follows up the narrative about Christ in the previous paragraph with a fresh appeal to the Philippians. He addresses them as **my dear friends** (literally, "my beloved," NRSV; see 4:1). Although Paul uses this term of endearment elsewhere (e.g., 1 Cor 10:14; 15:58), it is especially appropriate here. It reflects Paul's deep love and affection for this church (see 1:7-8).

The main clause in v 12 is the command to **work out your salvation with fear and trembling.** First, however, Paul gives his friends "an affirming vote of confidence" (Bockmuehl 1998, 150): **as you have always obeyed** (see 2:8). Paul does not call them to something new but rather to continue and build upon the obedience they have already shown.

But obedience to whom? At times Paul can talk about Christians obeying his own word as an apostle (e.g., 2 Thess 3:14; Phlm 21; compare 2 Cor 2:9; 7:15; 10:5-6), and that could be implied here (see the NRSV, which adds "me" as the object of the verb "obeyed"). In the present context, however, it is God who is working on behalf of those who are obedient (Phil 2:9, 13). Thus it is more likely that the Philippians' obedience is directed ultimately to God (see v 8). In the end, there is no need to drive a wedge behind the two ideas, since Paul's authority and admonitions as an apostle originate from Christ.

Consistent with their past obedience, Paul urges the Philippians to **continue to work out [their] salvation.** This exhortation is far less problematic than is sometimes thought. It poses no challenge to Paul's teaching that people are saved by the grace of God and not by human effort (e.g., Rom 4:5; Eph 2:8; but see Rom 2:13-16). Already in Phil 1:28, Paul has assured the Philippians that their salvation is "by God." And in 2:13 he gives a counterbalance to v 12 by reminding them that they can only work out their salvation because God is already at work in them. This, then, is not a question of working *for* their salvation but working *out* their salvation. The Greek verb *katergazomai* here means "to bring about" or "to carry out" something. The present tense of the verb indicates a consistent and ongoing effort. But what would it mean for the Philippians to do this?

One common way of reading Paul's appeal has been to take it in a wholly corporate sense: the Philippians are to work at the spiritual "health" or "well-being" of the community (e.g., Hawthorne and Martin, 2004, 139-40; Fowl 2005, 121). This view has in its favor that it fits well with Paul's concern in the context for unity and humility within the church (see 2:1-8, 14). The sticking point is that it requires an unusual interpretation of the word **salvation** (*sotēria*). Here, as elsewhere in this letter, it is *eschatological* salvation that is primarily in view (1:19, 28; see also 1:6; 3:20-21).

At the same time, Paul's imperative has to do with more than *simply* individual believers working out their personal salvation. Both the verb "work out" and the pronoun "your own" (*heautōn*) are plural in Greek. Paul's exhortation is directed to the people of God. Likewise, the wider context speaks of the Philippians living out their shared life as "children of God" in the midst of a crooked world (2:14-15). Paul, therefore, is concerned that the Philippians live out the salvation they have received from God in their common life.

Of course, that assumes that the Philippians must individually respond to Paul's appeal (Fee 1995, 235). Ultimately their salvation will be realized personally on the day of Christ. Furthermore, Paul has already set forth the responsibility of "each" member of the community toward one another (2:4). There is surely no divorce here between individual and corporate salvation (see Bockmuehl 1998, 151-52). But the thrust of this passage is not on how individuals get saved. It is rather on how the Philippians' shared gift of salvation is presently "worked out" in the context of the Christian community and the pagan world (Fee 1995, 235).

"Working out your salvation," then, is the community's intentional response to God's gracious action in Christ on their behalf (see 2:6-11). This requires a daily life of disciplined obedience—what Paul elsewhere calls the "obedience of faith" (Rom 1:5; 16:26; Hooker 2000, 512). According to the grammatical structure of Phil 2:12 (*"just as* you have obeyed . . . *so now* work out"), working out their salvation is an ongoing expression of the Philippians' obedience (see Fee 1995, 235-36). Verse 13 makes clear that working out their salvation involves cooperating in God's ongoing work of moral transformation within them, both individually and as a community.

If we want to know the specific shape that living out their salvation should take, Paul spells it out in this letter. Among other things, it means they will

- work together as a unified body and adopt a common mind-set (vv 1-4)
- stop bickering and live as God's holy people in a dark world (vv 14-16)
- fervently practice a lifestyle of cruciform love (vv 5-11)

Paul qualifies this call in a surprising way: his readers are to work out their salvation **with fear and trembling.** The language is borrowed from the OT, where it often refers to the terror people experience in the face of God's mighty acts (e.g., Exod 15:16; Deut 2:25; 11:25; Ps 54:6; Isa 19:16; compare 1 Cor 2:3; 2 Cor 7:15). In this case, however, the idea is hardly that of dread. Nor does it imply an anxious fear or uncertainty concerning their salvation. Rather, these words point to the reverence or awe that is the appropriate attitude of those who are living out their salvation in the presence of the living God.

Reverence for God is necessary not only because God is in their midst, enabling their obedience (v 13), but also because God will hold the church accountable for their actions and relationships with others (Witherington 1994, 72). Paul reminds his friends in Philippi that Christian obedience is not something to be taken casually. It demands full seriousness and determined effort.

Furthermore, the Philippians' commitment to carry out their salvation should not hinge on whether or not Paul is among them in Philippi. Paul's **presence** (*Parousia*) may refer both to his being with them in the past as well as to a possible future visit. The Philippians should continue to practice an obedient lifestyle, not only when their apostle is on hand to instruct and encourage them, but especially (**now much more**) in his **absence** (see 1:27).

■ **13** Left unguarded, Paul's robust exhortation in v 12 could be misunderstood to undermine his theology of grace. So he immediately solders the Philippians' work to a theological anchor in v 13: **it is God who works in you.** In the context, the phrase **in you** (*en hymin*) probably means in the first place "in your shared life," as God's people (see 1:6; 2:5). Again, however, this presupposes God's saving work in the Philippians individually. Thus, the nuance of "within you" cannot be excluded.

Paul spotlights God's indispensable role in the outworking of their salvation in a number of ways (see Silva 2005, 122-23).

First, the causal word **for** provides a link between the imperative of v 12 and the assurance of v 13. The Philippians can only work out their salvation *because* God is already working in them (Deasley 2007, 197).

Second, in Greek, **God** (*theos*) is given special emphasis at the beginning of the sentence. This puts the accent squarely on divine, not human action (literally, **the one who works in you is <u>God</u>,** *theos . . . estin ho energōn en hymin*).

Third, it is God's power that "energizes" (*energeō*) the community's "working out" (*katergazomai*) of their salvation. There is a striking play on words here; both verbs are based on a common root, *ergon*, "work" (Wagner 2007, 259). This divine work does not mean that God is doing everything for them. Rather, it shows that God is "working mightily" to supply the needed empowering (Fee 1995, 237). God's work underlies our work.

Fourth, God is the one who enables Christians both **to will and to act.** Through the Holy Spirit, God energizes the human will to desire the will of God. Chrysostom was quite right that God does not deprive us of free will but rather increases our willing (*Hom. Phil.* 8.2.12-16).

Moreover, the Spirit of God gives us the ability not only to *want* to do what pleases God (see Rom 7:15-24) but also to do it (Rom 8:3-4). Wesley puts it this way: "God breathes into us every good desire, and brings every good desire to good effect" (1979, 6:508). Here both God's work and the Philippians' work are evident. The same verb, *energeō*, is used of God's powerful work and that of Christians. As Adam Clarke insists, the power to will and to do comes from God; the *use* of that power is our human response (n.d., 497).

Fifth, the *motive* for God's empowering work is **his good purpose** (literally, "for the sake of *the good pleasure*"; *hyper tēs eudokias*). God's saving activity in the lives of the Philippians is his great purpose and pleasure for his people (see 1:6). This implies that God is moved to work in us, not because of anything we do, but solely because of his undeserved grace and for his glory. Verse 13 begins and ends with God.

2. Live as God's Holy People in a Dark World (2:14-16)

■ **14** How does Paul's appeal for the outworking of the Philippians' salvation work out in practice? Paul gives the call to Christlike obedience a face with distinct features in vv 14-16.

The Philippians must **do everything without complaining or arguing** (v 14). **Everything** (*panta*) has a place of emphasis in the Greek text. **Do everything** is a comprehensive command, embracing all that is involved in the church working out its salvation in reverence and obedience to God (v 12; see 1 Cor 10:31; Col 3:17). On the other hand, the words **complaining** and **arguing** may speak directly to issues that are troubling the body of Christ in Philippi.

Complaining (*gongysmos*—a striking example of onomatopoeia, in which the form of the word imitates the sound of the "grumbling" it represents) is probably a deliberate echo of Israel's grumbling in the wilderness (e.g., Exod 15:24; 16:2, 7-9; Num 14:27-29; 17:5, 10). The same word in its verb form also appears in 1 Cor 10:10, where the Corinthians are warned not to grumble like the Israelites did in the desert. Israel's murmuring, however, was directed against Moses, and ultimately God. Does the analogy with the wilderness story imply that the Philippians were complaining against their local leaders, such as the overseers and deacons mentioned in 1:1 (so, e.g., Osiek 2000, 71; Silva 2005, 124)? Is Paul warning his readers that such griping against leaders is tantamount to rebellion against God?

There is little to support this suggestion in the rest of the letter. More likely, the reference to grumbling makes a more general point: when faced with hardships in the desert, Israel murmured, doubting that God was truly leading them. By analogy, the Philippians must avoid a similar attitude as they now encounter opposition and difficulties (see 1:27-30). For Paul's readers, like the Israelites before them, a pattern of grumbling betrays a failure to see that God is the one who is truly working among them (2:13; Fowl 2005, 123). A complaining spirit is also self-focused and would surely have negative effects on their community life (see vv 3-4).

The second term, **arguing** (*dialogismos*), probably connects this command more directly to the facts on the ground in Philippi. If so, it highlights the kind of internal bickering and quarreling that sows division in the community (see 4:2-3). Given the allusions to the Exodus story in this passage, it is quite possible that this word recalls Israel's disputes with Moses and God in the wilderness (e.g., Exod 17:1-7; Hooker 2000, 512-13). The Philippians can learn from the misadventures of their spiritual ancestors in the desert: practices such as grumbling and bickering point to an attitude of rebellion against God. Furthermore, they contradict the mind-set of selfless humility modeled by Jesus. They must therefore be deported from the life of obedience (Phil 2:1-11).

■ **15** The purpose (*hina*) of forsaking a lifestyle of grumbling and arguing is that **you may become blameless and pure, children of God without fault in a crooked and depraved generation** (v 15a). This is a clear echo of Deut 32:5 (see 32:10), which vividly pictures the unfaithfulness of Israel during their wilderness wanderings. There Israel is described as a people who, literally, "acted corruptly toward [God]; not his children, blameworthy (*mōmēta*), a crooked and depraved generation." Paul now flips this characterization on its head. The Philippians have *become* God's children. As a result, their lives must be *blameless* (*amōma*) *in the midst* of a crooked and depraved generation (Hooker 2000, 512). Ironically, the "twisted and perverse generation" no longer refers specifically to disobedient Israel but to the mainly pagan society of Philippi that opposes the gospel (see Phil 1:28).

Paul's point in borrowing language from Deuteronomy is not that the church has replaced Israel as God's children (against O'Brien 1991, 294; see Bockmuehl 1998, 156-57). Rather, Israel once again serves as a negative example of what the Philippians should stay clear of if they are going to be the true people of God (Fowl 2005, 124).

The positive alternative to all this is that they **become blameless and pure.** The term **blameless** (*amemptos*) designates conduct that is above accusation or blame, both in the eyes of God and others. In 1 Thess 3:13 and 5:23, it is connected to holiness and is a condition to being ready for the return of Christ.

The second adjective, **pure** (*akeraios*), was sometimes used of unadulterated wine—not diluted. In the NT, however, it speaks of a sincere and innocent character (see Matt 10:16; Rom 16:19).

What is more, as **children of God without fault,** Christians are to reflect their Father's own holy character (see Matt 5:45, 48). In the OT, sacrificial animals were described as "without blemish" (*amōmos*). But Paul transposes this idea into the moral realm to express the holiness that is God's purpose for the church (Col 1:22; Eph 1:4; 5:27). Together, "blameless," "pure," and "faultless" (in Greek all three words begin with the same sound, the "*a*-prefix," for rhetorical effect) describe the life of holy integrity God has called his people to live (compare Paul's similar language, "pure," *eilikrineis*, and "blameless," *aprospokoi*, in 1:10).

The result of the Philippians' blameless lifestyle is that they currently **shine** (present tense) **like stars in the universe**. The word translated **stars** (*phōstēres*) can refer to anything that gives light. But here it especially pertains to heavenly bodies ("luminaries"), such as the sun, moon, and stars. Paul's thought is not simply that Christians stand out against the darkness. In a positive sense, they also illuminate the world around them, as luminaries bring light to an otherwise dark sky.

This is a familiar theme in Scripture. For example, Israel, as God's Servant, is called to be a light to the Gentiles living in darkness (Isa 42:6-7; 49:6; see Acts 13:47). And Jesus pictures his disciples as the light of the world, who let their light shine before others (Matt 5:14-16; compare 1 Thess 5:5).

In particular, Paul's words recall the language of Dan 12:3. This passage says that, in the coming age of the resurrection, the wise, who lead many to righteousness, will shine like the lights of the heaven. Here Paul applies Daniel's future vision to the present mission of the church in the world. The unity and integrity of God's people in Philippi will enable them to have a light-bearing witness among their pagan contemporaries, even as they dispel the darkness around them.

■ **16** The beginning of v 16 expresses *how* the audience will shine in a dark world: **as you hold out the word of life**. The NIV rightly takes this phrase with v 15 rather than with what follows in v 16 (as, e.g., the NRSV).

The meaning of this phrase is sharply contested. Does the verb *epechō* mean to "hold out/forth" the word in an evangelistic sense, as in the NIV, or to "hold fast" the word of life (e.g., NRSV, NASB)? There are good arguments on both sides. The majority of recent commentators favor the second option, given the theme of steadfastness in the face of adversity in the letter (see Poythress 2002). This reading also fits with Paul's desire that his work in Philippi will not be in vain on the Day of Judgment (v 16).

Nevertheless, the translation "hold forth" is preferable, for the following reasons:

- The evangelistic understanding of "offering" the word to others fits well with what Paul has just said about the Philippians shining as lights in the world (v 15).
- Daniel 12:3, which v 15 echoes, also has a missional thrust; it speaks of "those who lead many to righteousness."
- The distinctive phrase "word of life" refers to the gospel message that brings life to other people.
- "Hold forth" is the most basic sense of the word *epechō* in ancient

Greek literature (see Ware 2005, 256-70; for this reading, see most older commentators, e.g., Calvin, Lightfoot, Vincent, and recently Bruce, Marshall, and Thurston).

Verses 14-16a, then, call the church to engage in God's reconciling mission. If God's people in Philippi avoid internal grumblings and wranglings and conduct themselves in a way that is above reproach, their lives will shine like bright lights in a dark world. In so doing they will hold out to their pagan neighbors the life-giving gospel, not only by the words they speak, but also through the lives they live.

Did the Philippians *Hear* the Old Testament?

Philippians does not contain a single explicit OT quotation. Nevertheless, there are numerous allusions to OT texts, especially in 2:14-16 (see also Phil 1:19/Job 13:16; Phil 2:10-11/Isa 45:23; Silva 1993, 634-35). This is not surprising, given that Paul's thought is steeped in the OT. But can we expect the Philippians, coming out of a pagan background, to have been tuned in to such echoes from the Greek Bible?

This is not an easy question to answer with confidence. Certainly, there is no reason to assume that the Philippians would have been familiar with the OT prior to their coming to Christ. Nor would the majority of Christians in Philippi have been able to read the OT privately. This was not least because levels of literacy in the ancient world were low (see Fowl 2005, 125). At the same time, we can surmise that the Philippians, living in a largely oral culture, would have heard the Scriptures read again and again as part of their instruction in the Christian way. What is more, Paul's letter would surely have been read aloud to the church—not just once, but on repeated occasions. Conceivably, those who delivered the letter would have highlighted and explained the OT allusions for the faithful.

It is likely, then, that the Philippians' ears would have been trained over a period of time to hear Paul's allusions to Scripture. As Fowl observes, helping the Christian community to learn to recognize and reflect on such allusions to the OT within the NT remains a vital task of the church's discipleship ministry today (2005, 126).

In v 16*b* Paul gives the Philippians a further incentive for Christian obedience: if they maintain a blameless character and a faithful witness, he will be able to **boast** on their behalf **on the day of Christ.** Here Paul's attention suddenly shifts from how the Philippians must work out their salvation to his own stake in that process. Paul's "boasting" (*kauchēma*) in the Philippians parallels their own boasting on his behalf in 1:26. In both cases, however, the focus is squarely on what God has done in Christ (Fowl 2005, 127; see the comments on 1:26 above). Paul does not boast of his own ministry or achievements but in what Christ has done through him in the lives of his converts (see Rom 15:17-18; 1 Cor 15:10).

Paul's boasting has as its goal the coming day of final assessment, the **day of Christ** (see 1:6, 10). Then the Philippians will become his "crown of boasting" (1 Thess 2:19 NRSV), because their lives will give evidence that he **did not run or labor for nothing**. "Running" and "laboring" are two of Paul's classic images for his missionary work. The first, taken from the athletic games, pictures Paul's ministry as a race. The end-time reward awaits those who finish the contest (see 1 Cor 9:24-27; Gal 2:2; Phil 3:13-14; 2 Tim 4:7-8).

Paul's ministry also involves hard labor, as a tentmaker toils in the shop (see, e.g., 1 Cor 4:12; 15:10; Gal 4:11; Col 1:29; Fee 1995, 250). The apostle's concern here is that on the Day of Judgment, his missionary efforts will not prove to be *in vain* (see Gal 2:2; 1 Thess 3:5). Paul's language seems to recall Isa 49:4, where the Servant of the Lord says, "I have labored in vain, I have spent my strength for nothing and vanity" (NRSV). Clearly, Paul understands that the ultimate effectiveness of his ministry depends on the character and obedience of the Christian communities God has placed in his care.

3. Share in Paul's Sacrificial Ministry (2:17-18)

■ **17** The hope that Paul will be able to take satisfaction in the faithfulness of his readers on the final day apparently leads him to reflect once again on his own situation. He finds himself a prisoner, with execution a hovering possibility (see 1:12-26). Accordingly, in 2:17 he switches to a sacrificial metaphor. He would gladly pour himself out, even to the point of martyrdom, in order to make the Philippians' service acceptable to God.

Paul begins this thought with a conditional ("if") clause: **but even if I am being poured out like a drink offering on the sacrifice and service coming from your faith**. Unlike today's Western societies (but similar to many majority-world contexts), religious sacrifices were commonly practiced throughout the Roman world. We probably do not need to choose between a Jewish or pagan background for this image. Nevertheless, Paul's allusions to Scripture throughout 2:14-18 suggest that the OT sacrificial system may have been foremost in his mind.

Animal sacrifices were often accompanied by a **drink offering** of wine or oil, which was poured on top of the sacrifice or at the foot of the altar (e.g., Exod 29:38-41; Num 15:1-10; 28:1-15). In this case, Paul himself is the secondary drink offering that is being poured out on the main sacrifice of the Philippians' faith.

Is Paul talking about his impending martyrdom (so early church fathers and most modern commentators)? Or is this simply a general reference to his sufferings as an apostle (e.g., Fee 1995, 252-54; Hawthorne and Martin 2004, 148-49)? The answer seems to be both/and, rather than either/or.

On the one hand, nothing in the context *requires* that this is a reference to Paul's death. The verb **I am being poured out** (*spendomai*) does not signify the pouring out of blood or a *literal* death (see Hawthorne and Martin 2004, 149). Moreover, the present tense of the verb suggests that Paul is thinking about his ongoing ministry, not some future martyrdom.

On the other hand, the conditional **even if** implies that Paul is contemplating something he has not yet experienced, but is still a possibility. In two later settings (2 Tim 4:6 and Ign. *Rom.* 2.2) the language of **being poured out like a drink offering** is a reference to death.

What, then, should we make of Paul's hope that he will be able to visit the Philippians, which appears only a few verses later (Phil 2:24)? In the previous verse, Paul makes his release conditional on "how things go with me" (v 23). What is more, he has already mentioned the possibility of death in 1:20-26. The potential of martyrdom, therefore, seems to be on Paul's radar screen.

The focus of this vivid metaphor, however, is not on martyrdom itself. Paul is willing to be poured out in order to complete the sacrifice of his friends at Philippi, whatever that might involve. Should it mean ongoing hard labor as a missionary, should it lead to further imprisonment and suffering, **even if** it should cost him his life, he would offer himself with joy. He is ready "most gladly [to] spend and be spent" (2 Cor 12:15 NRSV) for the sake of his converts. Paul once again models the life of self-giving love (Phil 2:7), even as he follows the one who was "obedient to death—even death on a cross!" (v 8).

In the metaphor, Paul, as the libation, is being poured out on the more substantial sacrifice. Here the Philippians are pictured as priests offering their own **sacrifice** (*thysia*, see 4:18; Rom 12:1) **and service** (*leitourgia*, "priestly service," from which the word "liturgy" comes; see Phil 2:30) to God (Bockmuehl 1998, 161).

But what is the Philippians' sacrifice? Is their **faith** itself the offering? Or is it something that is *the result of* their faith? In the context, it seems best to take the sacrifice as a service that *arises from* faith (**coming from your faith**), not as faith itself (Hooker 2000, 514; Fee 1995, 254-55). **Faith** (*pisteōs*), in this case, probably refers to the Philippians' utter, trusting reliance on God (see comments on 3:9). Their sacrifice, then, flows out of that faith.

Later in the letter, Paul applies the language of **sacrifice** to the Philippians' gift of money to him (4:18; see 2:30). But given Paul's broad use of sacrificial imagery elsewhere (e.g., Rom 12:1; 15:16; Eph 5:1) there is no need to limit the Philippians' sacrifice to financial generosity alone (Bockmuehl 1998, 161-62; against, e.g., Hooker 2000, 514). Rather, it represents their whole life of obedience, humility, holiness, and witness that is the fruit of faith. In Romans Paul calls this the "obedience of faith" (Rom 1:5; 16:26).

Paul, then, sees his ministry as the completing capstone to the Philippians' life of obedience, even if that should demand the sacrifice of his own life. This "even if," however, is not a reason for sorrow, but joy: **I am glad and rejoice with all of you** (Phil 2:17b). Why? Surely because Paul's poured-out life helps to bring about the acceptable sacrifice that the Philippians offer. The faith and obedient service of the church is more important than the comfort—even the life—of the missionary.

■ **18** At the same time, joy is a two-way street. Paul exhorts his converts to **be glad and rejoice with me** (v 18). The use of the twin verbs "rejoice" (*chairō*) and "co-rejoice" (*sygchairō*) in v 17b and again in v 18 makes a point with an exclamation mark. Just as the Philippians are partners with him in the gospel (1:5) and in suffering for Christ (1:29-30), he urges them to also become partners in joy (see 1:25-26; 3:1; 4:4).

Certainly, this suggests that Paul's friends should rejoice in the midst of their own suffering, as Paul has already modeled before them (1:18). But it does more. In particular, it calls them to be joyful because of the apostle's faithful service, even if Christ should be exalted through Paul's death, rather than his life (v 20). As Bockmuehl notes, vv 17b-18 beautifully illustrate Bengel's summary of the whole letter: "I rejoice; you, too, rejoice!" (*gaude, gaudete;* Bockmuehl 1998, 162).

FROM THE TEXT

1. *Working out what God works in.* Verses 12 and 13 present us with a paradox. Do we work out our salvation or is it wholly the work of God? Because of the paradoxical way in which these ideas are stated, well-meaning Christians throughout the church's history have overemphasized one side or the other. Putting too much stress on v 12 shrivels God's role in our salvation. This error is particularly associated with the British monk Pelagius (fourth and early fifth centuries), who believed that people could "work *for*" their salvation. It is the result, taught Pelagius, of exercising our free will and living righteously.

Some Christians today live under the misconception that once they have received salvation, whether or not they keep it depends entirely on their own moral determination to do what is right. Or we might give lip service to God's role, but then act as if everything depended on our own abilities and efforts.

On the other hand, if the pendulum swings too far in the direction of v 13, we can so emphasize God's work in us "to will and to do" that we expect God to do everything. For example, the popular slogan "let go and let God" can be misunderstood to mean that we can put our lives on automatic pilot and passively expect God to carry us along.

It is crucial that we hold up *both* sides of the paradox. Paul gives us a glorious tension in vv 12 and 13. We must "work out our own salvation" with all seriousness and spiritual commitment precisely because God is already at work in us. He is enabling us through the Spirit's power to desire and do what pleases him. Historically, the Wesleyan-Arminian theological tradition has affirmed "responsible grace" (see Maddox 1994). This involves *both* God's primary work in initiating and energizing our salvation *and* our grace-enabled cooperation in the outworking of that salvation. John Wesley's memorable summary of the relationship between these verses in his classic sermon "Working Out Our Own Salvation" can hardly be improved upon:

God works; therefore you *can* work. . . .

God works; therefore you *must* work. (Wesley 1979, 6:511; on the implications of this passage, see Wagner 2007, 257-74)

We need to make two additional points here. First, this all means that Paul's understanding of salvation is more comprehensive than we often recognize. In a biblical sense, salvation is never limited to a past event of conversion ("When were you saved?"), or even to a present experience ("Are you saved?" see Silva 2005, 121). Rather, Paul can talk about salvation in three tenses: past ("you have been saved"—Rom 8:24; Eph 2:5, 8; 2 Tim 1:9; Titus 3:5), present ("you are being saved"—1 Cor 1:18; 15:2; 2 Cor 2:15), and future ("you will be saved"—Rom 5:9-10; 10:9; 13:11; 1 Cor 3:15; 5:5; 2 Tim 4:18).

But for Paul the emphasis is firmly on the future. Salvation in its fullness will come on the day of Christ, in relation to God's ultimate renewing and redeeming purpose for the whole world (see Phil 1:6; 3:20-21; Rom 8:18-25). And if salvation is a comprehensive process that will not be consummated until the final day, then working it out will involve living obediently and letting God do his work of moral transformation in light of that coming event. Similarly, 2 Pet 1:10-11 urges Christians: "Be all the more eager to make your calling and election sure. For if you do these things, you will never fall, and you will receive a rich welcome into the eternal kingdom of our Lord and Savior Jesus Christ."

Second, in cultures used to thinking strictly in terms of individual salvation based on personal decisions, it is easy to miss Paul's emphasis on the *church* working out its salvation in its shared life. There is both an individual and a corporate dimension to God's saving work. Paul would tell us that our personal salvation isn't worth much unless it is "worked out" in terms of promoting Christian unity, showing unselfish love toward others, and being a people of radical integrity within a crooked world. Salvation involves God's ongoing work of conforming his church to the pattern of Christ.

2. *Holiness and mission.* This passage makes a direct connection between the church's mission and its character as the holy people of God. Paul spotlights two things that are essential for the church to fulfill its evangelistic calling in the world.

The first is *unity.* A church that lives its communal life without "complaining and arguing" is a church that will shine like a beacon in the darkness. People who are searching for authentic, caring relationships will "see" the gospel being lived out. Jesus, as well, saw the church's unity as a testimony to those outside: "I pray . . . that all of them may be one, Father, just as you are in me and I am in you. May they also be in us so that the world may believe that you have sent me. . . . May they be brought to complete unity to let the world know that you sent me and have loved them even as you have loved me" (John 17:20-21, 23).

Unfortunately, just the opposite is too often the case. Divisions in the Christian community become a stumbling block to the church fulfilling its reconciling mission. The world watches, Christians bicker, the flame of witness smolders.

Second, Paul latches the church's witness in the world to its *moral integrity*. Our embodied holiness will be like a light-ray piercing a dark cavern. This testimony has a dual nature. On the one hand, the church's character must be different from that of the surrounding culture. It must stand over against the lifestyle of a twisted world. Too often, the church's light doesn't shine because it is indistinguishable from the darkness. We have no possibility of transforming the culture if we are too much like it. When the church *becomes* God's holy church, it can expose the surrounding darkness by its very difference.

On the other hand, a church that lives out its common life in blamelessness and integrity will positively give light to the world. Paul never imagines the church as a holy enclave, going on permanent retreat from the wicked world around it. Rather, the light shines "in the midst" of a bent and debased generation. We are reminded of Jesus' call for his disciples to be the "salt of the earth" (Matt 5:13) and the "light of the world" (v 14). A church that embodies the holy character of Christ will have a transforming influence on its world.

Christian families, for example, can model servanthood and fidelity in societies where families are too often characterized by conflict, abuse, and disposable relationships. Christian leaders who demonstrate integrity in speech, finances, and sexuality will provide an alternative to many cultural patterns of leadership. When the church is a distinctive community, it will both challenge the values of the culture and at the same time light a path to its Lord.

This does not downplay the need for a verbal testimony to the "word of life." But it does recognize that if our witness is not embodied, it will be both unconvincing and incomplete. As Jesus put it, "Let your light shine before others, that they may see your good deeds and glorify your Father in heaven" (Matt 5:16 TNIV).

3. Seeing ourselves in Israel's story. Using language from the OT, Paul draws an analogy between the experience of Israel in the wilderness and the present situation of the church in Philippi. Paul invites his Gentile readers to find themselves in Israel's story, for it is their story, as well. And they must allow that story to reshape their attitudes and behavior.

This speaks to the church today. We, too, must learn to see the continuity between Israel's sojourn in the desert and our pilgrimage as the people of God. We must allow that vision to defy our patterns of complaining and compromising with a crooked world. Part of the task of biblical preaching is to help congregations find themselves in the biblical narratives of Israel and the early church. Such a practice goes beyond simply "applying" a text as an outsider. Rather, we must learn to enter into the biblical story in such a way that God reshapes our stories and transforms our thinking and living (Hays 1997b, 173).

4. *Joy in the midst of suffering.* The final word in this passage, as well as Paul's whole appeal to gospel-worthy living (1:27—2:18), is a word of *joy*. As in 1:12-18, this is not joy *because* of suffering, or even *in spite* of suffering, but joy *in the midst* of suffering. It is an attitude of rejoicing "even if" (v 17). *Even if* Paul's labor for Christ leads to his death, he can rejoice.

This is oceans apart from superficial smiles or a trumped up triumphalism that fails to take suffering seriously. Joy, unlike circumstantial feelings of pleasure or happiness, is profoundly theological. It "has nothing to do with circumstances, but everything to do with one's place in Christ" (Fee 1995, 257). Joy is a pervasive mind-set that flows out of our relationship to Christ and to others in Christ. It accompanies lives and communities that are devoted to embodying and advancing the gospel of Christ—"even if" that involves adversity and affliction. This is why Paul can end this passage with an imperative: "Rejoice"! Joy is an intentional attitude, rooted in the knowledge that the sovereign God is at work in all of the contingencies of our lives.

IV. TWO CHRISTLIKE EXAMPLES: PHILIPPIANS 2:19-30

BEHIND THE TEXT

Paul follows his exhortations to unity and steadfast obedience in 1:27—2:18 with a much more practical section in 2:19-30. On the surface, it is about travel plans. Paul intends to send two of his coworkers, Timothy (vv 19-24) and Epaphroditus (vv 25-30), to the church in Philippi. He hopes to follow them in his own anticipated visit (v 24).

Paul often reserves news about his own travel designs and the movements of his companions for the end of his letters (see Rom 15:22-29; 1 Cor 16:1-12; Col 4:7-17). It might seem a bit odd, then, to find such relatively mundane material right in the middle of Philippians. The apostle, however, does not *always* hold discussions of travel plans until the end. At times he weaves them into the main body of his letters, when they advance his current argument (e.g., 1 Cor 4:17-21; 2 Cor 8:16-23; 1 Thess 2:17—3:6). That seems to be precisely what is happening here.

This section fits well into the flow of the letter. It resumes Paul's "narrative" of his own situation ("my affairs," 1:12; 2:23) and the progress of the gospel in Philippi, from 1:12-26. Closer to hand, it picks up on the language and themes of 2:1-18. Paul's reference, for example, to everyone seeking their own interests (v 21) echoes his exhortation in v 4 not to seek one's own interests but rather the interests of others. Timothy's faithfulness to serve (*douleō*) with Paul in the work of the gospel parallels the actions of Christ, who took the form of a servant (*doulos*). And Epaphroditus's act of risking himself and coming near to death (*mechri thanatou*, v 30) reminds us of Christ's obedience "unto death" (*mechri thanatou*; v 8 KJV) on the cross. Such interlocking language suggests that Paul is deliberately building on the theme of unselfish humility that we encountered earlier in the chapter (Culpepper 1980, 350).

Paul's reason, then, for including vv 19-30 at this point in the letter is more than simply to inform the Philippians about travel itineraries and his hopes for the church. Here information serves a higher aim. Paul holds up his coworkers Timothy and Epaphroditus as further examples of the kinds of attitudes he has been promoting throughout 1:27—2:18. These are lives

- whose conduct is worthy of the gospel (1:27)
- that are steadfast in their service to Christ, whatever the cost (1:28-30)
- that reflect the same unselfish mind-set as Christ himself (2:3-9)
- that are lived blamelessly in obedience to Christ (2:12-18)

As such, this passage shares much in common with the "letters of commendation" that we find in Paul's writings (e.g., Rom 16:1-2; 1 Cor 16:15-18; 2 Cor 8:16-24) and elsewhere in the ancient world. Paul commends these two brothers to the Philippians as worthy examples to follow. They are concrete embodiments of the narrative of Christ (Phil 2:6-11; Fowl 2005, 131).

Furthermore, this section has a transitional role in the letter. Not only do Timothy and Epaphroditus put "flesh and blood" (Thurston 2005, 117) on the mind-set of Christ described in 2:1-11, but they also provide a positive contrast to the negative examples in ch 3.

From a rhetorical standpoint, the passage has been considered either a "digression" in Paul's argument (Watson 1988, 71-72) or as the second development of the appeal to unity and humility that began with the example of Christ in 2:1-18 (Witherington 1994, 75; Williams 2002, 141). The latter seems closer to the mark. As always, however, we need to be careful not to jam Paul into rhetorical pigeonholes.

The passage divides readily into two parts:

The first (vv 19-24) explains Paul's hope to send Timothy to them soon, but not immediately. The phrases "I hope . . . to send" and "in the Lord" in v 19 are repeated in vv 23 and 24. This repetition brackets commendation of Timothy (vv 20-22) with a literary inclusion.

The second paragraph (vv 25-30) is more detailed. It relates Paul's intention to send back Epaphroditus as a worthy emissary who has risked his life on their behalf. There is a perceptible change in tone between the two paragraphs. Paul says "I hope" to send Timothy (vv 19, 23), but he finds it "necessary" (v 25) and is "all the more eager" (v 28) to insure the return of Epaphroditus (Deasley 2005, 28). Paul's heightened sense of urgency regarding Epaphroditus flows, as we will see, out of the particular circumstances that prompt the unexpected return of the Philippians' messenger.

IN THE TEXT

A. Timothy (2:19-24)

■ **19** The section begins with Paul's **hope . . . to send Timothy,** who is with him as he writes the letter (v 19). Paul grounds this hope **in the Lord,** a phrase that occurs three times in these twelve verses (vv 19, 24, 29). This implies that the **Lord Jesus** is the one who both directs these plans and will enable their fulfillment (Bockmuehl 1998, 164-65). Everything Paul does, he does in the sphere of his relationship with Christ.

That Paul wants to send Timothy **soon** (*tacheōs*) communicates some measure of urgency. At the same time, it makes clear that Timothy will not be the bearer of the letter. Timothy will be free to travel as soon as Paul gets further news about the outcome of his own situation (v 23).

Timothy is Paul's most trusted ministry partner and undoubtedly the one closest to his heart. According to Acts, Timothy hailed from the city of Lystra in Asia Minor. He was the son of a Jewish Christian mother and a Greek father. Joining Paul's ministry team after Paul had separated from Barnabas, Timothy was entrusted with a number of sensitive and difficult missions in places like Corinth (1 Cor 4:17; 16:10), Thessalonica (1 Thess 3:2, 6; see Acts 17:14; 19:22), and, according to the Pastoral Letters, Ephesus (1 Tim 1:3).

Given this colleague's experience and long-standing relationship with the church at Philippi (Acts 16:1, 11-13), it is hardly surprising that Paul proposes to dispatch Timothy as his representative. Timothy can be trusted to convey Paul's thoughts accurately and to provide a reliable report from the congregation (Fowl 2005, 132). Here the particular purpose (or *result*; *hina*) of Timothy's visit is that Paul will be **cheered** by good news about the Philippians (literally, "your affairs," *ta peri hymōn*). Fee makes the helpful point that in light of the occurrence of the same phrase in 1:27, Paul's interest in the Philippians' "affairs" is not simply with their general circumstances. He especially anticipates a positive report about the kind of "affairs" addressed in 1:27—2:18; that is, with matters like their unity and fidelity to the gospel in the face of adversity (1995, 265). That Paul will also (*kagō*) be encouraged when Timothy reports back to him suggests that he expects the Philippians to be cheered by news of his own circumstances, as well (see v 23).

■ **20** Paul's letter of commendation for Timothy follows in vv 20-22. Timothy is uniquely suited for his task for three reasons.

First, Timothy **genuinely cares** for the Philippians' **welfare** (literally, "your affairs," v 20). The verb **cares** (*merimnēsei*) is used in the negative sense of "worrying" in 4:6. Here, however, it expresses a positive, heartfelt concern for others.

In that way, Timothy is *like-minded* with Paul. At least that seems to be the best way to take the rare term *isopsychos* (literally, "having one soul"; NIV: **I have no one else like** him, i.e., *Timothy* [emphasis added]). Although this word occurs only here in the NT, the idea of friends sharing the same soul is commonplace in Greco-Roman descriptions of friendship (e.g., Aristotle, *Eth. Nic.* 9.8.2). Earlier Paul used a similar word when he called the Philippians to be "together in soul" (*sympsychoi*) in their common life (2:2; see 1:27). Now he says that Timothy, like none other, shares his own deep-seated love and concern for these converts. Timothy is truly "a man after Paul's own heart" (Clarke n.d., 498).

■ **21** Second, Timothy **looks out** for the interests **of Jesus Christ**, not for **his own interests** (v 21). This verse explains why Paul has no one else of like mind in caring for the Philippians (v 20). Timothy's unselfish concern is contrasted with all those (**everyone**) who seek after "their own thing" (*ta heautōn*; Thurston 2005, 101).

To whom does the word **everyone** refer? Every believer in Rome? All of Paul's coworkers who might have been available for a trip to Philippi (so most commentators)?

More likely, there is more than a dash of hyperbole in Paul's global language. Surely **everyone** would have included self-seeking people in Rome, like those already mentioned in 1:15-17. Yet 2:21 also takes us back to the contrast in vv 3-4 between those who look out for their own interests and those who look to the interests of others. Paul is implicitly setting Timothy apart from all those in Rome—or in Philippi—whose attitudes are self-serving (Fee 1995, 268; Marshall 1991, 69). In contrast, Timothy models for the Philippians an others-oriented mind-set, like that of Christ himself (vv 6-8).

■ **22** Third, Paul can commend and send Timothy because he **has proved himself** to be a faithful servant in **the work of the gospel** (v 22). Timothy's worth is well-known to the Philippians. Acts 16 recounts that he was at Paul's side when the church in Philippi was planted.

The term ***proven character*** (*dokimē*) refers to something that has been tested and approved as genuine. **As a son with his father,** Timothy has labored with Paul. Here the father-child image suggests not only a relationship of close, personal affection (see 1 Cor 4:17; 1 Tim 1:2; 2 Tim 1:2) but especially the role of a father teaching his son a trade (Fowl 2005, 134). The focus is not on Timothy serving Paul. Rather it is on their shared service (**with me**) in the cause **of the gospel**. Timothy has, literally, ***worked as a slave*** (*edouleusen*). This verb reminds us that Paul and Timothy are **slaves of Christ Jesus** (1:1). In particular, they pattern themselves after the one who became a slave for others (2:7).

In one sense, Paul's commendation of Timothy is hardly necessary. The Philippians are already well aware of Timothy's worth (v 22). This "character reference," then, seems to be primarily motivated by Paul's desire to give the Philippians an explicit example of someone who does not seek his own interests. Timothy models a Christlike love for others in an exemplary way.

■ **23** Paul resumes the concern of v 19, his hope to send Timothy to Philippi. Now, however, we learn why it will be "soon" (v 24), rather than right away. First, Paul must **see how things go** in his own situation (**with me**). This is undoubtedly a reference to when Paul can bring news about the outcome of his imprisonment, along with further instructions to the church.

■ **24** Paul views Timothy's visit as a prelude to his own. Paul's statement that he is **confident** that he himself **will come soon** echoes a similar expectation in 1:25. That persuasion, like his "hope" to send Timothy in v 19, is grounded **in the Lord** and God's ability to make it possible. At the same time, all things, including plans for what lies ahead, are subject to the will of the Lord; Paul's future is in the hands of God.

B. Epaphroditus (2:25-30)

■ **25-26** As we noted above, Paul's second letter of commendation has a more urgent tone than the first. Paul thinks it **necessary** (*anagkaion*, emphasized in Greek) to send Epaphroditus to the Philippians right away. But why is it *necessary*?

The answer lies in the situation behind Paul's statements in vv 26 and 28. We know that Epaphroditus was sent as a representative of the church in Philippi to minister to Paul's need. This help came both in terms of financial support (4:18) and presumably Epaphroditus's own companionship and practical service (2:25). Either *en route* or after he arrived, however, Epaphroditus contracted a life-threatening illness (vv 27, 30). Somehow the Philippians got wind of this crisis and became deeply concerned over the welfare of their beloved emissary. This, in turn, caused Epaphroditus to long to be reunited with the Christian community at home (v 26). His yearning ran deeper than simply a bad case of homesickness (against Barth 1962, 87-88; Hawthorne and Martin 2004, 164). Paul uses the same verb (*epipotheō*) to describe his own heartfelt "longing" for his dear friends in Philippi (1:8).

What is more, Epaphroditus became **distressed**, not due to his own serious sickness, but because of the anxiety *the Philippians* had suffered over it (2:26). **Distressed** (*adēmonōn*) is a word of intense emotion. Elsewhere it describes Jesus' anguish of spirit in the Garden of Gethsemane (Matt 26:37; Mark 14:33). In order to relieve both the Philippians' anxiety and that of his companion, Paul considered it **necessary** to release Epaphroditus from his care-giving mission and to send him home earlier than originally planned. (For the question of how much time would be required for the travel implied in this paragraph, as well as its bearing on the letter's origin, see the Introduction.)

At the same time, Paul commends Epaphroditus to the church with a profusion of praise. The apostle deploys no less than five terms in v 25 to express his positive regard for this valuable team member in the work of the gospel. The first three, all linked by the pronoun **my** (*mou*), picture the close relationship between Epaphroditus and Paul.

Brother can sometimes refer to all believers. But in this context, **my brother** indicates Paul's warm affection for Epaphroditus.

Paul regularly uses the term **fellow worker** (*synergon*) to describe those who have served alongside him in the work of the gospel (e.g., Phil 4:3; 2 Cor 8:23; 1 Thess 3:2).

The military metaphor, **my . . . fellow soldier,** is less common (Phlm 2; see 1 Tim 1:18; 2 Tim 2:3). It suggests a shared struggle in the midst of adversity and conflict. Perhaps it is no coincidence that Paul would invoke such an image for Christian service when writing to a Roman military colony such as Philippi (see Fowl 2005, 135). As Bonnie B. Thurston observes, the use of such terms for one of Paul's "teammates" suggests, not a hierarchy, but a mutually shared ministry in the cause of the gospel (2005, 103).

The final two terms in v 25 spotlight Epaphroditus's relationship to the Philippian church. The pronoun **your** (*hymōn*) is emphasized in the original text. **Messenger** is a translation of a Greek word generally rendered "apostle" (*apostolos*). Here it is used in a nontechnical sense of someone who is sent by others to fulfill a given task; in other words, an appointed envoy.

The specific role Epaphroditus has been commissioned to perform is to be a **minister** to Paul's need. The NIV's **to take care of my needs** does less than full justice to the Greek term **minister** (*leitourgos*). This word conveys the idea of someone who discharges a "priestly service." The related term, *leitourgia* (vv 17 and 30), denotes a sacred ministry or service. Paul uses these terms elsewhere to describe his own priestly ministry of declaring the gospel to the Gentiles (Rom 15:16). In the present context, he pictures Epaphroditus's ministry to him as a priestly offering to God (Hooker 2000, 520).

Epaphroditus's service to Paul surely involved delivering the financial gift from the church at Philippi (see 4:18). But it probably also included various kinds of personal and material help given during Paul's imprisonment. Such a ministry was vital, since Roman prisoners like Paul were dependent on family or friends to provide for their basic necessities (Rapske 1994, 426). Epaphroditus's sacrificial service to Paul shows that he, like Timothy, is someone who is willing to put the needs of others ahead of his own (Fowl 2005, 136).

■ **27** Verse 27 emphasizes (*for* **indeed**) the severity of Epaphroditus's illness. We can only speculate about the specific nature of the sickness. Whatever it entailed, the Philippians' messenger was at death's door. But this dire state of affairs was transformed when **God** extended his **mercy,** not only to Epaphroditus, but also to Paul.

Divine mercy for Epaphroditus meant physical recovery, most likely through God's healing intervention (Fee 1995, 279; Thurston 2005, 103). That same mercy spared Paul **sorrow upon sorrow.** Epaphroditus's narrow escape from death saved Paul from the pain of bereavement over a beloved "fellow soldier" on top of his other sufferings and disappointments. Bockmuehl is surely right that it is no contradiction to consider dying for the sake of the gospel to be "gain" (1:21), while at the same time seeing recovery from mortal illness as an expression of divine grace (1998, 172).

■ **28** Since Epaphroditus has been restored to health, Paul is **all the more eager to send him** to the Philippians—sooner than expected. His arrival will relieve the church's anxiety over the welfare of their emissary and so enable them to *rejoice again.* This reading takes "again" (*palin*) with the verb "rejoice," which follows it, rather than with the participle "seeing," which precedes it (vs. the NIV; see Fee 1995, 280-81).

Epaphroditus's early exit, however, will not only renew *the Philippians'* joy but also diminish *Paul's* **sorrow***.* The word translated **anxiety** (*alypoteros*) in the NIV is based on the noun "sorrow" (*lypē*) that appears in v 27.

Why would Epaphroditus's departure alleviate Paul's grief and not *increase* it? Hooker correctly notes that encouragement is tied to the shared experience of those who are "in Christ" (2000, 520). The Philippians' joy at being reunited with Epaphroditus will become Paul's joy as well. Their release from anxiety will mean the lessening of Paul's own sorrow.

■ **29** It follows "then" (NRSV) that the Philippians should **welcome** Epaphroditus **with great joy** and give him the **honor** he deserves (v 29). But why does Paul feel the need to urge Epaphroditus's home church to welcome and honor him? Does this hint at a strain in the relationship? Is Paul concerned that Epaphroditus has some critics among the Philippians who might interpret his early return as a failure to accomplish his mission? (so, e.g., Silva 2005, 139; Marshall 1991, 70-71). This is possible, but unlikely.

There is no compelling reason to read between the lines of Paul's praise for Epaphroditus and assume that his agenda is to correct a specific problem. Appeals to receive and esteem God's servants are not unusual in Paul's letters (e.g., Rom 16:1-2; 1 Cor 16:15-18; 2 Cor 8:24), and such exhortations are a standard feature of ancient letters of commendation (Fee 1995, 281). Consequently, the Philippians are to welcome Epaphroditus **in the Lord** (see Phil 2:19, 24); that is, in the spirit of the Lord Jesus shown in the story of Christ (vv 6-11; Hawthorne and Martin 2004, 166). The present tense of the verb "to welcome" (*prosdechesthe*) shows that Paul is not just thinking of the Philippians' initial reception of Epaphroditus; they are to give him an *ongoing* welcome (Bockmuehl 1998, 174).

Furthermore, Paul exhorts the Christian community to **hold such people in honor** (*entimous*). In the first-century world, **honor** was a foundational cultural value. People (esp. those with considerable status) were constantly competing for public recognition and praise. But the typical reasons for receiving honor in the eyes of others—noble birth, large public benefactions, personal patronage, athletic or military triumphs—are *not* why ministers like Epaphroditus deserve esteem. Instead, the church should recognize those who follow Christ on a path of *downward* mobility (vv 6-8; on honor and shame in the first-century Mediterranean world and the NT, see deSilva 2000, 17-119).

Epaphroditus had willingly taken the way of the cross—publicly identifying himself with Caesar's prisoner; putting his own life on the line in service to others. *This* is the kind of person, Paul says, who should be prized. By appealing to this familiar language, Paul speaks clearly to a culture obsessed with gaining honor. At the same time, he turns the values of the dominant culture on their head (see Fowl 2005, 138; Bockmuehl 1998, 174). In this, he is only following Jesus himself, who told his disciples not to seek the place of public honor, because those who exalt themselves will be humbled, and those who humble themselves will be exalted (Luke 14:7-11).

■ **30** Paul now explains why Epaphroditus should be held in honor: **because he almost died for the work of Christ.** Here the **work of Christ** (*ergon Christou*) refers above all to Epaphroditus's ministry to Paul as the representative of the Philippian church. Yet it is *Christ's* work in another sense. In the course of fulfilling that mission, Epaphroditus came **close to death** (*mechri thanatou*). This phrase echoes 2:8 (KJV), where identical words speak of Christ's obedience "unto death" (*mechri thanatou*). Epaphroditus has followed the example of his Lord in a pattern of costly, cruciform love.

The phrase **risking** (*paraboleusamenos;* the only NT occurrence) **his life** is a striking metaphor wrested from games of chance. Epaphroditus was willing to expose himself to great danger. In effect, he gambled with his own life in order to do God's work faithfully.

The purpose of this high-stakes risk, Paul insists, is **to make up for the help you could not give me** (literally, *to fill up what was lacking in your service to me*). Paul does not say this to criticize the Philippians. Nor does he assume that they were under *obligation* to correct some deficiency in their service to him (against Fowl 2005, 139). Rather, their help fell short because they were separated from Paul and could not minister to him in person. Only through Epaphroditus, their ambassador, could they fill in this gap in their ministry to Paul.

We find something similar in 1 Cor 16:17. There, the same language describes three representatives from the church in Corinth visiting Paul, who made up for the absence of the rest. Here Epaphroditus completes the Philippians' "priestly service" (*leitourgia;* see Phil 2:17, 25) to Paul. The emphasis, then, is not on the Philippians' shortcomings, but on Epaphroditus's practical ministry to the apostle. It is a service discharged at huge personal cost. This becomes a further reason to honor their faithful messenger and to hold high the welcome banners upon his return.

Epaphroditus, therefore, models faithfulness to Christ and the ministry of the gospel, no matter the cost (1:27-30; Geoffrion 1993, 143). No less than Timothy, he embodies the attitude of putting the interests of others before one's own (2:1-11). Both of these coworkers give the Philippians a tangible picture of what it is like to live out the story of Christ in service to the gospel (Bockmuehl 1998, 175).

FROM THE TEXT

1. *A theology for ordinary life.* Mundane travel arrangements. Commendations of first-century coworkers. Where in this do we find a word from God for the contemporary church? Clearly, this passage does not tender the same measure of direct theological and ethical teaching we encounter in 2:1-18. At the same time, these verses remind us that Paul's theology was a "theology of the road." It translated into everyday life.

The threefold occurrence of the phrase "in the Lord" in this passage (vv 19, 24, 29) is no happenstance. Here we find servants of Christ in the midst of their comings and goings, hopes and plans, sicknesses and sorrows, joys and friendships—and all of it lived out "in the Lord." Practical matters such as providing for financial and physical needs are viewed as a spiritual service, a form of worship (1:30). The "reality" narratives in this passage help us remember that our theology has little value unless it connects with day-by-day living and shapes our ordinary practices and relationships.

2. *"Love" stories.* This passage bristles with exemplary stories that narrate how real people embody the mind-set of Christ. This applies not only to Timothy and Epaphroditus, but also to the apostle himself. Paul cares deeply for his friends, and he shows it in his actions. Instead of insisting that Epaphroditus stay on to minister to him in prison, he puts the needs of the Philippians and of his coworker ahead of his own. Even with the threat of execution hanging over him, Paul "eagerly" sends back their emissary. He testifies that their joy at being reunited with Epaphroditus will also be his own.

Paul also demonstrates his love for his coworkers. His affirming language about them radiates it; his heartfelt pain over Epaphroditus's brush with death throbs with it. Finally, the Philippians' own self-giving love in action comes through, not only in their financial support for Paul, but also in their sending one of their own to care for his needs, when they themselves could not. In short, by telling a number of intersecting stories, this passage celebrates a mutuality of loving care for others. It brings concrete expression to the master "love story" of Christ (2:6-11).

I agree with Fowl that it is crucial for us, as well, to tell the stories of exemplary lives in order that those lives might shape how we live out the gospel today (2005, 142). In much of our world, including a postmodern context in the West, stories of people who live authentic and self-giving lives probably have more potential to form behavior than reams of ethical instruction. Whether narrated from Scripture, or from the lives of believers in the past or present, stories need to be told. Reflecting on my personal journey, the stories and testimonies of God's faithful servants have powerfully molded my own attitudes and behavior. Like the Philippians, we need concrete examples of lives that unselfishly seek the concerns of Jesus Christ (2:21).

3. *The true measure of significance.* Inhabiting a world in which rules about what brought people honor and dishonor shaped peoples' behavior, Paul consistently rewrote the cultural scripts in light of the gospel. He asked the Philippians to prize Epaphroditus, not because he represented the things that the dominant culture would have considered worthy of honor, but because he conformed to an alternative code of honor—that of Christ and the gospel (2:29).

Such language connects readily with Christians in many cultures today (e.g., Middle Eastern, Oriental, Latin). In these contexts, the values of public honor and shame continue to be strong motivators for how people act and think. Christians in North America and Western Europe may not live in honor-based cultures in the same sense. But those societies still promote a compelling set of values that define what brings individual members success and significance in the eyes of others. David A. deSilva observes that such definitions are transmitted

> by our families of origin, who were themselves perhaps only partially socialized into the Christian ethos; by our educators who motivated study by pointing to the promising, well-paying careers and potential for advancement it would bring; by the endless barrage of commercials telling us what we should aspire to possess and display; and by the role models our society selects and elevates through very public award ceremonies and other avenues of idolization. We still are raised to seek the approval of the group and to act so as to gain recognition. (2000, 85)

Christian communities in the global North find themselves in settings where the values of the majority culture often clash with those of Christ crucified. An essential aspect of Christian discipleship involves learning to discern the difference. This relates both to where we discover our own personal value (the same word *entimos* that Paul uses in 2:29 can mean "valuable," "having worth," as well as "honored"), as well as who receives approval and recognition from the church.

On a personal level, we are freed from having to measure our worth and success by the values on which the culture puts the highest price tags. In Western societies, these include such attributes as physical attractiveness, athletic prowess, wealth and upward mobility, acquisition of prestige items, professional success, celebrity, sexual conquest, independence, and beating the competition (see deSilva 2000, 86). If we are to resist computing our significance according to such standards of approval, we must learn to find our validation in the things that God honors and values—holiness, humility, *downward* mobility, courageously putting the interests of others first.

What is more, Christian communities must honestly ask themselves by what criteria they give out honor and acclaim. Do we esteem the wealthy who contribute large donations to Christian ministries more than the poor who cannot? Are well-known Christian recording artists or television personalities granted a celebrity status that borders on idolization? Do we reserve public awards and recognition for church leaders who have achieved position, influence, and numerical success?

We dare not forget that God deliberately chooses "the foolish things of the world to shame the wise" and "the weak things of the world to shame the strong" (1 Cor 1:27). The gospel of Christ calls the church to a countercultural estimation of greatness. True honor follows those who "make themselves nothing." Real success comes when we embody the narrative of Christlike love. This passage challenges us to more intentionally recall and find ways to honor those little-known, "unsung heroes" in our own lives—those who have modeled such cruciform love before us.

V. STANDING FIRM IN THE FACE OF THREATS TO THE GOSPEL: WARNINGS AND EXAMPLES: PHILIPPIANS 3:1—4:1

A. True and False Confidence (3:1-11)

BEHIND THE TEXT

The course of the letter now takes a surprising turn. Chapter 3 opens with the word **finally,** which sounds like Paul is about to wind things down. In reality, however, roughly half of the letter is still to come. On top of that, v 2 explodes on the scene with a dramatic change in tone: ***Beware of the dogs!*** This unexpected shift in mood and topic, immediately following what seems to be a conclusion, has led some scholars to think that 3:2 (or perhaps 3:1*b*) marks where the fragment of another letter has been inserted into the text of Philippians.

As we noted in the Introduction, however, there are plausible reasons for considering Philippians a unified composition, not a collection of different letters. Indeed, the Greek phrase the NIV translates as **finally** (*to loipon*) often signals a transition (see 1 Thess 4:1) rather than a conclusion. Here, ***as for the rest,*** or "in addition," is a better rendering. Its function, then, would be to introduce a new thought or series of issues to follow.

But why such an abrupt change in tone and topic? One suggestion is that in the course of writing, Paul suddenly recalled troublemakers who could threaten the Philippians. Others think that Paul is reacting to fresh news of the activities of Judaizing Christians elsewhere. Although we cannot rule out such explanations, they are unnecessary to make sense out of what is going on here.

In the first place, sudden shifts in tone are not unheard of in Paul's letters (see, e.g., Gal 3:1; 4:21; Rom 16:17; 1 Cor 15:58). Second, the intensity of Paul's warning against the opponents may be related to Paul's concern to protect a church for which he carries deep affection (Koperski 1996, 78). Third, the abrupt tonal shift is likely a deliberate rhetorical strategy. It is intended to spotlight the contrast between the opponents' identity and Paul's own modeling of the gospel that follows (vv 4-14; Geoffrion 1993, 200).

A weightier question concerns whether or not the subject matter of ch 3 fits with what precedes it in the letter. In one sense v 2 does introduce a "new" topic. But how Paul develops this theme in 3:2—4:1 is linked to what he has already written. For example, the section picks up on Paul's admonition in 1:27-30 to live out the gospel by standing firm (1:27; 4:1) in the face of opposition (now in the form of rival teachers; 1:28; 3:2-3) and suffering (1:29-30; 3:10).

Furthermore, ch 3 continues the pattern of good and bad examples for his audience that we have observed up to this point in the letter (e.g., 1:12-26; 2:5-11, 17, 19-30). Accordingly, we find the following sequence of examples in ch 3:

3:2-3: negative example—Judaizing teachers
3:4-6: negative example—Paul (in the flesh)
3:7-14: positive example—Paul (in Christ)
3:15-16: application and appeal to the Philippians
3:17: positive example—Paul
3:18-19: negative example—enemies of the cross
3:20-21: the goal of following Paul's example

Above all, Paul's personal history in 3:4-11 follows a V-shaped pattern of humiliation/exaltation, similar to the Christ hymn in 2:6-11. Like his Master before him, Paul renounces his high status and privileges (in Judaism), considering them to be total loss (3:4-8; compare 2:6-7). He embraces the obedient suffering and death of his Lord (3:10; see 2:8) and hopes to share ultimately in Christ's resurrection from the dead (3:11; see 2:9-11). Although the parallel is by no means identical, Paul's story in ch 3, both in its plot and its language, echoes the story of Christ. Overall, 1:27—2:18 and 3:1—4:1 follow a similar structure: each gives instructions to the Philippians, and both have a personal example at their core—Jesus in 2:6-11 and Paul in 3:4-11 (Thurston 2005, 109; see Kurz 1985, 117).

Paul's Story and Ancient Autobiography

Ancient philosophers and letter writers often made reference to their own histories. Unlike modern autobiographies, these personal accounts were not intended to be more or less objective historical records of one's life. Rather, the purpose of ancient autobiographical references was above all to persuade or exhort an audience (see Lyons 1985). In letters of the Greco-Roman period, autobiography is often a means of moral instruction, with the life of the writer serving as an example for the readers. The Roman writer Pliny expresses this well in one of his letters:

> My profession brought me advancement, then danger, then advancement again; I was helped by my friendship with honest men, then injured by it, and now am helped again.... This should be a warning never to lose heart and to be sure of nothing, when we see so many fluctuations of fortune following each other in rapid succession.
>
> It is a habit of mine to share my thoughts with you and to set out for your guidance the rules and examples which shape my own conduct. That was the purpose of this letter. (*Epistles* 4.24.4-7)

What is more, Greco-Roman philosophers often described their own positive actions and attitudes in contrast to others who displayed inferior motives and behavior (see, e.g., Dio Chrysostom, *Oration* 32.11-12; compare Phil 3:2-9; 1 Thess 2:1-12). Such descriptions gave their audience an ideal to imitate, as well as a negative example to avoid.

This sheds light on the function of Paul's references to his past. When Paul inserts pages from his life story into his letters (e.g., Gal 1—2; 4:12-20; 6:11-18; Phil 3:4-14; 1 Thess 1—2), they are not simply for historical or biographical interest. More importantly, they offer his converts a paradigm to follow as they learn to live faithfully before God (see Lyons 1985; Gaventa, 1986, 313-26).

Philippians 3:2-11, then, is not only intended to warn the Philippians about false teachers who could threaten their Christian existence but also serves Paul's broader purpose of bringing about Christian formation (see Gal 4:19) in the lives of his audience. It does this by giving them a cruciform pattern to follow. Paul himself has embodied the "Master pattern" of renunciation/suffering/resurrection. And his example encourages the Philippians to adopt this gospel mind-set, as well. Only then will they be able to stand united in the face of suffering and opposition that comes both from without and from within.

The rhetorical effect of Phil 3:1-11 is stunning. Verses 2 and 3 evidence a number of powerful rhetorical devices. These include intense irony and the repetition of the same word ("Beware") at the beginning of three staccato clauses (see Hawthorne and Martin 2004, 172). In v 4 Paul switches to the first person singular ("I") for the rest of the section. In the categories of ancient rhetoric, this is an argument based on *ethos*. Paul's own character and credibility become an important part of the message.

Paul uses the rhetorical strategy of "comparison" in vv 4-6, when he shows that his Jewish credentials surpassed that of his rivals. Verses 7-11 then bring the passage to a highly emotive, almost poetic climax. Paul employs a number of rhetorical techniques in these verses. In vv 7-8, 10, he uses chiasm.

Here, similar phrases alternate their positions in a crisscross pattern. Repetition also enhances the passage's rhetorical effect. This is especially evident in the extended interplay of the commercial imagery (**profit,** v 7, and **gain,** v 8; vs. **loss,** v 7, **lost,** v 8). The IN THE TEXT section of the commentary treats these and other rhetorical features of the passage more fully.

Turning to the historical background for 3:1-11, this passage is probably rooted in Paul's concern that Jewish Christian missionaries could threaten the church in Philippi with their false teaching (vv 2-4*a*). Apparently, these teachers tried to *supplement* the gospel of Christ crucified with the idea that Gentile believers needed to submit to the Jewish law, particularly circumcision, in order to be full Christians.

Such rival "Judaizing" teachers had baited Paul's ministry among the Gentiles in the past. In fact, Paul's sharp language in v 2 recalls Galatians, where Paul rails against agitators with a similar background who are endangering the life of the church (see Gal 1:8-9; 5:12; 6:12-13). We do not know whether these "dogs" (v 2) were already "hounding" the Philippians or whether this is still simply a potential threat. The latter scenario is probable, since Paul does not go into much detail in applying this danger to the church. Furthermore, his appeal to ***beware*** (v 2) of them sounds more like a preemptive warning than a reaction to people who had already invaded the community.

This passage can be divided into four parts:

1. a transition verse (v 1) that serves as a hinge between Paul's discussion about Timothy and Epaphroditus in 2:19-30 and the new section
2. a direct warning against the Judaizers, where Paul contrasts their defective message and practice with that of the true people of God (vv 2-4*a*)
3. Paul's appeal to his former life "in the flesh," which even outstrips that of his opponents (vv 4*b*-6)
4. a narrative of the great transformation that knowing Christ effected in his life (vv 7-11)

This final section is earmarked by what N. T. Wright calls "multiple, almost obsessive" references to Christ (2005b, 115). As elsewhere in Philippians, *Christ* is the center of it all.

IN THE TEXT

1. The Transition (3:1)

■ **1** Our passage begins with a transitional term, ***as for the rest*** [of what I need to say], and an exhortation to **rejoice in the Lord.** By this point in the letter, the theme of joy should come as no surprise. Here it forms a link to 2:12-18, where Paul urges the Philippians to rejoice with him in the midst of suffering (vv 17-18). Likewise in vv 19-30, they are called to welcome Epaphroditus, who has risked his life for the gospel, with a spirit of joy (vv 28, 29). Now Paul is about to warn the Philippians that further troubles are possible in the form of rival teachers. He desires that his friends would face that prospect, as well, with an attitude of joy (Thielman 1995, 166). The phrase **in the Lord** is linked to joy for the first time in the letter (see 4:4). This pinpoints both the source of their rejoicing and its object (see Pss 32:11; 35:9).

But this relatively straightforward exhortation is followed by a rather puzzling statement: **it is no trouble for me to write the same things to you again, and it is a safeguard for you.** What are the "same things" that Paul has in mind? Is he pointing backward to what he has just said about rejoicing in the Lord? This is possible, since Paul has already raised the issue of rejoicing a number of times in the letter (1:18; 2:17-18, 28, 29). But it is hard to see how the command to rejoice would be a **safeguard** for the Philippians.

Instead, Paul probably looks ahead to the warning and example he is about to give them. In that case, **the same things** would refer to information he has communicated to them previously, either in person or by letter.

The notion that what Paul is about to repeat is for their "security" (*asphales*; literally, "safe") suggests that the church is not presently in grave danger. Nevertheless, he seeks to warn them against the possibility (Hooker 2000, 524). Paul, then, starts this new section in the letter by reaffirming the Philippians' need to rejoice in the Lord. At the same time, he prepares them for the matter he is about to impress upon them.

2. A Warning Against "the Dogs" (3:2-4a)

■ **2** Paul fires a rhetorical cannon in v 2, with three successive cannon balls: ***Beware of the dogs; beware of the evildoers; beware of the mutilators!*** This is exceptionally strong language. The rhetorical force is boosted by three factors: (1) its sudden appearance; (2) the threefold repetition of the verb ***beware;*** and (3) the use of alliteration, in which each of the warnings has an object beginning with the letter *K* (*tous kynas . . . tous kakous ergatas . . . tēn katomēn*). It is almost impossible to reproduce the effect in English, but Frank Thielman's translation moves in that direction: "Beware of the curs . . . the criminals . . . the cutters!" (1995, 167).

Some have argued on the basis of grammar that the triple ***beware*** (*blepete*) has the weaker sense of "consider" or "take note of." In other words, the Philippians should observe and learn from their mistakes (e.g., Garland 1985, 165-66). But that does not fit either the tone or the context, which surely imply a warning.

Apparently, Paul's emotive language is aimed at one group of opponents, not three. Paul does not give us much specific information about them, but the best explanation is that the people he has in mind are Judaizing missionaries (for the identity of the rivals, see above, BEHIND THE TEXT). Readers of this invective today should keep the following considerations in mind:

- Name-calling was characteristic of ancient rhetoric (Gorman 2004, 441). The Jewish historian Josephus, for example, says of Apion that he "has the mind of an ass and the impudence of a dog, which his country men are wont to worship" (*Ag. Ap.* 2.7 §86; cited by Perkins 1991, 101; see also Titus 1:12, in which Cretans are labeled as "liars, evil brutes, lazy gluttons").
- Paul's frontal assault targets some Judaizing rivals, not Judaism or Jewish Christianity in general (see Bockmuehl 1998, 184).
- Paul's robust rhetoric indicates the seriousness of the issues at stake. The Judaizing message undercuts the heart of what it means to live out the gospel by bringing Gentile Christians under the yoke of the Law. Paul's language is intended to jolt his dear friends into recognizing the danger that may lie down this road.
- The specific terms Paul uses in v 2 are chosen for their striking irony. Language that Jews would have considered apt for Gentile outsiders comes back at them like a verbal boomerang.

Let us consider these terms individually. **Dogs** in the ancient cities were anything but "man's best friend." They were seen as unclean scavengers that prowled the streets, feeding on filth and garbage. Consequently, "dogs" was an intensely negative term (see, e.g., Deut 23:18; 1 Sam 17:43; 2 Sam 16:9; Matt 7:6; 15:26; Mark 7:27; Rev 22:15). Furthermore, it was sometimes used by Jews to show contempt for Gentiles. Paul the Pharisee (Phil 3:5) would no doubt have previously viewed Gentiles as unclean "dogs." Here, however, he turns the insult on its head; by trying to make the Gentile converts "clean" through circumcision, it is the *Judaizers* who become the impure "dogs" (Fee 1995, 295).

Evildoers (*kakous ergatas*) is probably also ironic. In the Psalms, "evildoers" describes God's enemies who fail to obey the Torah (e.g., Pss 5:5; 6:8; 14:4; 28:3). Once again, Paul seizes language that would ordinarily apply to Gentile outsiders (see Gal 2:15) and pins it on *Jews* who want Gentiles to submit to the Law.

The third disparaging term, **mutilators** (*katatomē*; literally, "mutilation") is a pun in Greek, which deliberately plays on the word **circumcision** (*peritomē*, v 3). This language may imply that the people Paul has in mind teach that Gentiles must be circumcised, like Jewish proselytes, to be full members of the people of God.

Here Paul's irony reaches its climax as he inverts the interlopers' point of greatest pride (Hooker 2000, 524). For Jews, circumcision was the mark of the covenant; it was the badge of membership in the people of God. Mutilation—"slashing" the flesh—was the practice of paganism (1 Kgs 18:28). Such ritual laceration was strictly forbidden to Jewish priests (Lev 21:5). But in Paul's mind, circumcision that is not a matter of the heart has no more value than pagan self-mutilation (see Gal 5:11-12; also the vivid paraphrase, "knife-happy circumcisers" [Phil 3:2 TM]). The very people who insist that circumcision is necessary for being *inside* the covenant—*they* are the outsiders, cut *off* from the people of God. Paul's threefold description, then, serves as a warning to the Philippians: don't be seduced by such "righteousness . . . in the law" (v 6 NKJV; Hooker 2000, 524-25).

■ **3** We see the flip side of this great reversal in v 3: **For it is we** [emphatic in Greek] **who are the circumcision.** In the upside-down world of the gospel, it is the Judaizers who are the real Gentiles, while all those who have faith in Christ—both Jews and Gentiles—are the genuine covenant community. Note that here Paul does not even say, "we are the *true* circumcision" (as, e.g., NASB and GNT), i.e., in contrast to a *false* Jewish one. Instead, he simply states, **we are the circumcision** (*hē peritomē*)—the *only* one.

This is an astounding claim for a Jew like Paul to make. Already in the OT, Israel was promised a "circumcision of the heart" (Deut 30:6; see also 10:16; Jer 4:4; 9:26), symbolized by physical circumcision. Paul sees this inward heart circumcision, which is the work of the Spirit of God, as a blessing of the new covenant (Rom 2:25-29; Col 2:11). Christ, not circumcision, becomes the passport into God's people. As a result, physical circumcision is now irrelevant for one's relationship to God (1 Cor 7:19; Gal 5:6; 6:15; Eph 2:11). The Gentile believers in Paul's audience are full children of the covenant and rightful heirs of all of God's promises to Abraham.

Paul goes on to characterize God's new covenant people in three ways.

First, they **worship by the Spirit of God.** The verb **worship** (*latreuō*) is used throughout Scripture of a religious service to God or to pagan deities. As the Jewish priests offered their "service" to God in the temple, so now God's people make the whole of life an act of service and worship to God (Bockmuehl 1998, 192). Romans portrays this ongoing way of life as a living sacrifice, which is the Christian's spiritual service (12:1; see Luke 1:74; Acts 24:14; Heb 12:28). This "service," then, is not so much an experience of corporate worship on a Sunday morning as it is daily life lived "in a manner worthy of the gospel of Christ" (Phil 1:27).

Significantly, Christians worship **by the Spirit of God.** This suggests an implied contrast: On the one hand, the Jewish teachers put their confidence in the "flesh," which represents life without the Spirit. On the other, the true people of God offer acceptable service through the power and guidance of God's Spirit.

This is similar to Jesus' teaching in John's Gospel that, since God is Spirit, true worshippers must worship God "in spirit and truth" (John 4:23). What is more, since the Spirit is the gift of the new era of salvation, spiritual worship is the privilege of *all* believers, regardless of whether they are physically circumcised or uncircumcised.

The second attribute of "the circumcision" is that they **glory in Christ Jesus**. As in Phil 1:26 and 2:16, the word for **glory** or **boast** (*kauchōmenoi*) is used positively in the sense of exulting or rejoicing in Christ. The crucial matter is one's basis for boasting. As we will see, boasting in oneself or one's own privileges is excluded (3:4-6; compare Rom 3:27). The only true grounds for boasting is Jesus Christ and his reconciling death on the cross (see Gal 6:13-14; 1 Cor 1:31).

Third, Paul highlights what God's people do *not* do (and, by implication, what the Judaizers *are* doing)—put **confidence in the flesh**. This is a key phrase, attested by its threefold appearance in vv 3 and 4. The verbs **glory** and **put confidence** (*peithō*) are near synonyms. Paul views having confidence in the flesh and putting confidence in Christ as mutually exclusive attitudes (Thielman 1995, 169). But what does it mean to put confidence **in the flesh**?

Flesh (*sarx*) is a term that Paul uses in a variety of ways. These include: the body's physical material; the weak human realm; and human existence on its own apart from God and opposed to the Spirit. In this latter sense, **flesh** characterizes the old life that is in league with sin (see Schweizer 1971, 7:98-151; Dunn 1998, 62-73). Here Paul may be playing on more than one sense of the term. On one level, it may refer to trusting spiritually in the rite of circumcision, which takes place literally, *in the flesh*.

Beyond that, putting confidence in the flesh means placing confidence in what is merely human, apart from the grace and Spirit of God. In the present context, this misplaced trust is centered on human status and achievements (vv 4-6).

■ **4a** Reinforcing the point, Paul turns to his own résumé. The first part of v 4 brings the present paragraph to a close. But it also leads into Paul's personal narrative to follow. The statement is striking: literally, ***though I myself have confidence even in the flesh***. Paul turns to his own sterling record in Judaism as "exhibit A" for the utter futility of relying on human attributes for acceptance by God. First comes the evidence for such a bold claim (vv 4b-6). This is followed by Paul's new perspective: such reasons for pride have become sewage in comparison to the grace of knowing Christ (vv 7-11; Fee 1995, 303).

3. Paul's Jewish Pedigree (3:4b-6)

■ **4b** For the rest of this passage (vv 4b-11), Paul draws from his own biography as a paradigm for the Philippians to follow. His rhetorical strategy is to compare the Jewish rivals' pride in the flesh with his own superior credentials in Judaism. To make his point, Paul is willing to indulge in some "mock boasting." If he can show that his own robust reasons for human confidence did him absolutely no good, surely that would be true of anyone who might come to the Philippians boasting about their Jewishness or fleshly assets (Marshall 1991, 83).

In v 4b Paul makes it clear that his dismissal of human advantages as a ground of boasting before God is not a matter of envy or "sour grapes." As Thomas Aquinas astutely observes, while many people scorn things they don't have, Paul scorns what he *does* have (1969, 96). In fact, Paul says, whatever reasons the Judaizers have **to put confidence in the flesh, I have more.** He is telling his rivals, in effect, "If you want to play that game, I can outscore you every time!" By any human standard of judgment, Paul's Jewish pedigree is impeccable.

■ **5** Paul proceeds in vv 5-6 to list the merely human advantages he once took pride in—his *curriculum vitae* as a Jew. First, he names his Jewish privileges, the things he inherited from his parents. *Religiously*, he was a full member of the covenant people; he was **circumcised on the eighth day,** as the Law required. This demonstrates that Paul was no convert to Judaism, who would have been circumcised as an adult.

In terms of *ancestry*, Paul was **of the people of Israel.** The Greek word *genos* (**people**) implies bloodline and racial descent. He was an Israelite by birth (see 2 Cor 11:22; Gal 1:14).

Paul had also taken pride in his *tribal identity* as a member **of the tribe of Benjamin** (see Rom 11:1). Benjamin was a favored son of Jacob (Gen 35:18), the only son to be born in the land of promise. This tribe had given Israel its first king, Paul's namesake, Saul. Being from such enviable stock could only enhance Paul's top-flight reputation as a Jew.

Paul's claim to be **a Hebrew of Hebrews** (see 2 Cor 11:22) brings his tally of inherited assets to a climax. Most likely, this expression means more than simply that he considered himself a pure Jew. The term **Hebrew** probably also implies that, although born outside of Palestine, Paul was taught to speak Hebrew or Aramaic in his home (Hengel 1991, 25-26). Many Diaspora Jews only spoke Greek. But "Hebrews" kept close cultural and linguistic ties to the Jewish heartland of Palestine (see Acts 6:1; Bockmuehl 1998, 197; Gutbrod 1965, 3:389-90), Paul, then, had taken great pride in his *ethnic, cultural,* and *linguistic* heritage.

In addition to these four inherited privileges, Paul lists three further claims. In contrast to the first group, these assertions testify to his personal devotion and achievements as a Jew. In Greek, each of them is introduced with the preposition *kata*, **in regard to.**

First, in his approach to the **law,** Paul was a **Pharisee.** The accent here probably falls on Paul's dedication to observing both the written and the oral Torah meticulously. It apparently also includes the Pharisees' commitment to maintain ritual purity and holiness. Hooker notes that Paul's identity as a Pharisee heaps further irony on his description of a group of *Jews* as "dogs," **evildoers,** and "mutilators" (v 2). The Pharisees would normally be the *last* ones to recognize such people as belonging to Israel (2000, 526; on the Pharisees, see Westerholm 1992, 609-14; Mason 2000, 782-87).

■ **6** Paul, however, was not just *any* Pharisee. His **zeal** for the Torah drove him even to the point of **persecuting the church** (v 6). Zeal for God and the purity of Israel was a positive attribute in the OT. Phinehas the priest modeled such godly zeal, when he killed an Israelite man and his Midianite mistress in order to purge Israel from idolatry (Num 25; see Ps 106:28-31). Similarly, Paul's exceptional passion for God and his law (see Gal 1:14; Acts 22:3-4) drove him to track down those he saw as a threat to the purity of Israel. Determined to exterminate the fledgling Christian movement (see Gal 1:13), Paul was on the radical edge of Pharisaic Judaism (see Bockmuehl 1998, 200).

Here Paul does not call attention to his persecuting activity in order to bemoan its sinfulness (compare 1 Cor 15:9; 1 Tim 1:13-14). On the contrary, he wants to convince his audience of the high level of devotion to Judaism he had achieved. According to his old perspective, Paul persecuted Christians, not because he was evil, but because he was "good"; he was a man inflamed with zeal for God's law (Hawthorne and Martin 2004, 186).

Here we have the first appearance of the term **church** (*ekklēsia;* literally, a "gathered people") in Philippians. In this context its meaning expands beyond a local gathering of Christians to a more general and universal understanding of the people of God (Fee 1995, 308, n 15).

The capstone of Paul's catalog of accomplishments in Judaism comes in what might strike us as an astonishing statement: *in regard to righteousness that is in the law, blameless* (v 6). We should note that this is how Paul would have evaluated himself *from the perspective of his Pharisaic past.* As a Christian, he would surely have given his past performance—in particular his persecuting activity (see 1 Cor 15:9)—a different verdict (Marshall 1991, 85). But Paul's present point is that, according to his understanding of what the Law required as a Jewish Pharisee, he met the standard; there were no black marks on his record.

The pre-Christian Paul, like most observant Jews, believed the commandments of the Law could be kept. If anyone sinned, the Law provided means of atonement and receiving forgiveness (Fowl 2005, 151; Bockmuehl 1998, 202). Consequently, Paul does not say he was "sinless." Rather, under the Law's standard of righteousness, he was "without fault" (*amemptos;* see Thompson 2002, 10-12). Luke's Gospel makes a similar evaluation of John the Baptist's parents, who observed "all the Lord's commandments and regulations blamelessly" (Luke 1:6; see Mark 10:20).

This claim, notes Fowl, debunks the image of the pre-Christian Paul as a Luther-like individual, tortured by a guilty conscience, searching desperately for a gracious God to liberate him from the legalistic yoke of Judaism (2005, 151; thus, the NIV's **as for legalistic righteousness** is an unfortunate translation). As Craddock describes it, "We do not have in this text the portrait of a man at war with himself, crucified between the sky of God's expectations and the earth of his own paltry performance. Paul is not in this scene a poor soul standing with a grade of ninety-nine before a God who counts one hundred as the lowest passing grade" (1985, 59). Paul's problem was not that he couldn't make the grade; it was that he *did* make it, only to find out that it was the wrong standard of assessment.

Righteousness (*dikaiosynē*) in the Law could not bring Paul a right relationship with God; it was an externally measured righteousness that could only give rise to "confidence in the flesh." Paul's immediate concern, of course, is to show that he had excelled in the kind of Law-based righteousness that would have been appealing to the Judaizers. Paul has demonstrated that he has utterly impressive Jewish credentials, both in pedigree and performance. Being a "poster child" for life "in the flesh," he is eminently qualified to show that trusting in human evaluations is a dead-end street.

4. The Surpassing Value of Knowing Christ (3:7-11)

■ **7** Paul's story now takes a dramatic turn. A great reversal took place in his life as a result of his transforming encounter with Christ on the Damascus road. Drawing on commercial language, Paul writes off the former assets he has just listed as losses: **but whatever was to my profit I now consider loss for the sake of Christ** (v 7).

The opening conjunction **but** is missing from a number of important early manuscripts, and it is not certain whether it is original. Either way, however, the contrast with what precedes is plain. When Paul adds up the value of his fleshly advantages and achievements—his "gains" (*kerdē*)—the sum total is *zero*. Whatever was formerly on the plus side of the balance sheet has now been transferred to the liability column. A radical revision has taken place in Paul's spiritual bookkeeping. This occurred not so much for Christ's sake (as in the NIV) as **on account of Christ** (*dia ton Christon*). It is because of who Christ is and what he has done (Fee 1995, 315 n 8).

It is important to notice what Paul does *not* say. He does not say that everything about Judaism or his life as a Jew is inherently silly or worthless. Elsewhere he affirms that his Jewish identity and heritage is something that is still of considerable importance to him (see Rom 3:1-2; 9:1-5; 11:1-2). Rather, from his new perspective in Christ, he has come to **consider** all such assets as utter loss. They have become losing investments because they are part of a way of life that trusts in the flesh rather than in Christ (see Bockmuehl 1998, 204-5; Wright 2000, 180).

The verb **consider** is in the perfect tense (*hēgēmai*, "I have come to consider") in Greek. This suggests that Paul came to count these things loss when he encountered Christ in his conversion, and that continues to be the case.

There is also an echo here of the Christ hymn in ch 2. As Jesus did not *consider* "equality with God as something to be exploited, but emptied himself" (2:7 NRSV), so Paul *considers* all of his former advantages to be loss for the sake of Christ (Wagner 2007, 268). Paul's story is patterned after the story of Christ.

Paul goes on to reinforce the basic contrast of 3:7. He does so both through repetition and by a crescendo of thought. This becomes clearer when we see that vv 7 and 8 form a carefully crafted literary chiasm (crisscross pattern, see 1:15), which plays different variations on the metaphor of gain and loss:

a *But whatever was <u>gain to me</u>*
  b *These things I have considered <u>loss on account of Christ</u>*
    c *More than that I also consider <u>all things</u> to be <u>loss</u>*
      d *Because of the <u>surpassing greatness of knowing Christ</u> Jesus my Lord*
    c' *Because of whom <u>I have lost all things</u>*
  b' *And I consider them <u>filth</u>*
a' *In order that <u>I may gain Christ</u>*

■ **8** Verses 8 through 11 comprise one long sentence in Greek. The sentence begins with an emphatic "not only so, but what is more" (Fee 1995, 317, *alla menounge kai*). The rest of v 8 then develops the thought of v 7, intensifying it in several ways.

First, the verb **consider** changes from the perfect tense (literally, "I have come to consider") in v 7 to the present (**I consider**; *hēgoumai*) in v 8. This emphasizes the current reality of Paul's past change in attitude.

Second, Paul expands what he considers loss from simply his fleshly assets in vv 5 and 6 to **all things** (*panta*). Paul does not spell out precisely what he has in mind. Presumably, however, **all things** embraces whatever might be a source of human confidence or stand in competition to Christ. For Paul, these losses are not just a matter of perception. He has actually renounced any gain connected with such assets, whether personal achievements, privileges, status, honor, material possessions, comforts, or security (Gorman 2004, 443).

The rhetorical impact of this claim builds even further with a third restatement of it, this time with a passive verb. Because of Christ (or **for whose sake**), Paul says, "I have suffered the loss [*ezēmiōthēn*] of all things" (NRSV). Paul's language recalls the teaching of Jesus, who warns that it is of no profit to gain the whole world and lose one's life (Mark 8:36). And Jesus' parables of the pearl of great price and the treasure in the field (Matt 13:44-46) make a similar point about "losing" everything that was once considered valuable for what is of supreme value. Calvin evokes another image, that of seamen who throw everything overboard so that the lightened ship may safely reach the harbor (1965, 272).

Third, Paul's last use of the word **consider** makes the strongest statement of all. Not only does he count the merely human assets he once trusted in as liabilities, but he regards them as vulgar and abhorrent. The NIV's **I consider them rubbish** is too weak a translation for the shocking word Paul uses (*skybala*). Found only here in the New Testament, *skybala* could refer to refuse, stinking and decaying food, or even human excrement (see Lang 1971, 7:445-47). It carries the idea of something that is only fit to be thrown out because it is so disgusting. As a result, ***filth*** or the coarse colloquial term "crap" better captures the detestable quality expressed in this term. Paul could hardly have stated his revulsion toward his former sources of pride and self-righteousness more emphatically.

Fourth, this great reversal has happened not simply ***on account of Christ*** (v 7), but because of **the surpassing greatness of knowing Christ Jesus my Lord** (v 8). This is the overwhelming value that renders everything else worthless and so much "dog dung" (TM) in comparison. The phrase also functions as the centerpiece (d) of the rhetorical chiasm in vv 7-8 (see above). This shows that it is the main point that Paul wants to stress (on literary chiasms, see Capes, Reeves, and Richards 2007, 64-65).

Paul identifies the content of ***the surpassing value*** (*to hyperechon*) as, literally, ***the knowledge of Christ Jesus my Lord*** (a phrase that piles up a series of Greek genitives). **Knowledge** (*gnōsis*) is a key term here and, in its verb form, in v 10. In the Greco-Roman world, *gnōsis* was widely prized in philosophical and religious circles. As Bockmuehl points out, it "was rapidly becoming one of the buzzwords for access to desirable religious 'inside information,' partly intellectual and partly mystical" (1998, 205). Some scholars have tried to trace Paul's interest in knowledge to such Greco-Roman sources, particularly the later philosophical and religious movement that came to be known as Gnosticism. But this has turned out to be a cold trail.

It is much more likely that Paul's thinking about knowledge is grounded in the OT idea of the knowledge of God, which has to do with a deep mutual relationship between God and his people. Such knowledge was expressed from God's side in his election (call) and grace. From the human side, knowledge is expressed in a response of loving obedience to God's self-revelation (see Jer 31:34; Hos 4:1; 6:6). To know God is more than having the "facts" about God. It is an intimate knowledge of deep personal relationship—like husbands and wives know each other. In fact, "knowing" in the Hebrew tradition could even be applied to sexual intimacy; for example, Adam *knew* Eve (Gen 4:1; for the background to the term, see esp. Bockmuehl 1998, 205-6).

Here Paul relates this personal knowledge to **Christ Jesus my Lord.** Immediately our thoughts are drawn back to Phil 2:6-11. The Christ whom Paul knows is the one who humbled himself in cruciform love and is now exalted as universal Lord. But Paul makes the remarkable claim that the same Jesus whose sovereignty will be confessed by the whole of creation is also **my** Lord (see Bockmuehl 1998, 206). Since this is the only occurrence in Paul's letters of the expression **my Lord,** it is worth our attention.

In the first place, it implies that Paul has submitted to Christ's lordship over his own life. This loyalty is rooted in Paul's experience of being captivated by Christ on the Damascus road, where he recognized Jesus as Lord (see Acts 22:8, 10).

Second, it reveals the intensely personal and experiential nature of Paul's relationship to Christ. Paul's language throbs with love and devotion. To know Christ in this way is also to be known and loved by Christ in return (see 1 Cor 8:3; Gal 2:20; 4:9). Such an intimate communion with Christ is the signature of Paul's life. It is so transcendent in value that it more than compensates for the loss of everything else (Bruce 1983, 88). At the same time, while Paul's relationship with Christ is personal, it is not individualistic. Later in the chapter he talks about the whole community awaiting its Lord Jesus Christ (3:20).

Paul goes on to state the purpose and goal of his decision to count everything as just so much muck in two ways.

First, he says, I reassess everything **that I may gain Christ.** This echoes the word "gain" (**profit**) in v 7. But it also turns everything upside down. What Paul used to consider gain has become a write-off because he has discovered the one true gain, Christ himself (Fee 1995, 320). We need to be careful not to misunderstand the metaphor. Paul does not think of Christ as a commodity to be acquired, like a high-yielding stock that might be added to one's portfolio (Fowl 2005, 153). Rather, *gaining* Christ goes hand in glove with *knowing* Christ.

What Paul desires to **gain** is the relationship with Christ this passage describes. The Greek purpose clause (*hina*, **in order that**) suggests that Paul's "gaining" of Christ has a future orientation (implied by the aorist tense of the verb). On one hand, Paul has already gained Christ through coming to know him in his conversion. On the other, he is still on a journey, which will only be completed when he gains Christ in a full and final sense on the last day.

■ **9** The second phrase, **and be found in him** (v 9), is parallel to knowing and gaining Christ (v 8). Here the emphasis is on *where* Paul desires to be found—**in Christ.** In the present context, this has to do with being united with Christ through sharing in his death and resurrection (3:10; on the phrase **in Christ,** see the comments on 1:1).

Once again, Paul echoes the language of the Christ hymn in 2:6-11 as he recounts his own spiritual autobiography. Just as Jesus was "found" in human form in 2:8, so Paul longs to be **found** in fellowship with Christ, conformed to his own likeness (3:10). Again we see both the *now* and the *not yet* in this ambition. He is already *in Christ*. But he still anticipates the future consummation of his faith. Thus, there is a real sense in which Paul continues to look forward to being **found in him** on the final day when he stands in the presence of God (see O'Brien 1991, 392; Hooker, however, limits this phrase to Paul's present experience of Christ, 2000, 527). This future hope is the goal of Paul's story. The passive voice of the verb "be found" (*heurethō*) shows that the chief actor in this ongoing drama is God.

The rest of v 9 further explains what it means to be found **in Christ**. Paul puts this in terms of two mutually exclusive kinds of **righteousness**. He defines the first as ***my own righteousness,*** which **comes from the law**. The second is **the righteousness that comes from God**.

The contrast with Paul's description in vv 5-6 of his former righteousness in the Law could not be more striking. There he lists the things in which he once placed his trust as the basis of his relationship with God. These include circumcision and, in particular, his blameless righteousness in the Law and zeal for the Torah. As impressive as it all was from a human perspective, it was his **own righteousness**; that is, his own achievement. It was a righteousness that puts confidence in human privilege and performance, a righteousness that was neither desired nor accepted by God (Bockmuehl 1998, 209). Similarly, Paul speaks in Rom 10:2-3 about his fellow Jews' misguided zeal for God, which leads them to seek "their own" righteousness instead of God's.

What is more, the old righteousness was based on **the law** (*ek nomou*). Ultimately, it made one's relationship with God dependent on being circumcised and performing the works of the Law, rather than on what God has done in Christ.

Paul, however, considers the old brand of righteousness to be dung (v 8). He has abandoned it in the past, buried under the dust of the Damascus road. In its place (**but,** *alla*), he embraced a new form of **righteousness,** which **comes from God and is by faith**.

Paul, then, is using the term **righteousness** (*dikaiosynē*) in two different senses in this verse. The old righteousness signifies something like upright behavior, as in v 6. In contrast, the new "righteousness" has to do, in the first place, with a *right relationship* with God (Fee 1995, 322).

In fact, the language of *righteousness* is exceptionally rich and flexible in Paul's letters, and its meaning has been hotly debated (on this, see Ziesler 1972; Onesti and Brauch 1993). Does the **righteousness that comes from God** refer to God's declaring sinners who deserve to be condemned, "not guilty," on the basis of what Christ has done (*forensic* justification)? Does it have to do with God making people ethically righteous? Or is it the saving work of God that has the power to transform those who are justified? (see Thielman 1995, 171-72).

Although the issues are complex, it seems best to find the background to Paul's understanding of righteousness in Paul's Bible, the LXX. In the Greek OT, righteousness is a covenant word. It operates within the sphere of the covenant relationship between God and his people (for the covenant context of righteousness in Paul, see, e.g., Dunn 1998, 340-46; Hays 1992, 1129-33; Wright 1997, 95-133). This relational understanding of righteousness has a number of dimensions, including (see esp. Talbert 2002, 37-39):

- God's righteousness often refers to God's faithfulness and love on behalf of his covenant people (see, e.g., Pss 5:7-8; 89:13-14; Isa 11:5; 16:5).
- God's righteousness is seen in his saving and delivering activity, which fulfills God's covenant obligation toward Israel (see, e.g., 1 Sam 12:7; Pss 65:5; 71:15; 98:2; Isa 45:23-24; 46:13; 62:1-2).
- God's righteousness "justifies" humans. That is, he "sets them right," allowing them to benefit from his righteousness. This can involve removal of the sinner's guilt; i.e., forgiveness (Ps 51:14; see Isa 43:25-26; 53:11), rewarding the righteous (1 Kgs 8:32), vindicating people before their enemies (Isa 50:8), or delivering/vindicating them in the end (e.g., Isa 51:5-8; 62:1-2; Mic 7:9-10). In addition, some Qumran texts talk about God's righteousness bringing purity to the believer (e.g., 1QH 11:30; 1QH 4:37).
- God's righteousness can be given to people so that they can act righteously. Psalm 72:1-2, for example, asks that God give his righteousness to the king, enabling the king to judge justly (see *Let. Aris.* 280).
- Israel's righteousness involves a response to God's covenant faithfulness—practicing justice and fulfilling the demands of the covenant (see, e.g., Isa 1:26; 16:5; Amos 5:7, 24; 6:12).

It is in this covenant connection that we must place Paul's understanding of righteousness in Phil 3:9. Elsewhere, especially in Romans, Paul speaks of the "righteousness of God" (*dikaiosynē theou*, Rom 1:17; 3:5, 21, 22; 10:3; 2 Cor 5:21). Although the emphasis varies from case to case, this term primarily refers to God's covenant love and faithfulness seen in his saving activity in Christ.

But in v 9 Paul speaks of the righteousness **from** God (*hē ek theou dikaiosynē*). Here Paul is not emphasizing God's own righteousness or righteousness as a divine activity. Rather, he stresses (1) the *source* of righteousness—God; and (2) the character of righteousness as a divine *gift* to believers (see also Rom 5:17; 10:3; 1 Cor 1:30). Paul contrasts his old achievement-oriented, Law-based righteousness with God's gracious gift of a restored relationship with himself.

At the same time, the vertical dimension cannot be divorced from the horizontal. God's gift of righteousness enables people to practice justice and live rightly in relation to others (Ps 72:1-2). For Paul, a right relationship with God that does not involve righteous living is unimaginable (Fee 1995, 322 n 35).

The "righteousness from God," therefore, means more than simply a legal *status* that God bestows upon the sinner (see Wesley n.d., 512). It is the restoring of a right *relationship* between persons through the work of Christ. In this relationship, people acknowledge God's claims upon their lives and live accordingly. And although Paul here speaks in the first person ("I"), a right personal relationship with God entails inclusion into the covenant community and expresses itself in right relationships with others.

Finally, righteousness has a future dimension. God's gift of righteousness is something Paul "has" (*echōn*). But it is also something that he *will* have, when he ultimately is **found** in Christ (v 9) at the time of the future resurrection (v 11). Here righteousness likely includes the biblical idea that the God who is faithful to his covenant will vindicate the righteous in the end. A right relationship with God offers the sure hope of acceptance by God on the final day, when God sets right the entire universe (Gorman 1991, 135-36).

But *how* does God bring about this new covenant relationship? This brings us to one of the most hotly contested phrases in the letter: **through faith in Christ.** Our problem is that the precise meaning of the Greek phrase *pistis Christou* (literally, "the faith of Christ") is far from clear.

In the first place, the word **faith** has a broader range of meaning in Greek than in English (it can sometimes mean "faithfulness"; see Rom 3:3). Second, the phrase "of Christ" (the Greek genitive) can be understood in two different senses. Should we take it as **faith <u>in</u> Christ** (an objective genitive) or as "the faith [or "faithfulness"] *of* Christ" (a subjective genitive)? The former, traditional translation is reflected in the NIV. The latter rendering is offered as an alternate translation in TNIV and NRSV. However, it has seen a rising swell of support among scholars over the past several decades (see especially Hays 1997, and Hays' bibliography). What makes it so hard to decide is that both readings are grammatically possible and both can make good sense out of the various passages in which the phrase occurs (see Rom 3:22, 26; Gal 2:16 [twice]; 3:22).

The second reading, which speaks of "the faithfulness *shown by* Christ," has several things in its favor. First, it avoids the redundancy of two references to human faith in the same verse. If "faith in Christ" refers to Paul's faith, then why would he need to add the phrase **by faith** at the end of the verse? Second, some interpreters argue that the instrumental use of the preposition **through** (*dia*) "the faith of Christ" fits best with divine, not human, action. That is, true righteousness is brought about **through** Christ's *faithfulness* on the cross, rather than through human faith (Bockmuehl 1998, 211). Third, the notion of "the faithfulness of Christ" fits nicely with the thought of Phil 2:6-11, where Paul emphasizes Jesus' faithful obedience to the point of death.

Without question, the balance this reading offers between God's initiative ("through the faithfulness of Christ") and the human response ("by faith") is theologically appealing. Nevertheless, the evidence favors the traditional reading. Consider the following:

- Although Paul refers to Christ's *obedience* (Phil 2:8; Rom 5:19), nowhere does he speak unambiguously of Jesus' own "faith" or his "faithfulness." Nor does Paul make Jesus the subject of the verb "to believe" (*pisteuō*). On the other hand, Paul often refers to believers having faith *in* Christ (see Rom 10:14; Gal 2:16; 3:26; Eph 1:15; Col 1:4; 2:5; Phlm 5), including earlier in this letter (Phil 1:29).
- Far from unnecessary, the two references to **faith** in 3:9 add emphasis and clarity. Paul repeats both "righteousness" and "faith" to reinforce his point: true righteousness comes not by human endeavor but by faith in Christ (see also Gal 2:16; Rom 3:22).
- The Greek grammar most naturally suggests that both references to "faith" refer to the same thing. The second occurrence of "faith" has an article [*tēi pistei*], which refers back to Paul's faith that was just mentioned. It seems unlikely that the Philippians would have recognized a sudden shift from Christ's faith to a human response of faith within the same clause (see Dunn 1997, 79).
- In the context of Phil 3, Paul contrasts two competing means of achieving righteousness: confidence or trust in what is merely human ("the flesh," v 3; "my own," v 9) and glorying or trusting *in* Christ (vv 3, 9; Deasley 2007, 225 n 2).

We must conclude, then, that in 3:9 the focus is on the faith of believers who trust in Christ rather than the faithfulness of Christ himself. At the same time, I cannot help but wonder, along with Robert Jewett, whether we *must* make an either/or decision (2007, 277-78). Grammarians recognize that it is possible for an author to intend for a Greek genitive to have both an objective (e.g., "faith in Christ") and a subjective (e.g., "Christ's faith/faithfulness") sense (e.g., Wallace 1996, 119-21). Perhaps we cannot rule out the possibility that Paul recognized the phrase's ambiguity and was quite happy for it to have a pregnant meaning for his audience.

In any case, Hays reminds us not to overstate the differences between these two options for the phrase "faith of Christ." Both maintain that righteousness does not come from the Law. Both hold that being rightly related to

God is grounded in God's gracious act in the death and resurrection of Christ. And both see faith as the appropriate response to what God has done (1992, 1131).

Paul draws special attention in v 9 to the reality that God's gift of righteousness is accepted **through faith** (*dia pisteōs*) **in Christ** and ***on the basis of faith*** (*epi tēi pistei*). Here **faith** is not a matter of merely assenting to a belief system. In the context, it means that Paul has abandoned all of the assets and assurances that propped up his own righteousness; he now relies utterly on God's saving work in Christ (Bockmuehl 1998, 213).

At the same time, faith is more than a one-time act of believing in Christ. Rather, it is a Spirit-enabled, ongoing response of trust, faithfulness, and obedience (see Rom 1:5; 16:26, "the obedience of faith"). Such a continuing response characterizes a right covenant relationship with God and the community's life "in Christ." This also means that "faith" is more than the individual choice to become a believer. It also means to participate in the shared life of a community, whose existence is defined by Christ (see 2:5-11).

■ **10** In this verse we come to the heart of Paul's spirituality: ***that I may know him*** [Christ] ***in the power of his resurrection and participation in his sufferings.*** The precise connection between this statement of purpose and what comes before it is not clear. Most likely it expresses the goal of being found "in Christ" and having a new God-given righteousness that depends on faith (so Vincent 1897, 103; Fee 1995, 327; for the view that this clause is parallel to "that I may gain Christ and be found in him," see O'Brien 1991, 400-401).

At the same time, v 10 picks up on the thought of "knowing Christ Jesus my Lord" in v 8 and gives it a more concrete definition. Paul had first come to **know Christ** years earlier in his world-shattering encounter with the risen Christ on the Damascus road. But for Paul this experience was not a distant memory to be preserved and admired like a fine museum piece. He discovered in Christ an inexhaustible fullness; he realized there was always more of Christ to come to know (Bruce 1983, 90). **To know Christ,** therefore, became "the overriding and unfading ambition of Paul's life" (Bockmuehl 1998, 213-14). As we saw in v 8, this is not a knowledge *about* Jesus but rather an intimate personal relationship with him.

Knowing Christ in this way transforms the person who knows him (Marshall 1993, 148). As a result, Paul further defines what it means for him to know Christ as knowing **the power of his resurrection** and ***participation in his sufferings.***

It is important that we see the structural relationship of the three objects of the verb **to know.** Paul is probably not listing three separate things he desires to know: Christ, his resurrection power, and the sharing of his sufferings (so NIV). Rather, Paul explains more precisely what knowing Christ means: *both* the power of his resurrection *and* partnership in his sufferings (taking the first "and" [*kai*] to be explanatory). In other words, these are two aspects of knowing Christ.

Before we look at the specific meaning of these phrases, we need to say a word about the order in which they appear in the text. Why is the sequence "counterchronological"—first resurrection, then suffering? Probably because Paul emphasizes that sharing in Christ's sufferings is only possible through the power of Christ's resurrection. According to Paul's "theological calendar," Easter comes *before* Good Friday (Craddock 1985, 61). Apart from the power and vindication of the resurrection, present suffering makes little sense.

To further underline the point, vv 10-11 form a chiasm, in which the two outer terms are "resurrection" and the two inner terms are "suffering" and "death":

a **power of his <u>resurrection</u>**
   b *participation in his <u>sufferings</u>*
   b' *being conformed to his <u>death</u>*
a' **attain to the <u>resurrection</u> from the dead**

Let us note two things here. First, there is a progression of thought within each of these pairs: from suffering to death; and from resurrection as a present empowerment to resurrection as a future hope. Second, Paul's participation in Christ's sufferings and death is surrounded by the reality of Christ's resurrection and his experience of it. For Christians living under the brilliant light of Easter, the resurrection is both the first *and* the last word (Bockmuehl 1998, 214).

What does it mean for Paul to know Christ in **the power of his resurrection**? The **power** (*dynamis*) that Paul has in mind is *God's* power, which raised Christ from the dead (see Rom 1:4; 1 Cor 6:14; 2 Cor 13:4; Col 2:12; Eph 1:19-20). Some commentators think this primarily refers to Paul's hope of sharing in the future power of the resurrection from the dead, as in v 11 (so Gorman 2001, 331; Koperski 1996, 184-85). But Paul *already* has a surpassing knowledge of Christ (see v 8). Consequently, the emphasis here is more likely on his ongoing experience of God's life-giving power. Paul wants to know the divine power that was supremely demonstrated in Christ's resurrection, not simply as a past fact, but as a present force.

But, paradoxically, Paul will experience the power of Christ's resurrection only if he is also willing to share in Christ's afflictions. Governed by a single article in the Greek text, the notions of the **power of his resurrection** and ***participation in his sufferings*** are intimately bound together. They are like flip sides of the same coin. On the one hand, we cannot expect to know Christ in his resurrection power apart from **sharing in his sufferings.** On the other, God's enabling power makes enduring sufferings for Christ's sake possible (see 2 Cor 12:8-10).

Paul uses the word *koinōnia* here in terms of active **participation** (see 1:5; 2:1; the NIV's **fellowship of sharing** is an overtranslation). For Paul, to know Christ intimately involves sharing in his sufferings. What kind of **sufferings** (*pathēmata*) does Paul have in mind? In the context, they are probably not the general sufferings that believers experience because they are in a fallen world (see Rom 8:18-25). More likely this is a reference to the difficulties and persecution the apostle endured on behalf of Christ and the gospel. Already Paul has assured the Philippians that it was a privilege to suffer *for* Christ (1:29). Now he affirms that Christians also suffer *with* Christ. In another letter Paul testifies, "the sufferings of Christ flow over into our lives" (2 Cor 1:5; see Col 1:24).

Once again, Paul's story is closely linked to Christ's story. Christ's resurrection and exaltation came by way of obedient suffering and the cross (Phil 2:6-11). And so, by analogy, Paul can only experience resurrection if he is willing to enter into Christ's sufferings and death (see Fee 1995, 322; Fowl 2005, 155). Knowing Christ intensely involves a profound identification with the Christ who suffered—a sharing of his very life and experience. There is a close parallel to this thought in 1 Pet 4:13: "But rejoice that you participate in the sufferings of Christ, so that you may be overjoyed when his glory is revealed."

A third aspect of knowing Christ is **becoming like him in his death.** Some commentators take this as a reference to literal martyrdom (e.g., Thurston 2005, 125, 128; Oakes 2001, 118-19). But the present tense verb, which refers to an ongoing experience, makes that highly unlikely. Rather, the thought is similar to that of 2 Cor 4:10-11, where Paul reminds his converts that he is "always carry[ing] around in [his] body the death of Jesus."

Paul uses a rare verb here. Literally, it means **being conformed** [*synmorphizomenos*] **to his death**. If we listen carefully, we will hear echoes of the Christ narrative in 2:6-8, where Jesus was found in the "form" (*morphē*) of a slave and became "obedient unto *death*" (KJV). **Being conformed to his death,** for both Paul and his audience, means living out the cross-shaped story of Christ. This surely involves God's work (the verb is in the passive voice: **being conformed**) of conforming Christians to the likeness of Christ, as they share in Christ's sufferings. But it goes beyond the previous phrase to include a cruciform attitude that characterizes the whole of life in Christ (see Fee 1995, 334; Fowl 2005, 155-56).

Just as Christ's way to the cross was a path of humility, obedience, and self-emptying love, so his followers embrace the same pattern of faithfulness. Michael J. Gorman calls this "cruciformity"—Christians living out their lives in conformity to the love story of the cross (2001). For Paul, to know Christ is to become like him. The more we share in Christ's sufferings and death, the more we are conformed to his likeness. And the more we are shaped into his likeness, the more we will experience the ongoing power of his resurrection.

■ **11** Yet the goal and climax of Paul's desire to know Christ lies in the future: ***if somehow I might attain the resurrection from the dead*** (v 11). Commentators have puzzled over why Paul uses the intensive form of the word for **resurrection** (*exanastasis*), which occurs only here in the NT (*anastasis* without the prefix is the usual form).

Some interpreters speculate that Paul is deliberately countering opponents who claimed that the resurrection had already taken place (e.g., Witherington 1994, 91; Thurston 2005, 125). But that must be read into the text. More likely, Paul's unusual word for resurrection, coupled with the phrase "out of (*ek*) the dead," emphasizes that this is a *future* rising from the dead. This implies a contrast with the present experience of Christ's resurrection power mentioned in the previous verse (Hawthorne and Martin 2004, 201; Fee 1995, 335 n 68).

Verse 11 holds another surprise. An unexpected ***if somehow*** (*ei pōs*) introduces the verse. Does Paul harbor a hint of doubt over whether he will indeed participate in the future resurrection? If so, how would that align with the apostle's robust confidence elsewhere that the resurrection is a certain hope for God's people (e.g., 1 Cor 15:20, 49-55; Rom 6:5; 2 Cor 5:1; 1 Thess 4:16-17)?

One popular interpretation is that Paul has no uncertainty about *whether* he will experience the resurrection. He is only unclear about what *route* he will take to get there—whether through martyrdom, some other form of death, or Christ's return in his lifetime.

This is possible, but Chrysostom has a better explanation: Paul's hesitation reflects his awareness that neither he nor the Philippians can presume on God's grace (*Hom. Phil.* 11.3.7-10). Earlier Paul called the church to work out their own salvation with fear and trembling in response to God's work among them (Phil 2:12-13). The verses that immediately follow this statement (3:12-14) are unequivocal that there is still a race to be run, a goal to be reached, and a prize to be gained. Elsewhere, Paul insists that he must dedicate himself to the gospel like an athlete in training. He wants to ensure that, even after preaching to others, he himself will not be disqualified from the prize (1 Cor 9:27).

The end-time resurrection is Paul's fervent and confident hope. But the ***if somehow*** reminds his audience that it is only those who continue to be conformed to Christ's obedience and suffering now who will share in Christ's resurrection to come (see Rom 8:17; Phil 2:6-11; 3:17-21; Hooker 2000, 529).

Paul's personal testimony in 3:10-11, then, serves as an example for his readers (see v 17). For both Paul and the Philippians, knowing Christ means a life of self-emptying service for others in conformity to the cross. Likewise, the power of Christ's resurrection becomes a present experience in the midst of afflictions. But they will only know that power in its fullness when they are conformed to the likeness of the glorified Christ in the resurrection from the dead.

FROM THE TEXT

This passage is undoubtedly one of the highpoints in the Pauline letters. What starts out as a stern warning against rival teachers ends up as a magnificent expression of Paul's spirituality and his understanding of the gospel. The core values and experience that Paul sets forth in these verses continue to challenge the church today.

1. *A vote of no confidence in the flesh.* We are still tempted to put confidence in what is merely human—the "flesh" (3:4). Although the particulars may be different, Paul's list of birth privileges becomes uncomfortably familiar when we look at the key concerns it reflects. Issues such as religion, family background, tribal or ethnic identity, nationality, language, and culture continue to be major sources of both pride and division in our world. Today we might also add matters like denominational affiliation, theological tradition, political loyalty, or gender to the mix.

Identity issues can still be used to draw borders between who is "in" and who is "out," or between first-class and second-class members of the Christian fellowship. For more than two decades, I have been involved in theological education within multicultural settings. The experience has shown me that nationalistic pride and cultural biases die hard, even among theological students and teachers—including the one I know best!

At the same time, it is important to note that Paul does not want to erase all cultural and social differences. Believers do not shed their cultural identities when they walk through the door of faith. Paul does not compel Jews to give up their Jewish lifestyle. God accepts Gentiles as Gentiles, not as Jewish proselytes. Privileges of birth and cultural identities are *relativized* by the gospel, not removed. For Christians, they cease to be a source of pride or confidence. Believers boast in Christ alone.

Likewise, this passage speaks forcefully to the human tendency to think that spiritual success is based on personal achievements rather than in knowing Christ. Ironically, this might involve the very things that we think are expressing our devotion to Christ. Perhaps they are "Christian" practices like keeping church rules or traditions, giving to the cause of missions, faithful church attendance, or zeal for evangelism. Whenever such activities become reasons for pride or spiritual confidence, they shift from the asset column to join our spiritual losses.

It is even possible for Christian leaders to use their ministries to establish their spiritual significance. As a fledgling pastor, I struggled with feelings that God's approval was all tied up with my *performance* in ministry. As a result, I was constantly afraid of failing God. When I didn't succeed according to whatever standards I set for myself or others set for me, I did not feel good about myself or my ministry. I was putting confidence in spiritual *successes* rather than in Christ. Paul's example has been teaching me, however, that all of my personal accomplishments amount to nothing when I view them as assets before God. Can we embrace the liberating news that our confidence in God's pleasure is not based on our human performance or spiritual exploits, but in "the surpassing greatness of knowing Christ" (3:8)?

2. *The sufficiency of salvation in Christ.* This passage raises another question, which is related to the previous discussion: Is what God has done in Christ truly *sufficient* for our salvation? Or is something else needed to make our salvation more complete or effective? For the rival teachers behind Phil 3, that "something else" was a deeper commitment to the Jewish law, especially the rite of circumcision. For us, "add-ons" to the gospel can take a multitude of forms.

Syncretism—combining incompatible beliefs or practices with the Christian faith—is one example. Thus, recent converts from paganism might continue to wear amulets, perform rituals, or visit the local diviner when they feel they need some "extra" help or power. But syncretism flourishes in the churches of the global North and West, as well. We find it in more blatant forms, like supplementing Christian faith with confidence in astrology or yoga. It also expresses itself in more subtle ways, such as tacking on a "gospel" of materialism and consumerism to the way of the cross.

In other cases, we place certain beliefs or practices alongside of knowing Christ. In effect, they become requirements for *real* salvation. For example, in some majority world settings, specific *ways of expressing the faith from a missionary's culture* are imposed on converts as indispensable supplements to a relationship with God. Sometimes a certain *interpretation of the Bible*—a particular view of end-time events, for instance—becomes a mandatory identity card for membership in the people of God. Or perhaps loyalty to a particular *political system or party* is seen as a litmus test of true Christian commitment. At times within the holiness tradition, distinctive *ways of behaving* (what we do or don't do) and *appearing* (what we wear or don't wear) have been confused with Christian essentials.

Or suppose particular *spiritual experiences*, whether we think about speaking in tongues, mystical prayer or visions, or anything else, are deemed necessary for being a "complete" Christian. When that happens, those experiences can crowd Christ out of the center of our relationship with God. The church must continually seek to discern between what is essential and what is not (Phil 1:10). With Paul, we must tenaciously resist the temptation to impose secondary norms on our fellow Christians. Our challenge is to keep what is *central* at the center—gaining Christ and being found in him.

3. *The righteousness from God.* Seeing the OT background to v 9, as well

as its context in ch 3, helps us move beyond the old battles between Protestants and Roman Catholics over the meaning of "the righteousness that comes from God." Luther championed the idea that God saves us by bestowing on us an *imputed* righteousness; that is, "a righteousness that comes completely from the outside and is foreign" (Luther 1972, 136). In other words, "God looks at me through the death of his Son, and he declares me just" (Carson 1996, 86).

In contrast, Roman Catholic theology traditionally affirmed that God *imparts* righteousness to us, actually transforming us within by his grace. This "infused" righteousness was normally seen as the *basis* for acceptance by God (Dunning 1988, 345; the 1999 "Joint Declaration on the Doctrine of Justification," signed by both Lutherans and Roman Catholics, goes a long way to bridge this historic divide).

I suspect that Paul would have been puzzled by such long-running debates within Christ's church. If Paul were asked, "Is that 'righteousness from God' you mentioned something God *declares* or something God *effects*?" perhaps his answer would have been, "Yes." In spite of the considerable theological freight the word "righteousness" carries, we should not forget that behind it all is a *relationship* with God (Thurston 2005, 127-28). And that covenantal relationship is wedded to knowing Christ.

This relational understanding will help guard us from viewing God's "right-wising" work in Christ as a kind of "legal fiction"; God counts people as righteous even though they are not. As Wesley recognized in his day, this is not just a theological question. It is also a pastoral concern: "What we are afraid of is this;—lest any should use this phrase, 'The righteousness of Christ is imputed to me,' as a cover for his unrighteousness. We have known this done a thousand times" (1978, 5:244).

For his part, Wesley tried to steer a *via media* that values both the Protestant insistence on justification by grace through faith and the Roman Catholic emphasis on sanctification or inward renewal (see, e.g., 1986, 3:505-7; sermon "On God's Vineyard"). For Wesley, and, I believe, for Paul, we are pardoned in order to participate in God's own nature (Maddox 1994, 168). Said differently, we are put right with God so that we can live rightly.

4. *Knowing Christ in his death and resurrection.* The goal of having God's righteousness, and everything else in Paul's life, is an intimate, growing, all-embracing knowledge of Christ (3:8, 10). This is the core of Christian spirituality. As Paul testifies earlier in the letter, "To live is Christ" (1:21). But it is *how* Paul defines what knowing Christ means for him, and by implication, for us, that gives us the most trouble: being conformed to *both* Christ's suffering and dying *and* his victorious resurrection. We can easily become unbalanced in either direction.

For instance, while living in the Philippines I observed that the most popular images of Christ were those of Jesus as an innocent child (the *Santo Niño*) and as the suffering or entombed Jesus. Such representations resonate powerfully with people who deal with ongoing physical and socioeconomic hardship. But they only communicate a half-truth when they deter people from experiencing the victory and power of Christ's resurrection. In the words of Filipina theologian Melba P. Magaay, "In our message we need to make the emphatic transition from the cross to the empty tomb! . . . Failure to do so consigns our people to the subtle demonic lie of seeing the work of Jesus, and life itself, as an endless passion, a picture of eternal defeat and unrelieved tragedy" (1987, 8). We are not left simply to *endure* hardships and suffering, apart from Christ's resurrection power and the enabling of the Spirit.

In contrast, the greater danger for Christians in the Western world is this: They embrace the victory of Christ's resurrection, while they at the same time avoid conforming to the cross in their own experience. Popular preaching and theology too often promise power without weakness, success without suffering, prosperity without sacrifice, salvation without discipleship, religion without righteousness. Paul's meaning is light-years from this kind of triumphalism. As Gorman frames it, the question is not *whether* we can experience the power of Christ's resurrection, but *how*; we experience it only by way of the cross (2001, 280).

Paul himself testifies in Galatians: "May I never boast except in the cross of our Lord Jesus Christ, through which the world has been crucified to me, and I to the world" (6:14). Christian spirituality is cruciform, or it is not truly Christian at all. Brennan Manning affirms: "The pattern is always the same. All roads lead to Calvary. We reach life only through death; we learn tenderness only through pain; we come to light only through darkness . . . we must be formed into the pattern of his death if we are to become Easter men and Easter women" (2002, 133). Cruciform living is a high-risk existence that will cost us *everything*.

How does this speak to the contemporary church, in which our passion for knowing Christ in both his suffering and his resurrection power is often distracted by the cultural "powers" of materialism and self-indulgence? Fee wisely observes that "a common return to 'the surpassing worth of knowing Christ Jesus our Lord' could go a long way toward renewing the church for its task in the post-modern world" (1995, 337). To do so, we must become a people who live out the Pauline paradox—empowered by the resurrection, conformed to the cross.

5. *Theology as biography*. In this passage, one of the most profound statements of the gospel in all of Paul's writings addresses us in the form of a personal testimony. By telling his story, the apostle unfolds the gospel of salvation by God's grace through faith and the reality of union with the crucified and

risen Christ. At the same time, Paul's autobiography is exemplary for others because it is shaped by the story of Christ crucified.

This marriage between theology and biography must characterize *our* lives, as well. Particularly in a postmodern context, our theological formulations about the gospel will have a hollow ring unless people can see them demonstrated in the lives of ordinary Christians. Our most cherished doctrines, such as justification by faith or sanctification, are no better than volumes on a dusty shelf if they are not translated into breathing biography. We cannot be satisfied to give lip service to doctrines that are no longer our personal testimony.

Like Paul, we must read our own life stories into the larger story of God's saving purposes for his creation (see Fowl 2005, 220-21). Our lives and our Christian communities must *be* the revolutionary, transforming story of God's grace revealed in Christ.

B. Pressing on Toward the Prize (3:12-14)

BEHIND THE TEXT

Paul's personal narrative continues in these verses. At the same time, it takes a new direction. He has just stated in 3:7-11 that his singular passion is to know and become like Christ. But perhaps someone might mistakenly think that this is already an accomplished fact. He, therefore, clarifies in these verses that the goal of fully knowing Christ lies in the future. His present life is one of constant pursuit, motivated by the prize that is ahead of him.

This final installment of Paul's autobiography in ch 3 is more closely connected to what comes before it than is often recognized. The NIV, for example, inserts a new heading before v 12, which implies a change of subject. But the section begins with the words **not that** (v 12*a*). This alerts us that what Paul is about to say is in some sense a contrast to what he has just stated in the previous verses (Fee 1995, 339). The expression **not that** implies *both* continuity *and* a shift in focus.

Some interpreters think there is a new subject here because of Paul's assurance in v 12 that he has not yet **been made perfect.** This verb, along with the related adjective "perfect" in v 15, is often read as evidence that Paul is countering "opponents" of some stripe in vv 12-16. Normally, these are thought to be people who claimed they had *already* reached a state of present perfection (for various suggestions by scholars as to the identity and views of these adversaries, see Fee 1995, 341, n 15). But such "mirror reading" runs ahead of the evidence.

All told, vv 12-14 make better sense if: (1) we treat them as a separate unit from vv 15-16, which begin to *apply* Paul's story (against most commentators, who take vv 12-16 as a single paragraph); and (2) we see that its basic purpose is to exhort the church, not to confront opponents (so Fowl 2005, 159; Oakes 2001, 119-20).

Paul lays out the dynamic character of his Christian life in the form of two striking parallel statements (emphasis added):

Not that I have already obtained (v 12*a*)
But I press on to take hold (v 12*b*)

I do not consider myself yet to have taken hold (v 13*a*)
But . . . I press on toward the goal (vv 13*b*-14)

In both sentences, the thought begins with a disclaimer stating what is not the case. This is followed by a positive assertion of Paul's determination to press forward (adapted from Silva 2005, 173). Likewise, in each sentence the main verb, **I press on** (*diōkō*), accents Paul's present perspective and mind-set.

From a rhetorical standpoint, this brief passage is elegant and packed with emotion. Paul calls into service a remarkable range of literary and rhetorical features, such as:

- repetition (e.g., **press on,** vv 12, 25)
- wordplay (e.g., the double use of the verb *katalambanō* in v 12*b*; Paul's aim is to **take hold** of that for which Christ has **taken hold** of him)
- contrasting parallelism (e.g., **forgetting what is behind . . . straining toward what is ahead,** v 13)
- direct address (**brothers,** v 13*a*)
- the dominant athletic metaphor of the footrace

Such persuasive strategies are intended to move his readers to change their attitudes and behavior.

As was the case in the first part of ch 3, Paul's story serves as an example for the Philippians to follow (v 17). Personal testimony becomes a powerful tool for urging his readers to pursue with a single-minded focus the ultimate goal of full communion with Christ.

IN THE TEXT

■ **12** The passage starts with an important qualification of what Paul has just said in the previous verses: **not that I have already obtained all this** (literally, *not that I have already received/attained*). The direct object in the NIV translation—**all this**—does not appear in Greek. Paul does not explicitly state what he has not yet obtained. Nevertheless, there has been no shortage of attempts to "fill in the blank." Is what Paul has not yet attained the resurrection from the dead he speaks about in v 11? Or does it look ahead to the "prize" mentioned in v 14? Or is it simply "Christ" himself (see O'Brien's discussion of various proposals; 1991, 420-21)?

More likely, what Paul is pursuing, but has not yet obtained, is the surpassing gain for which he has lost everything else, described in vv 8-11 (implied by the NIV's **all**). Above all, this involves knowing Christ and being found in him. Although it is Paul's ambition to know Christ now, both in Jesus' resurrection power and sufferings, a full knowledge of Christ must await Paul's participation in the end-time resurrection from the dead (vv 10-11; see vv 20-21).

The second verb describing the "not yet" of Paul's Christian experience is more controversial. The apostle assures his readers that he still has not **been made perfect** (*teteleiōmai*). The verb *teleioō* occurs only here in Paul's letters, but we encounter its adjective form, "perfect" (*teleios*), in v 15. Many interpreters think that Paul is co-opting the terminology of his opponents in order to correct some form of wrong-headed "perfectionism." One common explanation is that Paul is concerned about people in Philippi with a gnostic-type misunderstanding. We know that some deviating Christian groups held that they had already arrived at resurrection perfection in a spiritual sense (see 2 Tim 2:17-18; Hawthorne and Martin 2004, 206-7; Bruce 1983, 95).

Alternatively, Bockmuehl notes that members of the Jewish community at Qumran regarded themselves as "perfect" due to their observance of the Law (see Phil 3:6b). As a result, he thinks that Paul's Jewish rivals (see vv 2-3) may have used this language to make similar claims (1998, 221). The letter gives us no other indication, however, that there were people claiming "perfection" in Philippi. Furthermore, it is far from certain that Paul is talking about moral or spiritual perfection here.

The verb *teleioō* has a number of possible meanings, including "attaining the goal in view." In light of the race imagery that follows, this is probably what Paul has in mind. This verb, then, echoes the thought of the first one, making it more specific. The resurrection still lies in the future; therefore Paul has not yet **reached the goal** of full union with Christ.

In contrast to what he has not yet attained, Paul strenuously pursues the end that lies ahead. **I press on** (v 12b) translates a verb (*diōkō*) that in v 6 describes his relentless pursuit of the destruction of the church, thus, *persecuting* the church. Paul, however, can also use it in a positive sense: Christians must "strive after" virtues like peace (Rom 14:19), love (1 Cor 14:1), or good deeds (1 Thess 5:15). What is more, in Paul's world, this word could describe an army in hot pursuit of its opponents or hunters who persevere in stalking their prey (Liddell and Scott 1996, 440). But here (and more explicitly in Phil 3:14) the picture is more likely that of a runner who presses on with tenacity toward the finish line.

The object of Paul's ardent pursuit is **to take hold** (literally, "if indeed [*ei kai*] I might take hold") **of that for which Christ Jesus took hold of me.** There is a double play on words here. First, the verb **take hold** (*katalambanō*) is a compound form of the verb "obtain" (*lambanō*) that appears earlier in the verse.

Second, there is a skillful play on the active and passive forms of the verb "to take hold." Paul's striving to "capture" the eschatological prize (v 14) is only possible because he was first "captured" by Christ. This surely is an allusion to Paul's encounter with Christ on the Damascus road, when his life took a complete U-turn. As F. F. Bruce puts it, "Paul was conscripted into the service of Christ, but never was there a more willing conscript" (1983, 96). Now his whole life is focused on fulfilling the purpose for which Christ drafted him.

The Greek phrase behind the NIV's **that for which** (*eph' ho*) can be taken in two ways (see esp. Fitzmyer 1993). On the one hand, it could express the *reason* for Paul's hot pursuit of Christ (*"because* Christ Jesus has made me his own," NRSV; see Rom 5:12; 2 Cor 5:4; Wallace 1996, 342; O'Brien 1991, 425). On the other hand, the phrase could refer to the *aim* (**that for which**) of Christ's grabbing hold of Paul (NIV). Hooker shows that the second option fits the context better: "Paul's endeavors now are not simply the response to what Christ has done, but the completion of God's purpose for him" (2000, 533). In either case, however, the point is that God's work in Christ is first and foremost. As in 2:12-13, human striving, which is vital, must be grounded in the prior grace of God (see Silva 2005, 176).

■ **13** Quite unexpectedly, Paul draws his audience into his story. By appealing to them directly as **brothers and sisters** (v 13), he makes it clear that what he is narrating applies to them, as well.

Next, he stresses once again that he has not yet arrived, repeating the same verb ("take hold") that occurs twice in v 12: **I do not consider myself yet to have taken hold of it** (the object "it" does not appear in the Greek text).

At this point the athletic metaphor, only implied until now, becomes explicit. Like a runner in the midst of a footrace, Paul ignores what is behind him and fixes his gaze exclusively on the prize ahead. The Greek is startling—literally, **but one thing** (*hen de*)! Read out loud, this staccato statement could not help but grab the attention of the hearers. In 1 Cor 9:24-25, Paul uses the footrace metaphor to accent that only one of the competitors will gain the prize. But here the focus is not on the winning but on *how* the athlete runs the race (Fowl 2005, 161).

Paul and Athletic Competition

Paul's letters are peppered with images from the realm of athletics. These include allusions to stadium races (Gal 2:2; 1 Cor 9:24; Phil 2:16; 3:12-14; 2 Tim 4:7), boxing matches (1 Cor 9:26), athletic training (1 Cor 9:25, 27; 1 Tim 4:7-8;

compare 1 Tim 6:12; 2 Tim 4:7), and the victor's crown (1 Cor 9:25; Phil 3:14; 2 Tim 2:5; 4:8). This reflects the prominent role that athletic training and competition played within Greco-Roman culture. The most important venues for athletic events were the Greek games, such as the Olympic Games or the Isthmian Games, near Corinth, and Roman public festivals, held in numerous cities.

Knowing that his readers in Hellenistic cities like Philippi and Corinth would be familiar with the games, Paul uses them as analogies of the Christian struggle (Pucci 2000, 210; on Paul's use of athletic metaphors, see esp., Pfitzner 1967 and Williams 1999, ch 12). This is all the more noteworthy, since many Jews of Paul's time rejected athletic competition altogether. After all, athletic events were generally connected to pagan religious celebrations, and male athletes competed in the nude (Couslan 2000, 141). We cannot say whether or not Paul had firsthand knowledge of the games. Nevertheless, he does not shy away from using them as a point of contact with his Gentile audience.

Paul's deployment of athletic metaphors was not unique in the ancient world. Greco-Roman philosophers, especially the Stoics and the Cynics, were fond of athletic images to describe the virtuous and disciplined life (see Malherbe 2000, 138). The Stoic philosopher Epictetus, for example, pictures those who face their hardships with courage and perseverance as "Olympic victors" (*Discourse* 1:24.3).

Paul explains the "one thing" that is his focus in the rest of this verse and in v 14. He begins with two picturesque, parallel phrases. The first, **forgetting what is behind,** suggests a runner who refuses to steal a glance behind and become distracted, either by other competitors or by the ground already covered (compare Lucian, *On Slander* 12).

But what is it that *Paul* has "forgotten"? In the context, **what is behind** surely includes Paul's Jewish pedigree and performance. These are the things he once trusted in but wrote off as loss when he met Christ (3:4-6; but Thielman 1995, 196, 206, disagrees). Hence, the verb "forget" (*epilanthanomai*) can hardly mean that Paul "utterly forgets that [the past] ever existed" (Thurston 2005, 126). Paul has not deleted the past from his memory. Rather he has completely reevaluated it in light of his surpassing knowledge of Christ (v 8; Fowl 2005, 161-62). Consequently, the things he once valued and pursued are no longer his focus of attention; he leaves them behind and treats them as filth in view of the goal ahead.

But is it only his *pre*-Christian past that Paul has disregarded? Apparently not, since he is still in the process of **forgetting** (a present tense participle). This implies that he is also thinking of his labors and accomplishments to this point as an apostle of Christ. Good or bad, success or failure, the past will not distract him from reaching the goal.

The flip side of the parallel is that Paul is **straining toward what is ahead.** This vivid verb (*epekteinomenos*) conjures up the image of a runner in the final stages of the competition, every muscle and sinew fully stretched, body bent forward, hand extended, eyes fixated on the finish line. It is worth noting that the Eastern father Gregory of Nyssa appealed to this phrase repeatedly when describing the progressive nature of the spiritual life (e.g., 1995, 81, 144, 211). Whereas Paul's emphasis seems to be on running in a way that will reach the goal ahead (see v 14), Gregory stressed, not attainment, but an *attitude* of continual stretching out toward God; never satisfied, we are constantly moving forward in the pursuit of virtue and a deeper communion with God.

■ **14** With such intensity of desire and purpose, Paul testifies, **I press on** [see v 12] **toward the goal.** Figuratively, the **goal** (*skopos*) is the marker at the finish line on which runners fix their sight (see the verb *skopeō*, "to focus attention on," used in v 17 and 2:4). For Paul, reaching the eschatological goal results in gaining the victor's **prize** (*brabeion*), which is his "ultimate reason for running" (Fee 1995, 348).

But what is the **prize**? A precise answer to that question becomes more challenging in light of the rather ambiguous phrase that defines the term. The NIV renders it, **for which God has called me heavenward in Christ Jesus.** A more literal translation would be, *the prize of the upward call of God in Christ Jesus.* This may be another allusion to the Greek games. The picture would be of the presiding judge calling up the victor at the race's end to receive a prize, usually a laurel or celery wreath (Hawthorne and Martin 2004, 210-11; but see Bockmuehl 1998, 223). Yet this athletic image by no means exhausts the meaning of the phrase. For Paul, the notion of God's **call** (*klēsis*) is charged with theological current (see Kruse 1993a, 84-85; Coenen, 1975, 1:271-76).

Some interpreters take the call itself to be the prize (a genitive of apposition). In this case, the prize would consist of God's calling to be with Christ in heaven (see Heb 3:1; Eph 2:6). But in Paul's metaphor the goal is a *future* prize, not a call that he has already received in his conversion (Bockmuehl 1998, 222). It is better, then, to follow the NIV, in which the prize signifies what those who have obeyed God's call receive. In other words, it is the prize *promised by* the divine call (see, e.g., O'Brien 1991, 432-33).

Here the **call** is not a restricted calling to ministry. Rather, it is God's comprehensive call to salvation, a call into fellowship with Christ (1 Cor 1:9). Paul received this calling when his Christian race began on the Damascus road, and it has sustained him throughout. Moreover, it is an ***upward*** (*anō*) call. This is not so much because of its heavenward direction but because of its heavenly origin, character, and purpose (Bockmuehl 1998, 223; see Col 3:1-2). The goal of God's calling is to share in his eternal presence and glory when Christ returns (see vv 20-21; Eph 1:18: "the hope to which he has called you"; Phil 4:4).

Finally, God's call is **in Christ Jesus.** I take this to mean that Christ is the *sphere* in which the divine call is given and carried out. God's salvation call is **in Christ** from beginning to end.

In this light, we can now more specifically identify the **prize** toward which the call of God is directed. It is none other than knowing Christ in a full and ultimate sense. The magnificent goal toward which Paul strains every fiber of his being is not the calling as such; or heaven; or even eternal life. The prize is Christ himself. Being found "in Christ," fully and finally, is the supreme reward for which Paul has counted everything else as loss. And as the following verses will show, this is the prize he fervently desires for his audience to gain, as well.

FROM THE TEXT

1. *Living eschatologically.* Paul's picture of the Christian life as a dynamic process resonates well with contemporary Christians. What often does not suit us so comfortably is that all of his present efforts are oriented toward the final day. Paul stretches every sinew, not just to improve himself, or to become a more fulfilled Christian. Rather, it is because he sees ahead of him a glorious future, to which God has called him. This is often missed when Christians, especially in the West, appropriate these verses on a popular level. Fee's comments on this passage are worth quoting at length:

> The singular and passionate focus on the future consummation, which Paul clearly intends as paradigmatic, often gets lost in the church—for a whole variety of reasons: in a scientific age, it is something of an embarrassment to many; in a world "come of age," only the oppressed think eschatologically, for reasons of weakness we are told; in an affluent age, who needs it? But Paul's voice should not be muffled so quickly and easily. For a race who by their very nature are oriented to the future but who have no real future to look forward to, here is a strikingly and powerfully Christian moment. The tragedy that attends the rather thoroughgoing loss of hope in contemporary Western culture is that we are now trying to make the present eternal. (1995, 350)

God's grand purpose for his people and for the whole of creation is to carry his good work "to completion until the day of Christ Jesus" (1:6; see 3:11, 20-21; 4:5).

What are the implications of such an end-time perspective? I will mention three.

First, it reminds us that for Christians, the present has meaning only in light of the future. Gazing intently at the future gives us eyes to see how God's ultimate purpose of new creation for the whole world is already being worked out in Christ and his church.

Second, an eschatological orientation motivates and energizes us to endure faithfully to the end.

Third, Paul's perspective speaks to the tension that marks the holy life. On the one hand, our present spiritual lives should be characterized by an intentional, single-minded direction ("one thing I do," v 13), through God's enabling grace. As Kierkegard famously put it, "Purity of heart is to will one thing." On the other hand, the focus of our Christian formation is not on the present but on the future—what we *shall* be. We have not yet been made perfect/reached the goal (v 12; see Dunning 1998, 162). The pursuit of holiness is lived out in the teeth of this tension.

2. *Ensuring that "the prize is right."* As we saw above, this passage spotlights the dynamic character of life in Christ. We have not arrived. We are continually moving forward, reaching upward, pressing onward. But toward what end? What constitutes our goal is a matter of foremost importance. For Paul, and for us, the prize that beckons us forward "is not something—it is Someone" (Welch 1988, 109). The full knowledge of Christ—this is the prize that awaits us at the end of the race.

Unlike many popular notions of the future today, Paul did not conceive of the goal of his journey as something literal and tangible, such as simply "getting to heaven" or "walking on streets of gold" or "wearing a crown." Nor was his hope focused on the chance to be reunited with departed loved ones, as sincere as such longings may be. For Paul, living meant Christ (1:21). Knowing Christ and becoming like him was both his present passion and his supreme goal for the future.

The goal motivates the journey. If our purpose is merely "making it to heaven," we might be tempted to rest on our past laurels and passively coast along until we finally receive our reward. Even worse, eternity might become "nothing more than a selfish pursuit born of a fear of death or hell" (Walton 2001, 469). But when the fullness of Christ is the prize ahead, then the journey is earmarked by a deepening desire for communion with God.

The fact that Paul presently came up short of the goal did not discourage him. Rather, it spurred him on to continually strain toward a growing intimacy with Christ. Do we share that same passion to know more of Christ?

John Wesley on Life's Purpose and Goal

And let it be observed, as this is the end, so it is the whole and sole end, for which every man upon the face of the earth, for which every one of *you* were brought into the world, and endued with a living soul. Remember! You were born for nothing else. You live for nothing else. Your life is continued to you upon earth for no other purpose than this, that you may know, love and serve God on earth, and enjoy him to all eternity.... Therefore let your heart continually say, "This one thing I do." Having one thing in view, remembering why I was born, and why I am continued in life, "I press on to the mark." I aim at the one end of my being, God; even at "God in Christ reconciling the world to himself." He shall be my God forever and ever, and my guide even until death. (Sermon: "What Is Man?" Wesley 1987, 4:26-27)

3. *Putting the past behind.* Paul describes the spiritual journey with the image of a runner who forgets what lies behind (v 13). For the apostle, this included his enviable spiritual heritage, his regrettable activities as a persecutor of the church, his glowing successes in ministry, and his manifold sufferings as a servant of Christ. It is not difficult for us to find analogies to Paul's story in our own lives. For many contemporary Christians, the past is a hovering specter, threatening to impede their spiritual progress. "Forgetting" the past doesn't mean erasing it from our memory banks. Rather, it means that, by the Spirit's enabling, we no longer dwell on it as the focus of our attention. Letting go of the past gives us the freedom to press forward toward the future to which God has called us.

This surely involves "forgetting" bygone failures that can paralyze us with guilt or discouragement. But it also applies to past spiritual successes that might tempt us to become proud or complacent. A growing communion with Christ cannot live in harmony with a backward-looking focus. Jesus himself reminds us that "no one who puts a hand to the plow and looks back is fit for service in the kingdom of God" (Luke 9:62 TNIV).

C. Good and Bad Examples (3:15—4:1)

BEHIND THE TEXT

Paul now applies the story of his own experience of Christ (3:4-14) to the Philippians. We can describe Paul's flow of thought in 3:15—4:1 as follows:

1. In vv 15-16 he urges them toward a **mature** mind-set, the same attitude and actions he himself has embodied.
2. The "imitation of Paul" becomes even more explicit in v 17, when he invites them to emulate himself and others like him.
3. In sharp contrast, vv 18-19 warn the Philippians against *bad* examples—**enemies of the cross of Christ,** who are *not* to be imitated.
4. The section reaches a triumphant climax in 3:20-21. Unlike those whose mind-set is on earthly things, Paul and his readers possess a heavenly citizenship now. And they await a glorious resurrection in the future when the Savior returns. These verses build on the future-oriented focus of Paul's own story in vv 11 and 12-14.
5. Bursting with affectionate language, 4:1 draws the whole section together. Paul's appeal to **stand firm** in this verse also recalls the appearance of the same verb in 1:27. These two verses (1:27; 4:1) form literary bookends around the two major sections of exhortation in the letter (1:27—2:18; 3:1—4:1). At the same time, 4:1 marks a transi-

tion that paves the way for Paul's practical instructions to the congregation that follow (4:2-9).

Philippians 3:15—4:1 points back not only to Paul's personal history in ch 3 but also to the story of Christ in ch 2. The literary parallels between 2:5-11 and 3:15-21 are too striking to be coincidental. They include (emphasis added):

- The verb "to think/have a mind-set" (*phroneō*; 2:5; 3:15 [twice], 19)
- "cross" (2:8; 3:18)
- "earthly beings" (*epigeiōn*; 2:10) and "earthly things" (*epigeia*; 3:19)
- "is" (*hyparchei*; 2:6; 3:20)
- "Lord Jesus Christ" (2:11; 3:20)
- "form" (*morphē*; 2:6-7) and "conformed" (*symmorphos*; 3:21)
- "form, appearance" (*schēma*; 2:7) and "transform" (*metaschēmatizō*; 3:21)
- "to humble" (*tapeineō*; 2:8) and "humble" (*tapeinōsis*; 3:21)
- "glory" (2:11; 3:21)

In addition, the notion that Christ will subject "everything" to himself (3:21) reminds us that "every" knee will bow and "every" tongue confess the one whose name is above "every" name (2:9-11).

Note that the echoes of the Christ drama are especially concentrated in 3:20-21. Because of the similarities in vocabulary and the poetic character of vv 20-21, some interpreters think this is another example of an earlier hymn fragment that Paul adopted (e.g., Hawthorne and Martin 2004, 228-30). But as Bockmuehl points out, these verses are woven so tightly into both the immediate context and the whole letter, this suggestion has little to commend it (1998, 232-33; see also O'Brien 1991, 467-72).

Instead, it seems that once again Paul invites his audience to read themselves into the story of Christ's humiliation and exaltation. In this case, he spotlights the consummation of the story, Christ's glorious vindication (2:9-11). Paul has already urged the Philippians to be conformed to Jesus' suffering and death (2:5-8; see 3:10). Now he assures them that when Christ returns they will also share in his resurrection and vindication; they will become like him (3:21; see v 11).

Beside the rhythmic feel of vv 20-21, 3:15—4:1 has a number of other noteworthy rhetorical features. For example, Paul appeals to his *ethos*—the credibility and character of the speaker—when he holds up his own life before the Philippians as a role model worth imitating (3:16-17). Such calls to imitate worthy examples were commonplace among philosophers and letter writers in the Greco-Roman world (see, e.g., Ps-Isocrates, *Dem.* 4.11; 9-11; Seneca, *Epistles* 6.5-6; 7.6-9; 11.9; 52.8; Pliny, *Epistles* 7.1.7).

Paul also uses *pathos*, an appeal to the listeners' emotions, to intensify the contrast between his own godly example and the behavior of some "outsiders." With impassioned language, he talks about his **tears** over them (v 18). In addition, his dark description of these opponents as **enemies of the cross** who are headed for **destruction** stirs up feelings against them within his audience (Watson 1988, 75). The four staccato-like phrases that characterize them (v 19) add to the rhetorical punch.

There is striking *irony* here as well. When Paul talks about their "end/goal" (*telos*), their **god,** and their **glory,** he draws upon the vocabulary of faith. Ironically, however, each of these words is defined by a negative element of unbelief—their end becomes **destruction;** their god is their **belly;** and their glory turns into **shame** (Watson 1988, 75).

In addition, the language of Greco-Roman friendship is prominent in this paragraph. We see it in Paul's encouragement to have the same "mind-set" (*phroneō*, v 15), and above all in his expressions of ardent affection toward his dear friends in 4:1. At the same time, friends often warned each other about associating with dangerous "enemies" (Fitzgerald 1996, 155; Stowers 1991, 114-15). In this passage, Paul and his Philippian friends share common **enemies of the cross** (vv 18-19).

Perhaps the trickiest issue that lies behind this paragraph concerns the identity of these "opponents" in vv 18-19. Are these the same people whom Paul called "the dogs" earlier in ch 3, or are they a different group? Are they Christians or unbelievers? Have they already infiltrated the church or are they outsiders? Is Paul offering a specific description of their beliefs, or is he painting a more general and rhetorical portrait of what the Philippians should not be? Interpreters have come up with a variety of answers to these questions (see Hawthorne and Martin 2004, 221). The language Paul uses to describe these people is ambiguous enough that it is virtually impossible to be certain. What, then, *can* we infer about them?

First, Paul contrasts his own positive role model with the bad behavior of the "enemies." In this light, it is unlikely that the Philippians would have been tempted to pattern themselves after people who did not at least present themselves as Christians (Carson 1996, 91). Consequently, they were probably professing Christians whose behavior was in some way incompatible with the *cross* of Christ (v 18).

Second, Paul says that he has warned the Philippians on numerous occasions about these bad examples (v 18). This suggests that they were probably *not* a part of the Christian community at Philippi.

Beyond this, can we be more specific regarding their identity? Commentators usually opt for one of two alternatives. The first is that they are Judaizing Christians who were preoccupied with Jewish practices, such as circumcision and food laws (see vv 2-3). A second option views them as "libertines" who distorted Paul's doctrine of freedom in Christ into a license for shameful self-indulgence. How we come out on this issue will depend on our reading of the terms Paul uses to describe them in v 19, and I will take up the issue again when I discuss that verse. In any case, Fee wisely comments that, even if we cannot be certain about who these people are, their *function* in the passage is clear. They represent a pattern of thinking and behaving that is the polar opposite of the example found in Paul and others who faithfully run the race (1995, 352).

IN THE TEXT

1. Adopt a Mature Mind-set (3:15-16)

■ **15** Verses 15 and 16 are often taken together with Paul's testimony that he is pressing on toward the prize in vv 12-14 (see, e.g., NRSV, CEV). This is largely due to the appearance of the term "perfect" in v 15, which picks up on the verb form of the same word in v 12.

It is better, however, to see v 15 as the start of a new section in the letter, for two reasons:

First, the transitional word ***therefore*** (*oun*; not translated in the NIV) signals a fresh thought. Paul is saying, "As a result of the story I have been narrating, let us now hear its application" (Fee 1999, 158).

Second, Paul switches from the first person singular ("I") to the first person plural ("we"). He now includes his readers along with himself in the appeal: **all of us who are mature should take such a view of things.** Literally, the exhortation reads, ***as many as are perfect, let us have this mind-set.***

The key term ***perfect*** (*teleios*) in v 15 stands in tension with v 12. Why does Paul suddenly claim to be among the "perfect"? After all, he has just used this word's verb form to insist that he has *not* reached completion?

Due to this apparent inconsistency, some interpreters have read Paul's statement in v 15 in an ironic sense (e.g., Lightfoot 1953, 153; Hawthorne and Martin 2004, 211-12). In this case, Paul would be seizing the language of his opponents and turning it against them. He would be saying something like, "those who think they are already 'perfect' (but in fact are not), let them adopt this mind-set."

Although Paul is quite capable of speaking ironically (see, e.g., 1 Cor 4:8), it is unlikely that he is doing so here. It is not unusual for Paul to use related terms in somewhat different ways within the same context (Bruce 1983, 99; e.g., Phil 3:3, 5). Furthermore, Hooker's observation seems decisive: "The word can scarcely be ironic, since Paul includes himself among those who are 'mature'!" (2000, 533). What, then, does it mean for Paul and his readers to be ***perfect***?

English translations often render the word as **mature**. This should not be rejected—as long as we clarify what Paul means by "maturity." Alex R. G. Deasley rightly insists that for Paul, maturity "does not denote simply having been in process for a long time. It has a moral and ethical dimension" (2007, 218). We see this, for example, in 1 Cor 2:6, where Paul contrasts spiritual "adults" (*teleioi*) with "infants in Christ" who are caught up in jealousy and quarrelling (3:1-3; see also 14:20). In Ephesians and Colossians, to be perfect means to be spiritually "whole" or "complete," "attaining to the whole measure of the fullness of Christ" (Eph 4:13; see Col 1:28; 4:12; compare Matt 5:8; 19:21; Jas 1:4).

In the LXX, "perfect" (*teleios*) can describe those whose hearts are wholly devoted to God (2 Kgs 8:61; 11:4; 15:3, 14; 20:3) and so are blameless before him (Gen 6:9; Deut 18:13). The corresponding Hebrew word *tamim* is used in the Dead Sea Scrolls of those who wholly observe God's law and walk fully in his ways (see Schippers 1976, 2:59-66; and Delling 1972, 8:67-78). Consistently, the character aspect of Christian maturity is front and center (so also Polycarp, *Phil.* 12.1-3).

Above all, our understanding of what it means to be "perfect" in Phil 3:15 emerges from the context. The spiritually **mature** are those who adopt a certain attitude: **let us have this mind-set** (*touto phronōmen*, v 15). The word **this** (such a view of things) points the Philippians back to Paul's own attitude and orientation narrated in vv 4-14. It is a mind-set that is undivided in its pursuit of knowing Christ, being conformed to his sufferings and death, and striving toward the heavenly prize. The verb *phronōmen* (literally, "let us think") also recalls 2:5, where the Philippians are called to follow the humble and self-giving attitude of Christ.

To be **perfect,** then, means nothing less than to adopt the mind of Christ, which Paul himself has modeled. I agree with Hooker that in this context *teleios* probably means something more specific than what is expressed by the English word "mature" (2000, 533). It describes spiritual "wholeness," which is defined in terms of being like Christ in our character and practice.

According to v 15, such a mature Christian mind is both appropriate and available to Christians now. Yet those who are "perfect" in this sense are constantly and deeply aware that they have not yet reached their final goal, when they will be fully conformed to the likeness of Christ (vv 12, 21). Wesley aptly comments on these verses: "There is a difference between one that is perfect, and one that is perfected. The one is fitted for the race, ver. 15; the other, ready to receive the prize" (n.d., 512).

When Paul says, **as many of us are perfect,** he probably does not assume that every Philippian Christian currently fits that category. Rather, he leaves the door open for his readers to determine whether or not they match the description (O'Brien 1991, 435-36). Certainly, Paul desires that his readers would be spiritually mature and reflect a Christlike attitude.

Paul anticipates, however, that not all of them might fully share this way of seeing things. He, therefore, adds the qualification, **and if on some point you**

think differently, that too God will make clear to you (v 15b). Turning from the inclusive "we" to the "you all" of direct address, Paul speaks pastorally to the community as a whole. He assures them that if anyone has a different mind-set (*phroneō*, repeated from the first clause) than the one he has set forth in the previous verses, God will correct them. Here the term **differently** (*heteros*) has a negative connotation; in some sense, their attitude needs correction (see Lightfoot 1953, 153).

At the same time, Paul's gentle way of approaching the matter (Paul begins the sentence with "and" [*kai*], not "but") suggests that he does not view this as a fundamental departure from the mature Christian mind-set he has been advocating (Bockmuehl 1998, 226). Their inadequate outlook concerns a particular issue (*ti*, **on some point**), rather than their overall life direction. Paul's words are intended to encourage, not rebuke (Hooker 2000, 534).

Some interpreters think that Paul is again drawing on the language of ancient friendship. As friends, the Philippians have the freedom to disagree with him at various points (e.g., Fee 1995, 358-59; Thurston 2005, 131). But the focus here is not so much on their relationship with *Paul* as their relationship with *God* (see Fowl 2005, 165). Consequently, Paul is confident that if their basically sound Christian outlook goes awry at some point, then **even this** (*kai touto*) **God will reveal** to them (v 16).

Paul does not say precisely how this divine revelation will occur. The apostle can use the verb **reveal** (*apocalypsei*) and its related noun for various forms of divine communication. Often they describe God's saving revelation in Christ or the gospel (Rom 1:17; Gal 1:12, 16) or God's end-time judgment and salvation (Rom 2:5; 8:18-19; 1 Cor 1:7; 2 Thess 1:7). But this language can also refer to more specific divine revelations through visions and spiritual gifts (1 Cor 14:6, 26, 30; 2 Cor 12:1, 7; Gal 2:2; see Osiek 2000, 99; O'Brien 1991, 438-39). In Phil 3:15, Paul's meaning seems closer to this latter sense.

Here Paul probably has in mind the ongoing work of the Holy Spirit in the community to reveal the ways and will of God (see Eph 1:17). No doubt the Spirit could speak in a number of forms. In any case, Paul's plural address to the whole church suggests it will be more of a communal than an individual disclosure. Bockmuehl's observation is right on target that

> we find underlying this passage a doctrine of both the Spirit and the Church which is remarkably hopeful and robust: Paul trusts the Spirit to bring the Church to a knowledge of the truth, and to reveal to it the areas where its thinking is "out of step" (cf. v. 16) with the "pattern" (v. 17) of life in Christ. (1998, 228)

■ **16** Paul now brings the thought of v 15 to a conclusion by underlining its main thrust. Whatever "mind-set" deficiencies may need God's correction, the

Philippians (and Paul) should focus on what is essential: living up to what God has already made known. The verb **live up to** (*stoicheō*) draws on the military image of "keeping in step" or "marching in line," as for battle. Paul uses it to signify behavior that is conformed to a certain pattern or standard (see Rom 4:12; Gal 5:25; 6:16). Here the entire community is called to a common and unified way of living.

Paul urges his audience jointly to live up to what they *do* know; they are to conform to the level of Christian maturity they have already reached. Literally he says: *to what we have attained, [let us] live up to the same.* Paul's return to the first person plural (**we**) shows that he invites the Philippians to follow the same pattern of living that he himself pursues (see Phil 3:17; Fowl 2005, 166). This exhortation is also a form of encouragement. Paul seems to be saying, "We've come this far; let's keep making progress" (see Osiek 2000, 100).

2. Examples to Imitate: Paul and Others like Him (3:17)

■ 17 Verse 17 has no grammatical connection with what comes before it, and it is often taken as the beginning of a new section (e.g., O'Brien 1991, 443). But this seems unjustified. The appeal to "imitate me" in this verse comes hard on the heels of Paul's call for the Philippians to adopt the mind-set and lifestyle that he has demonstrated in his own story.

Paul's admonition, **join with others in following my example,** makes explicit what has been hinted throughout the letter to this point. Earlier, Paul affirms that the Philippians share in his own struggles (1:30). This reinforces that Paul's attitude toward suffering is an example for them (1:12-26; see 2:17-18). Subsequently, he models an unselfish love for others when he sends Epaphroditus back to the Philippians; he puts the needs of his colleagues and converts before his own (vv 25-30; see vv 3-4). And in ch 3, Paul's story of writing off all of his human achievements for the sake of knowing Christ his Lord (vv 4-14) is a superb example of embracing the mind-set of Christ (2:5-11).

Now Paul urges his Philippian Christian friends (literally, **brothers**) to **join with others** in imitating him. The word he uses (*symmimētai*; literally, "fellow imitators") is unique in ancient Greek literature, and its meaning is not fully clear. Possibly Paul says, "Be fellow imitators *with* me." This would imply that the Philippians should join Paul in imitating *Christ*. The other option is that the readers should collectively imitate Paul. Given what this verse goes on to say about following **the pattern we gave you,** the second alternative is more likely. Once again, Paul calls the congregation to be united in their Christian character and conduct (see 1:27; 2:2).

Taken on its own, Paul's admonition to "imitate me" might strike us today as an extreme case of arrogance. Three considerations, however, help to put his appeal in perspective.

First, the idea of imitating a teacher or moral example was a widespread form of learning in the ancient world, both in Greco-Roman and Jewish circles (see, e.g., Philo, *Virt.* 66; *Congr.* 70; *4 Macc.* 9:23; *T. Benj.* 3.1; 4.1). This reflected the belief that wisdom is embodied in a way of life (Hays 2000, 293). Students were expected not only to receive their teachers' instruction but also to put their examples into practice. Jesus himself urged his disciples, "I have set you an example that you should do as I have done for you" (John 13:15; see Luke 9:23).

Teaching by Example

In the Greco-Roman world, philosophers and moral teachers often stressed that people learned to live rightly by patterning themselves after good examples. An ancient handbook on letter writing, for instance, gives the following exhortation:

> Always be an emulator, Dear Friend, of virtuous men. For it is better to be well spoken of when imitating good men than to be reproached by all men while following evil men. (Ps.-Libanius, *Epistolary Styles*, cited by Malherbe 2000, 155)

Or consider this excerpt from a letter written by the Roman philosopher Seneca, a contemporary of Paul:

> Let us choose ... men who teach us by their lives, men who teach us what we ought to do and then prove it by their practice, who show us what we should avoid, and then are never caught doing that which they have ordered us to avoid. Choose as a guide one whom you will admire more when you see him act than when you hear him speak. (*Epistle* 52.8, cited by Malherbe 1986, 63-64)

Second, the call to imitate Paul is at the same time an invitation to walk in the footsteps of Christ (1 Cor 11:1; 1 Thess 1:6). We have seen that Paul's story in Phil 3:4-14 is a form of living out the story of Christ in 2:6-11. Paul does not urge the Philippians to imitate his own advantages or accomplishments. Rather, he wants them to emulate his willingness to share in Christ's sufferings (3:10; see 1:30; 2:17) and to give up his own interests out of love for Christ and others (3:7-9; see 2:3-8, 25-30). In short, when Paul says, "Imitate me," he is simply putting flesh on the invitation to embrace the cruciform pattern of Christ (2:5).

Third, Paul understood that young disciples need concrete examples of how to embody the gospel of Christ in their everyday lives. Craddock grasps this well: "To show them how to walk, those first generation believers, with no precedents or history, with no New Testament, with few preachers and most of them itinerant, struggling as a small minority in a pagan culture, no better textbook could be offered than the lives of those who stood before them as leaders" (1985, 67-68). Simply telling them to live in a manner worthy of the gospel (1:27) would be insufficient on its own. The Philippians needed to observe and reproduce what they saw in Paul and other mature Christians who were actually doing it (see Fowl 2005, 167). In today's language, Paul was a mentor to his friends in Philippi.

In the second part of the verse, Paul expands the company of Christian role models to include **those who live according to the pattern we gave you.** The last phrase literally reads, *just as you have us as an example* (*typos*; see 2 Thess 3:9). *Us* (*hēmas*) likely includes Paul and other members of his ministry team who are known to the Philippians, such as Timothy and Epaphroditus (see 2:19-30). But Paul's language is general enough to encompass a wider group of believers who live exemplary lives (so Fee 1995, 365-66; Bockmuehl 1998, 229).

Paul urges his friends to "notice carefully" or **keep [their] attention on** (*skopeite*; see 2:4) *those who walk in this way.* The verb **walk** (*peripateō*) is the apostle's signature word for an ongoing lifestyle that is pleasing to God (see, e.g., Rom 6:4; 8:4; Gal 5:16; 1 Thess 2:12). The call to imitate Paul and others focuses on their way of life (see Phil 1:27; 4:9). Believers must "walk the walk."

3. Examples to Avoid: Enemies of the Cross (3:18-19)

■ **18** Verses 18 and 19 give the reason (**for**) that following Paul's gospel-shaped example is all the more pressing. The Philippians must be alert to countermodels, who **live as enemies of the cross of Christ** (v 18; on the identity of this group, see BEHIND THE TEXT for this section).

As in 3:2, the language is intense. Paul has repeatedly warned the Philippians **before** about these people. Now, with a pastor's breaking heart, he does so **again with tears** (literally, "crying"). Fee suggests that Paul weeps *over* these people because they were professing Christians who ought to know better (1995, 369). Yet Paul's tears may stem just as much from the harmful influence such foes could have on the Philippians or on the progress of the gospel (Sumney 2007, 93; see Acts 20:30-31).

But why were they **enemies of the cross**? Most likely, these **many** did not openly challenge the message of the cross; nor would they have considered themselves to be its enemies (Fowl 2005, 172; Marshall 1991, 100). The repetition of the verb "walk" (**live**) from v 17 shows that the issue at stake is not so much wrong teaching as it is wrong *living.*

In the context of Philippians, Hooker's assessment seems to hit the nail on the head: "They are 'enemies of the cross,' because their whole manner of living is a denial of the revelation of God in Christ, whose self-emptying led to death on the cross. . . . They claim to be Christians, but fail completely to see the relevance of 2:6-11 for their own lives" (2000, 535). We might further assume that, unlike Paul, they sought to avoid the suffering and weakness that are a part of the way of the cross (see 3:10; 1 Cor 1:18—2:5).

■ 19 Paul drives home the point that these enemies of the cross model a lifestyle and a mind-set that are opposite of his own example. Four pithy phrases (the verbs are absent in Greek) describe them:
- *their end* [*telos*] *is destruction*
- *their god is their belly*
- their glory is in their shame
- their mind is on earthly things

The first of these characterizes their **destiny** on the day of judgment. Standing at the head of the list, it is intended to shock (Bockmuehl 1998, 230). In contrast to Paul's running toward the goal of the heavenly prize (v 14; see vv 20-21), these people are "walking" on a path that ends in disaster. The same language of **destruction** (*apōleia*) describes the fate of the Philippians' pagan opponents in 1:28. For Paul, ultimate spiritual loss, even for professing Christians, is a dangerous possibility (Marshall 1991, 251). By adopting an attitude and lifestyle that opposes the cross, these people have placed themselves on a road toward final ruin.

Paul's fourth description, **their mind is on earthly things,** summarizes the whole list. Once again we have an appearance of the key verb *phroneō*. They lack the "mind-set" of Christ (2:5). Instead, their attitudes are focused on earthly values, not on the heavenly call of God in Christ (3:14; see v 20; Col 3:2).

The second and third phrases are more specific and considerably harder to interpret. Not surprisingly, these expressions have kindled much speculation. One common view dates from the time of the church fathers (e.g., Ambrosiaster, Augustine). It is that **belly** (*kolia*, "stomach") is a sarcastic allusion to Jewish food laws; and **shame** (*aischynē*), a reference to the nakedness associated with the rite of circumcision. Phil 3:18-19 would then be an extension of Paul's attack on the "Judaizers," who are concerned with imposing Jewish practices on Gentile Christians (v 2).

This is not impossible. But there is no comparable use for the terms **belly** and **shame** anywhere in the NT. What is more, Paul never connects Jewish dietary laws with idolatry; nor does he call circumcision itself "shameful," even if it is irrelevant for Gentile Christians (see Fee 1995, 372, 373, nn 39, 46).

It is more likely that these "belly-worshipers" (Osiek's phrase; 2000, 102) are professing Christians whose ultimate concern was fixed on satisfying their bodily desires (**earthly things**), not the self-giving way of the cross. Elsewhere, Paul warns the Romans about troublemakers who serve their own "bellies," in reference to physical appetites (Rom 16:17-18; see 1 Cor 6:13).

Likewise, shamefulness can describe various forms of self-indulgent behavior that characterized the old life believers have left behind (e.g., Rom

1:27; 6:21; Eph 5:12; see Bockmuehl 1998, 231-32). The moral sensitivities of these people have been flipped on their head; they give honor and esteem (literally, **glory**; *doxa*; see Hegermann 1990, 1:345) to the very things of which they ought to be ashamed. In a culture in which honor and shame were of critical importance, this would have been a searing indictment indeed (Sumney 2007, 94).

In the end, we should probably resist the impulse to identify these **enemies of the cross** too specifically. Paul's description of them is highly rhetorical. The main reason for their cameo appearance in the letter is to sharpen the focus of the point Paul is making: "Believers must always be friends with the cross. They must identify with the message and the reality of the crucified Christ" (Gorman 2004, 444). It is to that Christ-centered orientation that the apostle now returns.

4. A Heavenly Commonwealth and a Hope for the Future (3:20-21)

■ **20** Over against those whose mind-set is fastened on earthly things, Paul describes the glorious future of those whose **commonwealth is in heaven** (vv 20-21). The Greek word order brings out the contrast: <u>our</u> **citizenship** (our is emphatic) separates Paul and the Philippians from the "many" (v 18), whose lives are controlled by earthly appetites and values. At the same time, the connecting word in v 20 is **for** (*gar*), not **but,** as in the NIV and most English translations. Verses 20-21 therefore pick up Paul's main argument in vv 15-17 (with vv 18-19 acting as a kind of parenthesis). These verses explain the ultimate reason why the Philippians should adopt a Christ-oriented mind-set and follow Paul's godly example: as citizens of Christ's heavenly kingdom now, they will share in his final victory to come.

Commonwealth (*politeuma*) is a powerful image with political overtones in the setting of Roman Philippi. This is the second time in the letter that Paul has co-opted the language of Roman citizenship to picture the character of the church (see on 1:27). The word *politeuma* was used in a variety of ways in the Greco-Roman world. Two, however, are particularly important for understanding Paul's thought in 3:20.

First, the most common use of the term in the Hellenistic period was as a "state" or **commonwealth,** especially as a power governing the lives of those who belong to it (Lincoln 1981, 97-101). This is probably closer to Paul's use of the word *politeuma* here than the idea of **citizenship** as such. Nevertheless, it would certainly have been implied that those who participate in the heavenly commonwealth should live as "citizens" of that realm (see 1:27; Silva 2005, 184). In the Roman world, citizenship defined both a person's ethical behavior (Acts 16:21) and one's true allegiance (Oakes 2001, 138).

Second, *politeuma* could refer to an organized group of people within a city. For example, it often described a group of citizens of one city living in a place that was not their home (see Lüderitz 1994).

Both of these uses are significant for Paul's readers in Philippi. As a Roman colony, the city's ruling "commonwealth" was Rome. Philippi was governed by the Roman Empire in nearly all respects. Furthermore, the city of Philippi prided itself in its status as a Roman colony and in the benefaction of Caesar. Paul, however, tells the church that its allegiance is to a different commonwealth, a *heavenly* one. The Philippians' ultimate loyalty is not to Caesar, but to Christ, the true Savior and Lord (see below for the political context of these titles).

Although Paul's readers are physically located within the Roman Empire, they are, so to speak, resident aliens (see 1 Pet 2:11). They live in a realm to which they do not really belong (Marshall 1991, 103). They are in the world, but not of it (see John 17:14-16). As citizens of heaven, their values will be determined, not by any earthly loyalty, but by the "counter-empire" of Christ.

For Paul's readers who were *not* Roman citizens—probably the majority—this would have been an especially compelling word. As Peter Oakes insists, "Paul announces a citizenship that surpasses the citizenship of Rome and Philippi, which they are prevented from attaining" (2001, 138). *All* believers, slave and Roman citizen alike, find a new identity and unity in the heavenly commonwealth.

Citizens of Heaven

The anonymous *Epistle to Diogenetus* (A.D. second century) reflects on the kind of alternative citizenship that Paul describes in Phil 1:27 and 3:20:

> But while they live in both Greek and barbarian cities, as each one's lot was cast, and follow the local customs in dress and food and other aspects of life, at the same time they demonstrate the remarkable and admittedly unusual character of their own citizenship. They live in their own countries, but only as nonresidents; they participate in everything as citizens, and endure everything as foreigners. Every foreign country is their fatherland, and every fatherland is foreign. They marry like everyone else, and have children, but they do not expose their offspring. They share their food but not their wives. They are in the flesh, but they do not live according to the flesh. They live on earth, but their citizenship is in heaven. (*Diogn.* 5:4-9; Holmes 2007, 703)

Notice that the church's true commonwealth currently **is** (*hyparchei*; literally, "exists") in heaven. According to Paul, **heaven** is not simply about where we go when we die (see Wright 2007). We are *already* citizens of the heavenly realm. The commonwealth in heaven rules, shapes, and determines our present life on earth.

But that present existence is oriented toward the future—what is yet to be (compare 3:11-14). As a result, the church lives in neck-stretching expectation of a coming Savior (v 20*b*). Paul makes a clear reference here to the Parousia, Christ's victorious return. The verb translated **we eagerly await** (*apekdechometha*) is a special word in Paul's usage. It consistently describes the intense anticipation of the church's future hope (see 1 Cor 1:7; Gal 5:5; Rom 8:19, 23, 25).

Bockmuehl notes that the idea of a Savior coming **from** heaven (see also 1 Thess 1:10) is similar to the apocalyptic belief that the New Jerusalem will descend to earth (e.g., Rev 3:12; 21:2; 1998, 235). In the present context, "going to heaven" is not the ultimate goal of Christians' salvation. Paul does not envision Christ taking believers with him back to their heavenly home. Rather, the picture is that of Christ bringing heaven to a transformed earth (see Rev 21:1), as part of his final subjection of all things to himself (v 21; see Lincoln 1981, 102, 108; Wright 2007, 111-12, 160-61).

The term **Savior** (*sōtēr*) is striking. In the first place, it is a title Paul seldom uses (outside of the Pastoral Letters, only here and Eph 5:23). But more importantly, it carries both christological and political implications. Old Testament texts often refer to God as the "Savior" of his people (e.g., Deut 32:15; 1 Chr 16:35; Ps 62:2, 6; Isa 12:2, and esp. Isa 45:15, 21, echoed in Phil 2:10-11). When Paul calls Jesus "Savior," he again bestows on Christ a role ascribed to the one God of Israel (see Fowl 2005, 173-74).

At the same time, "savior" was a title of honor frequently given the Roman emperor. Emperor Claudius, for example, was hailed as "god who is *savior and benefactor*" and as "*savior* of the universe" (cited by Oakes 2001, 140). In v 20 the coming "savior" is also called "lord" (*kyrios*), another common title for Caesar (see comments on 2:11). And there is a further parallel: a key role of the emperor toward the people of the Roman Empire—especially a Roman colony—was to come and rescue them from their enemies (Oakes 2001, 139).

Paul's Christian friends in Philippi could hardly miss the point. As citizens of the heavenly commonwealth, they await the arrival of a Savior greater than Caesar to deliver them—**the Lord Jesus Christ** (see 2:11). This Savior will come not from Rome, but from heaven itself (Witherington 1994, 99). Paul asks the Philippians to look at their world through a radically different lens. The new reality that governs their lives is not Caesar and his earthly empire of power, but Christ and his heavenly kingdom of love.

■ **21** This verse makes two further points about the character of the salvation that Christ will effect at his return. He **will transform our lowly bodies so that they will be like his glorious body** (v 21*a*; in the NIV, this clause comes at the end of the verse). Although not mentioned explicitly, this is about the future resurrection, which will take place at the time of Christ's return.

Paul has already spoken of his own resurrection in 3:11. Now he expands this hope to embrace all those who are in Christ. The thought is similar to that of 1 Cor 15, which declares that believers will be "changed" (vv 51, 52), when perishable bodies are raised imperishable, and the body sown in dishonor and weakness is raised in glory and power (vv 42-43; see vv 52-54).

In Phil 3, however, Paul's language echoes the Christ hymn of 2:6-11 (for parallels, see BEHIND THE TEXT for this section). Here he contrasts, literally, **the body of our humiliation** (*tapeinōsis*) with **the body of his glory**. These terms recall that Jesus "humbled (*etapeinōsen*) himself" as a man (v 8), and, as a result, he was exalted "to the glory of God the Father" (v 11).

The word **body** (*soma*) is a many-layered term in Paul's writings. It cannot be restricted to the physical body alone. Here it also implies the whole person (see Kreitzer 1993, 72-74). The phrase "body of our humiliation" does not suggest that the body is evil or inherently sinful but that in its fallen state it is subject to suffering, weakness, and death. For the Philippians, this includes the suffering they are presently experiencing at the hands of those who oppose the gospel in Philippi (see 1:28-29). "Their current status is to be a body characterized by 'humiliation,' as was that of their Lord while on earth (2:6-8)" (Gorman 2004, 444).

But that will change. God, Paul assures them, has a glorious future planned for the **body**. When Christ returns, our bodies will not be discarded, but "transformed" (*metaschēmatizō*, a word used only by Paul in the NT). This is poles apart from the Greek notion that the immortal soul will be released from the temporary prison of the body. Instead, Christ himself will refashion our lowly bodies into a **body of glory** (that is, a body characterized by glory), like his own. "The risen Jesus," affirms Wright, "is both the *model* for the Christian's future body and the *means* by which it comes about" (2007, 161). For Paul, salvation means the transformation of human life in its wholeness, including a bodily aspect that will not end with death (see 1 Thess 5:23; Deasley 2007, 224).

Paul does not go into detail about the nature of this change. He simply affirms that its pattern is the glorified body of Christ himself. Elsewhere Paul calls the resurrected body a "spiritual body" (1 Cor 15:44-46). By this he means a body "adapted to the final life of the Spirit" (Fee 1995, 383). Here, however, he spotlights the idea that when Christ transforms our humble bodies, they will be **conformed** (*symmorphon*) to the resurrection body of Jesus. This immediately takes us back to 3:10; those who are now being conformed to his suffering and death *will* be conformed to the glory of his resurrection (compare Rom 8:29: "conformed to the likeness of his Son").

The notion of being conformed to Christ's body also reminds us that Jesus "conformed" himself to our humanity when he took on the "form" (*mor-*

phē) of a slave (Phil 2:7)—another echo of vv 6-11. Indeed, Hooker is precisely right that 3:20-21 is a necessary completion of 2:6-11, which said nothing about how *we* share in Christ's exaltation. "Now we realize," she affirms, "that he was born in human likeness and shared our human death in order that Christians might be transformed into his likeness and share his vindication" (2000, 536).

But there is more. Paul's second point about the salvation Christ will accomplish at his Parousia is that it will take place **by the power that enables him to bring everything under his control.** Paul envisions the transformation of Christians' lowly bodies as a part of a much bigger event. Unfortunately, the NIV omits the word ***also,*** which appears in the Greek text. But Paul closely connects these two aspects of Christ's end-time work: according to the same power by which Christ will conform our weak and suffering bodies to his own, he will ***also*** exercise his sovereignty over all things.

Chapter 3, therefore, ends by viewing Christ's final reconciling work from a breathtaking cosmic perspective (see Rom 8:18-25). As in Phil 2:10-11, Christ's rule is universal ("all things," *ta panta*) and unchallenged (Fowl 2005, 174). The claim that he is able **to subject all things to himself** echoes Ps 8:6, which early Christians interpreted as a reference to Jesus Christ (1 Cor 15:27; Eph 1:22; Heb 2:6-9). According to 1 Cor 15:27, God the Father made everything subject to the Son. Here the same language is applied to Christ himself. This is a remarkable christological moment. Christ, the Lord and Savior from heaven, has ultimate **power** (*energeia*, "working") and rule over all things.

Once again, the Philippians may have heard in Paul's language a challenge to the claims of imperial Rome. The emperor's ability to save his people was anchored in his power to bring about universal submission to his rule (Oakes 2001, 140-45). But the power of Rome (and all its modern counterparts) is simply a parody of the true sovereignty of the true Savior, Christ the universal Lord. As Fee observes, he will "subject 'all things' to himself, including the emperor himself and all those who in his name are causing the Philippians to suffer" (1995, 384). For Paul's audience, this is a word of uncommon assurance and hope.

5. Stand Firm in the Lord (4:1)

■ 1 Despite the chapter break, 4:1 is closely linked to what comes before. **Therefore** (*hōste*) signals that Paul is about to apply what he has just said to the particular situation of the Philippians (similarly, 2:12). In light of the glorious future that awaits them as citizens of the heavenly commonwealth, Paul urges his readers to **stand firm in the Lord.**

But before Paul commands, he commends (Hawthorne and Martin 2004, 239). Paul's language is lavish in its affection. In fact, the way he heaps up the terms of endearment for the Philippians in this verse is without parallel in his letters to churches. These **brothers and sisters** are his **beloved** (repeated for emphasis at the end of the sentence; also 2:12) and **longed for** (*epipothētoi*, recalling the verb form in 1:8; compare 2:26). Such expressions of fondness are common in ancient letters of friendship (Stowers 1991, 109). But for Paul they are more than simply a convention; they reveal the depth of his feelings for these much-loved friends.

The Philippians are also Paul's **joy** and **crown**. The motif of "joy" runs through the bloodstream of the letter (e.g., 1:4, 18; 2:2, 17-18, 29; 3:1; 4:4, 10). **Crown** (*stephanos*) refers to the wreath awarded to the victorious athlete in the Greek games. The same two terms appear in 1 Thess 2:19 in an eschatological setting. Here as well, Paul apparently means that the Philippians will be his "pride and joy" on the day of Christ (see Phil 3:20-21), the fruit of his missionary efforts. At the same time, they are *already* his joy and crown. These converts are his constant delight (1:4). They are the source of his confidence (v 6) that one day he will be able to "boast on the day of Christ" that he has not labored in vain (2:16).

In the midst of these powerful words of affection and confidence, Paul calls his friends to **stand firm** (*stēkete*). This appeal repeats the same verb in 1:27, which begins the long section of exhortations in the letter. Standing firm **in this way** (*houtōs*), therefore, probably embraces everything Paul has said since. But it especially applies to the thought of the preceding verses: they are to resist any "enemies of the cross" and follow Paul's Christlike example, in view of their heavenly calling (3:15-21). Only the **power** of the Lord (v 21) will make this possible (Thurston 2005, 135).

FROM THE TEXT

1. *Can Christians be "perfect"?* "There is scarce any expression in Holy Writ which has given more offence than this. The word 'perfect' is what many cannot bear. The very sound of it is an abomination to them." These words open John Wesley's 1741 sermon on "Christian Perfection," which was based on Phil 3 (Wesley 1985, 2:97). But Wesley's eighteenth-century account of the reaction against the very notion of "perfect" Christians sounds quite contemporary. Surely one of the most universally accepted maxims of our age is that "nobody's perfect."

In spite of frequent calls to "perfection" in the NT (e.g., Matt 5:48; 19:21; 1 Cor 14:20; Eph 4:13; Col 1:28; 4:12; Jas 1:4 [*teleios*: "perfect"]; Col 3:14; Heb 6:1 [*teleiotēs*: "perfection"]), most of us would choke on claiming to be "perfect" ourselves. Besides that, anyone bold enough to make such a claim would be disqualified immediately in the eyes of others on the grounds of sheer arrogance! For the most part, the "sound of it" is still "an abomination."

Unfortunately, the popular understanding of the term "perfect" is almost always something like "flawless in performance"—a definition that hardly fits the concept of perfection in the NT (Craddock 1985, 63).

On a practical level, does this mean that we should drop the language of perfection from our religious discourse altogether? Is it too much of a stumbling block to have any value for preaching and teaching today? Should we simply substitute terms like "mature" or "whole" instead? Perhaps. Wesley, on the other hand, argued that, rather than simply getting rid of the biblical language of perfection, we should carefully explain it.

For his part, Wesley went to great pains to try to clarify what Christian perfection does and does not mean (see Wesley 1985, 2:97-121). As a result, he strongly resisted a *perfectionism* that claimed too much for the "perfect" Christian (e.g., that Christians had "arrived" spiritually; that they were no longer capable of committing sin; that they were free from temptation). This is still a point of confusion today. Thomas Oden points out that when we hear the word "perfect," we tend to think in the static terms of the Latin *perfectus*, upon which the English word is based. It is a perfection in which there can be no improvement, change, or growth (1994, 320).

Wesley, however, read the NT in Greek. He recognized that when NT writers like Paul talked about being "perfect" (*teleios*), they were envisioning something dynamic, not static, an ever-increasing maturity, a *perfecting* grace. There is no perfection, Wesley insisted, "which does not admit of a continual increase." No matter how much one has attained, that person has "still need to 'grow in grace' and daily to advance in the knowledge and love of God his Saviour" (1985, 2:104-5).

In this, Wesley stood within the tradition of Eastern church fathers, like Gregory of Nyssa and Macarius the Egyptian. Such writers encouraged believers to seek a present perfection that had the hallmark of continual growth—a perfection in process (see Bassett 1997, 119-58; Schlimm 2003, 140-42).

Wesley was convinced that a "perfect" heart, whole and undivided in its devotion to God (see, e.g., Matt 5:48; 19:21; Jas 1:4; 1 John 4:8), is a gracious possibility in this life. Above all, Christian perfection could be summed up as love: "the humble, gentle, patient love of God, and our neighbor, ruling our tempers, words, and actions" ("Brief Thoughts on Christian Perfection," cited by Maddox 1994, 187; see Col 3:14).

But such wholehearted love for God and others is not a fixed state to be achieved. It only has meaning within the context of the entire journey of being transformed by God's grace into the image of Christ. Maybe that is why Wesley typically described those who have attained perfection as adult, or mature Christians—those who have grown up to the measure of the fullness of Christ (e.g., Wesley 1985, 2:105; Wesley n.d., 497, 524; see Maddox 1994, 187).

Wesley's and Paul's developmental language suggests a perfection that is not absolute, but relative. Indeed, in his sermon "On Patience," Wesley defines perfection that is "entire" as enjoying "as high a degree of holiness as is consistent with your present state of pilgrimage" (Wesley 1986, 3:179). A "perfect" drawing by a six-year-old is not the same as a "perfect" drawing by a twenty-year-old.

This kind of "perfection"—real but relative—squares well with Paul's claim for himself and others in Phil 3:15. It is a "perfection of the interim" (Deasley 2007, 218), living in the dynamic tension between what can be now and what will be in the future. We are called to experience God's gift of spiritual wholeness—a mature, Christlike mind and character that accords with our present stage on the journey. But we continually press on toward that final wholeness, when we will be fully and gloriously conformed to the image of Christ.

2. *Dealing with those who think differently.* Paul is realistic enough to recognize that not all Christians are spiritually mature. Sometimes thinking and behavior need to be changed. How Paul handles this sensitive pastoral issue in 3:15-16 provides a valuable model for the church today:

- On the one hand, Paul takes immature attitudes seriously. "Think[ing] differently" (v 15) is not just a matter of personal preference. It becomes a significant concern for the church when it involves a departure from the mature mind-set of Christ as revealed in Scripture.
- On the other hand, Paul shows remarkable patience in how he deals with those who think "otherwise." In a case where apparently no life-or-death issue is at stake, he doesn't force the matter. Rather, he waits for *God* to transform their mind-set in God's time. As Christian leaders, we can teach, preach, exhort, encourage, remind, and reprimand. But, as Reuben Welch puts it, "Only God can make an 'otherwise' mind 'otherwise!'" (1988, 112).
- This passage gives a vote of confidence to the correcting ministry of the Holy Spirit within the community of faith. Elsewhere, Paul assures the Corinthians that it is the Spirit who graciously reveals to us the mind of Christ (1 Cor 2:10-16). And Jesus himself promises that the Spirit will guide his church into all truth (John 16:13-15).
- Whatever differences in thinking may exist within the Christian community, the church must fix its vision on what is essential (Phil 3:16). We are called to live in a way that is worthy of the gospel (1:27). This gospel is not something "novel" or innovative. It is rather the old, old story, centered in Christ, revealed in Scripture, and attested by the historic witness of the church. If we are to keep making progress as mature Christians, it is vital that, together, we live out the story of Christ that we have heard all along.

- It follows that Christian leaders must take great care in what they insist on as being "essential" and how much correction of other believers they undertake. It is far too easy to come up with our own "authorized version" of which beliefs and lifestyle issues are necessary for everyone.

    The annals of missions history, for example, abound with the stories of well-meaning missionaries who have insisted that new converts talk about the faith and live it out in identical ways to "how we did it back home." Yes, there are lines that should not be crossed. But we need to make sure that they are not barriers of our own making.

- One thing this passage does *not* directly address is the question of how much diversity in teaching and lifestyle is acceptable within the church. A full treatment of that thorny issue is beyond the scope of this commentary. Nevertheless, any attempts to decide such matters must be undertaken, not simply by individuals, but within the context of the Christian community.

    Our efforts to discern the limits of Christian difference must be rooted in Scripture, guided by the Spirit, informed by the historic and intercultural understanding of the church, and in line with the transforming mission of God in the world. (For one attempt to wrestle with these issues, see Flemming 2005, 302-5.)

3. *The power of example.* Paul's appeal to "imitate me" (3:17) can be easily misunderstood today. The English word "imitation" often suggests mimicry, an exact copy of the original. But this appeal does not mean, "Be like me in every respect." That would ultimately demand that everybody be the same. Paul, for instance, did not expect his friends in Philippi to follow him into full-time missionary work or to have identical visionary experiences (2 Cor 12:1-7; Best 1988, 68). Rather, they are called to follow his example of losing all for the sake of Christ (3:7-8), of desiring to know Christ and to be like him (vv 10-11), and of passionately pursuing the heavenward goal (vv 12-14). In short, imitating Paul means applying the same Christ-oriented mind-set to their own life stories as he has shown in his (see 2:5-11).

Perhaps the more challenging question is, may *we* also say, "Imitate me"? It would be easier for us if this appeal were tied to Paul's unique role as an apostle, or if it simply applied to a time when converts did not yet have the NT to tell them how to live. But that is not the case. The gospel is still communicated as much by lives as by words. Observing and reproducing godly examples is a powerful, and too often neglected, strategy for spiritual formation.

Granted, the church must call Christians to holy living. But often what that means only becomes intelligible when we see it embodied in daily life and in real communities of faith. We need guides on the highway of holiness. The American Puritan Cotton Mather described it this way:

Examples do strangely charm us into imitation. When holiness is pressed upon us we are prone to think that it is a doctrine calculated for angels and spirits whose dwelling is not with flesh. But when we read the lives of them that excelled in holiness, though they were persons of like passions with ourselves, the conviction is wonderful and powerful. (Cited by Carson 1996, 94)

It is especially crucial for believing parents, Christian leaders, and mature disciples to provide living examples to those who are younger in the faith. How, for instance, will children from broken homes know what a loving and enduring Christian marriage looks like unless they see such relationships modeled before them? (see Carson 1996, 94). Or what about young people raised in a sex-obsessed culture? Will they know it is possible to live full lives of purity and integrity without the examples of godly women and men who are doing so? Will young believers know what it means to live like Christ in the twenty-first century if they do not see mature Christians whose lives remind them of Jesus?

My own spiritual walk was profoundly shaped as I observed my parents reflecting Christ in the ebb and flow of everyday life. Whether or not they were conscious of it, their lives consistently beckoned: "Imitate me."

4. *Citizens of heaven.* Throughout the history of the church, Paul's assertion that "our citizenship is in heaven" in 3:20 (along with the similar language in 1:27) has carried a weighty influence on Christian attitudes toward living in this world (see Bockmuehl 1995, 82-87).

This is particularly evident in the writings of the early church fathers. Typically, they spoke about our citizenship in heaven in connection with NT passages about Christians being pilgrims and aliens on earth (e.g., 1 Pet 2:11; Heb 11:16; 13:14; see Ps 87:1-3) or about the "Jerusalem above" (Heb 4:26), the new city of God (Bockmuehl, 1995, 84; see esp. Augustine, *City of God,* e.g., 5.17; 19.17; 20.9). Later, Phil 3:20 was interpreted in popular medieval piety to mean that heaven is the Christian's true home (see Thomas à Kempis 1973, 52; see further Bockmuehl 1995, 85).

Philippians 3:20 contributed, then, to the development of the idea that Christians are foreigners on earth, but belong to the heavenly city, their true homeland. And there is truth in this, of course. But too often the assumption has followed that the sole purpose of being a Christian is simply to "get to heaven when you die" (Wright 2007, 102-3). What is more, if we don't belong here anyway, then why get involved in the present world and its challenges? Why spend our energies on concerns like hunger or homelessness or global warming, if our calling is merely to "save souls" and get them ready to go home to heaven?

Such Christian escapism misses the point of this passage. In the first place, going home to heaven when we die is not the *ultimate* hope of the

Christian. N. T. Wright points out that being "citizens of heaven" does not simply mean that "Christians look forward to the time when they will return and live there for ever" (2003, 229).

As Paul describes it, the Christian hope is much more sweeping and magnificent than that. Paul pictures Christ coming *from* heaven to earth. Jesus the Savior rescues his people, not by helping them to escape from earth to heaven, but by changing their present bodies to be like his own. And this will happen in the context of the transformation of the whole of creation, when Christ will reign over a new heaven and a new (transformed) earth (see Rom 8:18-25; Rev 21—22).

Second, our citizenship in the heavenly commonwealth calls us, not to escape this world, but to live out the life of heaven on earth. If we currently *are* citizens of heaven, then our daily life in Philippi or Philadelphia or the Philippines must embody the character and values of God's heavenly reign. Recall Jesus' prayer: "Your kingdom come, your will be done, *on earth as it is in heaven*" (emphasis added). The church is called to "colonize earth with the life of heaven" (Wright 2007, 305), in anticipation of the renewal of God's creation to come. Life in the redeemed community, then, should be a preview of life under the coming reign of God. It is a life of wholeness and healing and justice and purity and compassion.

Third, citizenship in heaven is largely a *countercultural* existence. Because our ultimate allegiance is to the coming Savior and not to the powers of this world, we will demonstrate a radically different lifestyle and value system than others in the culture around us. Although we belong to another commonwealth, we joyfully remain in the world to be the living presence of Jesus and his kingdom; to prophetically challenge the culture; to become kingdom change-agents from within.

As citizens of heaven, we will have one foot firmly planted *inside* our culture, so that we can identify with the people around us and speak in a way that makes sense to them. At the same time, we will have one foot *outside* of the culture, as we model a cross-shaped alternative to the spirit of the world (see Volf 1996, 49).

VI. FINAL EXHORTATIONS: PHILIPPIANS 4:2-9

BEHIND THE TEXT

The letter is on the road to its conclusion. At this point, Paul gives his friends in Philippi some final practical instructions (4:2-9), before wrapping up with some personal greetings and a benediction (vv 21-23). These are elements we find near the end of other letters he wrote (e.g., 1 Cor 16:13-21; 2 Cor 13:11-13; 1 Thess 5:12-28). Sandwiched in between is something unique to Philippians—an extended expression of thanks to the church for its financial support and partnership in the gospel (Phil 4:10-20).

Apart from the closing greetings, this final portion of Philippians (vv 2-20) serves as the conclusion to Paul's argument in the letter. In Greco-Roman rhetoric, a major function of such a concluding section (the *peroratio*) was to recap the main themes already discussed (Aristotle, *Rhet.* 3.19; Quintilian, *Orat.* 6.1.1-8; Watson 1988, 76). Paul seems to do this throughout the unit, but especially in the present passage, vv 2-9.

Commentators differ over how vv 2-9 fit into the overall structure of the letter. Some, for example, think it is a part of a new unit that starts with v 1 and Paul's appeal to "stand firm" (e.g., Watson 1988, 76; Black 1995, 48). Others take vv 1-3 as a concrete application of the argument of ch 3 (e.g., Fee 1995, 285, 385-86; Bockmuehl 1998, 237); Paul's conclusion would then begin with 4:4. Admittedly, this is not an easy portion of the letter to outline. But the absence of a grammatical connection between vv 1 and 2 suggests that v 2 starts a new section. It is the "beginning of the end" of the letter (Deasley 2007, 277).

At first glance, these various practical exhortations might appear to have little connection, either to each other or to the rest of the letter. But a closer reading reveals that vv 2-9 reprise a number of important themes that Paul has already written about. These subjects include:

- unity (4:2-3; 1:27; 2:1-4; 3:15)
- having a Christlike mind-set (*phroneō*) (4:2; 2:2, 5; 3:15)
- being "in the Lord" (4:2; 2:19; 3:1; 4:1)
- contending together in the gospel (4:3; 1:27; see 2:22)
- the gospel (4:3; 1:5, 7, 12, 16, 27; 2:22)
- the church's eschatological hope (4:3, 5; 1:10, 28; 2:16; 3:12-14, 20-21)
- joy, rejoicing (4:4; e.g., 2:17-18; 3:1; 4:1)
- Christlike attitudes as a witness to unbelievers (4:5; 2:14-15)
- prayer (4:6; 1:3-4, 9-11, 19)
- imitating Paul and Christ (4:9; 2:5-11; 3:17)

In sum, these final exhortations reinforce Paul's main appeal to the Philippians throughout the letter—to live a life that is worthy of the gospel in unity, joy, and Christlikeness. At the same time, vv 2-9 build on the immediate context of v 1: Paul's instructions to the church help to unpack what it means to "stand firm in the Lord."

This section is rhetorically powerful, using a variety of devices designed to persuade the hearers. It opens with an impassioned appeal (*pathos*) directed toward two individuals in the church (4:2-3). Paul's repeated use of the first person ("I") in these verses reinforces the highly personal nature of this plea to his friends in Philippi.

With v 4, Paul abruptly switches from entreaty to command. What follows is a series of rapid-fire imperatives on different topics (compare 1 Thess 5:12-22; 1 Cor 16:13; 2 Cor 13:11). Phil 4:4-6 features the stylistic technique of "asyndeton," where the commands stand grammatically unattached to one another in Greek. This device gives each statement special emphasis. Because of this, it was often used at the end of discourses in Paul's day (Thielman 1995, 218).

The rhetoric reaches a climax in vv 8-9, with two carefully constructed sentences (translated quite literally):

Verse 8		Verse 9
whatever is true		*what you have learned*
whatever	*worthy of honor*	*and received*
whatever	*just*	*and heard*
whatever	*pure*	*and seen in me*
whatever	*pleasing*	
whatever	*admirable*	

> *if there is any moral excellence*
> *and if there is anything praiseworthy*
> *let your mind dwell on these things   continually practice these things*

In v 8, Paul borrows a teaching method from the Greco-Roman world, a list of virtues (Thurston 2005, 146). Such lists enumerated the ethical qualities that teachers wanted their students to embrace. Once again, Paul drops the connecting words between these virtues (thus, an example of asyndeton), allowing each one to stand out.

The second sentence, v 9, shows just the opposite literary device ("polysyndeton"). Here the same linking word "and" (*kai*) is repeated over and over, also for emphasis (Thielman 2005, 220). In both verses, the real focus is on the command at the end—what the Philippians should think and put into practice.

Paul also continues his appeal to good and bad examples as a strategy for moral formation. The passage begins with the story of two valued church leaders who have lapsed into a negative pattern of dissension (vv 2-3); it ends with the positive model of Paul (v 9; compare 3:17). In the latter case, once again Paul invokes his own character and way of life (an argument based on *ethos*) in order to persuade his audience of the course they should follow.

We can divide Paul's concluding advice to the church into three parts:

1. an appeal for reconciliation between two feuding church members (4:2-3)
2. a series of more general exhortations concerning joy, prayer, and peace (vv 4-7)
3. two summary exhortations to think and live rightly as Christians (vv 8-9)

IN THE TEXT

A. An Appeal for Unity (4:2-3)

■ **2-3** Quite abruptly, Paul launches into an urgent appeal: **I plead with Euodia and I plead with Syntyche to agree with each other in the Lord** (v 2). Here Paul does something that is almost unprecedented in his letters to groups of Christians—he names names. Singling these women out in front of the whole church (recall that Paul's words would have been read aloud) is a bold move, perhaps reflecting the seriousness of the problem (Fitzgerald 1996, 157). But it does not mean that Paul considers them "opponents." In fact, that he names them at all would have expressed friendship in the ancient world, since enemies were devalued by being left anonymous (Fee 1995, 389-90; see 1 Cor 4:18; 5:1-13; Gal 5:10; 6:12). Even so, we must ask, what prompted this unusual course of action?

Some commentators see the conflict between Euodia and Syntyche as the key to the whole letter. In this view, everything that Paul has already said builds toward this attempt to defuse a dispute that threatens the church's unity (e.g., Garland 1985, 172, 173; Osiek 2000, 21, 112). But this travels well beyond the evidence. The issue of unity is important, but it is not Paul's sole purpose for writing the letter (see the Introduction).

At the same time, the problem behind 4:2-3 cannot be shrugged off as "just a case of two bickering women" (Furnish 1985, 103). Paul's exhortations to two female coworkers are a concrete application of his appeal to unity and humility in 2:1-11. At a time when Christians in Philippi were facing outside pressures (1:27-28), this internal rift may well have posed a danger to the well-being of the church.

Behind this paragraph is a particular story. It is well known to both Paul and the Philippians but is foggy at many points to us. The underlying narrative is about two prominent Christian women who once labored side by side with Paul but who now are at odds. Beyond these broad strokes, however, Paul's passing references raise several tantalizing questions:

- Who are Euodia and Syntyche?
- What is the specific nature of their quarrel?
- Who is the "true companion" whom Paul asks to help resolve the dispute (v 3)?
- Who is the "coworker" Clement, and why mention him (v 3)?

As Craddock admits, this is one of the places in Paul's letters that "we are reminded . . . that we are reading someone else's mail" (1985, 70).

As to the identity of **Euodia** and **Syntyche,** they were most likely leading Gentile converts in Philippi. Their Greek names (which can be roughly translated as "good journey" and "good luck") are well attested in ancient inscriptions and are always female (see Lightfoot 1953, 158). Of greater importance is that these two women apparently had prominent roles within the Christian community. This was recognized as early as Chrysostom, who remarked, "These women seem to me to be the chief (*kephalaion*) of the Church which was there" (*Hom. Phil.* 13.4.2, 3). There are a number of reasons to think that they were leaders in the believing community in Philippi (see Witherington 1994, 105-7; Luter 1996, 412-15):

First, Paul includes them among his ***coworkers*** (*synergoi*), along with Clement and others (v 3; Paul's grammar connects **these women** who labored at Paul's side with **the rest of my fellow workers**). Paul does not use this term for believers in general; instead, "coworkers" refers to those who have labored with him in the ministry of the gospel (e.g., Epaphroditus, 2:25; see also Rom 16:3, 9, 21; 1 Cor 3:9; 16:16, 18; 1 Thess 3:2; Phlm 1, 24; see further, Dahl 1995, 6).

Second, Paul says that these two women **contended at my side in the cause of the gospel** (v 3). The verb ***struggled alongside*** (*synēthlēsan;* see also 1:27) is an athletic or military metaphor. At times, it was used of gladiators fighting side by side in the arena (Williams 1999, 265-66, 284 n 71). The word suggests that Euodia and Syntyche were active partners in Paul's ministry while he was in Philippi. More specifically, the phrase ***in the gospel*** (*en tōi euangeliōi*) implies that they partnered with Paul in the ministry of pioneer evangelism and the spread of the good news (see 1:5, 27; O'Brien 1986, 227; Keener 1992, 243).

Third, according to Acts, women had key leadership roles in the Philippian church from the time of its founding (Acts 16; see the sidebar "Women Leaders in Philippi").

Fourth, it was not unusual for Paul to have female ministry colleagues. Note the following examples:

- *Phoebe* is called a "deacon" (*diakonos*) of the local church at Cenchrae (Rom 16:1). This probably indicates that she was a leader in the congregation (Jewett 2007, 944).
- *Junia*, along with her husband, Andronicus, are described as being "outstanding among the apostles" (Rom 16:7). Here the term "apostle" (*apostolos*) suggests that they were respected missionaries, engaged in the ministry of the word.
- *Prisca* (or Priscilla) and Aquila her husband are another missionary couple, who led house churches in Ephesus and Rome (1 Cor 16:9; Rom 16:5). Like Euodia and Syntyche, Prisca is a "coworker" in Paul's evangelistic ministry (Rom 16:3-4; see Acts 18:2-3, 18-21, 24-28).
- *Mary, Tryphena, Tryphosa, and Persis* are all commended as colleagues who have "worked hard" as servants of the gospel (Rom 16:6, 12; on all these women, see the NBBC on Romans).

For Euodia and Syntyche to have significant leadership roles in Philippi would have been fully in line with the practice elsewhere in the Pauline churches.

Fifth, it is doubtful that Paul would have spotlighted this spat in a letter to the whole Christian community, if it were simply a private squabble between two church members. More likely, Euodia and Syntyche are influential leaders, whose conflict has the potential to polarize the entire congregation.

The suggestion that these two women may have been among the "deacons" (e.g., Peterlin 1995, 106-11) or "overseers" (e.g., Osiek 2000, 111-12) mentioned in 1:1 is appealing but cannot be proven. In any case, the disagreement between them was public knowledge and church members in Philippi were probably taking sides.

Women Leaders in Philippi

From the beginning, women played key leadership roles in the church in Philippi. According to Acts, the church was founded among a group of Gentile women who worshipped the God of Israel (Acts 16:11-40). The leading figure was Lydia, an independent businesswoman who hosted the embryonic church in her home (vv 13-15, 40). Within the culture of the day, those who were heads of households generally assumed a leadership role in the church that met in their homes. It is hardly surprising, then, that Euodia and Syntyche are described in Philippians as leaders in the Christian community. Apparently, these women were in no way inferior to their male colleagues (Phil 4:2-3).

This should all be seen against the backdrop of the role of women in Macedonia and the Roman world in general. During the Hellenistic period that preceded the rise of Rome, many women in Macedonia had positions of considerable influence. Inscriptions from the time show that high-status women were prominent in social, political, and economic life. They founded clubs and were active in various social organizations (Witherington 1994, 107). As one classic study summarizes, "If Macedonia produced perhaps the most competent group of men the world had yet seen, the women were in all respects the men's counterparts" (Tarn and Griffith 1959, 98).

During the Roman period in which Paul wrote, the status of women in Philippi would have been a mixed bag. On the one hand, Roman society was highly patriarchal, and women lived under many oppressive legal and cultural restraints. On the other hand, by the time of the Empire, the influence of women was on the rise. They were enjoying more freedom in social and economic life than women did a century earlier (Osiek 2000, 110).

There is evidence that Macedonian women took high-profile roles as patrons and priestesses in pagan religious cults (Thurston 2005, 17-18; Peterlin 1995, 109-10). Since Philippi was a Macedonian city without a strong Jewish presence, it would probably not have seemed culturally strange for Gentile women converts to take leading roles in the church (Witherington 1994, 108).

If Euodia and Syntyche are proven church leaders, and if their dispute threatens to poison the unity of the whole fellowship, then Paul's call for reconciliation is all the more pressing. It comes, however, not as a stern rebuke, but as an impassioned plea. The verb **I plead with** (*parakaleō*), as well as its repetition, bring out the earnestness of Paul's appeal. Paul urges each woman individually **to have the same mind-set** (*to auto phronein*) in the Lord.

This is typical language for addressing the health of a friendship in Paul's world (Stowers 1991, 112). But it is more than that. It also echoes Paul's call to unity, humility, and Christlikeness in 2:1-5 (see 2:2, 5; compare 3:15). What Paul urges goes much deeper than a superficial truce. He wants both parties to apply to their conflict the cruciform attitude of Christ himself (see Gorman 2004, 445).

Whatever the specific cause of the quarrel—and we cannot be sure (see Osiek 2000, 112-13, for various possibilities)—Paul's language implies that it was connected to their leadership roles in the church. In any event, Paul pleads with these valued leaders to set aside their personal agendas and exchange a self-promoting mind-set for the self-giving attitude of Christ. Paul's appeal to reconcile rests on three grounds.

First, the two women are to agree **in the Lord** (4:2). This phrase suggests that their unity is rooted in their common relationship to the Lord Jesus. Furthermore, they must live in a way that is fitting for those who are under his lordship. In particular, that involves following Christ's example of self-emptying love toward others (2:6-11).

Second, an important reason for helping these women settle their differences is that they have shared together in the work of advancing **the gospel** (v 3; the relative pronoun *haitines* probably means "for" [NRSV], rather than simply **who** [NIV]. It expresses one *reason* they should be assisted). Paul does not criticize their ministry on behalf of the gospel; on the contrary, he commends it. It is therefore urgent that their lives are consistent with the good news they represent (1:27).

Third, their unity is based on the fact that, along with other Christian coworkers, their **names are in the book of life** (v 3). This is unusual language for Paul. But it is well-attested within his Jewish heritage (e.g., Exod 32:32-33; Ps 69:28; Dan 12:1; Enoch 47:3; Rev 3:5; 13:8; 17:8; 20:12, 15; 21:27).

The image would also have been familiar to citizens of Philippi, whose names would have been listed in a civic register. Here the metaphor builds on Paul's eschatological reference in 3:20-21. It reminds Euodia and Syntyche that their conflict is out of character for citizens of the heavenly commonwealth, who await a Savior from heaven (3:20-21; see Fee 1995, 396-97).

Paul recognizes, however, that these two female leaders need assistance from the community to resolve their differences. Being absent himself, he asks another unnamed coworker to **help** (*syllambanō*) them embrace a common mind-set.

Paul addresses this person simply as a ***true companion*** (literally, **yokefellow**). Since "yoke" was a metaphor for the bond of friendship in the Greco-Roman world, Paul may be calling this person a "genuine friend" (Fitzgerald 1996, 149-51). This would imply a close relationship with Paul. But who is this mysterious mediator? The answer to this question was apparently clear enough to the Philippians, but it has given rise to all manner of speculation since (see the discussion in Bockmuehl 1998, 240-41).

Some have argued that the term **yokefellow** is actually a proper name, *Syzygus* (NIV margin). But the lack of any record of such a name in antiquity weighs against this. Other early proposals include the brother or husband of one of the women (Chrysostom), Epaphroditus, the bearer of the letter (Marius Victorinus; see 2:25), or even Paul's wife (Clement of Alexandria; Origen). The last suggestion arose because *sysygos* could occasionally refer to wives. But a female yokefellow seems to be ruled out by the *masculine* form of the adjective "genuine" (*gnēsie*). Additional candidates include Timothy, Luke (Fee 1995, 394-95), and the whole Philippian church (Hawthorne and Martin 2004, 242; Silva 2005, 193). In all likelihood, the question of whom Paul had in mind will remain an unsolved mystery.

We know little more about **Clement** (other than that his name is Latin) and **the rest of [Paul's] fellow workers** (v 3). All we are told is that they labored side by side with Euodia and Syntyche as the gospel took root in Philippi. Perhaps Paul is giving a gentle reminder to the two female leaders: they will only be able to continue their common struggle on behalf of the gospel, along with their coworkers, if they once again share the mind-set of Christ (Fowl 2005, 179).

Although there is much we do not know about the story behind this brief paragraph, one thing seems clear. Paul believes that these are reconcilable differences. As Fowl comments, "Despite the fact that Euodia and Syntyche are at odds with each other, Paul assumes that the common life of the Philippian church is capable of surviving this disagreement and generating the practices needed to reconcile these two leaders" (2005, 180). Knowing this, he can now return to exhorting the congregation as a whole.

B. A Call to Joy and Peace in All Circumstances (4:4-7)

■ **4** Verse 4 marks a sudden shift from appeal to imperative. The rather jerky grammar in Greek (created by the lack of connecting words) makes this series of commands and promises memorable. Verses 4-7 continue to work out Paul's aim for the moral formation of the church. These exhortations are tailored to the context in Philippi (Fee 1999, 172). In the face of external opposition and internal strife, Paul calls his friends to rejoicing, gentleness, and prayerful trust, which will enable them to experience God's surpassing peace.

The first imperative reinforces a theme that is by now familiar to the readers: **Rejoice in the Lord always. I will say it again: Rejoice!** Paul has repeatedly testified to his own attitude of joy (1:4, 18; 2:2, 17; see 4:10) and urged the Philippians to share in his rejoicing (1:25; 2:18, 28-29; 3:1). This verse especially picks up on the command to "rejoice in the Lord" in 3:1, but heightens the intensity. A number of features of this exhortation are striking:

- It is not an option, but a command: **Rejoice!**
- It rings with emphasis, both because the imperative is repeated and

because in Greek the word **rejoice** comes at the beginning and the end of the verse.
- The present tense verb **rejoice** (*chairete*) signals that this is the continual attitude of the believer. Joy is not so much a spontaneous outburst of emotion as a life practice (Fowl 2005, 182).
- The plural verb suggests that this is to be not only an individual but also a corporate experience. The entire community is called to rejoice *together*.
- The ground of our rejoicing is **in the Lord.** This is the third occurrence of this critical phrase in the first four verses of ch 4 (see 4:1, 2). Christian joy flows out of a relationship with the Lord, not from outward conditions. It "is thus an abiding, deeply spiritual quality of life" (Fee 1995, 404).
- We are to rejoice **always**—at all times and in all circumstances.

This final point deserves elaboration. The word **always** is highly significant in the context of Philippians. As Paul speaks these words, he is an imprisoned apostle with a capital charge hanging over him. He writes to a suffering church that is staring at opposition from without (1:27-30) and potential enemies from within (3:2-3, 18-19). As Barth memorably puts it, "'Joy' in Philippians is a defiant 'Nevertheless!'" (1962, 120). As a fruit of the Spirit (Gal 5:22), this joy is coterminous with problems, pressures, and tears.

The Spirit of Paul's hope-filled imperative to **rejoice in the Lord** is superbly expressed in Charles Wesley's hymn "Rejoice, the Lord Is King":

> *His kingdom cannot fail; He rules o'er earth and heav'n.*
> *The keys of death and hell are to our Jesus giv'n.*
> *Lift up your heart; Lift up your voice!*
> *Rejoice; again I say: rejoice!*

■ **5** The second exhortation in the series is to **let your gentleness be evident to all.** The word **gentleness** (*epieikēs*) is difficult to translate. In the LXX it is used to describe God's patient forbearance toward human failings (Ps 86:5; Bar 2:27). It speaks in the Pastoral Letters of a gentle and peaceable spirit—the inverse of being "quarrelsome" (1 Tim 3:3; Titus 3:2). But Paul's use of the term here seems closer to that of Wis 2:19 in the LXX, where the righteous answer persecution with a spirit of gentle forbearance.

Above all, Paul takes his cue from Jesus Christ, who showed "meekness and gentleness" (2 Cor 10:1; see 1 Pet 2:23), even in the face of insults and abuse. Gentleness, then, is the opposite of self-assertion and demanding one's rights (Deasley 2007, 230). The second-century *Epistle to Diognetus* thus testifies that God sent his Son, not "to rule by tyranny, fear, and terror," but "in gentleness (*epieikeiai*) and meekness . . . as one who saves by persuasion, not compulsion, for compulsion is no attribute of God" (*Diogn.* 7.3-4; Holmes 2007, 707).

Paul says that this Christlike quality should be **evident to all** (literally, "to all people"). That is, both those inside and outside the church should know of it. Certainly, an attitude of gentle forbearance is a medicine for the kind of internal discord described in Phil 4:2 and 3. But here the emphasis seems to be on the contagious influence of a gentle spirit within a pagan culture. When Christians lay down their right to retaliate, even in the face of opposition and suffering, their lives "speak." Their gentleness bears witness to a gospel about a Savior whose unwillingness to assert his rights led him all the way to the cross (2:6-8).

The next phrase is unexpected: **The Lord is near** (v 5*b*). This crisp assertion breaks up the sequence of exhortations and lacks any grammatical link with what comes before or after it. At the same time, there seems to be a connection in thought with what precedes and what follows. Believers can rejoice, endure suffering with gentleness, and live free from worry (vv 4-6), precisely because "the Lord is near."

But what does it mean that **the Lord is near** (*ho kyrios engys*)? Is Christ "close by"; that is, spiritually present among his people (e.g., Pss 34:18; 145:18)? Or is he **near** in the sense that his return is close at hand? These two options are not mutually exclusive, and both make good sense in the context. But Paul's reference to the Lord's expected return a few verses earlier (Phil 3:20-21) and the eschatological thread that runs throughout the letter (e.g., 1:6, 10, 28; 2:10-11, 16; 3:11-14; 4:3), suggests that the emphasis may be on the latter (see Rom 13:11; Jas 5:8).

Paul injects this simple but forceful phrase into his string of imperatives as an encouragement to a church under pressure. "Since their present suffering is at the hands of those who proclaim Caesar as Lord, they are reminded that the true 'Lord' is 'near'" (Fee 1995, 408). They can choose the path of gentle forbearance and need not worry (v 6). They have the assurance that the Lord's coming is at hand, and he will vindicate his people.

■ **6** Paul resumes his exhortations with the striking command, **Do not be anxious about anything.** On one hand, there is a positive concern about people and situations that is appropriate for Christians. We find an example of it in Timothy's deep care (*merimnēsei*) for the welfare of the Philippians (2:20). In this case, however, Paul is talking about an unproductive anxiety regarding worldly affairs that betrays a failure to trust God (Marshall 1991, 112). The command can mean, literally, "Stop worrying about anything" (*mēden merimnate*; a present tense verb).

Like the call to "rejoice always" in v 4, these are remarkable words, coming from someone who is languishing in prison. Moreover, the Philippians themselves had plenty of reasons to be anxious: persecution and economic hardship, a clash between leaders in the church, the potential threat of rival teachers, uncertainty surrounding Paul's future. What is more, "Most of them were poor, many were slaves, and few of them would have known the meaning of security" (Hooker 2000, 534). Worry is excluded, not because their problems are "not so bad after all," but because God is greater than their problems. There is likely an echo here of Jesus' own command not to worry about physical needs and the future (Matt 6:25-34).

Paul prescribes an antidote to worry: prayer. Instead of responding to trying situations with a harried anxiety, Christians must **in everything . . . present** [their] **requests to God** (v 6*b*). Note that both the scope of our praying (**in everything:** *en panti*) and the exclusion of fretting (**not about anything:** *mēden*) are all-embracing. **Everything** covers all needs and all circumstances. R. Rainy puts it well: "The way to be anxious about nothing is to be prayerful about everything" (cited by Michael 1928, 197).

To reinforce the point, Paul stacks up the words for prayer. He exhorts his audience: **by prayer and petition, with thanksgiving, present your requests to God.** There is probably not a large difference in the three terms for prayer. **Prayer** (*proseuchē*) is the more general word, while **petition** (*deēsis*) and **requests** (*aitēmata*) have to do with specific needs that are brought before God. The thought here is not unlike Jesus' teaching in the Sermon on the Mount that asking for daily bread (Matt 6:11) goes hand in hand with freedom from anxiety over the needs of life (Matt 6:25-34; Bockmuehl 1998, 247).

In addition, the attitude that should accompany all prayer is **thanksgiving** (*eucharistos*). Our gratitude for what God has done in the past enables us to trust that he will answer our prayers and supply our needs in the present. As Barth wisely reflects:

> To begin by praising God for the fact that in *this* situation, as it is, he is so mightily God—such a beginning is the *end* of anxiety. To be anxious means that we ourselves suffer, ourselves groan, ourselves seek to see ahead. Thanksgiving means giving God the glory in everything, making room for him, casting our care on him, letting it be his care. (1962, 122-23)

Thanksgiving, observes Wesley, is "the surest mark of a soul free from anxiety" (n.d., 513).

■ **7 And,** at the beginning of v 7, is more important than it first appears. It signals the *consequence* of praying with gratitude, which is **the peace of God** (*hē eirēnē tou theou*). This phrase appears only here in the NT. It stands for both the peace God *has* and *is* (see Judg 6:24: "the LORD is Peace") *and* the peace that God *gives* (Rom 14:17; 15:13; Col 3:15; 2 Thess 3:16). God's **peace** in the biblical sense means much more than the absence of conflict. It is God's *shalom* (in Hebrew), the wholeness and complete well-being that comes from God.

Such peace, Paul affirms, **transcends all understanding.** Does this mean that God's peace is above and beyond human comprehension (e.g., Chrysostom)? Or is Paul saying that God's peace "totally transcends the merely human, unbelieving mind" (Fee 1995, 410)? If Paul is stressing that God's peace surpasses human reasoning, which leads to anxiety, the latter could be his meaning. However, it is more likely that here he spotlights the uniqueness of God's *suprarational* peace (see Eph 3:20). This peace exceeds all understanding, comments Silva, "precisely because believers experience it when it is unexpected, in circumstances that make it appear impossible: Paul suffering in prison, the Philippians threatened by quarrels within and by enemies without" (2005, 196).

Verse 7 ends with a promise. God's all-surpassing peace **will guard your hearts and your minds in Christ Jesus.** Paradoxically, Paul uses a military term (**guard**, *phroureō*) to picture God's *peace* (Craddock 1985, 72; see 2 Cor 11:32). The image of "guarding" would have connected well with the Philippians. The military garrison that was stationed in Philippi was responsible for guarding the Pax Romana ("Roman peace"). But in contrast to the coercive force that secured the people of Philippi in the name of *pax*, Paul promises a radically different defense. The **peace of God** himself stands on duty, protecting the thoughts and hearts of his people (Fowl 2005, 184).

What, then, do they need to be "guarded" from? Certainly the fears and anxieties that threaten to overpower their **hearts** and their ***thoughts***. In addition, this divine peace is able to protect the Christian community from the kinds of fusses and frictions the Philippians are now experiencing (4:2-3). Bockmuehl points out the slight variation on this theme in Col 3:15. There Paul urges Christians to let the "peace of Christ *rule*" or "referee" their hearts collectively, "since as members of one body you were called to peace" (1998, 248).

Once again, the phrase **in Christ Jesus** is not simply an afterthought. The unfathomable peace of God that garrisons our hearts, individually and corporately, is a blessing of union with Christ (the phrase **in Christ Jesus** is attached to the main verb **will guard** rather than simply ***your thoughts***). We receive God's peace in and through the one who *"is* our peace" (Eph 2:20; see Col 1:20; Rom 5:1).

C. A Call to Focus on the Excellent and Follow Paul's Example (4:8-9)

■ **8** Verses 8 and 9 are summary injunctions, which function as a capstone for the specific demands of vv 4-7. Paul has just said that the peace of God would guard his readers' hearts and minds. Now he draws out some practical implications of that promise for their life in Philippi—how they are to think and what they are to do (Bockmuehl 1998, 249).

Finally (*to loipon*) in v 8 could, therefore, signal the conclusion to the exhortations leading up to it. Or it could simply mean "beyond that" or "in addition," as in 3:1. In any case, it does not introduce a new section of the letter.

What follows in v 8 is a list of virtues. This type of moral instruction appears in one form or another in nearly all of Paul's letters (see Kruse 1993, 962-63). But the *content* of the list is unexpected, as well as unique in the writings attributed to Paul. In some ways, Paul sounds here more like a Stoic philosopher than a Christian apostle: **whatever is true, whatever is noble, whatever is right, whatever is pure, whatever is lovely, whatever is admirable—if anything is excellent or praiseworthy—think about such things.**

These eight qualities are part of the common stock of popular moral teaching from the pagan culture of the day. But this raises a question. After all that Paul has said in this letter that challenges popular Roman values (see, e.g., 2:1-11), why does he suddenly appear to stamp his seal of approval on the ideals of the dominant culture?

Three considerations qualify Paul's endorsement of popular Greco-Roman morality. First, by and large, these virtues are not the exclusive property of pagans. All of them except the term **admirable** (*euphēma*) are part of Paul's Jewish heritage in the Greek Bible.

Second, Paul does not tell the Philippians to embrace *all* Greco-Roman values, but only "what he considers the *highest* and the *best* in pagan thought and culture" (Gorman 2004, 446).

Third, the exhortation that follows in v 9 puts these cultural virtues in the context of imitating Paul, as he embodies the cruciform story of Christ. Plainly, Paul does not embrace all of the Stoic assumptions behind these terms; Christians are called to "think about" such qualities only to the extent that they reflect the "mind of Christ" (2:5).

Nevertheless, we should not miss that Paul calls the Philippians to think and act Christianly *in the language of their own Greco-Roman culture*. In effect, he tells his audience, "Recognize the good wherever it is found and employ it in the service of Christ and the gospel." Verse 8 implies that Paul does not brand all of the ideals of the surrounding culture as automatically incompatible with the gospel. Christians can embrace the positive values and virtues of their world, provided these are viewed in light of the self-giving story of Christ (v 9).

Furthermore, in v 8 Paul risks formulating Christian truth in the language of the wider culture, *in spite of its links with Greek moral philosophy*. Here the apostle speaks the language his readers would still encounter in their daily interactions with pagan friends (Bockmuehl 1998, 250). But Paul does not want his Christian readers to understand what is "true" or what is "lovely" just like the pagans do. The language that Christians share with the dominant culture is always transformed in some way by the gospel of Christ crucified (see v 9). In other words, Paul intends for each of these "pagan" virtues to be filled with *Christian* content.

Having laid this foundation, we can turn to the meaning of the individual virtues in the list. In spite of the Hellenistic "sound" of these terms, there is no close parallel to this particular tally of virtues in the writings of the day. The list begins with six adjectives. Paul urges the Philippians to focus their thoughts on **whatever is** (literally, "whatever things are"):

- **true** (*alēthē*). "Truth" was a prime virtue in the Greco-Roman world (see Thiselton 1978, 874-77) but is also a characteristic notion of Paul. Since all of the terms in this list are moral qualities, what is "true" involves more than "correctness" or intellectual assent to a creed. It has to do with what is authentic, reliable, and real. Earlier in the letter, Paul contrasts those who preach Christ with false pretenses and those whose motives are true (1:18). For Paul, truth is always rooted in God (Rom 1:18, 25; 3:7) and revealed in the gospel (e.g., Gal 2:5, 14; Col 1:5; see Morris 1993, 954-55).

- **noble** (*semnos*). In the Greco-Roman world, this word often referred to what was sacred, majestic, or awe-inspiring. For Aristotle, it represented a "mild and seemly gravity" (*Rhet.* 2.17.4). In the NT it occurs only here and in the Pastoral Letters (1 Tim 3:8, 11; Titus 2:2). In both contexts, it probably signifies a moral quality of that which is worthy of respect and honor, in contrast to the crude and the sleazy.

- **right** (*dikaios*). "Justice" (*dikaiosynē*) was one of the four cardinal virtues of the ancient Hellenistic world. In general, the term "just" described people who lived up to their duties in relation to God, others, or the Law (see Schrenk 1964, 2:182-83). But for Paul, that which is "right" (see 1:7) is defined by God and God's righteousness, not by human understandings of justice (Fee 1995, 417-18). Consequently, we should take this quality in a comprehensive sense. This includes being righteous before God and reflecting God's own justice in our relationships with others.

- **pure** (*hagnos*). In Greek thought, as well as in the OT, this language could refer to both ritual purity and to ethical holiness and integrity (e.g., Ps 12:6; Prov 20:9; *hagnos* is from the same cognate family as the Greek words for "holy" [*hagios*], "holiness," etc.). In the NT, it is sometimes specifically tied to sexual purity (2 Cor 11:2; Titus 2:5). Here, however, the meaning is broader. It speaks of uprightness and integrity in our motives, actions, and all of life (see Phil 1:17; 1 Tim 5:22; 1 Pet 3:2; 1 John 3:3).

- **lovely** (*prosphilēs*). The next two words are more at home in the world of Hellenism than that of the Bible. This first term appears nowhere else in the NT. Nor does it show up on any list of ancient moral virtues. Its usage embraces both what is "lovely" (i.e., "beautiful") as well as what is "lovable" or attractive to others (see Sir 4:7). As Bockmuehl perceptively observes, "Of all the words in Paul's list, this one gives the clearest indication that the range of qualities that should shape a Gentile Christian mind includes a dimension not just of moral but of *aesthetic* truth as well" (1998, 253). Christians are to reflect on what is beautiful and pleasing, both in creation and in the spiritual lives of God's people.

- **admirable** (*euphēmos*). The last of the six adjectives occurs only here in the Greek Bible. In classical Greek texts, it meant something like "well-sounding" (hence, the English word "euphemism") and, as a result, attractive and winsome (see Lightfoot 1953, 161-62). It therefore overlaps in meaning to the previous word, **lovely.** Both terms imply that believers should concentrate on speaking and living in ways that are winsome to others in the wider community.

Now the pattern changes. Paul draws on two nouns that sum up the previous six qualities and sharpen their focus. He says, literally, ***if there is any moral excellence and if anything praiseworthy.*** These are both umbrella terms. The first word refers to "virtue" (*aretē*). It was a flagship expression of the Greek ethical ideal (see Link and Ringwald 1978, 3:925-28; Bauernfeind 1964, 1:457-61). Originally it was used for any kind of excellence or achievement. But in Greek (especially Stoic) philosophy it came to stand for the highest good, which people should devote themselves to attaining.

Given this focus on virtue by means of human achievement, it is not surprising that both the LXX and the NT writers tended to shy away from the term (but see 2 Pet 1:5, where it refers to human virtue; compare 1 Pet 2:9; 2 Pet 1:3). Its unexpected appearance at the climax of this virtue list underscores that Paul was not afraid to co-opt the language of Hellenistic moral philosophy. But here, as elsewhere, Paul infuses "virtue" with a distinctly Christian meaning (see v 9; Fee 1995, 419). For Paul, ***moral excellence*** comes not through human striving but by adopting the mind of Christ.

The second noun (*epainos*) in this setting refers to something that is worthy of praise. It is possible that Paul is exhorting the Philippians to think about things that are worthy of *God's* praise (see Rom 2:29; 1 Cor 4:5). But here, coupled with ***moral excellence,*** it probably speaks of a life that is recognized as **praiseworthy** by others.

The verb to which these eight qualities are related (*logizomai*) comes at the end of the list, for emphasis. Here it means not simply to **think about** but to "continually let your minds dwell on" such things (see Bauer 1979, 476; O'Brien 1991, 507). Paul is saying, "Fill your mind with these virtues. Concentrate on them. Make them your focus of attention." The implication is plain: when we carefully reflect on things that are true, noble and so forth, they become internalized and shape how we live. Deasley puts it well: "Thought leads to action, and what we open our minds to quickly becomes our master" (2007, 232).

It seems, then, that Paul wants to impress on his audience that the Christian mind is not closed to the highest moral values and ways of articulating them in their Gentile culture. Indeed, such publicly recognized virtues can serve as points of contact with the pagan society around them. They must live lives that are authentically winsome and morally excellent. This will help them fulfill their calling to shine as beacons in the midst of a crooked world (2:14-16; 4:5). But, as always, the litmus test for discerning what is morally excellent and what is not is the gospel of Christ, the message they have heard from the beginning. Hence, v 8 is incomplete without v 9.

■ 9 Verse 9 gives concrete definition to the more general qualities of the previous verse in terms of imitating Paul. This is reflected in the change in Greek pronouns from the indefinite "whatever things" (*hosa*) in v 8 to the definite "which specific things" (*ha*) of v 9. The latter explains the former more specifically in terms of the gospel the Philippians have learned from Paul (Bockmuehl 1998, 254). Paul says, in effect, "Read this list through the lens of what you have learned from me and seen in me" (Fee 1995, 420).

Appropriately, Paul concludes his exhortations in the letter by returning to the theme of imitating worthy examples (see on 3:17). In particular, 4:9 picks up on Paul's call to follow his own example in 3:17. Once again, "Paul offers his own life as a screening room" (Craddock 1985, 74): **whatever you have learned or received or heard from me, or seen in me—put it into practice.** But, as in ch 3, this invitation has meaning only to the extent that Paul is faithful to the pattern of life seen in the example of Christ (2:6-11). Ultimately, then, all of the virtues listed in 4:8 are embodied in Christ.

Paul uses four verbs to describe his ministry to the Philippians. The first two, **learned** (*manthanō*; see the cognate form, *mathētēs*, "disciple" which appears 264 times in the NT) and **received** (*paralambanō*), probably both refer to the instruction in the gospel and its implications that Paul gave them when he was initially in Philippi (see O'Brien 1991, 508-9). In his second-century letter to the church in Philippi, Polycarp speaks of how Paul, "when he was with you . . . accurately and reliably taught the word concerning the truth" (Pol. *Phil.* 3.2; Holmes 2007, 285).

The second verb, **received,** is more specific than the first. Here Paul uses a technical term from Judaism and early Christianity. It implies that he carefully handed on to them the Christian tradition he had received (see 1 Cor 11:23; 15:1-5; 2 Thess 3:6; see also Gal 1:9; 1 Thess 4:1). This refers to something more than ordinary classroom instruction, which students might choose to ignore. Paul's moral teaching served as an authoritative guide for how his beloved friends would live out the gospel in Philippi (see Green 2002, 184).

The next pair of verbs also go together. **Heard** and **seen** could portray two ways the Philippians learned from Paul—hearing what he said and watching how he lived. This is how the NIV takes it, adding the words **from me** after **heard**. But it is also possible that the text refers to what they heard *about* his conduct and character from others (perhaps Timothy or Epaphroditus) when Paul was not present. This seems the better reading, particularly since Paul has already used the same two verbs in 1:30 in relation to his example before the Philippians.

If this is the case, then both what they **heard** and "saw" have to do with how Paul embodied the gospel he taught (**in me**). Paul's life preached. He could, therefore, say without a hint of arrogance or embarrassment, "Follow my example" (Hawthorne and Martin 2004, 253).

What the Philippians have learned, listened to, and observed, they must continually **put into practice** (*prassete*). Verse 8 set before the Philippians a guide for how they should *think*. Now Paul gives them a pattern of what they must *do*. Both are essential for the church's moral formation.

It is fitting that the last word in Paul's concluding exhortation in this letter is not a command, but a promise. Paul, in effect, says, "If you will adopt a Christian mind and follow my Christlike example, you have this assurance: **the God of peace will be with you.**" The apostle often invokes the "God of peace" in prayers and promises for his converts near the end of his letters (Rom 15:33; 16:20; 2 Cor 13:11; 1 Thess 5:23). Already in v 7 Paul has assured his audience that the **peace of God** would guard and protect them. Now he promises that the **God of peace** himself will be present with them. The symmetry is exquisite.

As the **God of peace,** God is both the source and the giver of peace. This is no small assurance for a church facing frightening opposition from without (1:28) and disharmony from within (4:2-3).

FROM THE TEXT

1. *Dealing with disunity.* Conflict between church members or church leaders is an age-old problem. Granted, we do not know the details of the problem between Euodia and Syntyche (4:2-3). And circumstances will vary from case to case today. Nevertheless, we can still learn from the way Paul handles the disharmony between these two first-century leaders. This brief passage yields several important implications for dealing with discord in the church:

a. Addressing the problem instead of ignoring it. When tensions bubble up within the church, our tendency is often to avoid "rocking the boat." We shy away from confronting the people or the problem. Our text implies, however, that the stakes are too high to let disunity go unchecked, especially among church leaders. Unresolved conflicts endanger the spiritual health of those who are quarreling, the well-being of the congregation, and the church's witness to the world. Furthermore, to tolerate strife or self-promotion would be to fly in the face of the gospel itself (2:1-11; Ezell 1980, 375). Bonhoeffer observes that in such situations to say nothing can itself be an act of cruelty; to correct a Christian sister or brother is a ministry of love and grace (1954, 103-8).

b. Urging the offenders rather than denouncing them. Paul approaches his fellow workers who are at odds with an impassioned plea, not a heavy club of condemnation. Furthermore, he commends, as well as corrects. If we follow Paul's lead, our approach to disagreements within the church will flow out of love and pastoral concern. It should be done in a spirit of gentleness (4:5), affirming the value of those involved. The goal is to reconcile, not to punish.

c. Dealing with the issue evenhandedly. Paul's approach to conflict resolution is remarkable for its impartiality. He refuses to take sides. Nor does he get into the question of who is right and who is wrong. Such an evenhanded attitude does not trivialize the problem. Neither does it suggest that peoples' disagreements are unjustified. Rather, it assumes that reconciliation is paramount. For that to happen will require humility and confession from both sides.

d. Allowing the community to help with the healing. Encouraging fellow believers to resolve conflicts is a vital ministry of the body of Christ (see Matt 18:15-20; Gal 6:1). In many cultures today, Paul's approach of enlisting a gifted and trusted mediator (Phil 4:3) is a natural way of helping to reconcile those who are at odds. In the Western world, however, individuals are more apt to try to work out their problems on their own. But whatever the culture, strife within the community, especially when it involves leaders, is not simply a private matter. It is the concern and responsibility of the whole church (Thielman 1995, 223). The community must be willing to come alongside and be a part of the healing process. We are called to be reconcilers toward one another.

e. Focusing on agreement in the Lord. In the face of tensions among leaders or divided opinions in the church, the mind-set of Christ (v 2) must serve as our basis for unity. This does not mean that Christians will in the end agree on all matters of doctrine or practice. But it does mean that what we have in common—our shared life in Christ and partnership in the ministry of the gospel—is far greater than whatever divides us. Congregational leaders, in particular, need to model a willingness to lay aside their cherished opinions and personal preferences. The unity of the church and the progress of the gospel come first.

This is no simple matter, especially when disagreements create hurt feelings and ruptured relationships. But this passage takes us back to what is essential. What truly counts is that we embrace the same mind-set *in the Lord*, the one who humbled himself for the sake of others.

2. *Women in leadership.* Paul does not consciously set out to address the subject of "women in ministry" in this passage. Nevertheless, vv 2-3 speak to that contemporary debate. They give us a snapshot of two women serving as influential leaders in their local Christian community. This is all the more significant because Paul mentions it so incidentally (on the role of women in the NT church, see Witherington 1998; Keener 1992; France 1995).

But not everyone agrees. Inevitably, what we believe about the appropriateness of women in ministry will color our interpretation of individual texts like the one before us. Consequently, interpreters who apparently doubt that women could have exercised such prominent ministry roles in the church read these verses quite differently. The early church father Theodore of Mopsuestia, for instance, made Euodia into a man (Euodias) and Syntyche "his" wife (see v 2 KJV). Others have argued that when Paul calls these women **fellow contenders** in the gospel (v 3), he is referring to their suffering and possible martyrdom in the cause of Christ, not to their gospel ministry (e.g., Blum 1972, 66).

Such readings, however, have little support in the text. Fee reflects on the implications of the passage: "Here is evidence that the Holy Spirit is gender-blind, that he gifts as he wills. Our task is to recognize his gifting and assist all such people, male and female, to 'have the same mindset in the Lord'" (1999, 171). It is a sad situation when women are called by God, gifted by the Spirit, theologically and spiritually equipped—and shut out of many ministry roles in the church, purely on the basis of their gender.

My own Wesleyan theological tradition has been historically open to women serving as congregational leaders. But we often struggle in practice, especially when it comes to local churches accepting women in certain leadership roles. On the other hand, while serving as a missionary in the Philippines, I witnessed many female pastors and leaders whose ministries bore extraordinary fruit. Such service becomes a thrilling possibility, when doors are open for women and men alike to strive side by side in the work of the gospel (v 3).

3. *Abandoning worry.* This passage exhorts us not to worry about *anything* (v 6). Yet our natural tendency is to worry about *everything* (Hooker 2000, 547). We become anxious over personal concerns—financial strains, a rebellious child, marital stresses, the *lack* of a companion, pressures at work, academic deadlines, and the like. What is more, the simple act of turning on a television or surfing the Internet triggers a bombardment of worrying realities, whether the threat of terrorism, global warming, widespread poverty and disease, natural disasters, or ethnic-based conflicts. How is it possible for twenty-first-century Christians *not* to worry?

Fortunately, the command against worrying does not stand on its own. Paul's alternative to anxiety is *prayer*, in an attitude of *thanksgiving* (v 6). If the formula, "Don't worry . . . but pray," sounds a bit too simple, we need to recall the kind of prayer that Paul is talking about. It presupposes a deep reliance on the Heavenly Father, who is faithful to care for his children (Matt 6:25-34). Such trust is nourished by gratitude for what God has lavishly given and graciously done on our behalf. Anxiety, on the other hand, is self-focused; it exposes a failure to give things over to God. Bockmuehl's observation is perceptive: "Worry can be the delayed symptom of a practical atheism that grows from persistent neglect of prayer and addictive belief in self-sufficiency" (1998, 247).

Just as living in a state of worry is a choice, so we can *choose* to cast all our anxiety on the one who cares for us (1 Pet 5:7). This is not an invitation blissfully to ignore our pressures or to escape from our responsibilities. Nor does Paul say that God will relieve our anxiety by getting rid of what we are anxious about (Welch 1988, 121). Too many Christians bear the scars of false promises that God will take away all of their problems. The cares and concerns we carry are real. But just as real is the possibility of being liberated from the ogre of anxiety. This comes only through grateful prayer and trust in a God who can be trusted. Wesley rightly insisted that "anxiety and prayer cannot stand together" (n.d., 513).

The result of such prayerful trust is stunning: The *shalom* of God, "which is far more wonderful than the human mind can understand" (Phil 4:7 TLB), will grant us protection and rest in Christ. This divine peace is not only the experience of individual believers but also the shared blessing of the Christian community. The words of the old hymn ring true:

> O what peace we often forfeit,
> O what needless pain we bear,
> All because we do not carry
> Everything to God in prayer.
> —Joseph M. Scriven
> "What a Friend We Have in Jesus"

4. *Engaging the culture.* Philippians 4:8-9 has important implications for the church's relationship with the surrounding culture today. In v 8, Paul tallies a set of virtues that were widely valued in the pagan world and uses them to instruct Christians about how they should think and live. Underlying such a move is the belief that the whole world belongs to God. God is present and active in the world he has created, including our human cultures. Although sorely sinful, the world is capable of being remade by the God who made it.

As a result, the church's calling is not to completely reject the culture around it. Whenever cultures and their moral and religious values reflect God's truth, this is evidence that God's grace is at work (Dyrness 1995, 58). We are therefore free to celebrate what is good and true and lovely in our cultures. As the second-century apologist Justin Martyr claimed, "The truth which men in all lands have rightly spoken belongs to us" (*2 Apol.* 2.13). We should not be afraid to value and learn from what is good in "secular" art, music, cinema, literature, proverbs, or customs, or to enlist them into the service of Christ.

Likewise, we can recognize that all cultures have virtues and values that overlap with those of God's kingdom. While living in the Philippines, I was intrigued by the way the Filipino people named their shared cultural values. One such core value is called *pakikipagkapwa-tao* (literally, "being a fellow to others"). It involves notions like sharing, treating others with respect, extending a helping hand to those in need. These attributes have much in common with the Christian notion of *koinōnia* (partnership). The church today, like Paul, can affirm such positive values and use them as points of contact for the gospel (Flemming 2005, 130).

At the same time, v 9 reminds us that we do not embrace the ideals of the wider culture uncritically. Under the Spirit's guidance, we must discern when to say no to popular values. When the church allows the world around it to dictate its moral agenda, it speeds down what Jesus called the wide road to destruction (Matt 7:13).

Our text calls us to sanctified thinking. The final test for what is true and good in the art forms or values of our culture is this: Are they compatible with the cruciform mind of Christ revealed in the gospel? (For more on how the NT informs the church's engagement with culture, see Flemming 2005.)

5. *A pattern of discipleship.* Verses 8 and 9 also convey something vital about the character of our discipleship. These concluding exhortations reveal a beautiful balance between right *thinking* and right *practice.*

The text urges Christians to fix their minds on things that are pure and excellent (v 8). Thoughts are powerful. To a large extent, we *are* what our minds dwell on. If we focus on Christlike thoughts, we will be Christlike; if we fill our minds with rubbish, we will live like rubbish. Jesus makes the point vividly in the Sermon on the Mount: behind impure actions are lustful thoughts, and below acts of murder are hateful attitudes (Matt 5:21-30).

The text implies that there are things that Christian disciples should *not* be thinking about. An often-neglected aspect of Christian formation is the disciplining of our thoughts. Do we allow our minds to dwell on the pure or the sordid? The right or the wrong? Do our thoughts about others edify or tear them down? Growth in conformity to Christ involves being transformed by the renewing of our minds (Rom 12:2).

Negatively, pursuing a transformed mind may require us to eliminate from our lives certain conversations, movies, television programs, Internet sites—whatever prompts us to dwell on unhealthy and impure thoughts. Positively, it will mean filling our minds with the Word of God and Christian teaching—as Paul puts it, "the things you have learned and received" (v 9).

Our thinking must be nurtured through time-tested spiritual disciplines, such as meditating on Scripture and attentively reading the classic devotional texts. The goal of these "holy habits" is that our minds and imaginations would be profoundly re-formed in the shape of the mind of Christ.

On the other hand, this passage calls us not only to think holy thoughts but also to live holy lives (v 9). Thinking cannot be separated from doing. If our minds are absorbed by what is pleasing to Christ, then action will follow (Ezell 1980, 378). Christian discipleship involves diligently pursuing practices of devotion and service that help us live out the cross-shaped pattern of Christ. J. Ross Wagner observes that "such practices are best learned through imitation and sustained through significant, ongoing, face-to-face and heart-to-heart relationships" (2007, 273). The great need of the body of Christ today is not for more megaministries. It is for more communities of growing disciples, who authentically embody the gospel in their daily interaction with one another and with a needy world.

For Paul, and us, Christian maturity involves both "forming right habits of mind" (Wagner 2007, 269) and practicing a cruciform way of life. And lest we imagine that the task is too demanding, this section ends with the assurance that the "God of peace" himself will be present with us (v 9).

VII. CONCLUDING MATTERS: PHILIPPIANS 4:10-23

A. Gratitude for the Philippians' Gift (4:10-20)

BEHIND THE TEXT

Paul's "thank-you note" to the Philippians in 4:10-20 is one of the most personal sections of the letter. Behind it lies the story of the Philippians' long-standing generosity on Paul's behalf. The latest chapter in that story is their recent gift through Epaphroditus (vv 15-18). His main exhortations and warnings to the church behind him, Paul now turns to expressing gratitude for their support.

But how the apostle says thanks raises some intriguing questions: If acknowledging the Philippians' financial gifts is an important reason for the letter (see the Introduction), then why does Paul postpone the subject until the very end? And why does he seem to "thank" (he never actually uses the word) them in such a lukewarm fashion? After all, he makes it plain that he did not really need their gift, nor did he seek it (vv 11, 17).

For some commentators, the best answer to such questions is that vv 10-20 were originally part of a separate letter, sent as soon as Paul received the gift (e.g., Beare 1959, 150). Others think that Paul's reticence betrays a certain embarrassment to speak about the touchy subject of money (e.g., Martin 1976, 161; Hawthorne and Martin 2004, 258-59). But many of the problems that scholars have with this passage are better explained when we view these verses in the context of Paul's cultural and social world. In particular, we need to understand (1) the unit's rhetorical function in the letter; and (2) the background of gift-giving in the Greco-Roman world.

As for the first issue, this is not the only time in the letter that Paul makes reference to the Philippians' gift. Both 1:5 and 2:25-30 allude to it indirectly. But Paul leaves the main development of the subject until near the end of the letter. This is almost certainly a deliberate strategy, which supports Paul's persuasive aims in Philippians.

As we noted in the last section, 4:10-20 makes up the final part of Paul's rhetorical conclusion (*peroratio*) to the letter (vv 2-20). According to Aristotle, the *peroratio* seeks to recapitulate some of the main themes, to help the audience be well-disposed toward the speaker, and to strengthen the argument by appealing to the audience's emotions (*Rhet.* 3.19). We find evidence of all three of these functions in Paul's expression of gratitude.

First, the passage reinforces a number of themes Paul has already developed, including:

- joy (4:10; e.g., 1:4, 18; 2:18; 3:1; 4:1)
- the long-standing partnership (*koinōnia*) that binds Paul and the Philippians together (4:14, 15; 1:5, 7; see 2:1)
- suffering for the gospel (4:14; 1:29-30; 2:17, 25-30; 3:10)
- having an others-oriented "mind-set" (*phroneō*; 4:10; 1:7; 2:2, 5)
- a willingness to be "humbled" (4:12; see 2:3), even as Christ "humbled himself" (2:8)
- experiencing the enabling work of God (4:13; 1:6; 2:13)
- gratitude for the Philippians and for Epaphroditus their messenger (4:10-20; 1:5; 2:25-30)
- Paul as an example of cruciform living (4:11-13; 1:12-26; 3:17; 4:9; see 2:5-8)

Second, Paul helps to ensure a positive hearing from his audience by telling the story of their past generosity and by expressing his gratitude to them.

Third, Paul arouses the empathy of his readers through a positive emotional appeal (*pathos*). This happens when he narrates his afflictions (4:12, 14) or recalls the unique bond of caring between them (vv 10, 15-16). At the same time, Paul is not limited to the aims of the rhetorical handbooks. He uses this rhetorical conclusion as an opportunity to model the cruciform gospel (see vv 11-13) and ultimately to bring glory to God (v 20).

Paul's careful rhetorical arrangement also comes to light in the parallels between his "thank you" in vv 10-20 and his thanksgiving in 1:3-11. In addition to the common themes mentioned above, Paul, for example, talks about his partnership with the Philippians "from the first day until now" (1:5) and *in the beginning of the gospel* (4:15). And both sections end by giving glory to God (1:11; 4:20; for further parallels, see Peterman 1997, 91-92). In superb symmetry, 1:3-11 and 4:10-20 frame the entire Epistle.

Furthermore, placing Paul's expression of gratitude at the end of the letter signals that finances are only one aspect of the gospel partnership he and the Philippians share, not the main point of the letter (Gorman 2004, 447; against Fitzgerald 1992, 322). At the same time, its final position gives this passage emphasis, particularly when read aloud to the gathered community of faith. As Fee offers, "These are intentionally the last words left ringing in their ears as the letter concludes, words of gratitude, theology, and doxology that simply soar" (1995, 17). It is clear, then, that Paul's "thank-you note" in 4:10-20 is hardly an afterthought or a misplaced item. Rather, it is a carefully crafted conclusion to the letter.

Let us turn now to the first-century context of giving and gratitude. Paul's tone in this passage is likely to be puzzling if we read his words through our own cultural glasses. To an ancient Hellenistic reader, however, Paul's restrained approach to thanking his audience would have made much more sense. Recent scholarship has shown that the high concentration of financial language in this passage (e.g., **the matter of giving and receiving** [v 15]; **what may be credited to your account** [v 17]; **full payment** [v 18]) is not just about money.

In the Greco-Roman world, the giving and receiving of gifts was shaped by a whole network of social rules and relationships. The exchange of material benefits (gifts and services) played a vital role in both friendships between social equals and in relationships between socially superior patrons and inferior clients (Peterman 1997, 197; see Bormann 1995 on 4:10-20 in light of Greco-Roman patron-client relationships).

Gifts in antiquity had strings attached. Normally, accepting a gift would put the receiver in the giver's debt (a socially inferior position); it carried the obligation to repay in kind or even more (Witherington 1994, 127). On the other side, giving a gift could increase the status of the giver. It was one way of gaining a commodity of much greater importance: honor (Fowl 2005, 24). As a result, the giving and receiving of benefits could easily degenerate into a kind of "power game," in which one party held the upper hand over the other (Fee 1995, 444). Because the mutual exchange of gifts was tied up with the relative power and status of the parties involved, Paul understandably handles the matter with care (Fowl 2005, 190).

In particular, verbal thanks for gifts played a different role in the Greco-Roman world than it does in modern Western societies. For Paul to thank the Philippians directly or effusively for their gift might suggest that he was binding himself to pay them back (Peterman 1991, 264). Paul, therefore, walks a fine line between appearing to be ungrateful and saying something that would hold him in the spider's web of social conventions regarding reciprocity and patronage (Blomberg 1999, 205).

Consequently, if Paul's expression of gratitude is not as straightforward as we might be accustomed to, it is because he is dealing with cultural expectations about giving and receiving that could negatively affect his relationship to the Philippians. Part of his aim in this passage, then, is to recast typical cultural understandings of giving and receiving in light of the gospel (for more on the social practice of "giving and receiving," see Peterman [1997]; Berry [1996]).

Paul and Financial Support

It is important to see Phil 4:10-20 in the context of Paul's wider financial dealings with his churches. In 1 Cor 9, Paul argues vigorously for the right to receive support for his ministry. But, in general, he refuses that right (e.g., 1 Cor 9:12-18; 2 Thess 3:9), choosing instead to support himself by working with his hands.

Paul gives two main reasons for this strategy: First, he does not want to be a burden to the churches (2 Cor 11:9; 12:13-16; 1 Thess 2:9; 2 Thess 3:8). Second, he is concerned not to erect any obstacles to the progress of the gospel (1 Cor 9:12). Such obstacles might come if he were charged with impure motives for preaching. Paul's world had no shortage of charlatan philosophers, like the Sophists, whose trademarks were greed and the habit of bilking their followers.

Furthermore, if Paul had taken funding from a church like Corinth, he risked being drawn into the cultural convention of patronage. Accepting patronage would force Paul into an inferior client status, under perpetual obligation to his well-to-do patrons. Such a relationship could restrict his ability to preach the gospel freely (1 Cor 9:18), as well as to carry out his itinerant ministry.

Paul, however, makes two exceptions to his general policy of refusing support. First, he apparently accepted travel expenses to "send him on his way" (1 Cor 16:6; 2 Cor 1:16; see Rom 15:24). Second, Paul entered into an ongoing relationship of missionary support with one congregation, the church in Philippi (Phil 4:15-18). Paul apparently did not view this as a patron-client relationship but rather as a mutual partnership of equals in the gospel (v 15; on Paul's financial dealings, see Witherington 1994, 123-24).

We looked earlier at the rhetorical function of 4:10-20 in the letter. But what are some of the specific ways Paul makes this section persuasive to his audience?

Once again, Paul argues from his own character and credibility (*ethos*), especially in vv 11-13. This is actually the third (and briefest) autobiographical scene of the letter, following 1:12-26 and 3:4-14. Hard on the heels of Paul's call to imitation in 4:9, his story of poverty and plenty becomes an example for his audience. His words of testimony imply that they, too, can face their current hardships and suffering with the assurance of Christ's enabling power (v 13).

Other literary and rhetorical conventions strengthen Paul's argument. In v 12 we find an abbreviated list of afflictions (see Rom 8:35; 1 Cor 4:9-13; 2 Cor 4:8-9; 11:23-29; 12:10). Such catalogues were familiar to both Hellenistic and Jewish writings of the period (see Kruse 1993b, 18-19). In this case, Paul frames the list in a series of contrasting pairs (**to be in need/to have plenty, well fed or hungry, in plenty or in want**). The sevenfold repetition of the linking word *kai* in this verse (the literary device of *polysyndeton*) only heightens the emphasis. Read aloud to the gathered assembly, the effect would have been powerful and persuasive.

At the same time, Paul spotlights key ideas through repetition (e.g., "all" [*panta*], five times in vv 12, 13, 18, 19; words of "need" [vv 11, 12, 16, 19] and "abundance" [vv 12, 18, 19]). Finally, the paragraph as a whole is framed by Paul's rejoicing in the Lord (v 10) and his exulting in the glory of God (v 20). It is therefore hard to deny that Paul's letter/sermon ends with a piece of exceptional artistry and persuasive power.

The passage naturally divides into three parts: (1) vv 10-13; (2) vv 14-17; and (3) vv 18-20. The first two follow a similar pattern (laid out nicely by Fee 1995, 424-25). First, Paul acknowledges the Philippians' gift (vv 10*a*, 14). Then he immediately qualifies what he has said about them (v 10*b*, you were concerned, but had no opportunity to show it; vv 15-16, a reminder of your past record of giving and receiving). Finally, he adds two sharper qualifiers, beginning with **not that** (vv 11-13: not that I am in need; v 17, not that I desire the gift).

The third unit begins like the first two. Paul acknowledges their gift (v 18) and adds a qualification: the promise that God will provide for their own needs (v 19). This time, however, the third element is not another qualifier but rather a canticle of praise to God (v 20).

IN THE TEXT

1. Rejoicing and Contentment (4:10-13)

■ **10** The section begins with the familiar theme of Paul's rejoicing over the Philippians (1:4; 2:2; 4:1). Here Paul assures them, ***I rejoiced in the Lord greatly because now at last you revived your concern for me*** (v 10). The NIV takes this as a present joyful attitude (**I rejoice**; an "epistolary aorist"). But more likely it refers to the joy Paul experienced when Epaphroditus arrived with the Philippians' gift. The adverb **greatly** (*megalōs*; only here in the NT) shows the intensity of Paul's "*mega*-joy."

As Fowl points out, "Expressing joy is not the same as expressing thanks" (2005, 192). Philippians 4:10-20 has sometimes been called a "thankless thanks" (e.g., Lohmeyer 1929, 178, 183), since Paul never actually uses a Greek equivalent to "thank you." But following the normal cultural conventions for expressing thanks would draw him into an obligation to repay the gift, or else risk hurting the relationship (Fowl 2005, 230; see above, IN THE

TEXT). Instead, Paul transforms the conventional assumptions about reciprocity in two ways.

First, he tells his friends that his joy is **in the Lord**. Paul and the Philippians are not in a normal two-way relationship of giving and receiving. Theirs is a "three-way bond" (Fee 1995, 428). They are partners together in the service of Christ and the gospel.

Second, the reason for Paul's great joy is that they have shown the kind of unselfish **concern** that he has encouraged throughout the letter (Fowl 2005, 230). The English word **concern** translates the now familiar verb *phroneō* ("think" in 1:7; 2:2, 5; 3:15-16, 19; 4:2), which means to have a certain mind-set. It is the mind-set that Paul has toward them (1:7), and which they see above all in the self-emptying love of Christ (2:5-11). By caring for the apostle in his suffering, they are demonstrating the kind of Christlike attitude Paul wants them to have toward one another (Fowl 2005, 230).

The verb **you have renewed** (*anethalete*) is a lively botanical metaphor that literally means to "bloom again"—like perennial flowers blossom in the spring after lying dormant through the winter. **At last** (*ēdē pote*) might sound like Paul is chiding them a bit for taking so long to revive their concern for him (so Chrysostom, *Hom. Phil.* 15.4.10-14; "after so long," NEB). But that is not how Paul intends it, so he immediately adds a qualification: **about which indeed you have been concerned, but you had no opportunity to show it**.

The phrase that connects this clause to the previous one ("about which indeed," *eph' hōi kai*) is not easy to translate. Similar to its use in 3:12, *eph' hōi* probably shows the *aim* of the Philippians' concern for Paul ("to which end"), rather than the *reason* for it ("because"; see comment on 3:12; Fee 1995, 430, n 28; Fitzmyer 1993, 331).

Paul makes it clear that the Philippians are not to blame for the gap in their material care for Paul. Both the verbs **concerned** (*ephroneite*, the second occurrence of the verb in v 10) and **lacked opportunity** (*ēkaireisthe*) are in the Greek imperfect tense. This indicates that the Philippians' concern was consistent, but they were continually hindered from expressing it. *Why* they could not help Paul, he does not tell us. Perhaps it had something to do with their poverty (2 Cor 8:1-2; for other possibilities, see Hawthorne and Martin 2004, 262-63). In any case, Paul does not hold it against them.

■ **11** Paul now heads off a second potential misunderstanding (**not that**). His joy is not based on the fact that the Philippians have met his physical **need** (*hysterēsis*; see Mark 12:44) through their gift.

From one standpoint, Paul *did* need his friends' help. Prison rations in the Roman world were so miserable, both in quantity and quality, that they often put the prisoner's survival at risk. As a result, prisoners relied on friends and family to provide food and other necessities (Rapske 1994, 209-14, 426).

At the same time, *talking about* one's needs was a delicate matter in Paul's world. For instance, the Stoic philosopher Seneca writes that merely mentioning a need could be taken as a request (*Ben.* 2.2.1-2; 7.24.1-2; Peterman 1997, 134-35). Paul, it seems, wants the Philippians to understand that by rejoicing at their generosity, he is not angling for more money. What is more, Aristotle and others saw friendships based on need or "usefulness" as the least desirable type (e.g., Aristotle, *Eth. Nic.* 8.3.3; 8.4.2-3; 13.2, 4, 13; see Fitzgerald 1996, 157-59). Very likely, Paul wants to make it clear that his relationship with the Philippians is not about what he can get out of them but is of the highest level of friendship.

The reason (*gar*), Paul explains, he does not speak out of need is that he has **learned to be content whatever the circumstances.** The adjective **content** (*autarkēs*; see 2 Cor 9:8; 1 Tim 6:6, where the noun form appears) can also mean "self-sufficient" (Bauer 1979, 122).

From the time of Aristotle on, philosophers discussed self-sufficiency in relation to friendship (see Fitzgerald 1996, 152-53; Berry 1996, 112-14). But the ideal of being self-sufficient was particularly linked to Stoicism, one of the most popular philosophical movements of the day. For the Stoics, self-sufficiency meant becoming independent from all external circumstances and from material goods. As Seneca expressed it, "The happy man is content with his present lot, no matter what it is, and is reconciled to his circumstances" (*Vit. Beat.* 6.2). Through discipline and inner strength, individuals could master their own universe. The Stoics' aim was to become serenely indifferent to anything fate tossed their way.

When Paul claims to be **content whatever the circumstances,** is he simply taking over a moral virtue from the Philippians' culture (so Thurston 2005, 152-53)? Does he suddenly put on the toga, so to speak, of a Stoic wise man? On the contrary, Paul redefines the familiar language of "self-sufficiency" in a distinctively "non-Stoic" way. The whole letter shows that Paul does not see himself as an independent soul, but as one who is truly *interdependent* with his friends in Philippi. Nor does the apostle seek detachment from life's circumstances. Instead he has learned to see his hardships as a part of God's great drama of salvation (Fowl 2005, 195; see 1:12-26).

Above all, 4:13 reveals that Paul's contentment comes not from his own inner resources, but from God. Fee puts it well: "[Paul] uses the language—and outwardly assumes the stance—of Stoic 'self-sufficiency,' but radically transforms it into Christ-sufficiency. The net result is that Paul and Seneca, while appearing to be close, are a thousand leagues apart" (1995, 427).

This kind of contentment is something that Paul has **learned** (*emathon*; a constative aorist, which views Paul's Christian experience as a whole; it did not break in on him in a flash of insight; against Martin 1976, 163). Contentment does not come automatically. We find the same verb in v 9, in reference to the Philippians learning from Paul's example. Here, as well, Paul's personal testimony invites his audience to follow him into the school of contentment.

■ 12 This verse sketches the kinds of "circumstances" (v 11) in which Paul has learned to be content. His language is eloquent and rhythmical. It begins with two balanced clauses: **I know both how to be abased and I also know how to abound.** In light of the context, most commentators think that Paul is referring specifically to economic poverty and plenty.

But the verb **abased** (*tapeinousthai*; literally, "to be humbled" or "to be made low") suggests a somewhat broader meaning. For the Stoics, "humiliation" was a demeaning, slave-like mentality, something to be avoided at all costs (see comments on 2:3). For Paul, however, the abasement of poverty was part of an entire cross-shaped way of life—a life in conformity to the one who "made himself low" for others (2:8; Fee 1995, 433).

Whatever the situation (literally, **in everything and in all things**), Paul testifies: **I have learned the secret of being content** (the word "content" is not in the Greek text but is added by the NIV for clarification). The verb Paul uses (*mueō*) occurs only here in the NT. Originally, it described the process of initiation into the secrets of the mystery cults. His statement in v 12 probably plays on that meaning, which we can assume would have been familiar to his pagan audience. He has been "initiated" into the opposite conditions of being "well fed or hungry . . . living in plenty or in want." Paul's lists of personal hardships elsewhere testify that he was indeed intimate with deprivations like hunger and thirst, rags and homelessness (1 Cor 4:11; 2 Cor 11:27).

It is striking, however, that he also talks about learning the secret of coping with fullness and abundance (*perisseuein*; the second occurrence of the verb in v 12). A number of church fathers suggest that abundance can be every bit as challenging as poverty. Chrysostom, for example, observes that "[m]any who have become affluent have become derelict. They do not know how to bear their good fortune" (*Hom. Phil.* 15.4.10-14; cited by Edwards 1999, 285).

Furthermore, "material abundance does not alleviate anxiety. Abundance simply shifts one's focus from getting things to keeping the things one has" (Fowl 2005, 195). Scripture tells us little about Paul's experience of plenty. The point is that Paul has learned to experience a deep-level contentment that transcends any circumstances in which he found himself.

■ 13 How is this possible? Verse 13 uncovers the secret of Paul's lifestyle of contentment. **I am able to do all things,** Paul affirms, **in the one who enables me.** Here is where the roads part most sharply between Stoic self-sufficiency and Christian contentment. The source of Paul's contentment is not inner strength but divine empowerment.

We need to make two further observations about this familiar text. First, it is important not to take Paul's testimony out of its context. This verse is not a blanket assurance that Christians can do *anything.* **Everything** (*panta,* which picks up *in everything and in all things,* v 12) refers in the first place to Paul's God-given contentment in poverty or plenty (Bockmuehl 1998, 262). But since this is a life attitude for Paul (see 1:21), **all things** probably applies to more than the immediate issue of material want or wealth. It embraces whatever situations he might face, whether temptations, slander, imprisonment, even potential death (Fee 1995, n 50).

Second, the common translation **I can do everything through him** (e.g., NIV, NRSV, NASB), is possible, but it is probably not the best way to read the Greek preposition *en.* Paul, it seems, makes the point that the power to be content in all circumstances lies *in* his relationship with Christ (see 3:10), not *in* his own power (Bockmuehl 1998, 262; O'Brien 1991, 527). It is only as he is in union with Christ that this divine empowerment is available to him. Later scribes made this explicit by adding the word "Christ" to the text (see KJV). The present tense participle Paul uses (*tōi endynamounti*) indicates that Christ continually supplies all the **strength** that we need.

2. A Partnership in Giving and Receiving (4:14-17)

■ **14** The word ***nevertheless*** (*plēn;* yet) signals a shift in thought (Thurston 2005, 153; see 3:16; Bauer 1979, 669). Paul resumes his commendation of the Philippians from 4:10. At the same time, he wants to fend off another misunderstanding. What he has just said about being content with his lot does not mean that he is ungrateful for his friends' generosity (see Seneca, *Ben.* 2.24.2-3 for a contemporary criticism of such ingratitude). On the contrary, they ***did well*** (*kalōs epoiēsate;* **it was good of you**). Paul affirms them with "positive and generous praise" (Vincent 1897, 146), even if he does not directly express thanks, which would acknowledge his social debt to them (Peterman 1997, 145).

Paul commends his dear friends specifically for participating in his affliction (**you . . . share in my troubles**). In the ancient world, true friendship was demonstrated by a willingness to share another's storms and adversities (e.g., Isocrates, *Demonicus* 26; Cicero, *Amic.* 22; cited by Berry 1996, 117). But here "sharing together" (*synkoinōneō*) in Paul's hardships is more than *simply* an act of friendship; it is also an expression of their active "partnership" (*koinōnia*) in the gospel (1:5, 7).

In this context, the term ***affliction*** (*thlipsis*) primarily refers to Paul's imprisonment (Fowl 2005, 196). In 1:7 Paul talks about his friends sharing in his "chains," and he directly links affliction and imprisonment in 1:17. But how do the Philippians "partner" in Paul's sufferings? Perhaps in four senses:

- They have helped to alleviate his misery through their gifts.
- In the Greco-Roman world, showing solidarity with a prisoner like Paul would have meant that they themselves experienced the shame and disgrace of his bonds (see Rapske 1994, 293-95).
- Paul's friends participated in his affliction by virtue of their own suffering for Christ in Philippi (1:29-30).
- The Philippians shared in the blessings of the advance of the gospel that resulted from Paul's imprisonment (1:5, 12-18).

■ 15 Having raised the matter of the Philippians' participation with their apostle, Paul now focuses on the primary expression of that solidarity: their material support. The church's recent gift is part of a longtime partnership in the gospel. Paul recalls this relationship by telling his friends' story. Verse 15 begins with the highly emphatic reminder, **now you yourselves, Philippians, indeed know** (*oidate de kai hymeis, Philippēsioi*). He is, in effect, saying, "Sit up and take notice of what I am about to say" (Fee 2007, 439, n 10). **Philippians** is a Latin-based form, appropriate for residents of a Roman colony. In this case, it is a term of affection for the audience (Bruce 1983, 129).

The key clause in the verse expresses *what* they know: **not one church shared with me in the matter of giving and receiving, except you only.** Here the Greek text gives special emphasis to the Paul's exclusive partnership with this congregation (**not one church . . . except you only**; see the sidebar "Paul and Financial Support" in the BEHIND THE TEXT section above).

But what does it mean that they **shared with [Paul] in the matter of giving and receiving**? The terms **giving** (*dosis*) and **receiving** (*lēmsis*) were part of the commercial vocabulary of the ancient world; it is the language of credits and debits. As a result, some have understood this as a one-sided financial transaction: the congregation gave (money) and Paul received (e.g., Wesley n.d., 514; Lightfoot 1953, 165; "you . . . gave me financial help," NLT). But that does not fit the idea of the Philippians' mutual "sharing" with Paul.

In Paul's world, business language was often used to describe the mutual exchange of benefits between true friends (e.g., Cicero, *Amic.* 26, 58; see Fitzgerald 2007, 294; Peterman 1997, 147-51). **Giving and receiving** had become a common way of talking about the *social* practice of reciprocity in gifts and services. "Sharing in the matter of giving and receiving," then, "is not primarily a financial expression, but rather a social metaphor" (Peterman 1997, 196).

The idea of "sharing" (*koinōnia*) also helped define ancient friendships (e.g., Aristotle, *Eth. Nic.* 8.12.1; 9.12.1; Berry 1996, 117-18). Here Paul's use of that language (**shared**; *ekoinōnēsen*) reinforces the idea of mutuality in Paul's relationship of giving and receiving with his friends in Philippi. Their friendship is beneficial to both parties. Thus, Paul co-opts the language of social relationships in his cultural world to describe the special partnership he shares with his audience.

At the same time, Paul transposes his partnership in **giving and receiving** into a key different from that of the dominant culture. Above all, this partnership is not simply between Paul and the Philippians. It is a three-way relationship between the apostle, the congregation and Christ (Fee 1995, 444). Because giving and receiving happens in union with the crucified and risen Lord, the whole matter is transformed (see Peterman 1997, 149, for differences between Paul's description and Greco-Roman expectations). Giving gifts is no longer a means of "social climbing" or putting others in one's debt. In Christ, the relative status of giver and receiver becomes insignificant. Both are "partners in the gospel" (1:5). In fact, throughout 4:14-20, "Paul does not stress the relationship the gift might create between himself and the Philippians, but the relationship between the Philippians and God that it symbolizes" (Gorman 2004, 448; see vv 17-20).

Two additional phrases in v 15 clarify the nature of the unique partnership that Paul and the Philippians share. The first, literally, ***in the beginning of the gospel,*** speaks of the origins of the relationship. But precisely when the gospel "began" has puzzled commentators. Among the various suggestions (see Hawthorne and Martin 2004, 269), the most plausible is the one reflected in the NIV: **in the early days of your acquaintance with the gospel.** In other words, this long-term partnership goes back to their beginnings as Christians (Fee 1995, 441; see 1:5 and *1 Clem.* 47.2, where the identical phrase has a similar meaning). Given the second qualifying phrase, **when I set out from Macedonia,** we should probably understand the **early days** as the period of Paul's first mission to Greece proper, especially in Corinth (see 2 Cor 11:8-9; Acts 17:10—18:18).

■ **16** After what Paul has just said, this verse is surprising. **Thessalonica** is another Macedonian city. Why, then, does Paul mention the Philippians' support while he was in that location *after* he talks about leaving Macedonia (v 15)? Perhaps he means it to be a further justification (**for,** *hoti*) of what he has just said in v 15 (O'Brien 1991, 535). **Even** (*kai*) while he was still in Macedonia, Paul's long-standing partnership with the Philippians in giving and receiving had begun. What is more, they sent material help ***more than once*** (literally, "both once and twice") during Paul's rough times in Thessalonica (see 1 Thess 2:2; Acts 17:1-7). By recalling the exemplary history of the Philippians' generosity, Paul expresses his grateful affection for these partners in the gospel.

■ **17** Echoing the pattern of v 11, Paul begins v 17 with a disclaimer (**not that**). Once again, the apostle sets out to correct a possible misunderstanding, ***not that I desire the gift.*** Although he commends his friends for their support, he is not interested in financial gain. He did not solicit their gift, nor is he indirectly requesting more. Throughout this passage, Paul walks a tightrope between showing, on the one hand, that he is grateful for their gifts; but, on the other, that he does not need (v 11) or seek them (v 17). *Epizētō*, the verb translated **looking for** in the NIV, is a strong term that means something like *desire* or "strive for" (Bauer 1979, 292; see Rom 11:7).

Paul follows this denial with the positive affirmation, ***I desire the profit that is accumulating into your account.*** In the first part of this sentence, we see a perfectly balanced contrast to the preceding clause:

Not that	I desire	the gift
But	I desire	the profit

Paul plays on two complementary images. First, he seeks, literally, "the fruit (*karpos*) that increases for your account." The Philippians' gift is concrete evidence of the kind of growing spiritual "fruitfulness" that Paul prays God will grant them in 1:11 (Fee 1995, 447).

Second, the term "fruit" commonly served as a financial metaphor in the ancient world, representing *profit* or "credit" (**what may be credited**). In tandem with the business language of **your account** (*logon hymōn*; see also v 15), the primary metaphor here is that of a bank account receiving compound interest (Thielman 1995, 237). But it soon becomes clear that this is a spiritual account held by God (see v 19), not unlike Jesus' image of "storing up treasures in heaven" (Matt 6:20; 19:21). Paul, then, gives the Philippians' material support a *theological* interpretation.

Considering the conventions about "giving and receiving" in Paul's world, this is a countercultural perspective. In Greco-Roman society, the gift-giver would normally expect a return benefit. It would come either in the form of a tangible gift of equal or more value or as an increase in honor. Here Paul affirms that the Philippians' gift does indeed bring them a return. The benefits they reap, however, are neither material gifts nor earthly honor, but *spiritual* dividends for their heavenly account (Peterman 1997, 149, 159). The "interest" they receive is, therefore, of far greater value than the original gift. The idea that God grants spiritual blessings to those who give to others in need is a familiar theme throughout the NT (e.g., Matt 6:4; 19:21; Luke 6:38; 14:12-14; 2 Cor 9:6-14; Fowl 2005, 198). From this perspective, Chrysostom was right that the Philippians' "giving and receiving" (v 15) involved giving material gifts and receiving spiritual benefits in return (*Hom. Phil.* 15.4.15).

But *when* do the Philippians receive this spiritual *profit*? Now or in the future? There is no reason to choose between the two. Paul desires that the fruit of God's gracious work in their lives, of which their loving generosity is evidence, will continually increase until it reaches full expression on the day of Christ (Fee 1995, 447; O'Brien 1991, 539; see 1:10-11).

3. Gratitude and God's Provision (4:18-20)

■ **18** For the third time in the passage, Paul commends the Philippians for their gifts (see vv 10, 14). But this is by far the most direct and the most exuberant of the three. Paul begins by stacking up three verbs that describe his positive response to the gift.

The first verb, **I have received** (*apechō*), carries on the banking metaphor from 4:15, 17. In commercial documents of the day, it was often used as a receipt for a payment; something like, "Paid in full" (Bauer 1979, 84-85). Paul Sampley takes this verb and other financial terms as evidence that Paul entered into a contractual arrangement (*societas*) with the Philippians: Paul preached and the Philippians paid him (1980, 51-77). But this is unlikely. The term (*apechō*) could also function in a less technical sense in a variety of social contexts (e.g., Phlm 15; Fowl 2005, 199). This broader understanding of what Paul **received** fits this passage's emphasis on the mutuality of his partnership with the Philippians (see Peterman's fuller critique of Sampley; 1997, 123-27).

Paul may simply be saying that he had gotten "everything" (*panta*) that the Philippians had sent through Epaphroditus. Such an acknowledgment was common in the ancient world, due to the distances and uncertainties involved in transporting goods (Peterman 1997, 142). In light of what follows, however, it is more likely that he means, **I have received all things** (I need), **and even more** (Bockmuehl 1998, 265). **I have more than enough** (*perisseuō*), picks up on a verb that Paul used twice in v 12. Despite being in prison, his friends' generosity has put him in the place of "abundance" he describes in that context.

Paul drives home the point with still another verb, **I am filled to overflowing** (*peplērōmai*, **I am amply supplied**). The same term describes God's full supply of the Philippians' need in v 19. Here, however, it is Paul who is "filled to the full" as result of his friends' provision through their surrogate **Epaphroditus**.

Interpreters who accuse Paul of a halfhearted, "thankless thanks" in this passage (see comment on v 10) have surely missed the point of Paul's words in v 18. He may not say "thank you" as such, but his language radiates an attitude of gratitude.

Without warning, Paul "switches the metaphorical location from the bank to the temple"; the Philippians' gift is now a sacrifice offered to God (Osiek 2000, 122-23). The rest of the verse resumes Paul's theological interpretation of the gift. Although Paul has been enriched by their generosity, much more important is how God sees it. Piling up the language of Israel's worship, he describes the gift as **a fragrant offering, an acceptable sacrifice, pleasing to God.**

The first image is especially striking. The picture of God taking pleasure in the "smell" of the burning flesh of animals may seem strange to many modern readers. However, **fragrant offering** (*osmēn euōdias*) is a metaphor for God's approval that surfaces repeatedly in the OT from Gen 8:21 onward. **Fragrant**, therefore, is similar in meaning to the terms **acceptable** and **pleasing**. The combination of **fragrant offering** and **sacrifice** (*thysian*) may constitute a deliberate echo of Lev 1:9, 13, 17, where Israel's burnt offerings have a pleasing odor to the Lord (Sumney 2007, 118). The same language describes the self-giving death of Christ in Eph 5:2. Although this language comes directly from the OT, it would not have been lost on Paul's Gentile audience. Sacrifices were a regular feature of religious practice in the Greco-Roman world. The point here is that the Philippians' gifts have enormous value in God's eyes.

■ **19** The passage reaches a majestic climax with the promise of God's working (v 19) and the praise of God's glory (v 20). These verses, therefore, provide a fitting conclusion, not just for Paul's "thank-you note" in vv 10-20, but also for the whole letter.

The opening conjunction **and** (*de*) links v 19 closely to what Paul has just said. The promise that follows is "the divine response to the Philippians' generosity" (Deasley 2007, 236). Paul also makes the connection by repeating language that described their care of him. He says, in effect, "Even as you have 'fully supplied' (v 18) 'my need' (v 16), **God will *fully supply*** (*plērōsei*) every need *of yours*."

In the Greco-Roman world, acknowledging the receipt of a gift would normally obligate *the receiver* to return the favor. But in this verse Paul "rewrites the rules." He has already recast the Philippians' gift to him as primarily an offering to God (v 18). As a result, it is not Paul, but *God* who will repay them (Peterman 1997, 157; Fowl 2005, 199-200). Those benefits come, not out of social obligation, but as the gracious blessing of God. What is more, the Philippians will receive a far greater return than Paul could ever pay, since their divine Benefactor is the one who lavishes his riches on humanity in Christ (Fowl 2005, 200).

With the highly personal language of **my** God (1:3; "my Lord," 3:8), Paul speaks as one who has a long experience of God's gracious provision (vv 11-13; Bruce 1983, 131). He can therefore assure his friends with confidence that God will fully **meet all** [their] **needs**. But which *needs* are covered in this promise? Certainly the context suggests that God will supply the Philippians' material needs. But Paul's language (*every* need of yours) and the place of this promise at the climax of the letter point to a more sweeping reference. God is sufficient for *all* their needs: contentment in the face of adversity (4:11-13); steadfastness in the midst of opposition and suffering (1:27-30); divine joy and peace as an answer to anxiety (4:4-7); purity in a crooked world (1:10-11; 2:15), just to name a few.

The last part of the verse explains *how* God will supply their every need:

according to his riches in glory in Christ Jesus. This is the language of extravagant abundance. "Since God's riches are immeasurable, God is able to meet every conceivable human need" (Hooker 2000, 545). These riches, Paul assures us, exist in the sphere of God's glory (*en doxē*). Here the more literal translation *in glory* is better than changing the phrase into an adjective, **glorious** riches (as in the NIV). This expression probably means that the riches of God's grace belong to God's own glory—the eternal splendor and majesty in which he dwells (Fee 1995, 451-52).

Furthermore, God has made these unbounded treasures available to his people **in Christ Jesus.** This phrase, given special emphasis in Greek, is the key to it all. Christ is the source and the sphere of God's limitless provision. We receive all of the riches of God's lavish love only as we are in union with Christ (see 1 Cor 1:5; Eph 1:7-8; 2:7). Should it surprise us, then, that the letter begins (1:1) and ends **in Christ Jesus** (see Fee 1995, 454)?

■ **20** At this point, there is only one fitting response. So Paul spontaneously breaks out into worship and praise: **To our God and Father be glory for ever and ever.** This concluding doxology, we should not forget, would have been read aloud within the gathered community (Fee 1998, 86). It is a community response. Appropriately, then, Paul's *my* **God** in v 19 becomes *our* **God and Father.** When God's people catch a glimpse of God's glory, the only thing to do is to give glory to God. When the church reflects on God's inexhaustible provision for its every need in Christ, it can only worship such a God (Thurston 2005, 156).

The worshipping community will continue to extol God's glory and grace **for ever and ever,** literally "unto the ages of ages" (see Gal 1:5; Eph 3:17; 1 Tim 1:17; 2 Tim 4:18). This eschatological language comes directly out of Paul's Jewish heritage. Likewise, the doxology closes with the Hebrew affirmation, **Amen.** Although traditional, it voices Paul's (and our) deepest desire: let it be so!

FROM THE TEXT

1. *The grace of giving.* Richard Foster cites Martin Luther as recognizing the need for three conversions: the conversion of the heart, the mind, and the purse (Foster 1985, 19). The matter of "giving and receiving" (v 14) money is still a sensitive issue for Christians, one that requires genuine discernment. Money is a paradox. It can become either an idol or a channel of grace, depending on how we treat it.

This passage affirms that giving our material resources to meet the needs of others is an act of worship directed primarily to God (v 18). It is no less "spiritual" a practice than any other aspect of the Christian life (Silva 2005, 208). In fact, what Paul elsewhere calls "the grace of giving" (2 Cor 8:7) is ultimately of greater benefit to those who give than to those who might be helped by the gift. Generosity toward others is sure evidence of God's gracious "fruit" in our lives (Phil 4:17). This is so not least because money is a rival power to God that seeks to own us (Matt 6:19-21, 24; 1 Tim 6:10). Fundamentally, if God has our purses and wallets, he has *us*.

Generosity in material things is also one way we embody the loving and self-giving story of Christ (2:5-11; 4:10). It is, therefore, curious that many preachers are unwilling to tackle the subject of money. When we neglect this essential element of our discipleship, we rob believers of the spiritual growth and freedom that goes hand in hand with the grace of giving (see 2 Cor 8 and 9). John Wesley understood this; he has more sermons on money than on Christian perfection (for a listing of Wesley's sermons that are devoted entirely or in part to the subject of money, see Lyons 1996, n 2).

Our text offers a particular challenge to communities of faith in the affluent societies of our world. What will it mean to "share in the affliction" (v 14) of others in a world of intolerable poverty and human misery? How will we become "partners in giving and receiving" (v 15) with the global body of Christ at a time when the chasm between the "haves" and the "have nots" is dramatically on the rise? It is hard to be prescriptive. But for those of us who are blessed with relative riches, surely we need to pray that God would convict and empower us to give more of those riches away (see Blomberg 1999, 253).

2. *Giving counterculturally.* This passage teaches that in money matters, as in all aspects of Christian discipleship, our lives must reflect the gospel and not the values of our culture. Paul understood that certain completely normal practices of giving and receiving in his world needed to be transformed by the gospel of Christ. Likewise, we must learn to discern when the ways of God's kingdom conflict with the narratives of our cultures. The specifics, of course, will vary. But money still gets tangled up in issues of power, status, and control, including within the church.

Consider, for example, the relationship between a minister and a congregation. As Fowl points out, today it is common for churches to adopt popular managerial models, in which the minister is primarily the employee of the congregation. If the minister "performs" well enough, he or she gets paid. If not, there are consequences (Fowl 2005, 231-32). But are the power relationships in this cultural model consistent with the kind of partnership in the gospel that Paul talks about in Philippians?

Even more worrying is the tendency to inject the values of a consumer culture into the church. In this case, members of a congregation become consumers of religious "products." If their felt needs are met, they stay and support the church financially. If they are unsatisfied with the product, they withhold their money or take it to the "competition."

Examples of giving with "strings attached" abound: a donor to a Christian university who makes his gift entirely conditional on having a building named after him; or churches that want to retain control of what they give to mission work by deciding just how their money is spent. Giving with self-serving conditions has little in common with the self-giving love of Christ. If we are fellow sharers in the gospel, we will embrace different perspectives on handling money than those of the culture around us.

3. *Christ-centered contentment.* Philippians 4:13 is perhaps the most frequently quoted verse in the letter. Yet those who cite it often wrench it from its context. "I can do *all things* through Christ who strengthens me" (NKJV, emphasis added) becomes everything from a slogan to boost one's self-image to a motto for an underachieving Christian high school basketball team! But Paul's "everything" is about finding God-given contentment in all of the ups and downs of life. In the first place, this speaks to our physical and material circumstances.

How we hear this word will depend on the particular life experiences we face. African theologian Eshetu Abate reminds us that for some Christian communities, these will be challenging words, heard in the midst of social upheaval, poverty, epidemics, natural disasters, and conflict (2006, 1448). Other Christians must learn to cope with affluence. Being well off may tempt us to rely on ourselves rather than God. The taste of material success may give us a craving for more. Wesley became convinced that, in general, "the more people increase in goods, the more they decrease in grace" (1979, 4:303). We need God's enabling power as much in abundance as in abasement.

In either situation, the key to contentment is not a Stoic (or Western individualistic) self-sufficiency. It is a Christ-dependency. Learning to face challenging circumstances with joy doesn't come through building up our spiritual muscles. In fact, no matter how long we are in the faith, "W*e never become spiritually strong*" (Welch 1988, 138). Just the opposite, Paul would say: it is only when we are weak that we are strong (2 Cor 12:10). True strength comes in humbly surrendering our need to be strong. Whether we find ourselves eating crumbs or caviar, whether in tragedy or in triumph, we do not have to be "strong" to cope. Christ is our strength.

4. *God's supply for our needs.* Throughout Christian history, Phil 4:19 has given God's people the assurance that God's rich resources are sufficient for every human need. Sadly, that blessed promise has often been misread. One misunderstanding is to limit the assurance only to God's provision of physical or material blessings. Far worse, the modern "prosperity gospel" has sometimes mangled Paul's words into a promise that God will supply believers with earthly wealth out of his "glorious riches" (see Thielman 1995, 240, 242).

But Paul does not say that God will fulfill all our desires or requests. The apostle himself prayed for God to alleviate his physical suffering. Instead, God gave him the assurance, "My grace is sufficient for you" (2 Cor 12:9). Part of our growth in discipleship involves learning to discern the difference between our "wants" and our genuine "needs" (see 1:10). In light of the wider context of Phil 4:19, those needs extend far beyond our physical and financial requirements.

That understanding became personal for me some years ago during my graduate studies. After much prayer, I sensed a growing conviction that I should continue my education at a university in Scotland. Exploring all possible sources of funding, I still came up far short of what was necessary. My only course was to release the matter to God and trust him to supply the need. Philippians 4:19 became very precious to me during the time of waiting on God that followed. In ways that were completely unexpected and amazing to me, God provided the resources to fund both my tuition and my living expenses. I gratefully testified to God's faithful and abundant supply.

But the story doesn't end there. During the course of my studies, I faced discouragement, loneliness, and many months of serious illness. I came to doubt my ability to complete the task. I questioned why God had led me into a place where failure seemed the only conceivable outcome. But in the midst of my personal darkness, I felt the Holy Spirit gently drawing me back to Phil 4:19. Can you trust your loving Father, the Spirit seemed to say, to meet *all* your needs according to his abundant riches? The need for money that God had graciously supplied appeared small in comparison to what I was currently facing. Once again, I had no other recourse but to trust God's provision in God's way and God's time. His divine resources became fully sufficient for all I lacked. Through that experience, I learned that the riches God makes available to us in Christ reach far beyond meeting our material needs.

And since this is a promise to the church, we can depend on God's provision for our *corporate* needs—wisdom, unity, maturity, generosity, a consistent and courageous witness, and more—*all* fully supplied out of God's lavish grace.

> *His love has no limit,*
> *His grace has no measure,*
> *His power has no boundary known unto men,*
> *For out of his infinite riches in Jesus,*
> *He giveth and giveth and giveth again.*
> —Annie Johnson Flint

5. *Friendship in the company of Christ.* The relationship between Paul and the Philippians we see in this passage has implications for Christian friendships today. Viewed through the prism of 4:10-20, Christian friendships:

- rejoice in God's working in the lives of one another (v 10)
- stand the test of time (vv 10, 15-16)
- are centered around a common relationship to Christ (vv 10, 13, 19)

- are not based on what we can get out of each other, but on serving one another; they are patterned after the self-emptying attitude of Christ (vv 10-11)
- model Christ-oriented attitudes and practices before one another (vv 11-13)
- are willing to share in one another's burdens and suffering (v 14)
- are grounded in a common partnership in the gospel (v 15)
- are characterized by mutual care, not on exercising power over others (vv 15, 17-18)
- are willing to minister to others in practical and material ways, according to our ability (vv 15-17)
- seek the spiritual health and growth of one another (vv 17-18)
- do not demand help from friends but gratefully accept it (vv 10-11, 14, 17-18)
- are not ultimately dependent on each other for joy and contentment but find these in our friendship with God (vv 11-13)
- affirm the value and positive actions of others (vv 10, 14-17)
- help others discern how they fit into God's ongoing saving work (vv 19-20)

Such Christian friendships share elements in common with relationships outside of the community of faith. Nevertheless, the two are not the same. Christian friendship is "friendship in the company of Christ" (Houston 2006, 167). And that makes all the difference.

B. The Letter Closing (4:21-23)

BEHIND THE TEXT

Paul ends his letter with a brief formal closing. This was typical of letters of the period, although the specific features of letter endings could vary.

Many Greco-Roman letters contained closing greetings. These took three forms: direct greetings from the sender ("I greet all who love you," Hunt and Edgar 1970, 302, 304); a request for the receiver to pass on greetings ("Greet your mother," *PTebt.* 412 in Richards 2004, 131); and greetings sent by a third party ("Serenus greets you," *BGU* 423). In Philippians, we find both the second (**Greet all the saints in Christ Jesus,** v 21) and the third (**All the saints send you greetings,** v 22) types (compare Rom 16:3-16, 22, where all three forms of greetings occur). As in other letters to churches he founded personally, here Paul does not greet any individuals by name (e.g., 1 and 2 Corinthians, Galatians, 1 and 2 Thessalonians; Bockmuehl 1998, 267).

Following the greetings, ancient letters often closed with a health-wish, like "I pray for your health," and/or a simple "farewell." In place of these formalities, Paul ends his letters with a final blessing, as in v 23. Typically, Paul modifies the standard letter conventions for his own theological purpose (see 1:1-11; on Paul's letter closings, see Weima 1994).

Paul probably penned this letter ending in his own hand (Bruce 1983, 132). It was common for ancient letter-writers, after dictating the letter to a scribe, to add a personally written postscript (see Richards 2004, 171-75). This would function as a sign of authenticity, similar to a signature today ("the distinguishing mark in all my letters," 2 Thess 3:17). In some cases, Paul explicitly draws attention to his closing autograph (1 Cor 16:21; Gal 6:11; Col 4:18; 2 Thess 3:17).

The closing of Philippians is notably simple (compare, e.g., Romans, 1 and 2 Corinthians, Galatians, Colossians). It is limited to a brief greeting (4:21-22) and a grace benediction (v 23). But after Paul's stirring promise and doxology in vv 19-20, something longer might seem unnecessary and intrusive (Fee 1995, 456).

These final verses feature a striking example of rhetorical bookends (*inclusio*), in which the ending reprises the language of the letter's beginning. In v 21, Paul greets **every saint in Christ Jesus,** just as he addressed the letter to **all the saints in Christ Jesus** (1:1). And Paul's opening blessing of **grace . . . to you from . . . the Lord Jesus Christ** (1:2) now becomes a closing wish that **the grace of the Lord Jesus Christ be with your spirit** (4:23). Like the front and back cover of a book, these literary brackets bind the letter into a single unit (see Black 1995, 25-26).

IN THE TEXT

■ **21** Paul's letter closing begins with a general greeting to **every saint in Christ Jesus.** For the meaning of **saint(s),** see the comment on 1:1. The Greek has the singular form **every saint** (*panta hagion*), rather than the NIV's **all the saints.** This may be Paul's way of greeting each of his friends individually ("each of God's holy people," NLT), even though he does not single anyone out by name (Bockmuehl 1998, 268).

It is unclear whether **in Christ Jesus** relates to the greeting itself (so Fee 1995, 458) or to **every saint.** In light of the similar phrase in 1:1, the latter is more likely. Paul gives his audience a final reminder that they are set apart as God's holy people only by virtue of their union with Christ (on the phrase **in Christ** see the comment on 1:1).

But who is to do the greeting? A number of commentators think that Paul's plural imperative **greet** (*aspasasthe*) is directed to the "overseers and deacons" mentioned in 1:1. In this case, the "leadership team" would see that the letter is read publicly and would convey Paul's regards to the rest of the church. This is possible. But since the letter is addressed to the church as a whole, this could simply be his way of sending greetings to each member of the congregation (Sumney 2007, 122; Fee 1995, 457, n 6). Most likely, he wants them to extend a greeting and expression of friendship to one another on his behalf.

The circle widens as Paul extends greetings from **the brothers and sisters who are with** [him]. Given the broader reference to **all the saints** in v 22, the **brothers and sisters** (literally, "brothers," *adelphoi*; see comments on 1:12) seem to refer to Paul's team of coworkers at his place of imprisonment. Paul does not name names, but this inner circle would at least include Timothy and Epaphroditus (2:19-30; for other possible candidates, see Phlm 23-24; Col 4:7-14; and Lightfoot 1953, 11).

■ **22** Expanding the circle still further, Paul conveys the greetings of **all the saints** in the area of his confinement. That is followed by a reference to the only group he singles out for special attention (**especially**) in the greetings, **those who belong to Caesar's household.**

This intriguing phrase has sparked a flurry of speculation about the identity and location of the Christians Paul has in mind. Although the church fathers often viewed them as high status members of the royal household, Lightfoot showed convincingly that such was not the case (see Lightfoot 1953, 171-78). In light of evidence from ancient inscriptions, **Caesar's household** (*Kaisaros oikias*) refers to the extensive network of civil servants, clients, and soldiers in the imperial service. Although some were of high rank, the vast majority were freedmen or freedwomen and slaves.

The emperor's civil servants were scattered throughout the empire, but the highest concentration would have been in Rome. Consequently, the reference to **Caesar's household** is one pillar of support for the view that Paul was writing from Rome (see the Introduction). Lightfoot points out the extensive connections between the names Paul lists in Rom 16:6-16 and those found in ancient inscriptions relating to members of Caesar's household (1953, 174-77).

This reference to **Caesar's household** would have had special meaning for a church in the imperial colony of Philippi. Paul's audience had suffered opposition from compatriots in Philippi who hailed Caesar as Lord (see 1:27). Paul himself is a prisoner of the empire in Rome. "For both Paul and his friends, it would have been a source of hope and reassurance to know that the gospel was penetrating in the very heart of the Roman imperial apparatus" (Bockmuehl 1998, 270). Even in Caesar's own household, there are fellow **saints** who proclaim Jesus as Lord (2:11).

■ **23** Paul's letter to his dear friends concludes with a final blessing, **the grace of the Lord Jesus Christ be with your spirit.** Similar grace-benedictions conclude all of the letters attributed to Paul. But these are not merely conventional formality.

As Morna Hooker reminds us, we can hardly read these words without recalling **the grace of our Lord Jesus Christ** that Paul narrated in ch 2 (2000, 546).

The phrase **with your spirit** (*meta tou pneumatos hymōn*; see Gal 3:18; Phlm 25; 2 Tim 4:22) uses a singular noun (**spirit**) to stand collectively for the whole church. This may express Paul's desire that the congregation would be united in God's grace as they share a single spirit. Although omitted in most modern translations, the concluding **Amen** has strong manuscript support and may be original (see Bockmuehl 1998, 271).

Fittingly, the letter ends where it began. Paul's closing blessing echoes his opening greeting (1:2). For Paul, **the grace** of God **in Christ** is both the first and the last word.

FROM THE TEXT

Two implications from this short letter closing stand out as words for our world. First, these greetings between the "saints" are an expression of Christian unity (see, e.g., 1:27; 2:1-4; 3:15; 4:2-3). They testify that the body of Christ bridges geographical distances, cultural differences, social inequalities, even political power and powerlessness (see Thurston 2005, 162-63).

This is all the more remarkable in light of the social research of scholars like Wayne A. Meeks (1983). Unlike every other known community in the ancient world, what distinguished the Christian church from its beginning was its heterogeneous character. It was not social status, racial identity, profession, gender, or any other human characteristic that united the church. What Christ had done for all of them made them one.

It may be true that churches with members of a particular age-group, socioeconomic status, or cultural background are more likely to attract people who are like them. But an intentionally homogeneous church, in which everyone comes from the same age or demographic group, is not the NT model of the "church of Jesus Christ." "We must learn, however painfully, to sing the gospel in all the rich harmonies that enhance the beauty of the song" (Flemming 2005, 53).

Second, Paul's final blessing reminds us that the call to live in a way that is worthy of the gospel (1:27) is and will always be a response to God's grace. It is no coincidence that the letter's closing words speak of God's gracious work and God's eternal glory: **My God will fully supply all your needs according to his riches in glory** (4:19). **To our God and Father be glory for ever and ever** (v 20). **The grace of the Lord Jesus Christ be with your spirit** (v 23).

What is more, God's great work of salvation comes to us solely **in Christ Jesus** (vv 19, 21). God's grace is from **the Lord Jesus Christ** (v 23). Throughout Philippians, Paul calls us to a Christ-centered existence. At the very least, this involves:

- knowing Christ Jesus as Lord (3:8, 10; see 1:21)
- reflecting Christ's self-emptying love in our attitudes and actions (2:5-11)
- living our shared life in joyful expectation of our future with Christ (1:6; 3:20-21)
- embodying and proclaiming the gospel of Christ (1:5, 7, 27-30; 2:14-16)

All of this is by **the grace of our Lord Jesus Christ.** It is my prayer that this same grace may be with you, the readers of this commentary. May you discover the joy that comes on the path of downward mobility and the fellowship of self-giving mutual service, following Christ.